I SENSE A COLDNESS TO YOUR MENTORING

I SENSE A COLDNESS TO YOUR MENTORING

DILBERT™

by **SCOTT ADAMS**

Andrews McMeel
PUBLISHING®

Andrews McMeel Publishing
a division of Andrews McMeel Universal
1130 Walnut Street, Kansas City, Missouri 64106
www.andrewsmcmeel.com

17 18 19 20 21 SDB 10 9 8 7 6 5

ISBN: 978-1-4494-2938-6

Library of Congress Control Number: 2013933514

www.dilbert.com

ATTENTION: SCHOOLS AND BUSINESSES

Other DILBERT® books from Andrews McMeel Publishing

Your New Job Title Is "Accomplice"
ISBN: 978-1-4494-2775-7

I Can't Remember If We're Cheap or Smart
ISBN: 978-1-4494-2309-4

Teamwork Means You Can't Pick the Side that's Right
ISBN: 978-1-4494-1018-6

How's That Underling Thing Working Out for You?
ISBN: 978-1-4494-0819-0

Your Accomplishments Are Suspiciously Hard to Verify
ISBN: 978-1-4494-0102-3

Problem Identified and You're Probably Not Part of the Solution
ISBN: 978-0-7407-8534-4

I'm Tempted to Stop Acting Randomly
ISBN: 978-0-7407-7806-3

14 Years of Loyal Service in a Fabric-Covered Box
ISBN: 978-0-7407-7365-5

Freedom's Just Another Word for People Finding Out You're Useless
ISBN: 978-0-7407-7815-5

Dilbert 2.0: 20 Years of Dilbert
ISBN: 978-0-7407-7735-6

This Is the Part Where You Pretend to Add Value
ISBN: 978-0-7407-7227-6

Cubes and Punishment
ISBN: 978-0-7407-6837-8

Positive Attitude
ISBN: 978-0-7407-6379-3

Try Rebooting Yourself
ISBN: 978-0-7407-6190-4

What Would Wally Do?
ISBN: 978-0-7407-5769-3

Thriving on Vague Objectives
ISBN: 978-0-7407-5533-0

The Fluorescent Light Glistens Off Your Head
ISBN: 978-0-7407-5113-4

It's Not Funny If I Have to Explain It
ISBN: 978-0-7407-4658-1

Don't Stand Where the Comet Is Assumed to Strike Oil
ISBN: 978-0-7407-4539-3

Words You Don't Want to Hear During Your Annual Performance Review
ISBN: 978-0-7407-3805-0

When Body Language Goes Bad
ISBN: 978-0-7407-3298-0

What Do You Call a Sociopath in a Cubicle? Answer: A Coworker
ISBN: 978-0-7407-2663-7

Another Day in Cubicle Paradise
ISBN: 978-0-7407-2194-6

When Did Ignorance Become a Point of View?
ISBN: 978-0-7407-1839-7

Excuse Me While I Wag
ISBN: 978-0-7407-1390-3

Dilbert—A Treasury of Sunday Strips: Version 00
ISBN: 978-0-7407-0531-1

Random Acts of Management
ISBN: 978-0-7407-0453-6

Dilbert Gives You the Business
ISBN: 978-0-7407-0003-3

Don't Step in the Leadership
ISBN: 978-0-8362-7844-6

Journey to Cubeville
ISBN: 978-0-8362-6745-7

I'm Not Anti-Business, I'm Anti-Idiot
ISBN: 978-0-8362-5182-1

Seven Years of Highly Defective People
ISBN: 978-0-8362-3668-2

Casual Day Has Gone Too Far
ISBN: 978-0-8362-2899-1

Fugitive from the Cubicle Police
ISBN: 978-0-8362-2119-0

It's Obvious You Won't Survive by Your Wits Alone
ISBN: 978-0-8362-0415-5

Still Pumped from Using the Mouse
ISBN: 978-0-8362-1026-2

Bring Me the Head of Willy the Mailboy!
ISBN: 978-0-8362-1779-7

Shave the Whales
ISBN: 978-0-8362-1740-7

Dogbert's Clues for the Clueless
ISBN: 978-0-8362-1737-7

Always Postpone Meetings with Time-Wasting Morons
ISBN: 978-0-8362-1758-2

Build a Better Life by Stealing Office Supplies
ISBN: 978-0-8362-1757-5

Introduction

I've tried to be a mentor. Apparently I'm not good at it. None of my saplings have grown into majestic redwoods that touch the sky. My mentoring victims usually end up more like kindling, or whatever pokes your eye out if you're not careful.

I don't know what I'm doing wrong. I have dispensed my finest advice with Moses-like self-assurance. But it turns out that I rarely say anything that people want to hear. My mentoring usually goes like this:

Me: You will need to work hard to achieve your dreams.

Young Person: I think we're done here.

Or

Me: I worked ten years without taking a day off.

Young Person: Is there someone else I could talk to?

My mentoring is also burdened by the fact that I genuinely don't know how much of my career success has been due to pure luck. That causes me to make unhelpful statements about our fates being determined fifteen billion years ago during the Big Bang. Some people find that demotivating.

I also have a bad habit of putting things into gloomy perspective, as in, "No one will remember you after you've been dead for a hundred years. And you'll stay dead for infinity . . . if you're lucky." I have it on good authority that five minutes with me can make your spine feel like it dissolved into your back fat. Mentoring is harder than it looks.

I don't know if anyone has ever died from following my advice. But just to be on the safe side, I avoid putting my sage-like guidance in writing. If I recommend bolstering your confidence by running with the bulls in Pamplona and you end up with a yard-long horn in your upper GI tract, I don't want a paper trail back to me. I'd like to be able to tell your surviving family members that I recommended you should read more, but you flipped out, and I don't know what happened after that.

The only thing I know for sure is that you should follow *Dilbert* on social media. I can't promise it will help your career, but I'm confident it won't turn out worse than my other advice.

Twitter: twitter.com/dilbert_daily

Facebook: facebook.com/Dilbert

S. Adams

Scott Adams

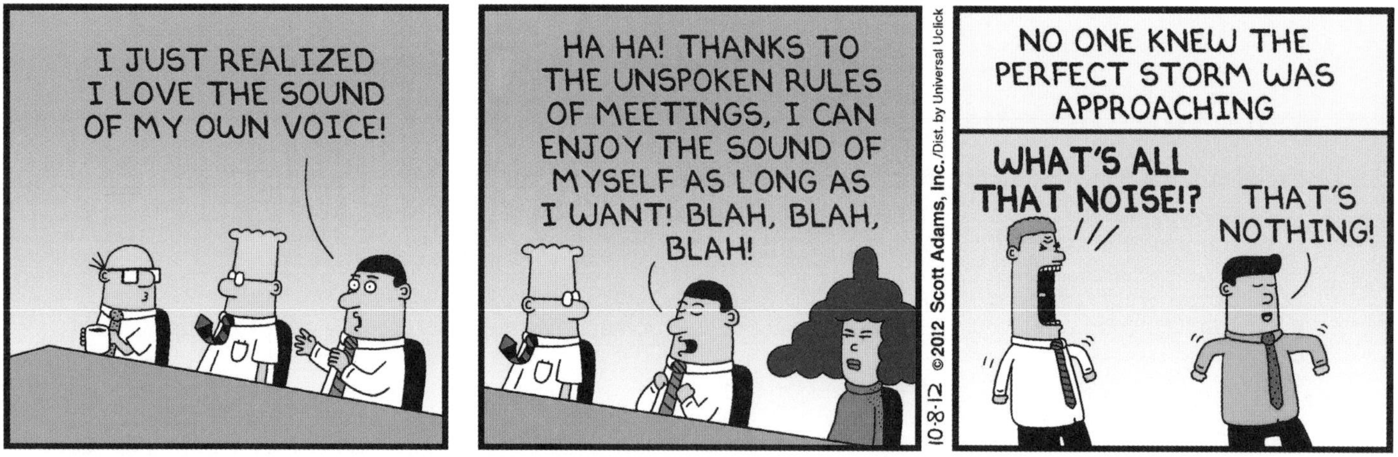
I JUST REALIZED I LOVE THE SOUND OF MY OWN VOICE!
HA HA! THANKS TO THE UNSPOKEN RULES OF MEETINGS, I CAN ENJOY THE SOUND OF MYSELF AS LONG AS I WANT! BLAH, BLAH, BLAH!
10·8·12 ©2012 Scott Adams, Inc./Dist. by Universal Uclick
NO ONE KNEW THE PERFECT STORM WAS APPROACHING
WHAT'S ALL THAT NOISE!?
THAT'S NOTHING!

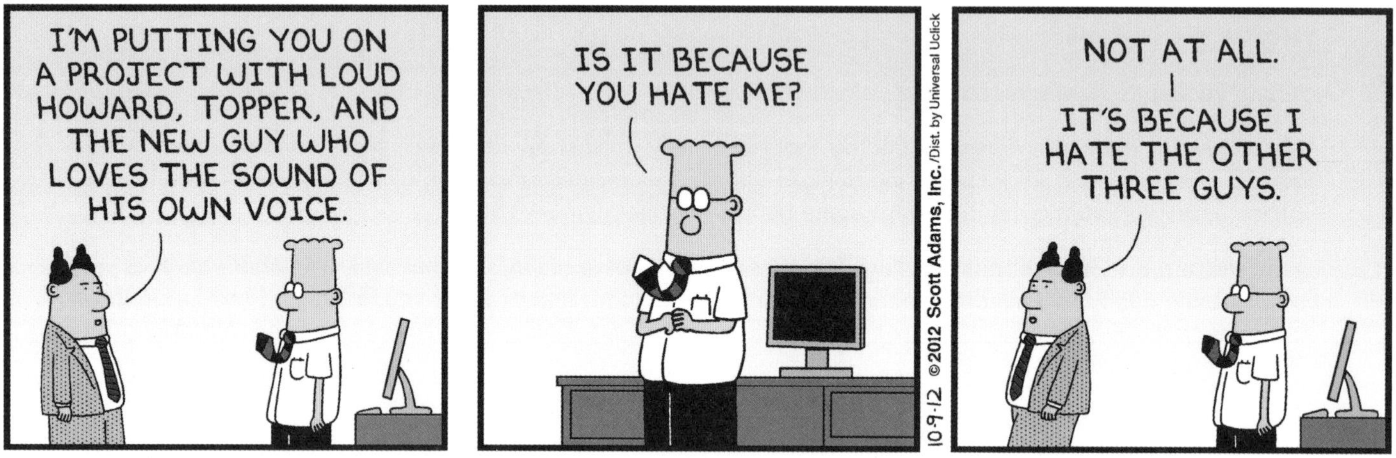
I'M PUTTING YOU ON A PROJECT WITH LOUD HOWARD, TOPPER, AND THE NEW GUY WHO LOVES THE SOUND OF HIS OWN VOICE.
IS IT BECAUSE YOU HATE ME?
10·9·12 ©2012 Scott Adams, Inc./Dist. by Universal Uclick
NOT AT ALL.
IT'S BECAUSE I HATE THE OTHER THREE GUYS.

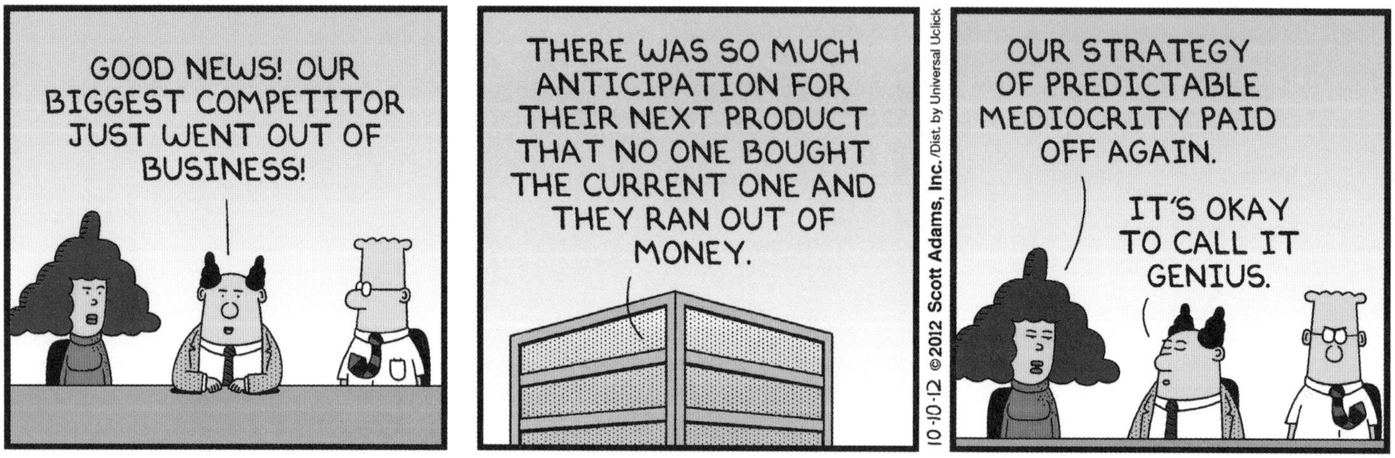
GOOD NEWS! OUR BIGGEST COMPETITOR JUST WENT OUT OF BUSINESS!
THERE WAS SO MUCH ANTICIPATION FOR THEIR NEXT PRODUCT THAT NO ONE BOUGHT THE CURRENT ONE AND THEY RAN OUT OF MONEY.
10·10·12 ©2012 Scott Adams, Inc./Dist. by Universal Uclick
OUR STRATEGY OF PREDICTABLE MEDIOCRITY PAID OFF AGAIN.
IT'S OKAY TO CALL IT GENIUS.

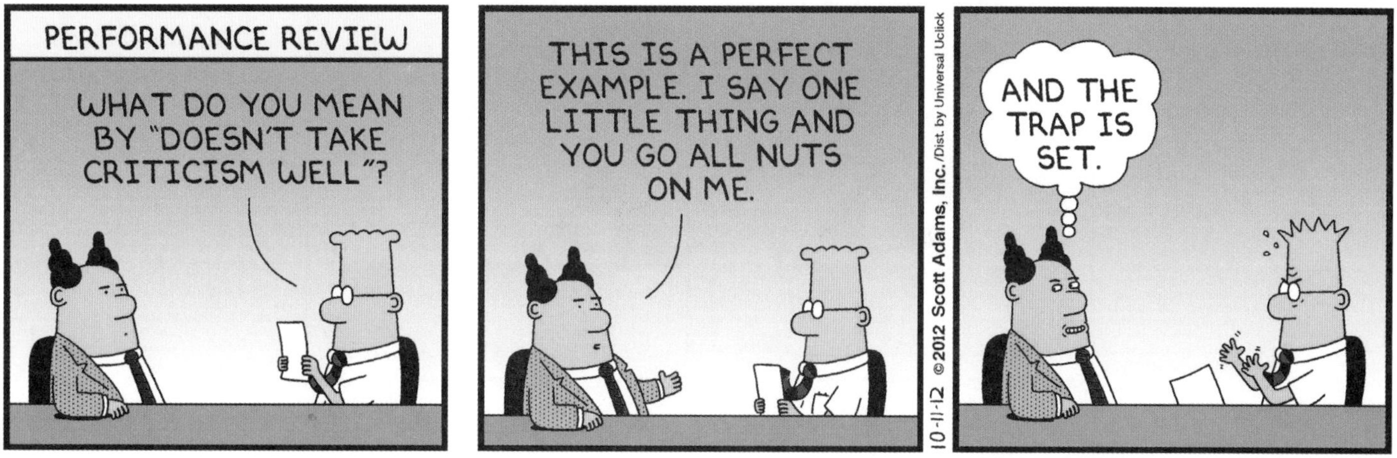
PERFORMANCE REVIEW
WHAT DO YOU MEAN BY "DOESN'T TAKE CRITICISM WELL"?
THIS IS A PERFECT EXAMPLE. I SAY ONE LITTLE THING AND YOU GO ALL NUTS ON ME.
10-11-12 ©2012 Scott Adams, Inc./Dist. by Universal Uclick
AND THE TRAP IS SET.

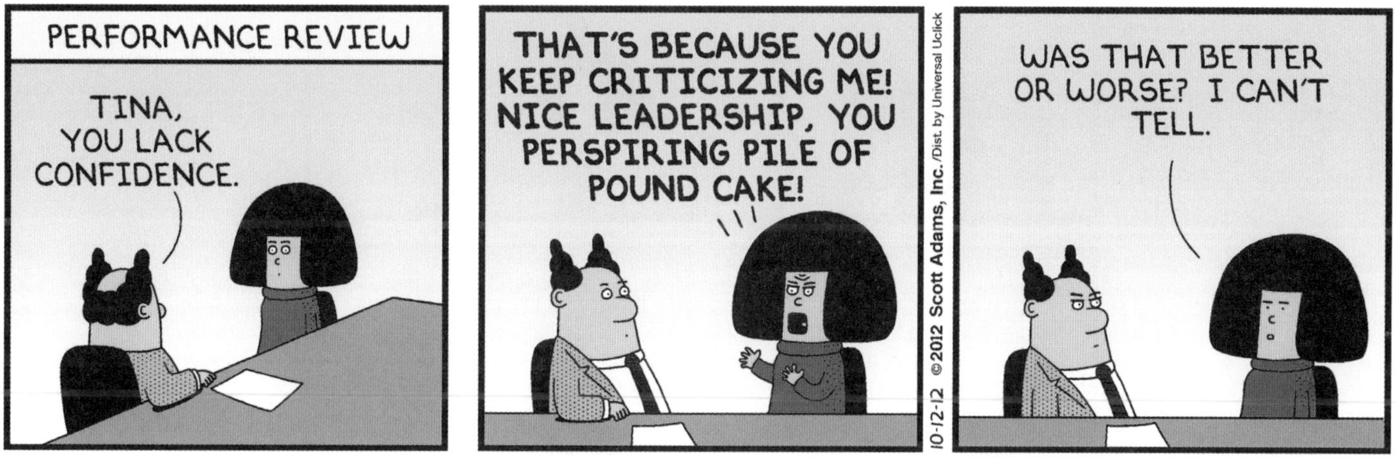
PERFORMANCE REVIEW
TINA, YOU LACK CONFIDENCE.
THAT'S BECAUSE YOU KEEP CRITICIZING ME! NICE LEADERSHIP, YOU PERSPIRING PILE OF POUND CAKE!
10-12-12 ©2012 Scott Adams, Inc./Dist. by Universal Uclick
WAS THAT BETTER OR WORSE? I CAN'T TELL.

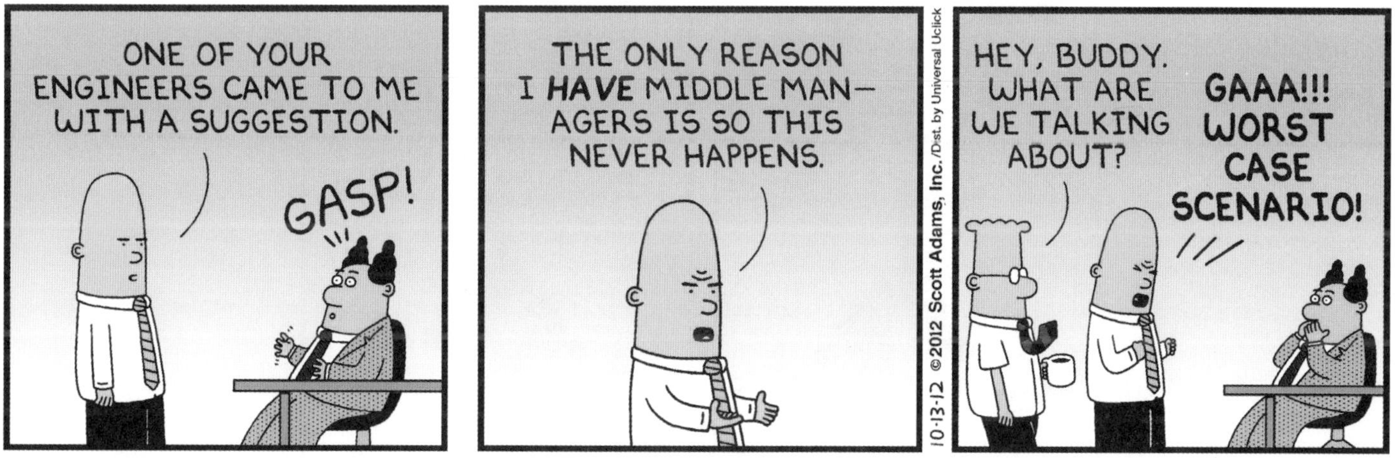
ONE OF YOUR ENGINEERS CAME TO ME WITH A SUGGESTION.
GASP!
THE ONLY REASON I HAVE MIDDLE MAN-AGERS IS SO THIS NEVER HAPPENS.
10-13-12 ©2012 Scott Adams, Inc./Dist. by Universal Uclick
HEY, BUDDY. WHAT ARE WE TALKING ABOUT?
GAAA!!! WORST CASE SCENARIO!

TAKE A LOOK AT THIS RESUME.
HA HA! THIS GUY IS A PIECE OF WORK!
LIE. . . LIE. . . EXAGGERATION. . . MISSPELLING. . . BAD FORMAT. . . WORKED ON FAILED PRODUCTS.
OOH! HE'S ALSO A CHAMPION SALSA DANCER. WHAT A TOOL!
WAIT. WHY AREN'T YOU JOINING IN THE TRADITIONAL MOCKING OF THE APPLICANT'S RESUME?
I'M WAITING TO FIND OUT IF HE'S THE HANDSOME FELLOW STANDING BEHIND YOU.
SCOOT OVER. YOU'RE BLOCKING MY VIEW OF A HANDSOME GUY.
©2012 Scott Adams, Inc./Dist. by Universal Uclick
10-14-12

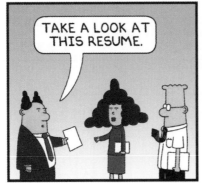

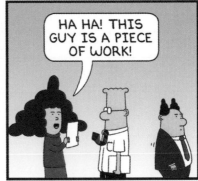

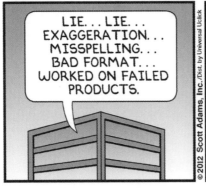

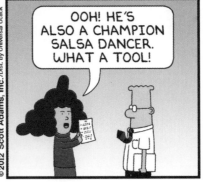

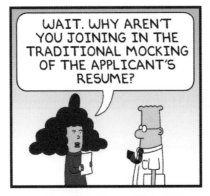

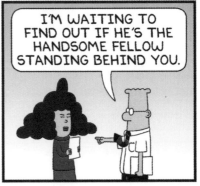

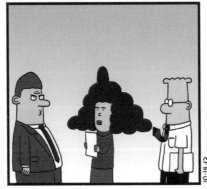

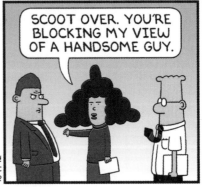

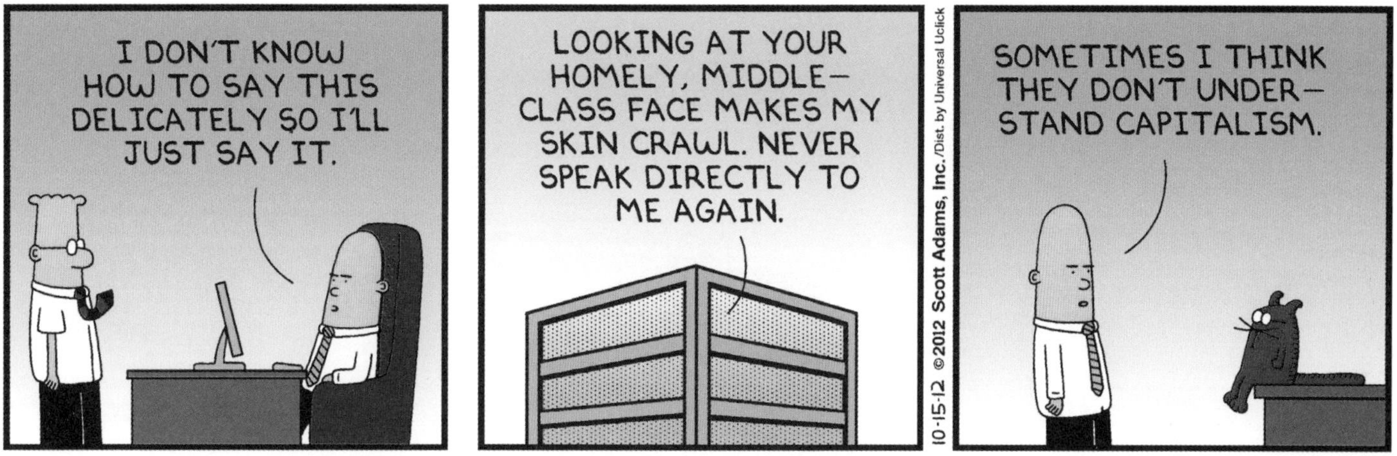
I DON'T KNOW HOW TO SAY THIS DELICATELY SO I'LL JUST SAY IT.
LOOKING AT YOUR HOMELY, MIDDLE-CLASS FACE MAKES MY SKIN CRAWL. NEVER SPEAK DIRECTLY TO ME AGAIN.
10-15-12 ©2012 Scott Adams, Inc./Dist. by Universal Uclick
SOMETIMES I THINK THEY DON'T UNDERSTAND CAPITALISM.

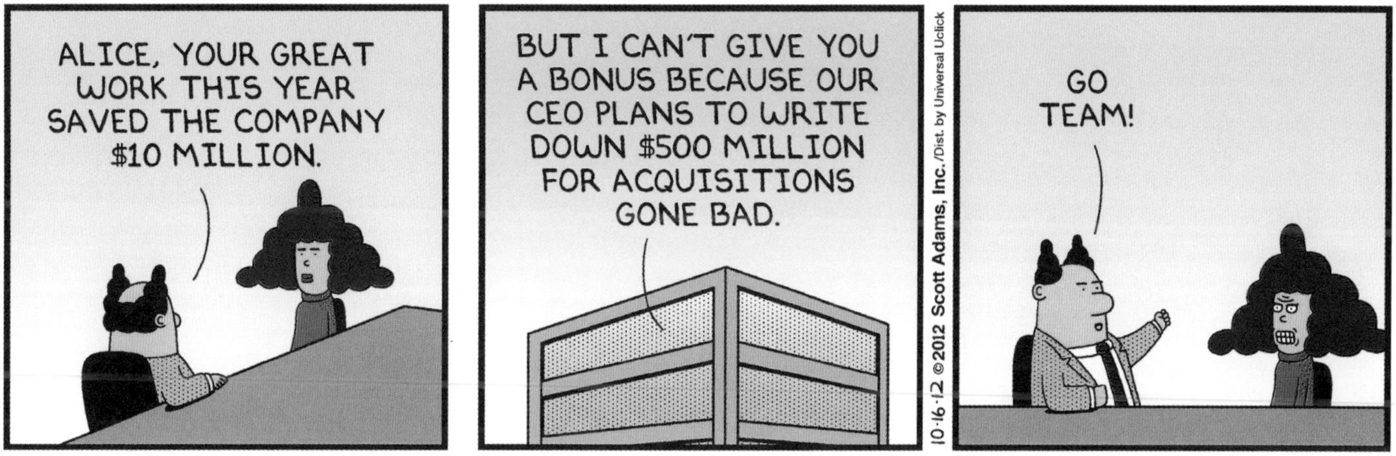
ALICE, YOUR GREAT WORK THIS YEAR SAVED THE COMPANY $10 MILLION.
BUT I CAN'T GIVE YOU A BONUS BECAUSE OUR CEO PLANS TO WRITE DOWN $500 MILLION FOR ACQUISITIONS GONE BAD.
10-16-12 ©2012 Scott Adams, Inc./Dist. by Universal Uclick
GO TEAM!

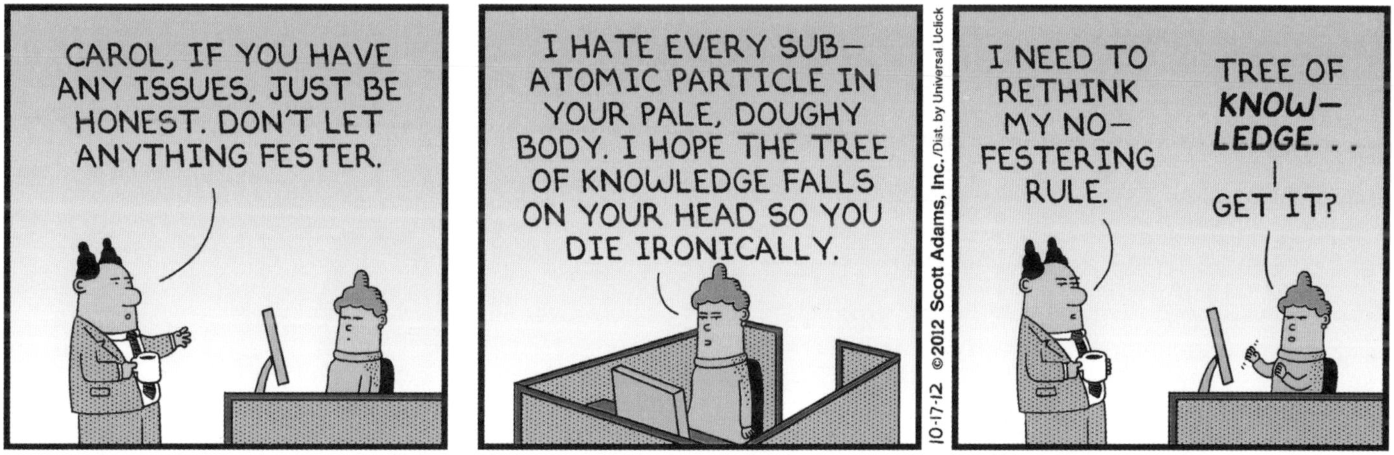
CAROL, IF YOU HAVE ANY ISSUES, JUST BE HONEST. DON'T LET ANYTHING FESTER.
I HATE EVERY SUBATOMIC PARTICLE IN YOUR PALE, DOUGHY BODY. I HOPE THE TREE OF KNOWLEDGE FALLS ON YOUR HEAD SO YOU DIE IRONICALLY.
10-17-12 ©2012 Scott Adams, Inc./Dist. by Universal Uclick
I NEED TO RETHINK MY NO-FESTERING RULE.
TREE OF **KNOWLEDGE**...
GET IT?

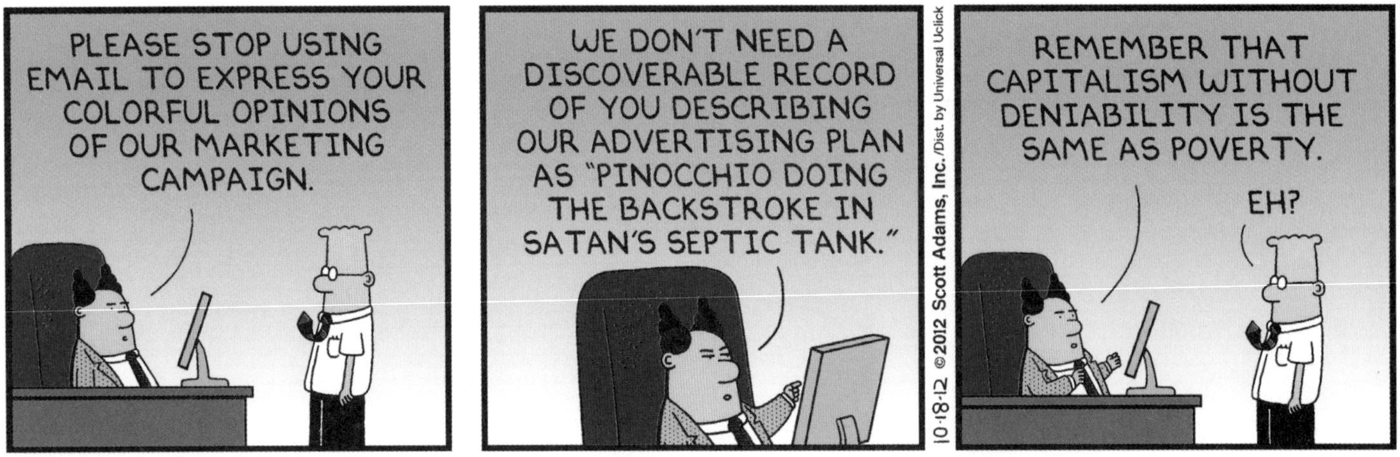
PLEASE STOP USING EMAIL TO EXPRESS YOUR COLORFUL OPINIONS OF OUR MARKETING CAMPAIGN.
WE DON'T NEED A DISCOVERABLE RECORD OF YOU DESCRIBING OUR ADVERTISING PLAN AS "PINOCCHIO DOING THE BACKSTROKE IN SATAN'S SEPTIC TANK."
10-18-12 ©2012 Scott Adams, Inc./Dist. by Universal Uclick
REMEMBER THAT CAPITALISM WITHOUT DENIABILITY IS THE SAME AS POVERTY.
EH?

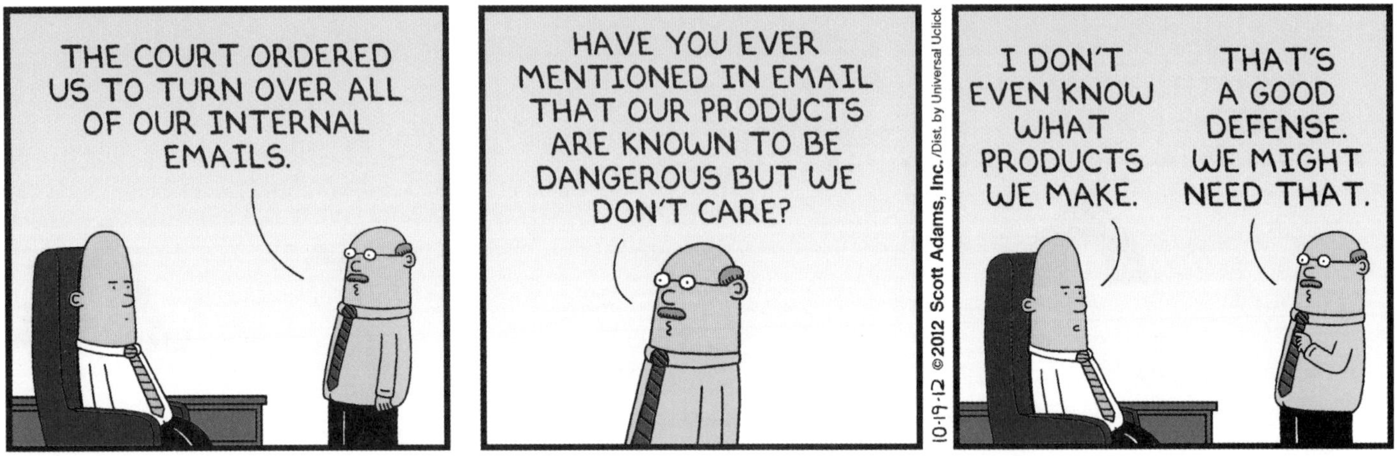
THE COURT ORDERED US TO TURN OVER ALL OF OUR INTERNAL EMAILS.
HAVE YOU EVER MENTIONED IN EMAIL THAT OUR PRODUCTS ARE KNOWN TO BE DANGEROUS BUT WE DON'T CARE?
10-19-12 ©2012 Scott Adams, Inc./Dist. by Universal Uclick
I DON'T EVEN KNOW WHAT PRODUCTS WE MAKE.
THAT'S A GOOD DEFENSE. WE MIGHT NEED THAT.

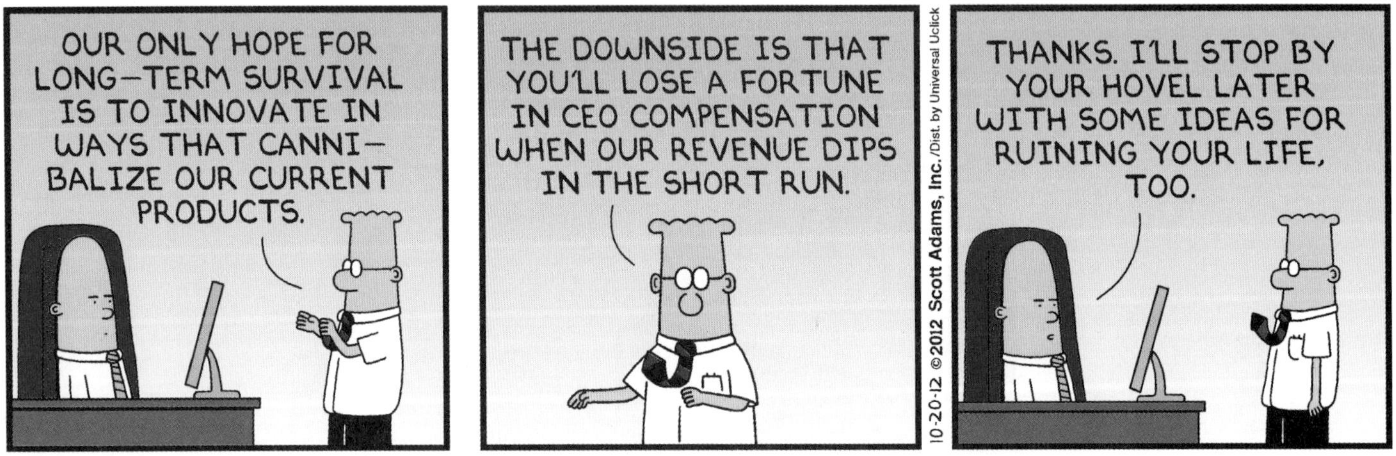
OUR ONLY HOPE FOR LONG-TERM SURVIVAL IS TO INNOVATE IN WAYS THAT CANNI-BALIZE OUR CURRENT PRODUCTS.
THE DOWNSIDE IS THAT YOU'LL LOSE A FORTUNE IN CEO COMPENSATION WHEN OUR REVENUE DIPS IN THE SHORT RUN.
10-20-12 ©2012 Scott Adams, Inc./Dist. by Universal Uclick
THANKS. I'LL STOP BY YOUR HOVEL LATER WITH SOME IDEAS FOR RUINING YOUR LIFE, TOO.

I NEED YOU TO CLOUDWASH OUR SOFTWARE.
CLOUDWASH?
MOVE SOME OF ITS FUNCTIONS ONTO THE INTERNET. BUT CALL THE INTERNET A CLOUD.
NO ONE WILL TAKE US SERIOUSLY UNLESS WE'RE DOING SOME-THING IN THE CLOUD.
WILL PEOPLE TAKE US SERIOUSLY IF WE MAKE TECHNOLOGY DECISIONS BASED ON JARGON?
WE DON'T CARE WHAT SMART PEOPLE THINK. THERE AREN'T THAT MANY OF THEM.
WE ONLY NEED TO CONVINCE OUR DUMB CUSTOMERS.
DUMB PEOPLE BELIEVE ANYTHING.
DO YOU BELIEVE I MOVED OUR SOFT-WARE TO THE CLOUD YESTERDAY?
YOU DID?
I'M GOING TO SAY YES.
©2012 Scott Adams, Inc./Dist. by Universal Uclick
10-21-12

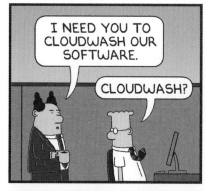

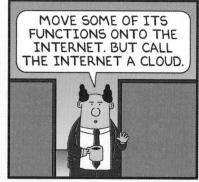

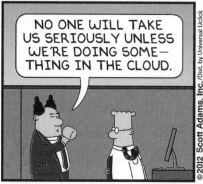

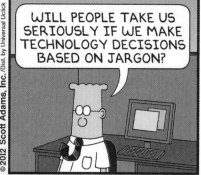

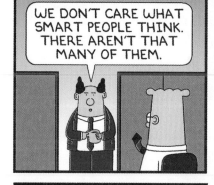

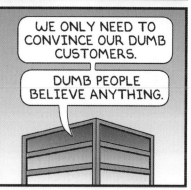

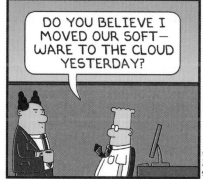

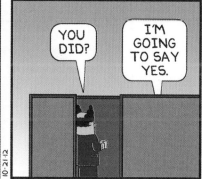

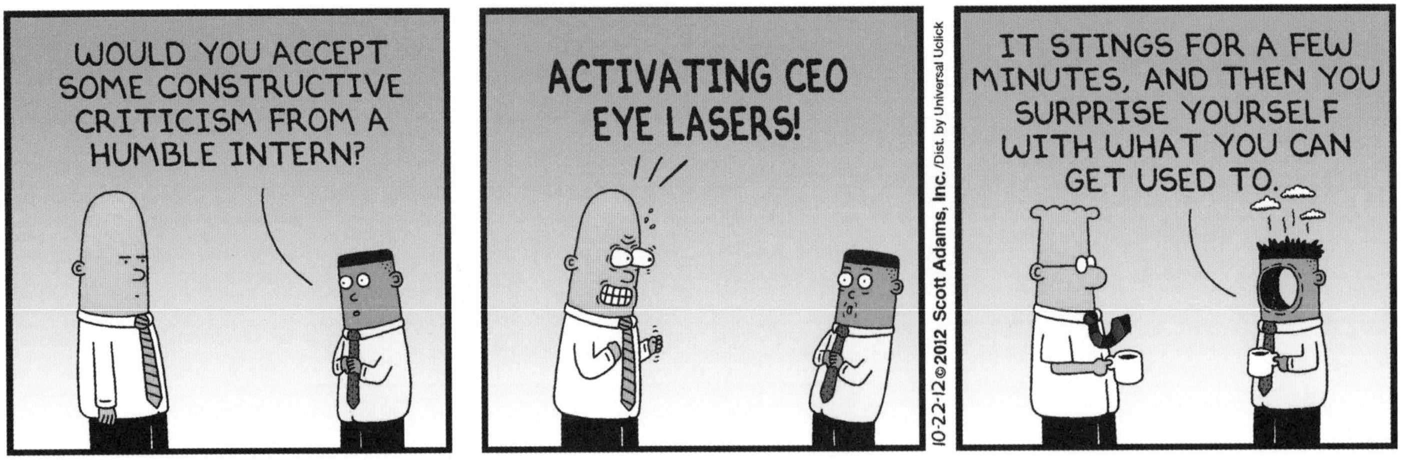
WOULD YOU ACCEPT SOME CONSTRUCTIVE CRITICISM FROM A HUMBLE INTERN?
ACTIVATING CEO EYE LASERS!
10·22·12 ©2012 Scott Adams, Inc./Dist. by Universal Uclick
IT STINGS FOR A FEW MINUTES, AND THEN YOU SURPRISE YOURSELF WITH WHAT YOU CAN GET USED TO.

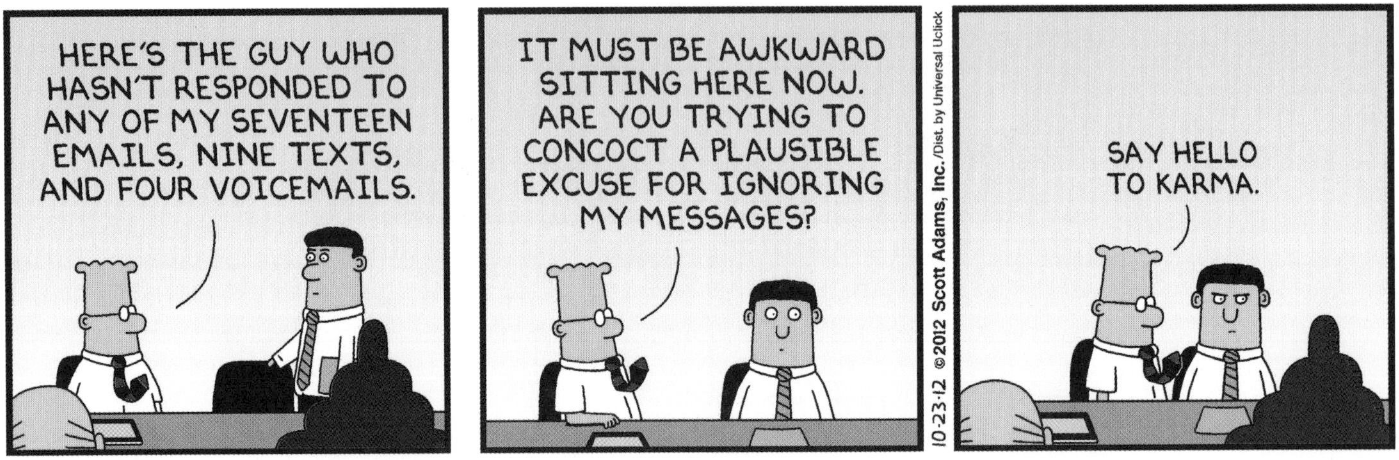
HERE'S THE GUY WHO HASN'T RESPONDED TO ANY OF MY SEVENTEEN EMAILS, NINE TEXTS, AND FOUR VOICEMAILS.
IT MUST BE AWKWARD SITTING HERE NOW. ARE YOU TRYING TO CONCOCT A PLAUSIBLE EXCUSE FOR IGNORING MY MESSAGES?
10·23·12 ©2012 Scott Adams, Inc./Dist. by Universal Uclick
SAY HELLO TO KARMA.

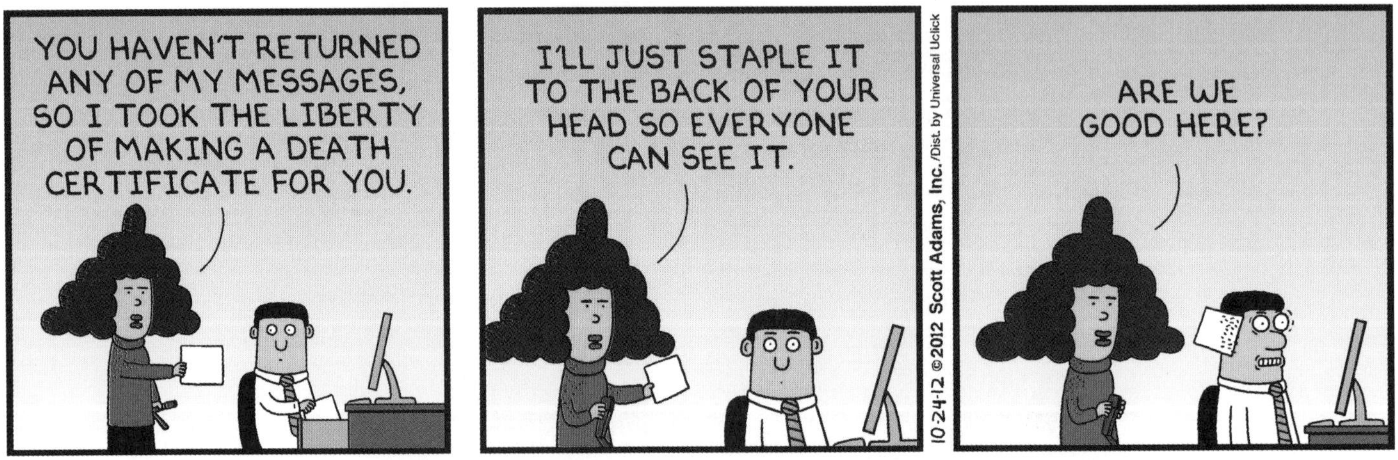
YOU HAVEN'T RETURNED ANY OF MY MESSAGES, SO I TOOK THE LIBERTY OF MAKING A DEATH CERTIFICATE FOR YOU.
I'LL JUST STAPLE IT TO THE BACK OF YOUR HEAD SO EVERYONE CAN SEE IT.
10·24·12 ©2012 Scott Adams, Inc./Dist. by Universal Uclick
ARE WE GOOD HERE?

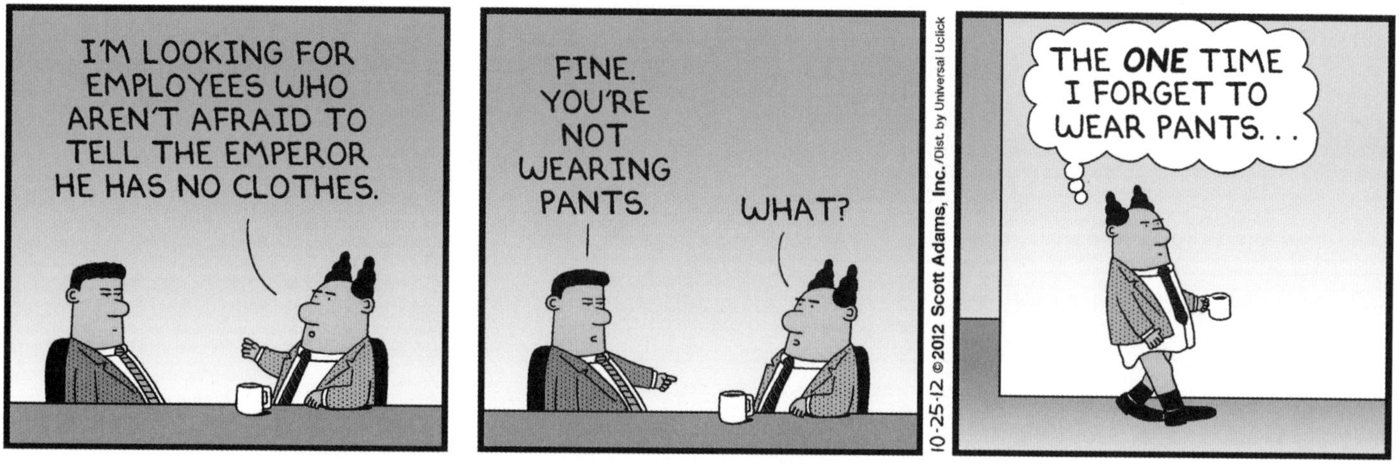
I'M LOOKING FOR EMPLOYEES WHO AREN'T AFRAID TO TELL THE EMPEROR HE HAS NO CLOTHES.
FINE. YOU'RE NOT WEARING PANTS.
WHAT?
10-25-12 ©2012 Scott Adams, Inc./Dist. by Universal Uclick
THE **ONE** TIME I FORGET TO WEAR PANTS. . .

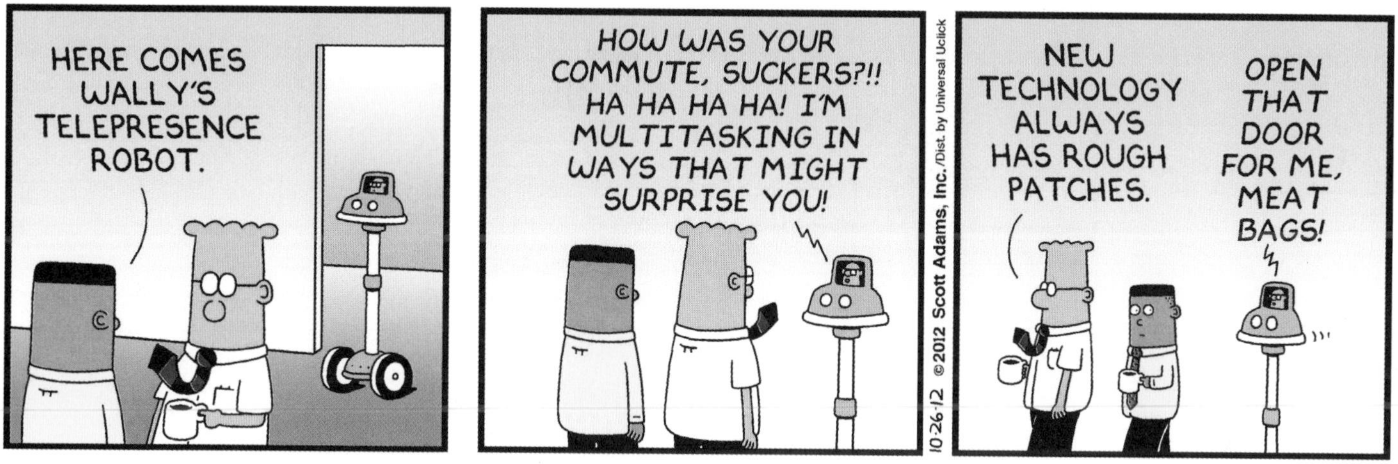
HERE COMES WALLY'S TELEPRESENCE ROBOT.
HOW WAS YOUR COMMUTE, SUCKERS?!! HA HA HA HA! I'M MULTITASKING IN WAYS THAT MIGHT SURPRISE YOU!
10-26-12 ©2012 Scott Adams, Inc./Dist. by Universal Uclick
NEW TECHNOLOGY ALWAYS HAS ROUGH PATCHES.
OPEN THAT DOOR FOR ME, MEAT BAGS!

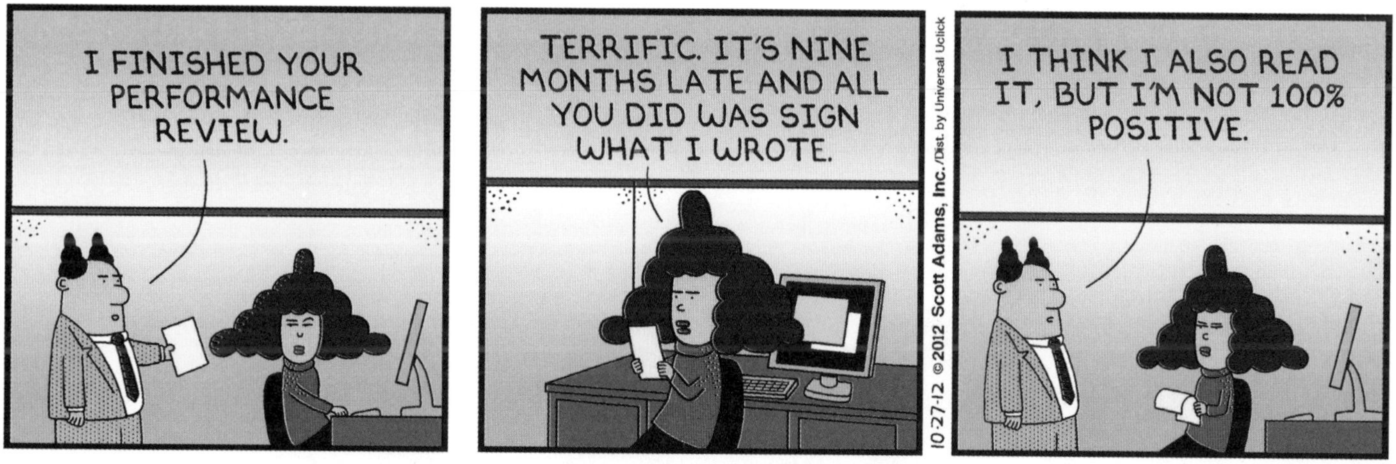
I FINISHED YOUR PERFORMANCE REVIEW.
TERRIFIC. IT'S NINE MONTHS LATE AND ALL YOU DID WAS SIGN WHAT I WROTE.
10-27-12 ©2012 Scott Adams, Inc./Dist. by Universal Uclick
I THINK I ALSO READ IT, BUT I'M NOT 100% POSITIVE.

. . . AND THAT'S OUR MARKETING PLAN FOR THE COMING YEAR.
RESEARCH SHOWS THAT CONSUMERS REJECT THIS SORT OF APPROACH.
RESEARCH IS STUPID.
ARE YOU SAYING THE STUDIES ON THIS PARTICULAR TOPIC ARE FLAWED?
OR ARE YOU JUST GENERALLY OPPOSED TO SCIENCE, RATIONAL THINKING, AND ALL MANIFESTATIONS OF COMMON SENSE?
STOP BEING PEDANTIC WITH YOUR SEMANTICS.
DID YOU GET BUY—IN?
YES, IN THE SENSE THAT THEY STOPPED TALKING.
©2012 Scott Adams, Inc./Dist. by Universal Uclick
10-28-12

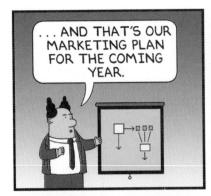

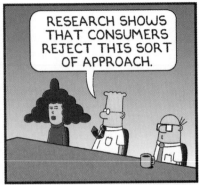

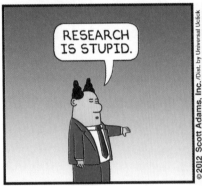

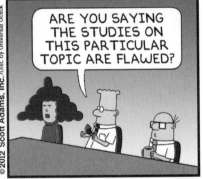

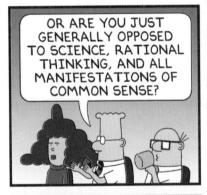

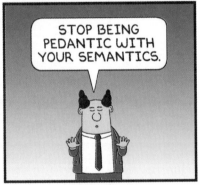

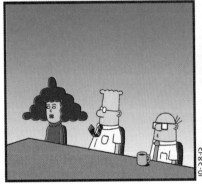

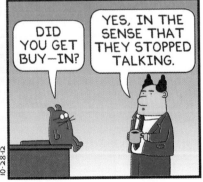

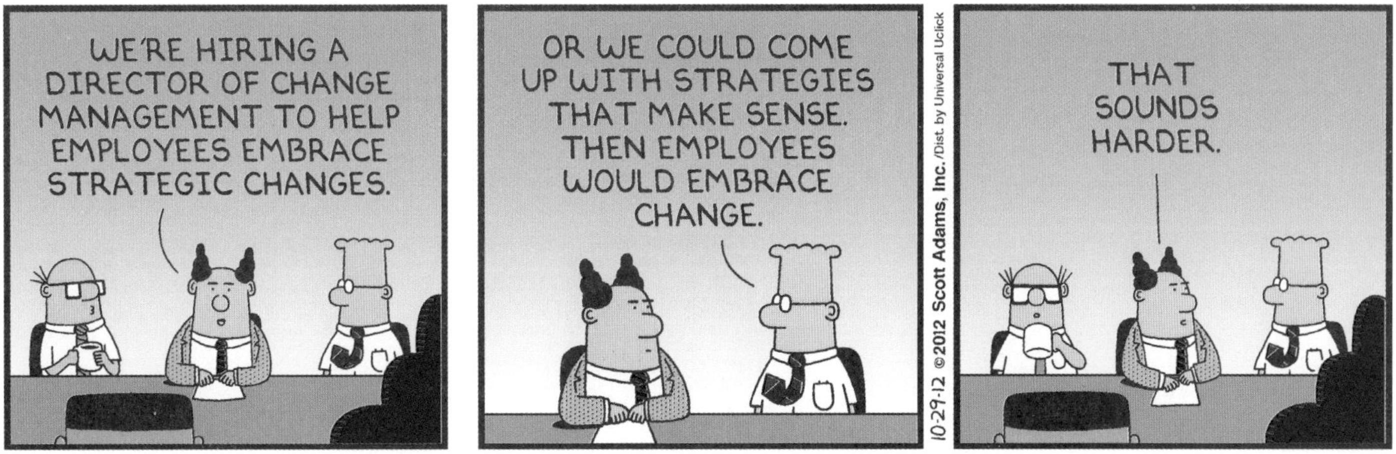
WE'RE HIRING A DIRECTOR OF CHANGE MANAGEMENT TO HELP EMPLOYEES EMBRACE STRATEGIC CHANGES.
OR WE COULD COME UP WITH STRATEGIES THAT MAKE SENSE. THEN EMPLOYEES WOULD EMBRACE CHANGE.
THAT SOUNDS HARDER.
10·29·12 ©2012 Scott Adams, Inc./Dist. by Universal Uclick

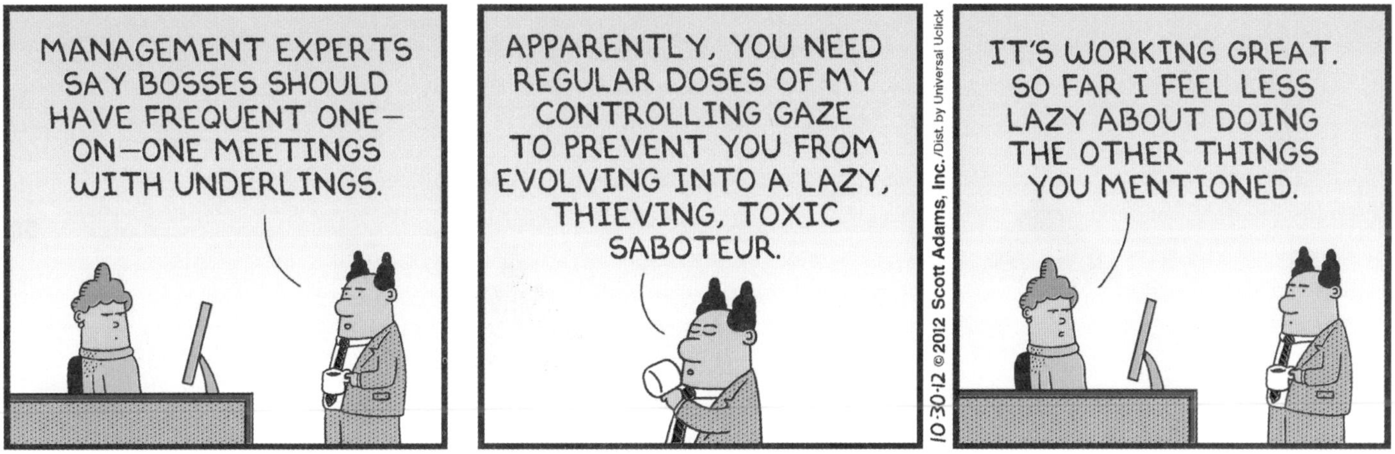
MANAGEMENT EXPERTS SAY BOSSES SHOULD HAVE FREQUENT ONE-ON-ONE MEETINGS WITH UNDERLINGS.
APPARENTLY, YOU NEED REGULAR DOSES OF MY CONTROLLING GAZE TO PREVENT YOU FROM EVOLVING INTO A LAZY, THIEVING, TOXIC SABOTEUR.
IT'S WORKING GREAT. SO FAR I FEEL LESS LAZY ABOUT DOING THE OTHER THINGS YOU MENTIONED.
10·30·12 ©2012 Scott Adams, Inc./Dist. by Universal Uclick

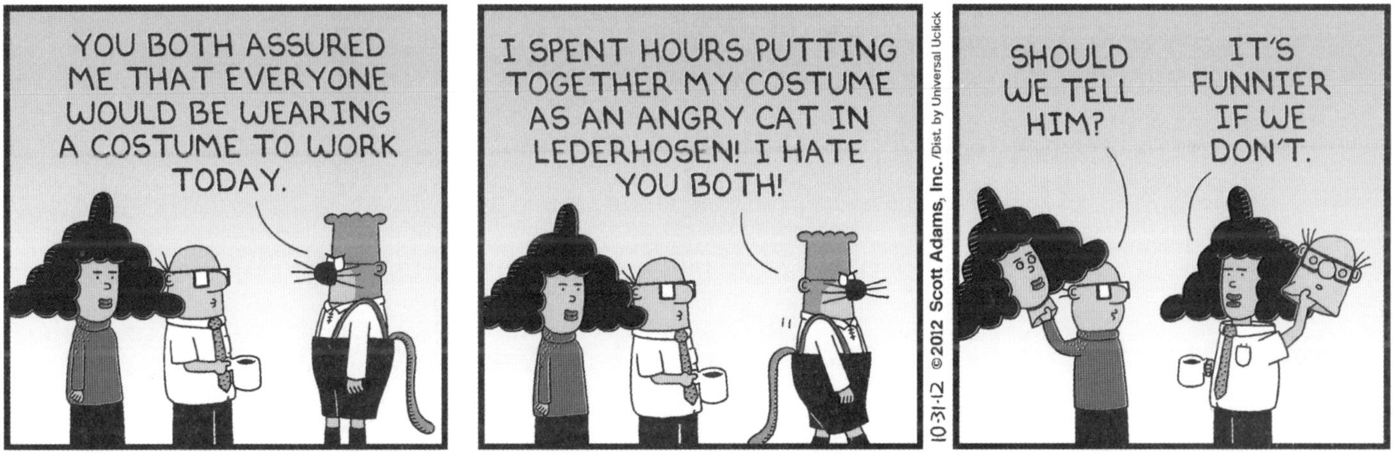
YOU BOTH ASSURED ME THAT EVERYONE WOULD BE WEARING A COSTUME TO WORK TODAY.
I SPENT HOURS PUTTING TOGETHER MY COSTUME AS AN ANGRY CAT IN LEDERHOSEN! I HATE YOU BOTH!
SHOULD WE TELL HIM?
IT'S FUNNIER IF WE DON'T.
10·31·12 ©2012 Scott Adams, Inc./Dist. by Universal Uclick

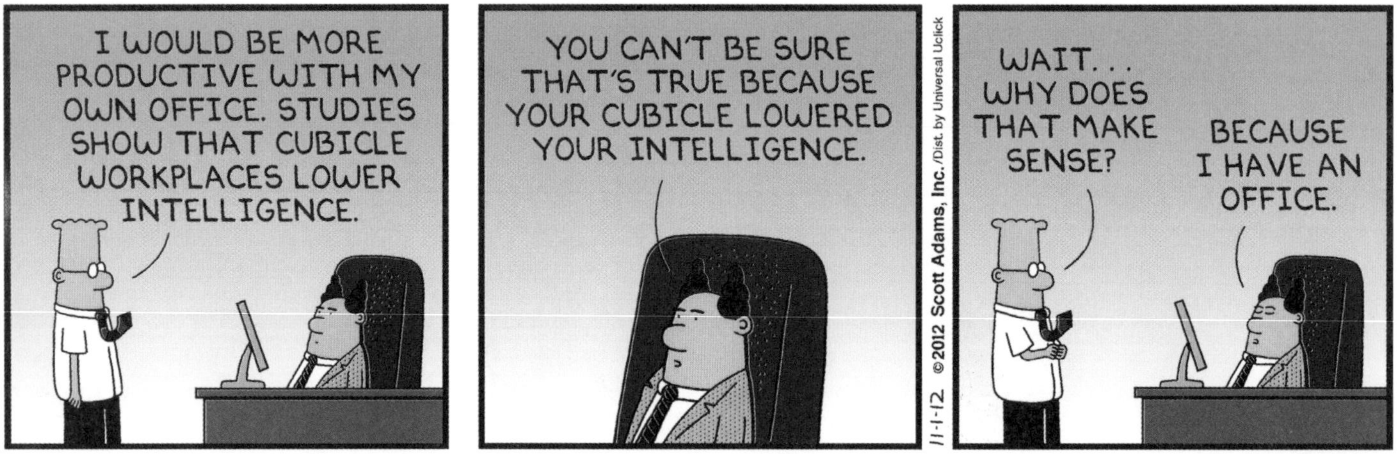
I WOULD BE MORE PRODUCTIVE WITH MY OWN OFFICE. STUDIES SHOW THAT CUBICLE WORKPLACES LOWER INTELLIGENCE.
YOU CAN'T BE SURE THAT'S TRUE BECAUSE YOUR CUBICLE LOWERED YOUR INTELLIGENCE.
11-1-12 ©2012 Scott Adams, Inc./Dist. by Universal Uclick
WAIT... WHY DOES THAT MAKE SENSE?
BECAUSE I HAVE AN OFFICE.

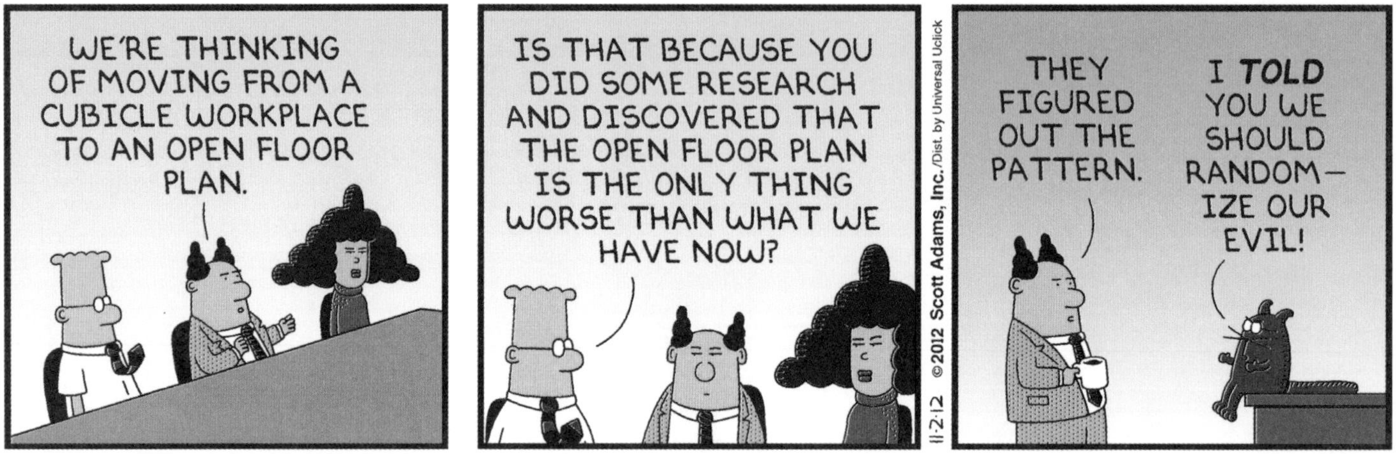
WE'RE THINKING OF MOVING FROM A CUBICLE WORKPLACE TO AN OPEN FLOOR PLAN.
IS THAT BECAUSE YOU DID SOME RESEARCH AND DISCOVERED THAT THE OPEN FLOOR PLAN IS THE ONLY THING WORSE THAN WHAT WE HAVE NOW?
11-2-12 ©2012 Scott Adams, Inc./Dist. by Universal Uclick
THEY FIGURED OUT THE PATTERN.
I TOLD YOU WE SHOULD RANDOM-IZE OUR EVIL!

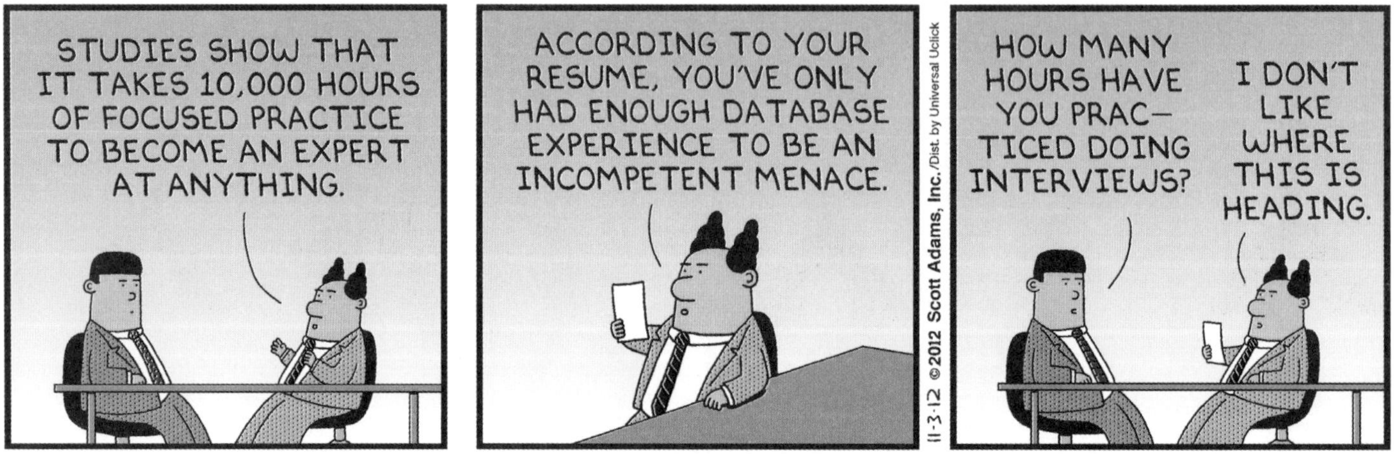
STUDIES SHOW THAT IT TAKES 10,000 HOURS OF FOCUSED PRACTICE TO BECOME AN EXPERT AT ANYTHING.
ACCORDING TO YOUR RESUME, YOU'VE ONLY HAD ENOUGH DATABASE EXPERIENCE TO BE AN INCOMPETENT MENACE.
11-3-12 ©2012 Scott Adams, Inc./Dist. by Universal Uclick
HOW MANY HOURS HAVE YOU PRAC-TICED DOING INTERVIEWS?
I DON'T LIKE WHERE THIS IS HEADING.

THE FIRST QUESTION ON THE EMPLOYEE SURVEY IS. . .
DO YOU FEEL YOU ARE VALUED AND TREATED WITH RESPECT AND DIGNITY?
WELL, LET ME PUT IT THIS WAY. . .
YOU KNOW HOW SOME-TIMES YOU STEP IN SOMETHING GROSS AND THEN YOU HAVE TO WIPE IT OFF YOUR SHOE WITH A PAPER TOWEL?
SO. . . YOU FEEL LIKE THE PAPER TOWEL?
NO, THE PAPER TOWEL HAS A PURPOSE.
SO. . . YOU FEEL LIKE THE GROSS STUFF ON THE SHOE?
NO, THE GROSS STUFF GETS TO LEAVE.
I FEEL LIKE A SHOE THAT HAS GROSS STUFF ON THE BOTTOM AND A SWEATY FOOT SHOVED ALL THE WAY TO THE END OF ITS SOLE.
I'LL LEAVE THIS ONE BLANK.
BECAUSE MY OPIN-IONS DON'T MATTER?
© 2012 Scott Adams, Inc./Dist. by Universal Uclick
11-4-12

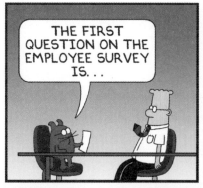

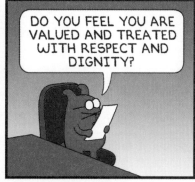

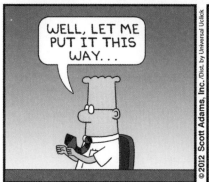

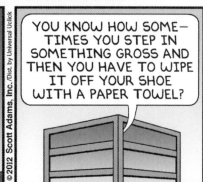

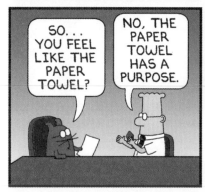

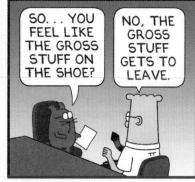

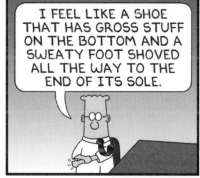

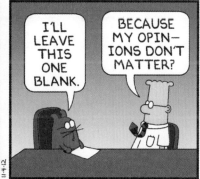

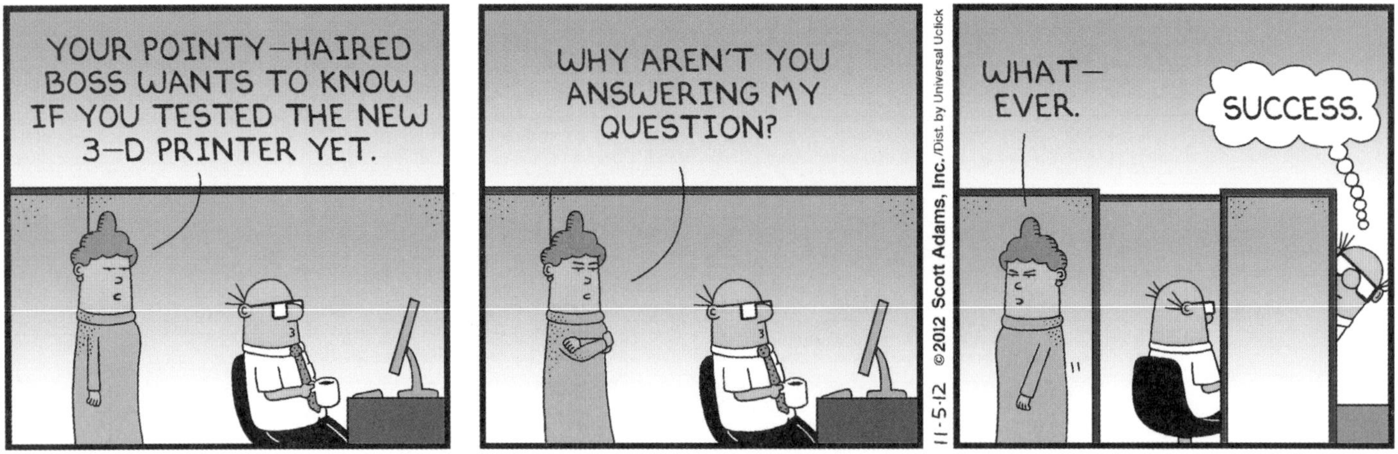
YOUR POINTY—HAIRED BOSS WANTS TO KNOW IF YOU TESTED THE NEW 3—D PRINTER YET.
WHY AREN'T YOU ANSWERING MY QUESTION?
11-5-12 ©2012 Scott Adams, Inc./Dist. by Universal Uclick
WHAT—EVER.
SUCCESS.

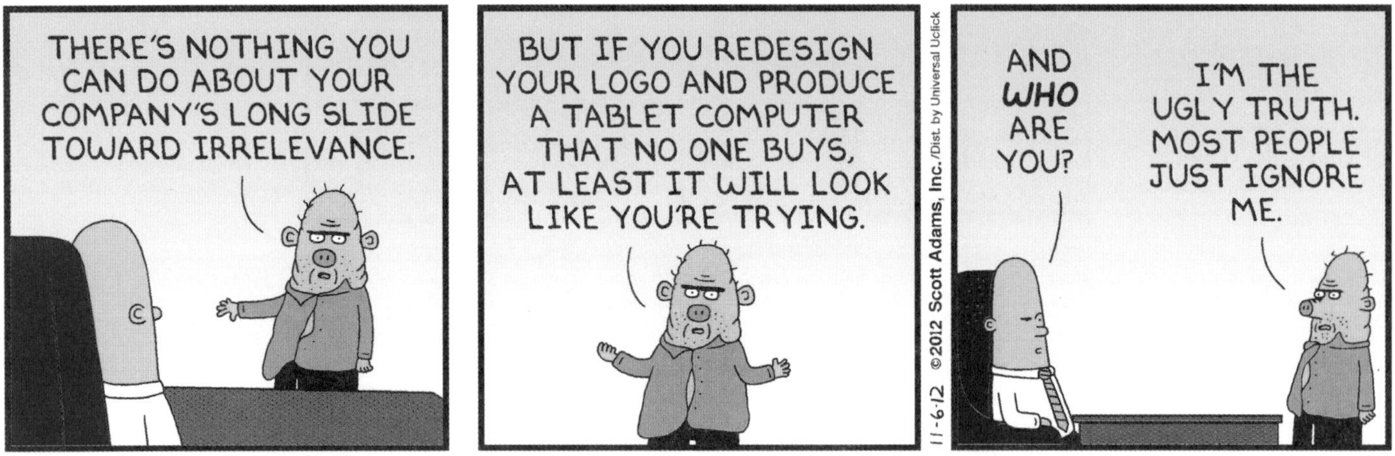
THERE'S NOTHING YOU CAN DO ABOUT YOUR COMPANY'S LONG SLIDE TOWARD IRRELEVANCE.
BUT IF YOU REDESIGN YOUR LOGO AND PRODUCE A TABLET COMPUTER THAT NO ONE BUYS, AT LEAST IT WILL LOOK LIKE YOU'RE TRYING.
11-6-12 ©2012 Scott Adams, Inc./Dist. by Universal Uclick
AND *WHO* ARE YOU?
I'M THE UGLY TRUTH. MOST PEOPLE JUST IGNORE ME.

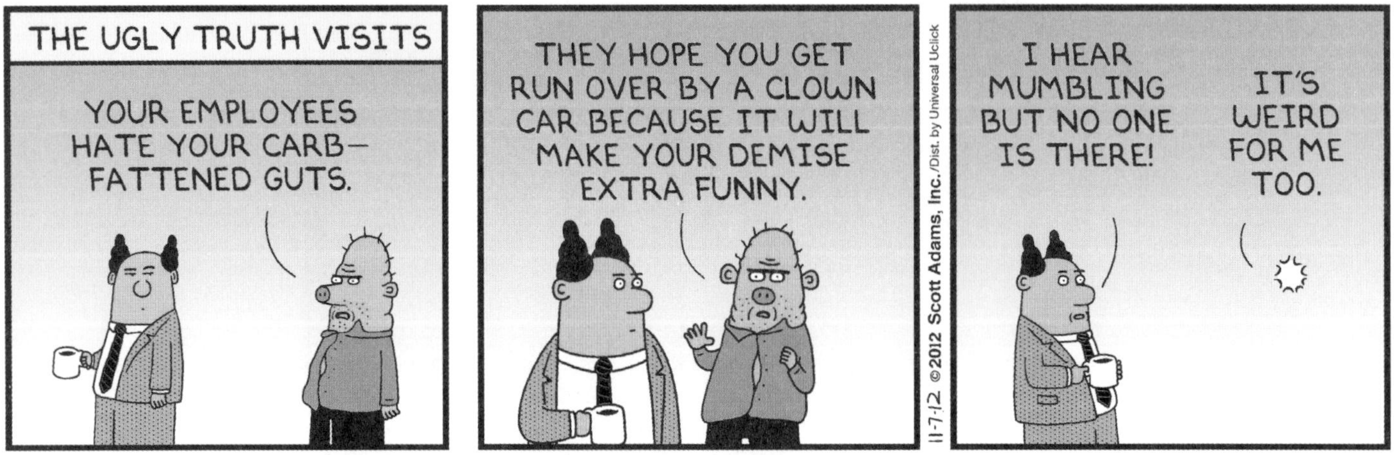
THE UGLY TRUTH VISITS
YOUR EMPLOYEES HATE YOUR CARB—FATTENED GUTS.
THEY HOPE YOU GET RUN OVER BY A CLOWN CAR BECAUSE IT WILL MAKE YOUR DEMISE EXTRA FUNNY.
11-7-12 ©2012 Scott Adams, Inc./Dist. by Universal Uclick
I HEAR MUMBLING BUT NO ONE IS THERE!
IT'S WEIRD FOR ME TOO.

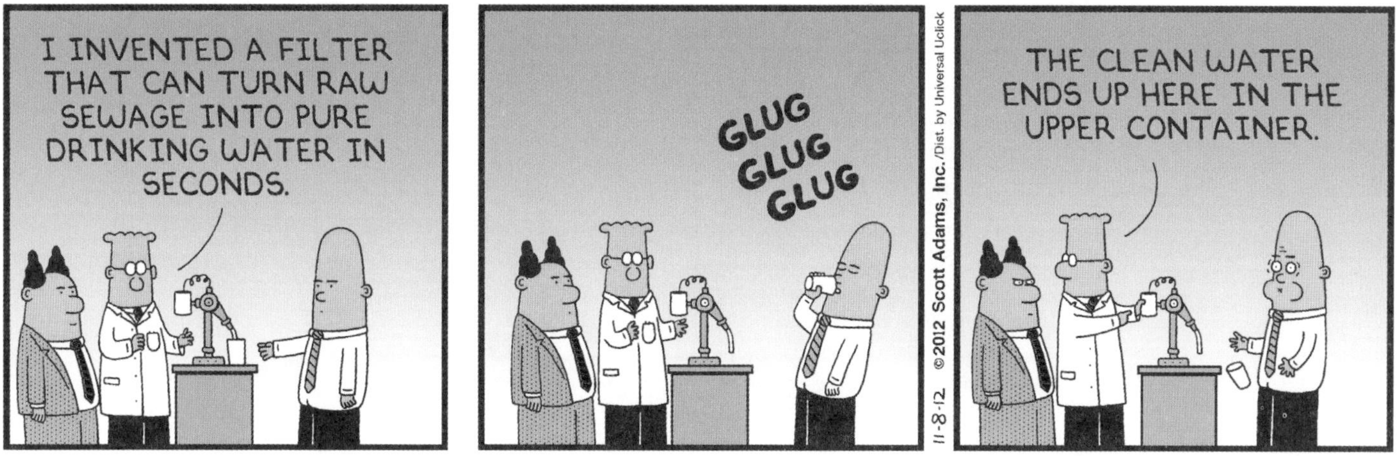
I INVENTED A FILTER THAT CAN TURN RAW SEWAGE INTO PURE DRINKING WATER IN SECONDS.
GLUG GLUG GLUG
THE CLEAN WATER ENDS UP HERE IN THE UPPER CONTAINER.
11-8-12 ©2012 Scott Adams, Inc./Dist. by Universal Uclick

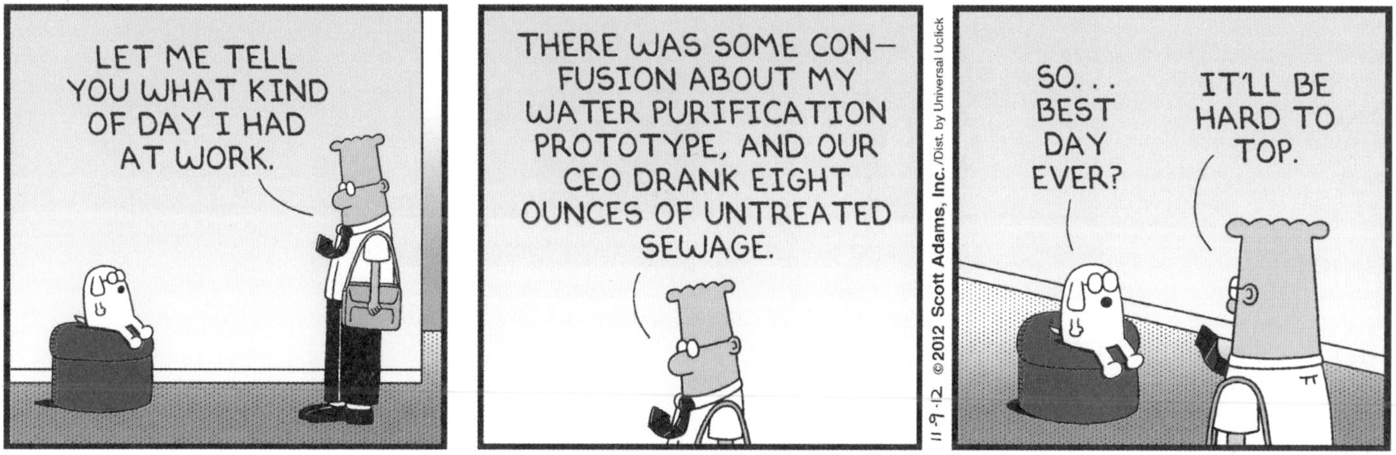
LET ME TELL YOU WHAT KIND OF DAY I HAD AT WORK.
THERE WAS SOME CON-FUSION ABOUT MY WATER PURIFICATION PROTOTYPE, AND OUR CEO DRANK EIGHT OUNCES OF UNTREATED SEWAGE.
SO... BEST DAY EVER?
IT'LL BE HARD TO TOP.
11-9-12 ©2012 Scott Adams, Inc./Dist. by Universal Uclick

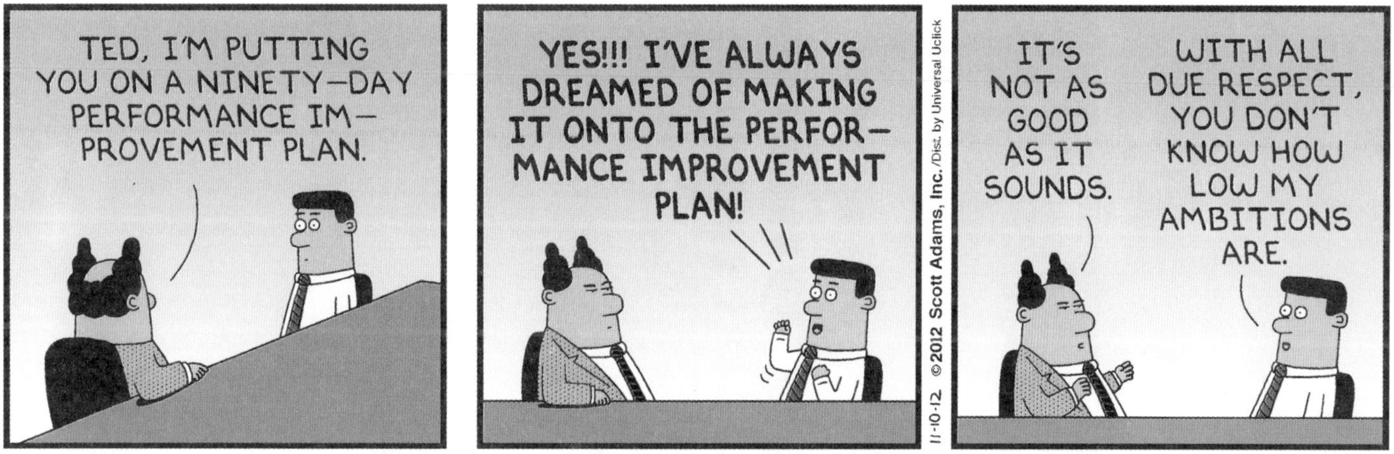
TED, I'M PUTTING YOU ON A NINETY-DAY PERFORMANCE IM-PROVEMENT PLAN.
YES!!! I'VE ALWAYS DREAMED OF MAKING IT ONTO THE PERFOR-MANCE IMPROVEMENT PLAN!
IT'S NOT AS GOOD AS IT SOUNDS.
WITH ALL DUE RESPECT, YOU DON'T KNOW HOW LOW MY AMBITIONS ARE.
11-10-12 ©2012 Scott Adams, Inc./Dist. by Universal Uclick

EXECUTION IS A GAME OF INCHES! YOU MISS 100% OF THE SHOTS YOU DON'T TAKE!
INNOVATION IS EVERYONE'S FULL-TIME JOB! BE THE DOG, NOT THE TAIL!
EXCELLENCE IS THE ONLY MARKET THAT ISN'T CROWDED!
WHY DON'T ANY OF YOU LOOK INSPIRED BY MY LEADERSHIP?
I DIED ON THE INSIDE YEARS AGO.
NOW I'M JUST A FLESHY CONTAINER FULL OF COFFEE AND RESENTMENT.
THIS GUY WAS BORN WITHOUT A SOUL. THE SHE-DEVIL AT THE END IS THE CHEMICAL FORMULA FOR HATRED.
DID YOU GET THROUGH TO THEM?
I DRILLED UNTIL I HIT BILE.
©2012 Scott Adams, Inc./Dist. by Universal Uclick
11-11-12

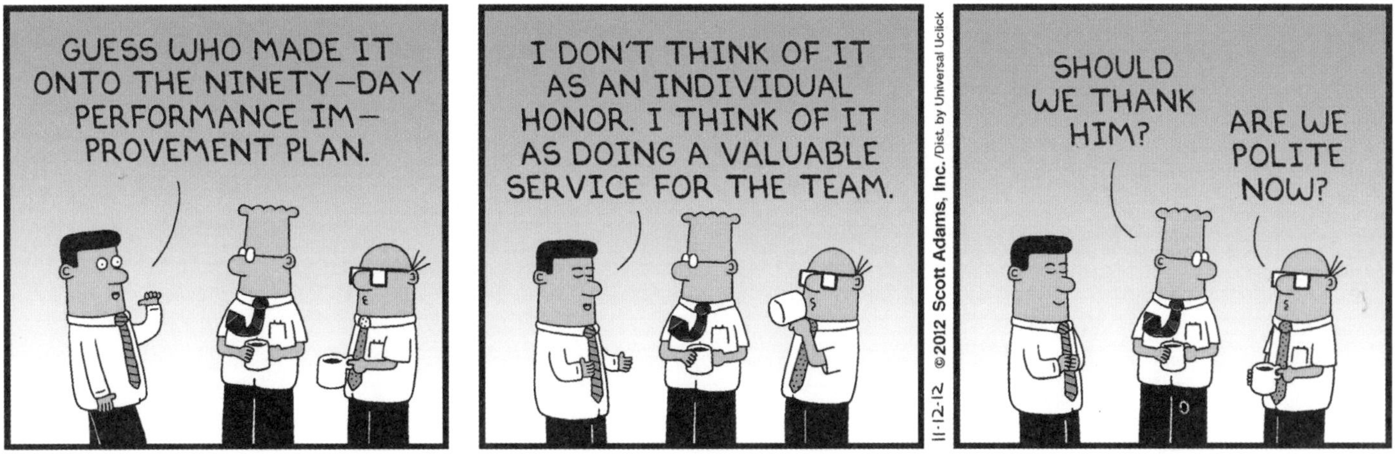
GUESS WHO MADE IT ONTO THE NINETY-DAY PERFORMANCE IM-PROVEMENT PLAN.
I DON'T THINK OF IT AS AN INDIVIDUAL HONOR. I THINK OF IT AS DOING A VALUABLE SERVICE FOR THE TEAM.
11-12-12 ©2012 Scott Adams, Inc./Dist. by Universal Uclick
SHOULD WE THANK HIM?
ARE WE POLITE NOW?

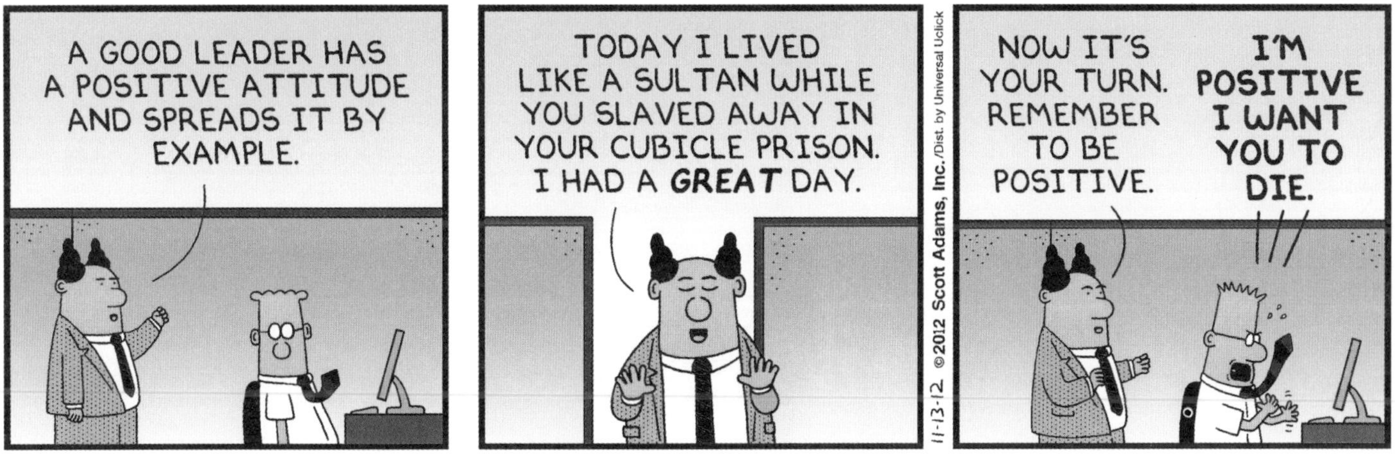
A GOOD LEADER HAS A POSITIVE ATTITUDE AND SPREADS IT BY EXAMPLE.
TODAY I LIVED LIKE A SULTAN WHILE YOU SLAVED AWAY IN YOUR CUBICLE PRISON. I HAD A **GREAT** DAY.
11-13-12 ©2012 Scott Adams, Inc./Dist. by Universal Uclick
NOW IT'S YOUR TURN. REMEMBER TO BE POSITIVE.
I'M POSITIVE I WANT YOU TO DIE.

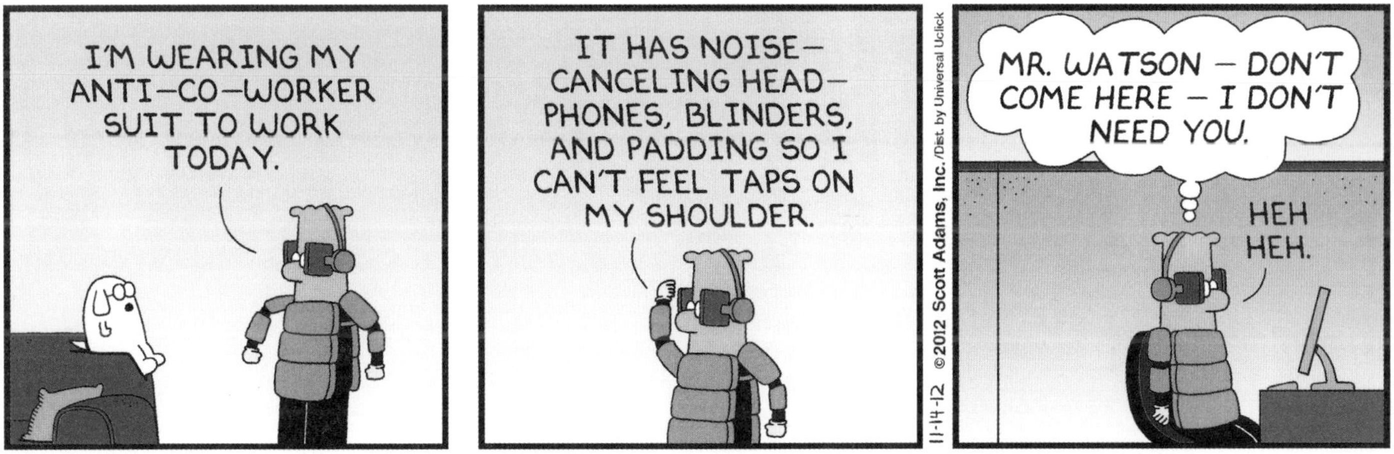
I'M WEARING MY ANTI-CO-WORKER SUIT TO WORK TODAY.
IT HAS NOISE-CANCELING HEAD-PHONES, BLINDERS, AND PADDING SO I CAN'T FEEL TAPS ON MY SHOULDER.
11-14-12 ©2012 Scott Adams, Inc./Dist. by Universal Uclick
MR. WATSON – DON'T COME HERE – I DON'T NEED YOU.
HEH HEH.

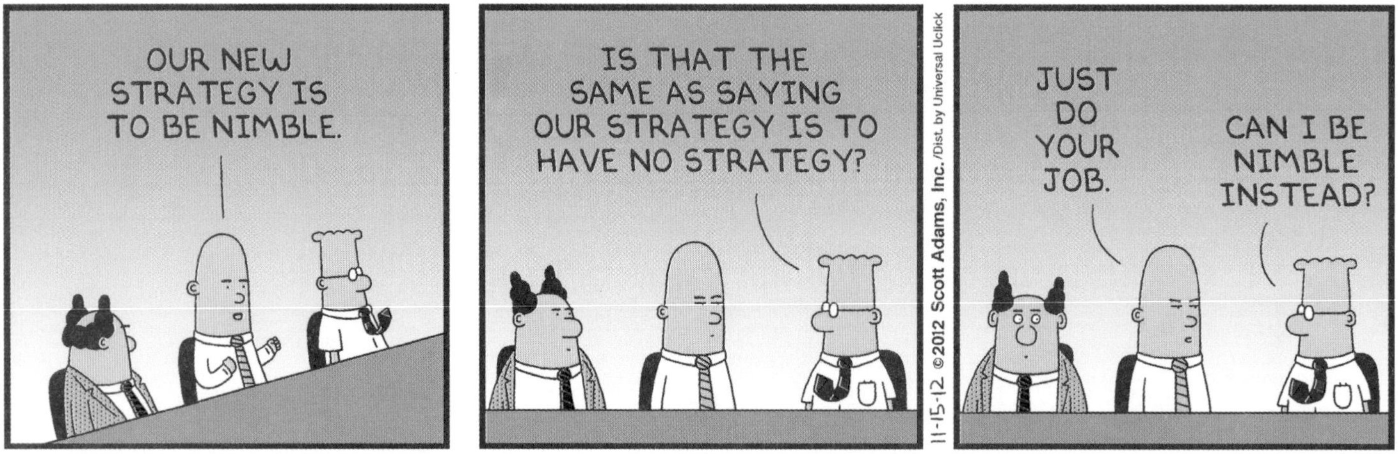
OUR NEW STRATEGY IS TO BE NIMBLE.
IS THAT THE SAME AS SAYING OUR STRATEGY IS TO HAVE NO STRATEGY?
JUST DO YOUR JOB.
CAN I BE NIMBLE INSTEAD?
11-15-12 ©2012 Scott Adams, Inc./Dist. by Universal Uclick

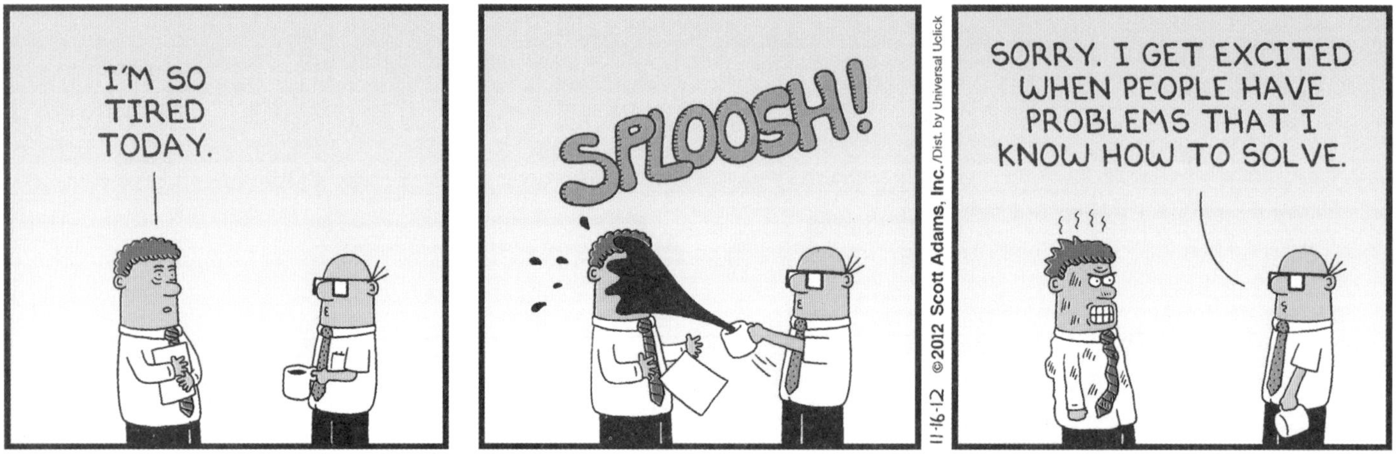
I'M SO TIRED TODAY.
SPLOOSH!
SORRY. I GET EXCITED WHEN PEOPLE HAVE PROBLEMS THAT I KNOW HOW TO SOLVE.
11-16-12 ©2012 Scott Adams, Inc./Dist. by Universal Uclick

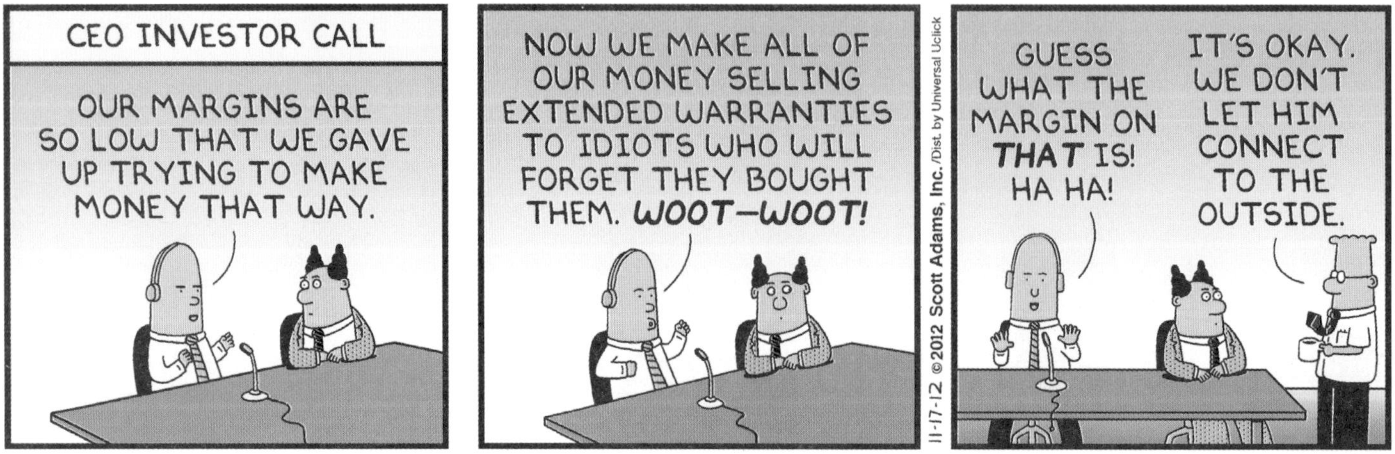
CEO INVESTOR CALL
OUR MARGINS ARE SO LOW THAT WE GAVE UP TRYING TO MAKE MONEY THAT WAY.
NOW WE MAKE ALL OF OUR MONEY SELLING EXTENDED WARRANTIES TO IDIOTS WHO WILL FORGET THEY BOUGHT THEM. WOOT-WOOT!
GUESS WHAT THE MARGIN ON THAT IS! HA HA!
IT'S OKAY. WE DON'T LET HIM CONNECT TO THE OUTSIDE.
11-17-12 ©2012 Scott Adams, Inc./Dist. by Universal Uclick

DO YOU HAVE A MINUTE TO ANSWER AN ENGINEERING QUESTION?
MY WIFE IS OUT OF TOWN VISITING HER SISTER.
SHE ASKED ME TO PUT UP THE HOLIDAY LIGHTS WHILE SHE WAS GONE.
I HIRED A HOMELESS GUY TO DO IT AND HE FELL OFF THE ROOF. WHAT'S THE EASIEST WAY TO GET RID OF THE BODY BEFORE MY WIFE COMES HOME?
YOUR QUESTION IS DISTURBING, BUT I'M INTRIGUED BY THE ENGINEERING PART.
HERE'S A DESIGN FOR A CATAPULT YOU CAN BUILD AT HOME.
AND HERE'S A SATELLITE MAP SHOWING THE BEST FLIGHT PATH TO A NEIGHBOR'S POOL.
DID HE DIE RIGHT AWAY?
NO, JUST A BROKEN LEG.
©2012 Scott Adams, Inc./Dist. by Universal Uclick
11-18-12

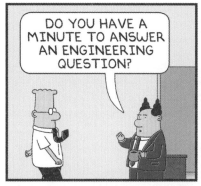

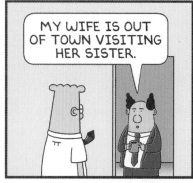

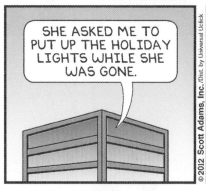

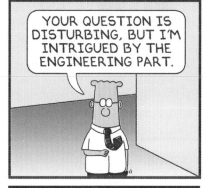

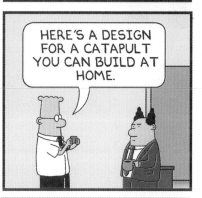

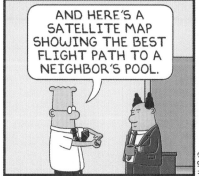

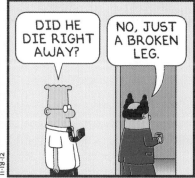

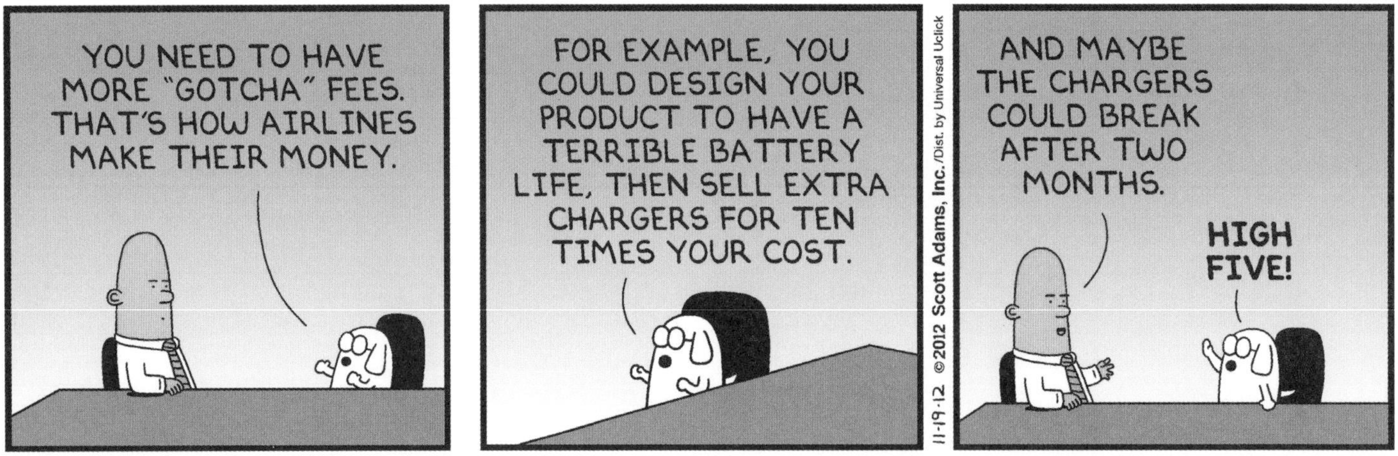
YOU NEED TO HAVE MORE "GOTCHA" FEES. THAT'S HOW AIRLINES MAKE THEIR MONEY.
FOR EXAMPLE, YOU COULD DESIGN YOUR PRODUCT TO HAVE A TERRIBLE BATTERY LIFE, THEN SELL EXTRA CHARGERS FOR TEN TIMES YOUR COST.
11-19-12 ©2012 Scott Adams, Inc./Dist. by Universal Uclick
AND MAYBE THE CHARGERS COULD BREAK AFTER TWO MONTHS.
HIGH FIVE!

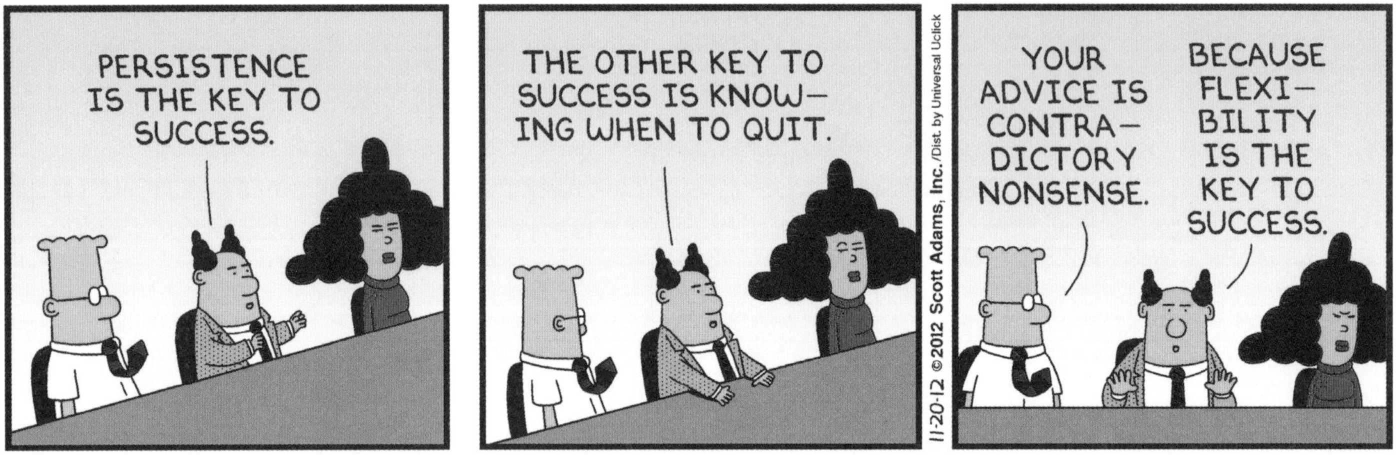
PERSISTENCE IS THE KEY TO SUCCESS.
THE OTHER KEY TO SUCCESS IS KNOW–ING WHEN TO QUIT.
11-20-12 ©2012 Scott Adams, Inc./Dist. by Universal Uclick
YOUR ADVICE IS CONTRA–DICTORY NONSENSE.
BECAUSE FLEXI–BILITY IS THE KEY TO SUCCESS.

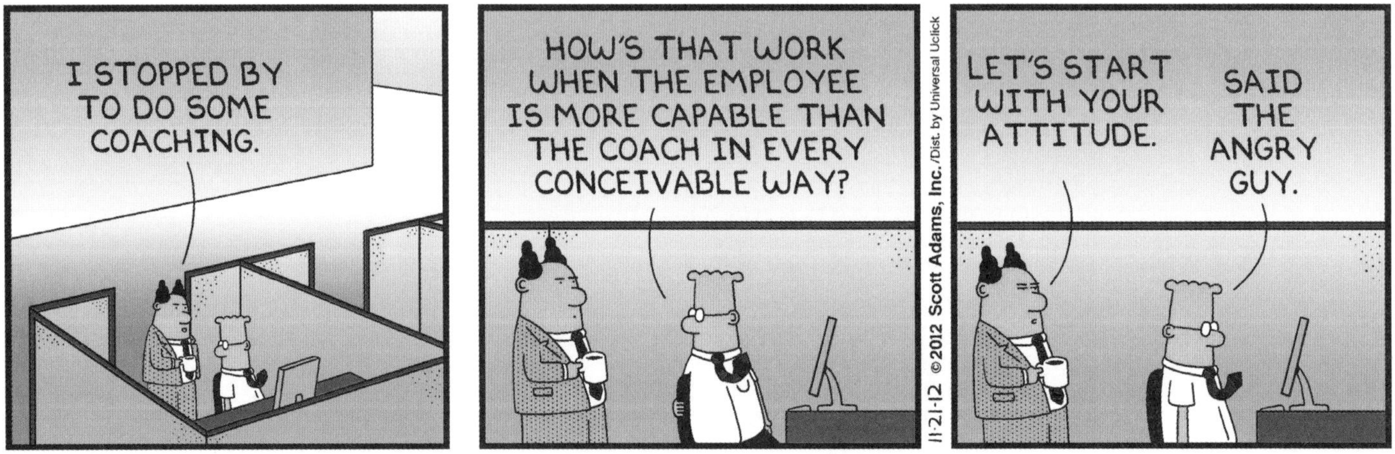
I STOPPED BY TO DO SOME COACHING.
HOW'S THAT WORK WHEN THE EMPLOYEE IS MORE CAPABLE THAN THE COACH IN EVERY CONCEIVABLE WAY?
11-21-12 ©2012 Scott Adams, Inc./Dist. by Universal Uclick
LET'S START WITH YOUR ATTITUDE.
SAID THE ANGRY GUY.

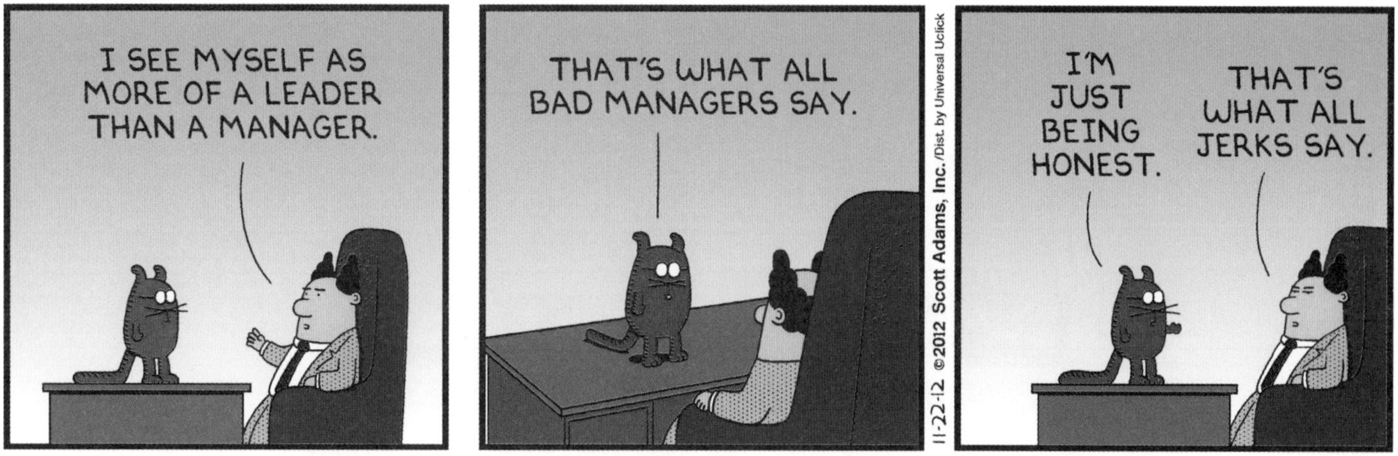
I SEE MYSELF AS MORE OF A LEADER THAN A MANAGER.
THAT'S WHAT ALL BAD MANAGERS SAY.
I'M JUST BEING HONEST.
THAT'S WHAT ALL JERKS SAY.
11-22-12 ©2012 Scott Adams, Inc./Dist. by Universal Uclick

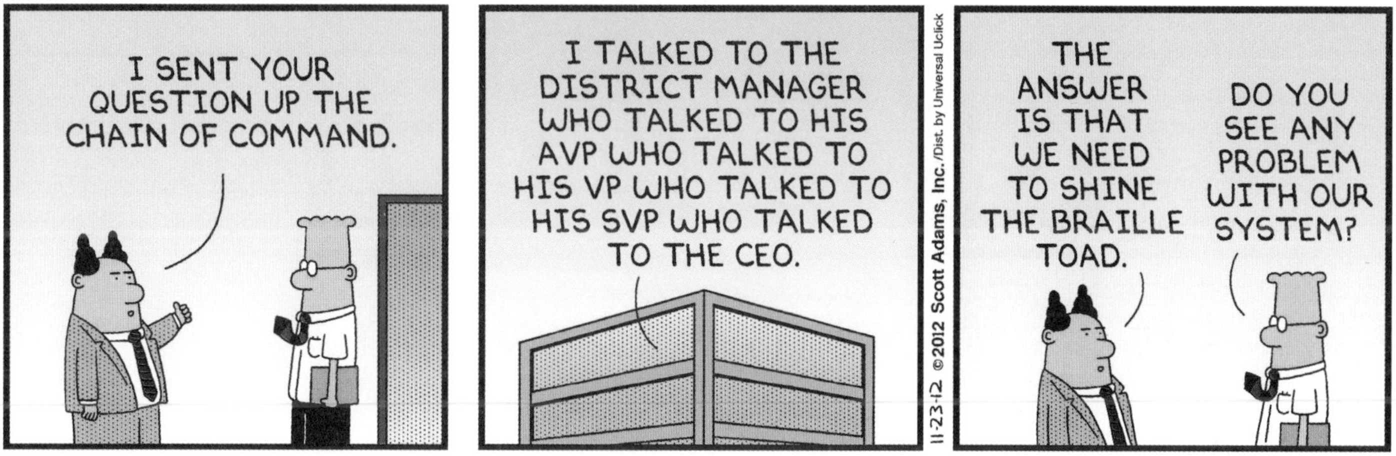
I SENT YOUR QUESTION UP THE CHAIN OF COMMAND.
I TALKED TO THE DISTRICT MANAGER WHO TALKED TO HIS AVP WHO TALKED TO HIS VP WHO TALKED TO HIS SVP WHO TALKED TO THE CEO.
THE ANSWER IS THAT WE NEED TO SHINE THE BRAILLE TOAD.
DO YOU SEE ANY PROBLEM WITH OUR SYSTEM?
11-23-12 ©2012 Scott Adams, Inc./Dist. by Universal Uclick

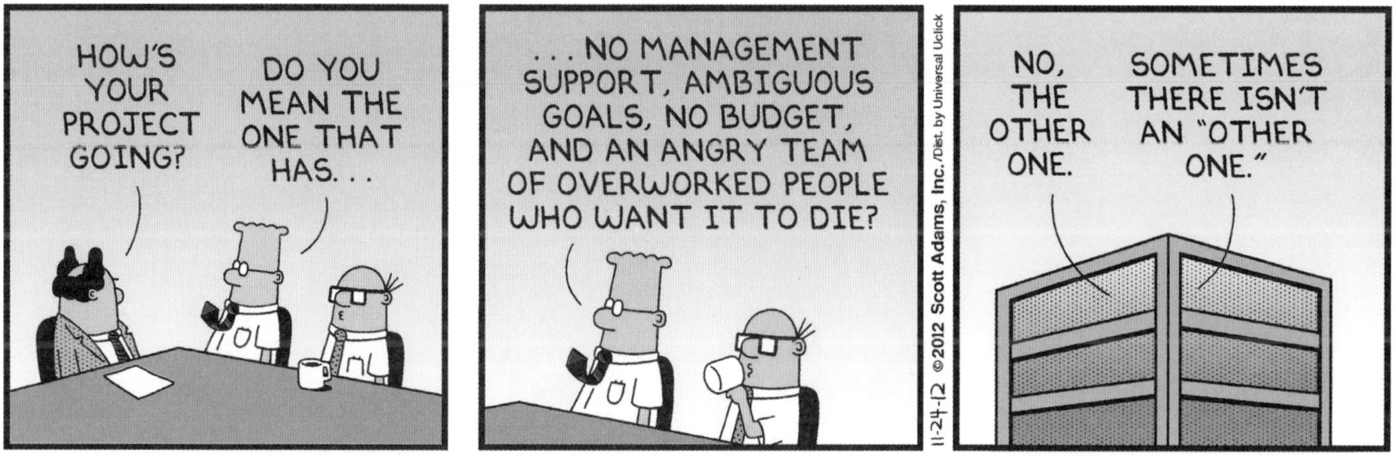
HOW'S YOUR PROJECT GOING?
DO YOU MEAN THE ONE THAT HAS. . .
. . . NO MANAGEMENT SUPPORT, AMBIGUOUS GOALS, NO BUDGET, AND AN ANGRY TEAM OF OVERWORKED PEOPLE WHO WANT IT TO DIE?
NO, THE OTHER ONE.
SOMETIMES THERE ISN'T AN "OTHER ONE."
11-24-12 ©2012 Scott Adams, Inc./Dist. by Universal Uclick

FIRST ON THE AGENDA, WE'RE STANDARDIZING ALL SCREEN SAVERS TO BE OUR COMPANY LOGO.
SECOND, OUR CEO IS HAVING A CONTEST TO SEE WHO CAN SUGGEST THE MOST USELESS CORPORATE RULE TO ELIMINATE.
I NOMINATE THE NEW SCREEN-SAVER RULE.
YOU CAN'T NOMINATE THAT ONE. IT'S TOO NEW.
WHY DOES THAT MATTER? ISN'T IT BETTER TO KILL IT BEFORE IT GETS IMPLEMENTED?
IT'S TOO SOON! IT'S JUST TOO SOON!
FINE.
FINE.
I NOMINATE WHATEVER IS NEXT ON THE AGENDA.
© 2012 Scott Adams, Inc./Dist. by Universal Uclick
11-25-12

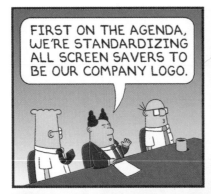

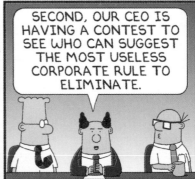

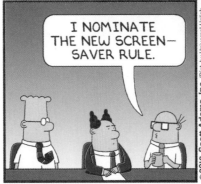

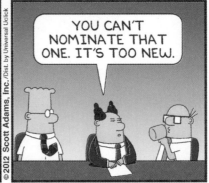

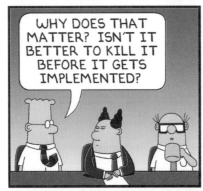

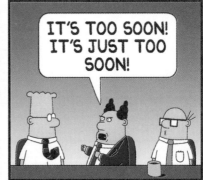

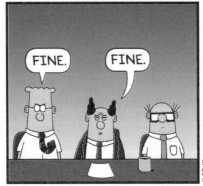

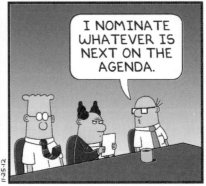

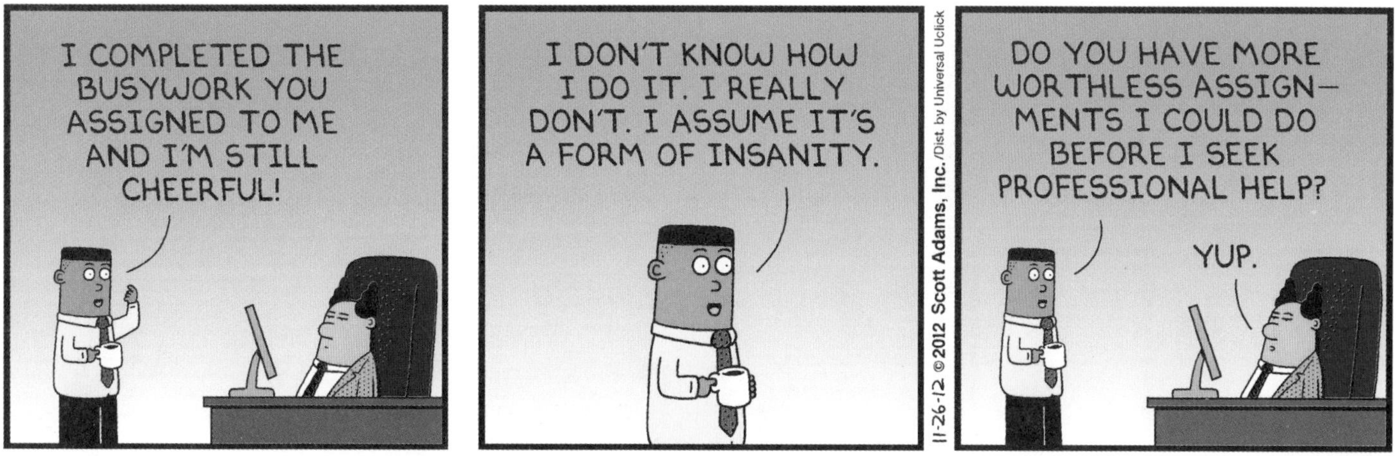
I COMPLETED THE BUSYWORK YOU ASSIGNED TO ME AND I'M STILL CHEERFUL!
I DON'T KNOW HOW I DO IT. I REALLY DON'T. I ASSUME IT'S A FORM OF INSANITY.
11-26-12 ©2012 Scott Adams, Inc./Dist. by Universal Uclick
DO YOU HAVE MORE WORTHLESS ASSIGN- MENTS I COULD DO BEFORE I SEEK PROFESSIONAL HELP?
YUP.

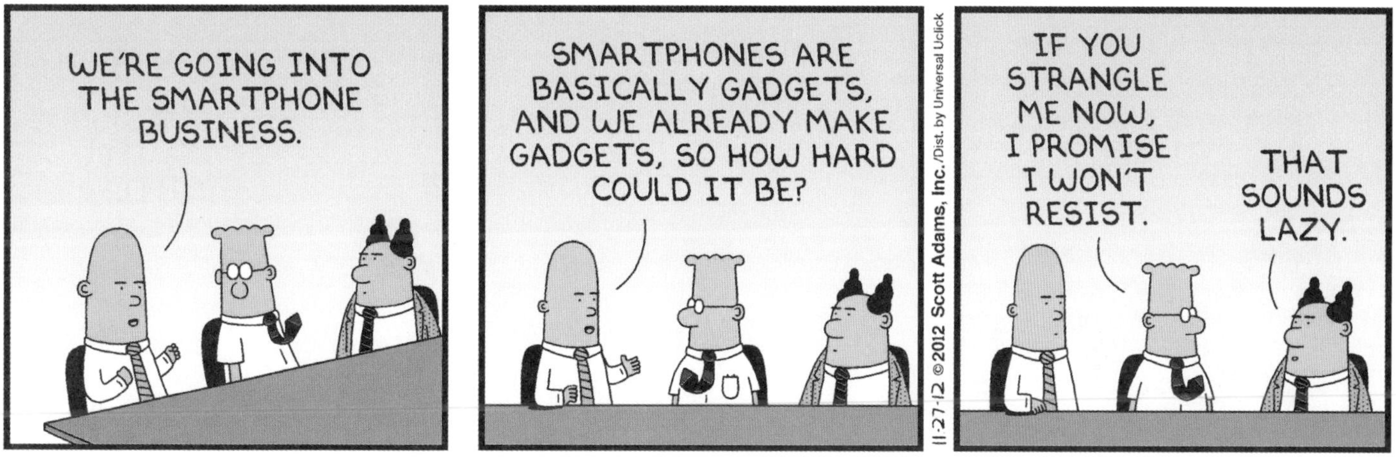
WE'RE GOING INTO THE SMARTPHONE BUSINESS.
SMARTPHONES ARE BASICALLY GADGETS, AND WE ALREADY MAKE GADGETS, SO HOW HARD COULD IT BE?
11-27-12 ©2012 Scott Adams, Inc./Dist. by Universal Uclick
IF YOU STRANGLE ME NOW, I PROMISE I WON'T RESIST.
THAT SOUNDS LAZY.

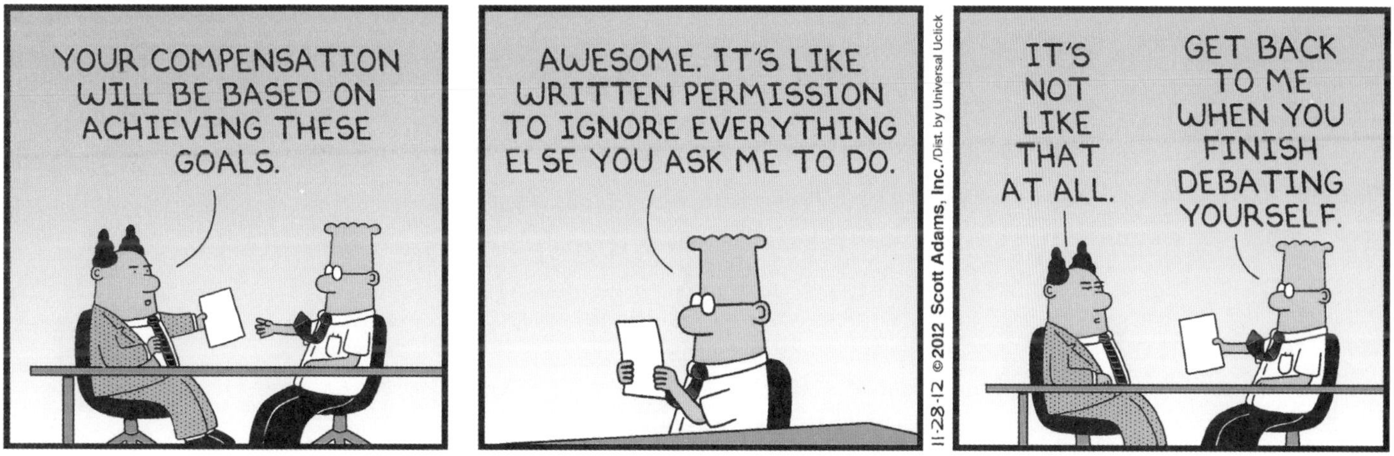
YOUR COMPENSATION WILL BE BASED ON ACHIEVING THESE GOALS.
AWESOME. IT'S LIKE WRITTEN PERMISSION TO IGNORE EVERYTHING ELSE YOU ASK ME TO DO.
11-28-12 ©2012 Scott Adams, Inc./Dist. by Universal Uclick
IT'S NOT LIKE THAT AT ALL.
GET BACK TO ME WHEN YOU FINISH DEBATING YOURSELF.

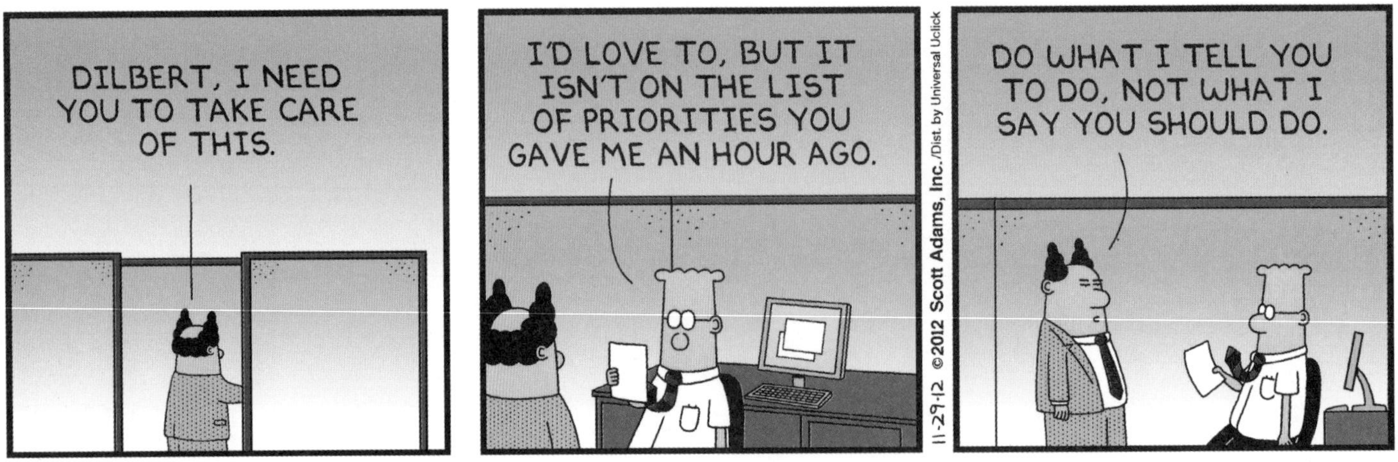
DILBERT, I NEED YOU TO TAKE CARE OF THIS.
I'D LOVE TO, BUT IT ISN'T ON THE LIST OF PRIORITIES YOU GAVE ME AN HOUR AGO.
11-29-12 ©2012 Scott Adams, Inc./Dist. by Universal Uclick
DO WHAT I TELL YOU TO DO, NOT WHAT I SAY YOU SHOULD DO.

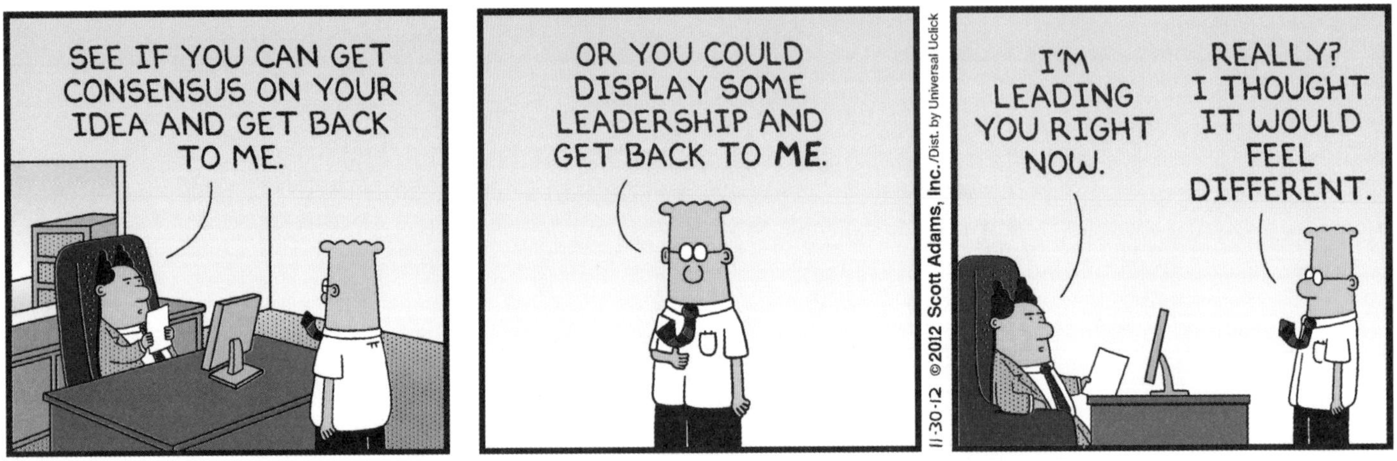
SEE IF YOU CAN GET CONSENSUS ON YOUR IDEA AND GET BACK TO ME.
OR YOU COULD DISPLAY SOME LEADERSHIP AND GET BACK TO **ME**.
11-30-12 ©2012 Scott Adams, Inc./Dist. by Universal Uclick
I'M LEADING YOU RIGHT NOW.
REALLY? I THOUGHT IT WOULD FEEL DIFFERENT.

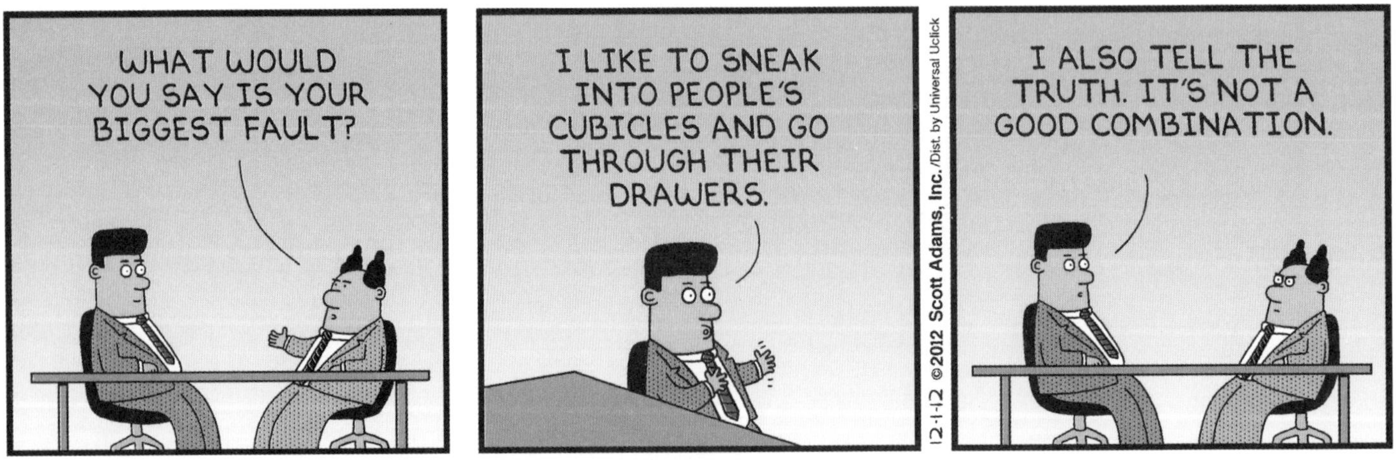
WHAT WOULD YOU SAY IS YOUR BIGGEST FAULT?
I LIKE TO SNEAK INTO PEOPLE'S CUBICLES AND GO THROUGH THEIR DRAWERS.
12-1-12 ©2012 Scott Adams, Inc./Dist. by Universal Uclick
I ALSO TELL THE TRUTH. IT'S NOT A GOOD COMBINATION.

I WOULD LIKE TO BE EVALUATED ON MY OUTPUT, NOT THE HOURS I WORK.
OKAY. THAT SOUNDS REASONABLE.
IT DOES? WOW.
AND I'D ALSO LIKE TO WORK AT HOME WHERE THERE ARE FEWER DISTRACTIONS SO I CAN BE MORE PRODUCTIVE.
©2012 Scott Adams, Inc./Dist. by Universal Uclick
OKAY. THAT MAKES SENSE.
REALLY? I MEAN. . . GREAT!
I'D ALSO LIKE TO WORK ON LONG-TERM PROJECTS THAT HAVE NO NEAR-TERM DELIVERABLES.
HOLY GRAIL, HOLY GRAIL, HOLY GRAIL.
GO BACK TO YOUR CUBICLE AND DON'T LEAVE UNTIL FIVE O'CLOCK.
12-2-12
I WAS THIS CLOSE TO RETIRING AT FULL PAY.

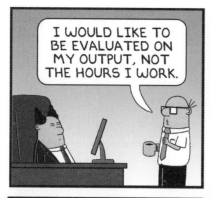

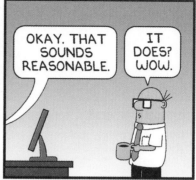

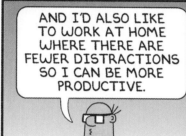

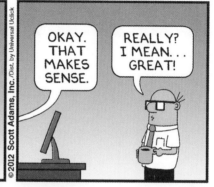

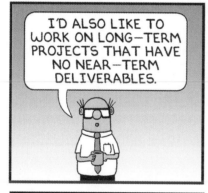

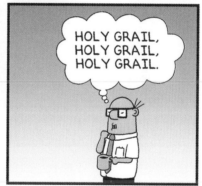

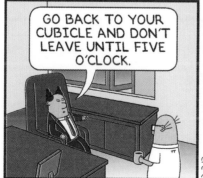

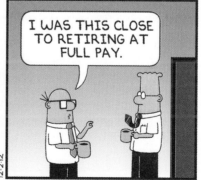

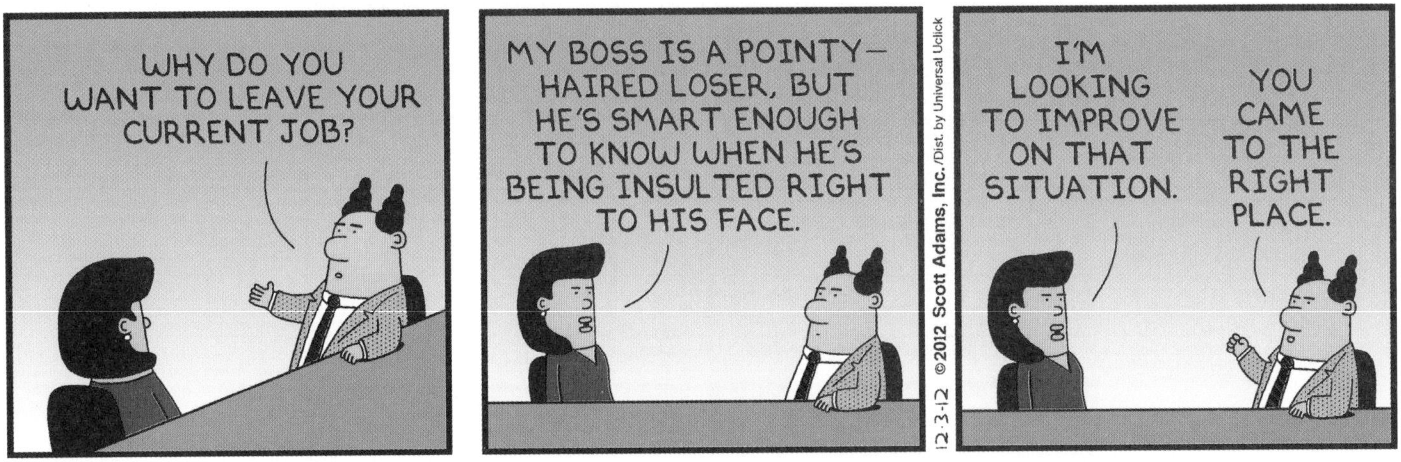
WHY DO YOU WANT TO LEAVE YOUR CURRENT JOB?
MY BOSS IS A POINTY-HAIRED LOSER, BUT HE'S SMART ENOUGH TO KNOW WHEN HE'S BEING INSULTED RIGHT TO HIS FACE.
12-3-12 ©2012 Scott Adams, Inc./Dist. by Universal Uclick
I'M LOOKING TO IMPROVE ON THAT SITUATION.
YOU CAME TO THE RIGHT PLACE.

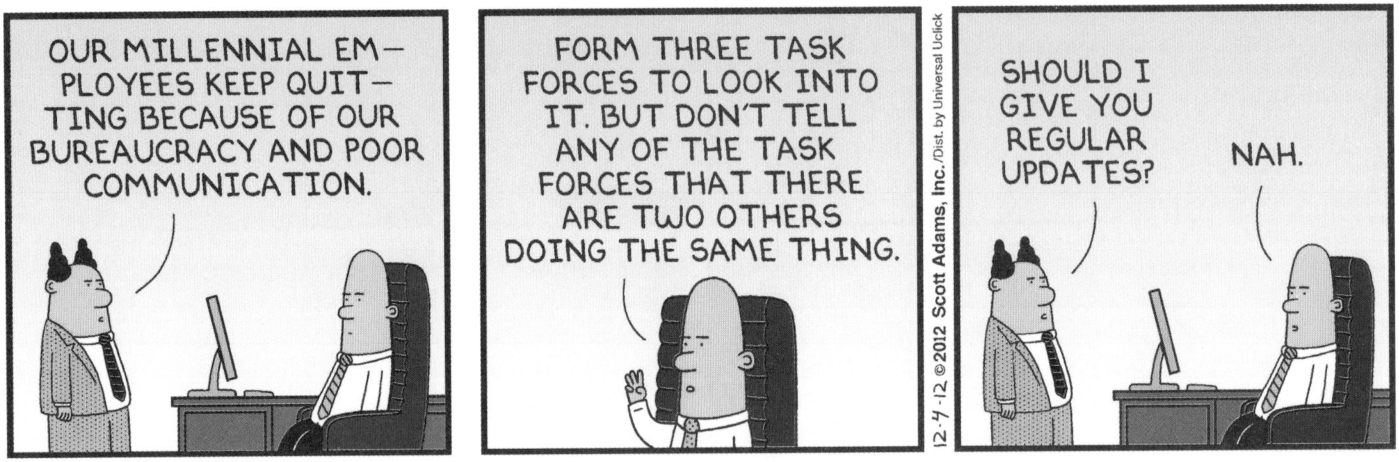
OUR MILLENNIAL EM-PLOYEES KEEP QUIT-TING BECAUSE OF OUR BUREAUCRACY AND POOR COMMUNICATION.
FORM THREE TASK FORCES TO LOOK INTO IT. BUT DON'T TELL ANY OF THE TASK FORCES THAT THERE ARE TWO OTHERS DOING THE SAME THING.
12-4-12 ©2012 Scott Adams, Inc./Dist. by Universal Uclick
SHOULD I GIVE YOU REGULAR UPDATES?
NAH.

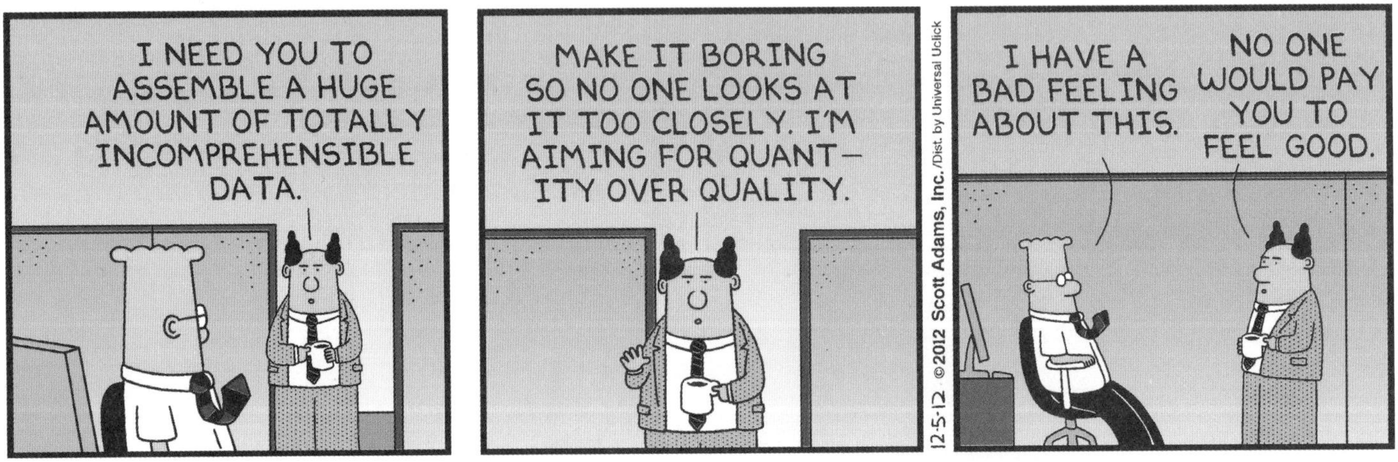
I NEED YOU TO ASSEMBLE A HUGE AMOUNT OF TOTALLY INCOMPREHENSIBLE DATA.
MAKE IT BORING SO NO ONE LOOKS AT IT TOO CLOSELY. I'M AIMING FOR QUANT-ITY OVER QUALITY.
12-5-12 ©2012 Scott Adams, Inc./Dist. by Universal Uclick
I HAVE A BAD FEELING ABOUT THIS.
NO ONE WOULD PAY YOU TO FEEL GOOD.

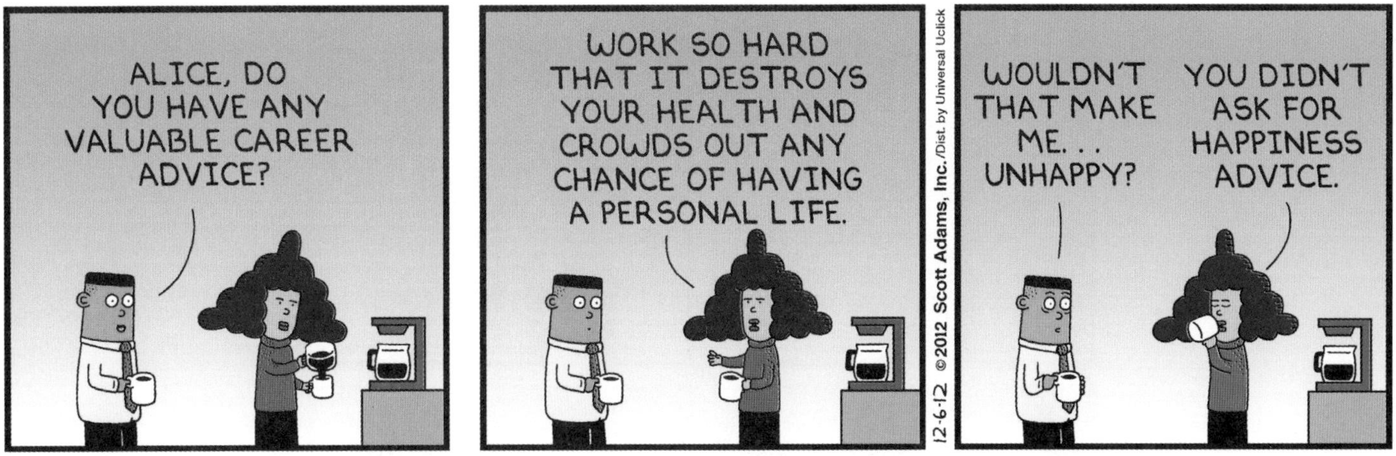
ALICE, DO YOU HAVE ANY VALUABLE CAREER ADVICE?
WORK SO HARD THAT IT DESTROYS YOUR HEALTH AND CROWDS OUT ANY CHANCE OF HAVING A PERSONAL LIFE.
12-6-12 ©2012 Scott Adams, Inc./Dist. by Universal Uclick
WOULDN'T THAT MAKE ME. . . UNHAPPY?
YOU DIDN'T ASK FOR HAPPINESS ADVICE.

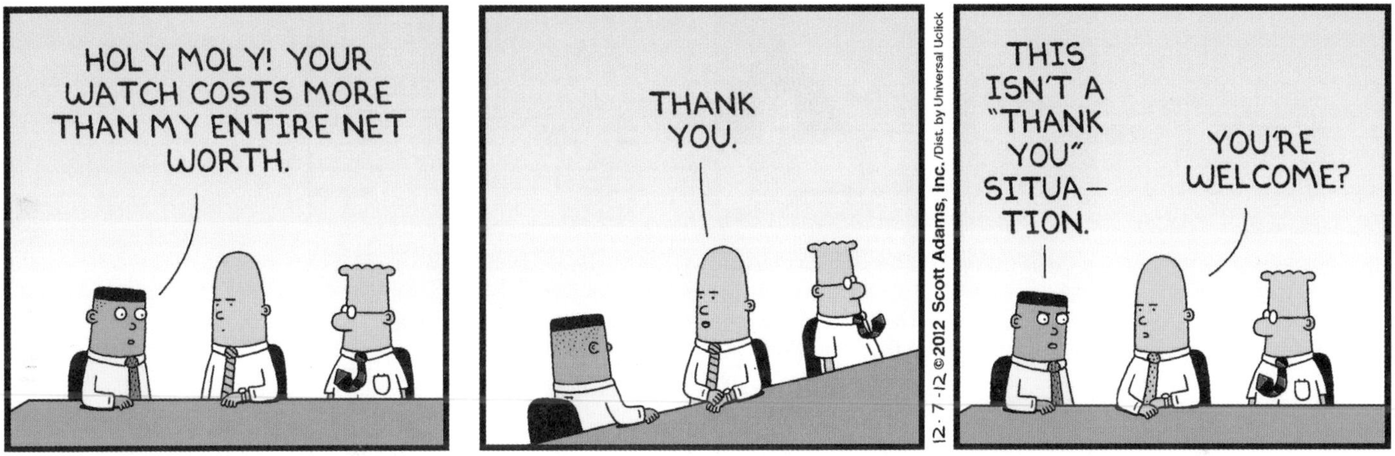
HOLY MOLY! YOUR WATCH COSTS MORE THAN MY ENTIRE NET WORTH.
THANK YOU.
12-7-12 ©2012 Scott Adams, Inc./Dist. by Universal Uclick
THIS ISN'T A "THANK YOU" SITUA-TION.
YOU'RE WELCOME?

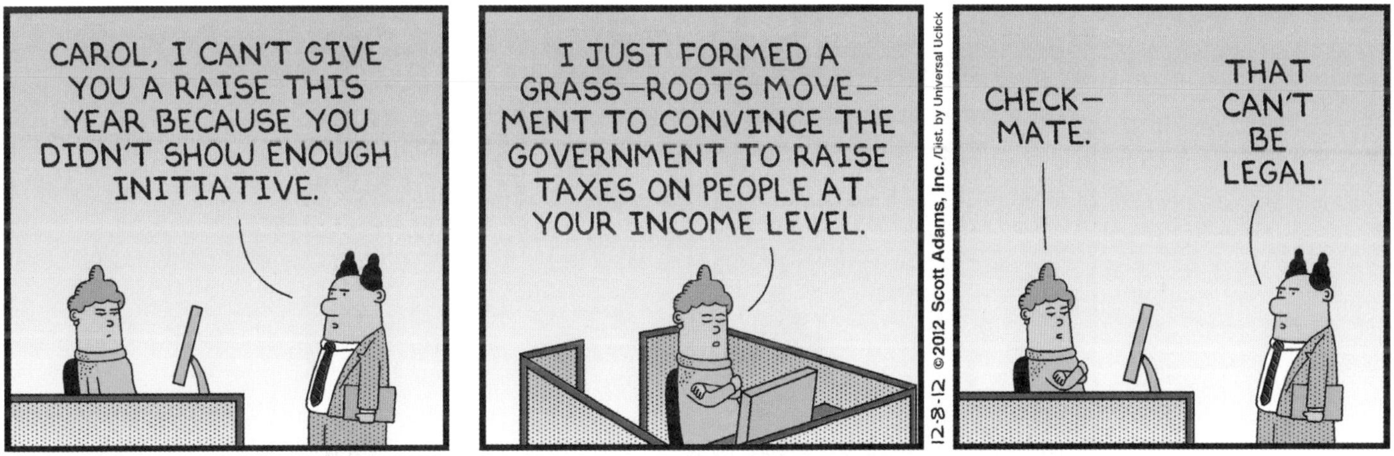
CAROL, I CAN'T GIVE YOU A RAISE THIS YEAR BECAUSE YOU DIDN'T SHOW ENOUGH INITIATIVE.
I JUST FORMED A GRASS-ROOTS MOVE-MENT TO CONVINCE THE GOVERNMENT TO RAISE TAXES ON PEOPLE AT YOUR INCOME LEVEL.
12-8-12 ©2012 Scott Adams, Inc./Dist. by Universal Uclick
CHECK-MATE.
THAT CAN'T BE LEGAL.

WE CAN MAKE THIS A GREAT PLACE TO WORK BY FOLLOWING THE GOLDEN RULE.
Golden Rule
TREAT OTHERS AS YOU WOULD WANT THEM TO TREAT YOU.
Golden Rule
THAT'S DUMB.
©2012 Scott Adams, Inc. /Dist. by Universal Uclick
IT'S NOT DUMB!
LET'S TEST YOUR RULE.
WOULD YOU LIKE IT IF SOMEONE GAVE YOU A HUNDRED DOLLARS?
YES.
OKAY. SO GIVE ME A HUNDRED DOLLARS.
OR ELSE FOREVER LIVE AS A HYPOCRITE WHO DOESN'T FOLLOW HIS OWN DUMB RULE.
SNORK!
SNORK!
12-9-12
I HATE YOUR ENGI– NEERING GUTS!!!
AT LEAST YOU'RE MAKING SENSE NOW.

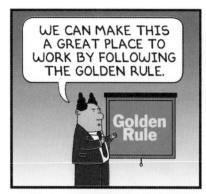

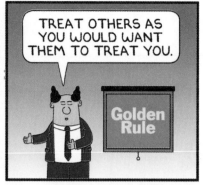

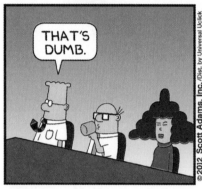

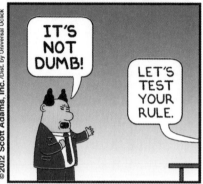

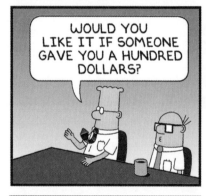

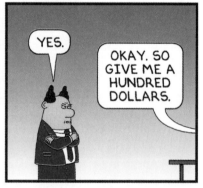

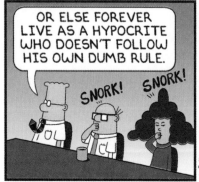

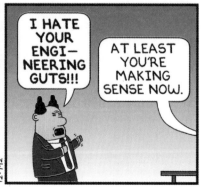

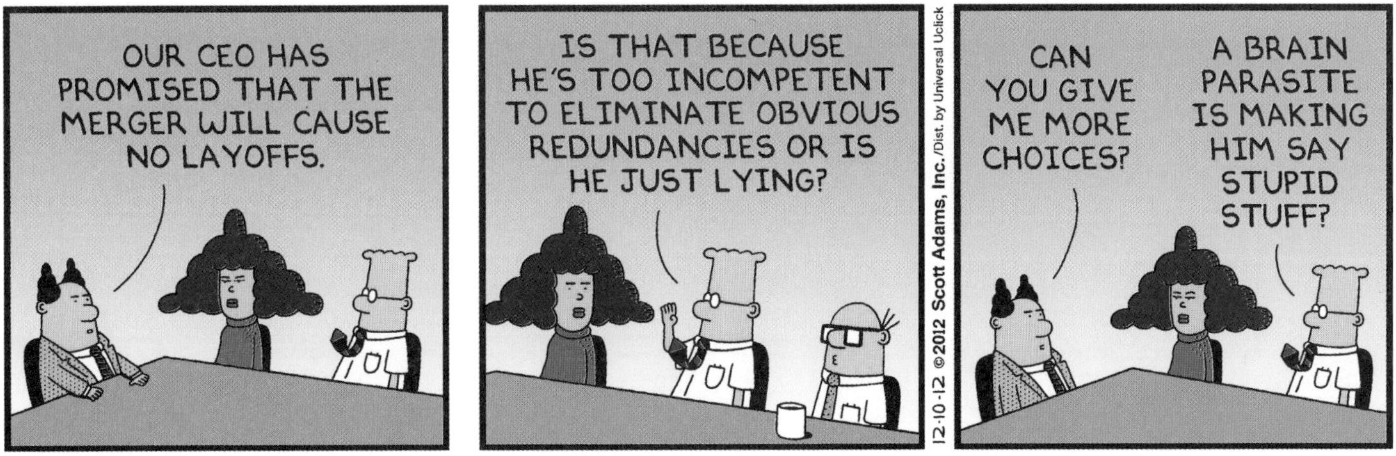
OUR CEO HAS PROMISED THAT THE MERGER WILL CAUSE NO LAYOFFS.
IS THAT BECAUSE HE'S TOO INCOMPETENT TO ELIMINATE OBVIOUS REDUNDANCIES OR IS HE JUST LYING?
12-10-12 ©2012 Scott Adams, Inc./Dist. by Universal Uclick
CAN YOU GIVE ME MORE CHOICES?
A BRAIN PARASITE IS MAKING HIM SAY STUPID STUFF?

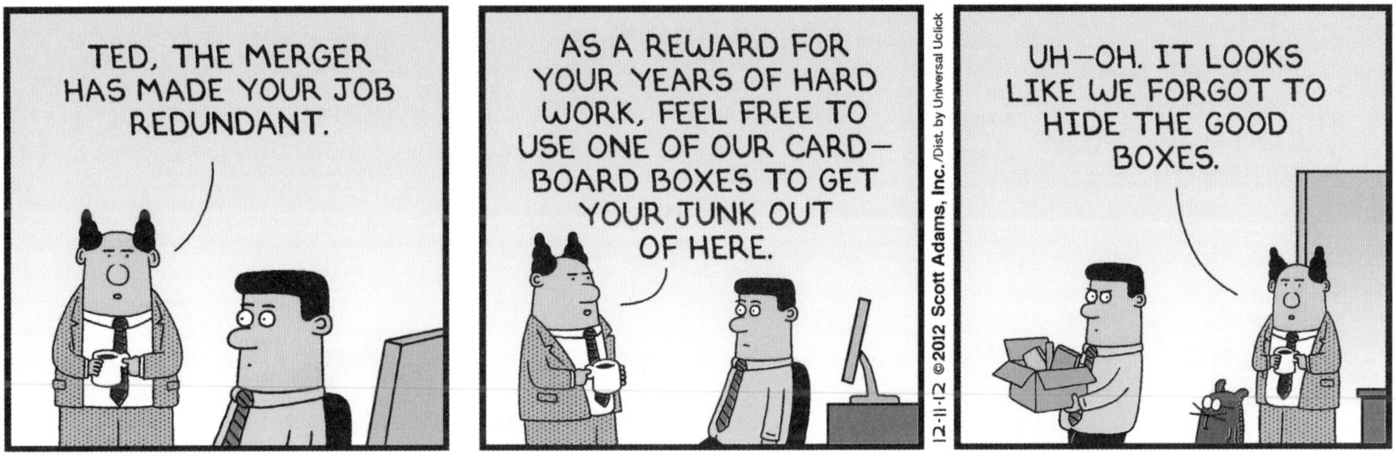
TED, THE MERGER HAS MADE YOUR JOB REDUNDANT.
AS A REWARD FOR YOUR YEARS OF HARD WORK, FEEL FREE TO USE ONE OF OUR CARD-BOARD BOXES TO GET YOUR JUNK OUT OF HERE.
12-11-12 ©2012 Scott Adams, Inc./Dist. by Universal Uclick
UH—OH. IT LOOKS LIKE WE FORGOT TO HIDE THE GOOD BOXES.

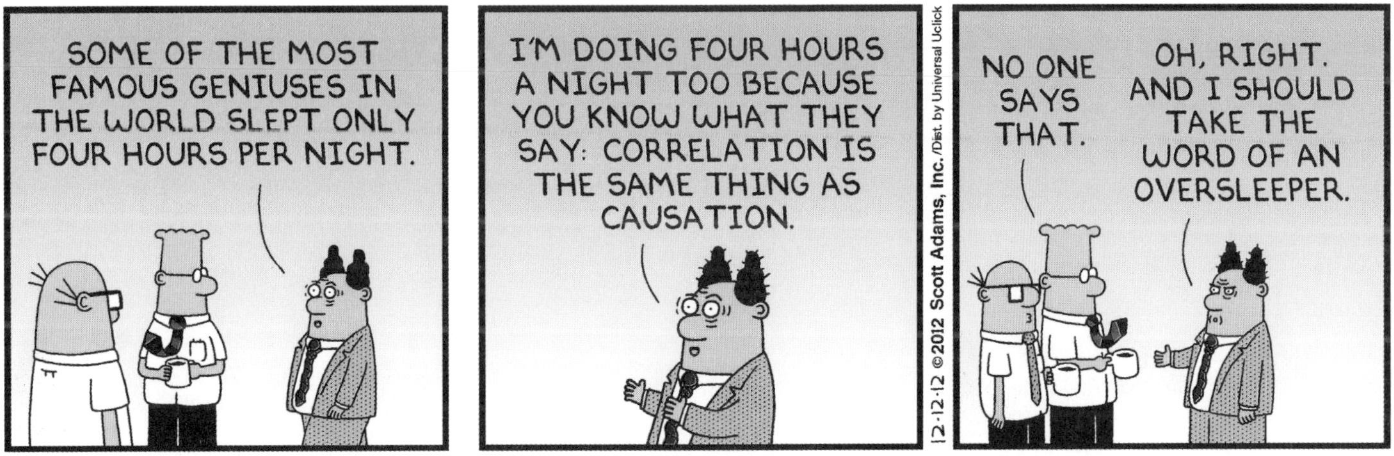
SOME OF THE MOST FAMOUS GENIUSES IN THE WORLD SLEPT ONLY FOUR HOURS PER NIGHT.
I'M DOING FOUR HOURS A NIGHT TOO BECAUSE YOU KNOW WHAT THEY SAY: CORRELATION IS THE SAME THING AS CAUSATION.
12-12-12 ©2012 Scott Adams, Inc./Dist. by Universal Uclick
NO ONE SAYS THAT.
OH, RIGHT. AND I SHOULD TAKE THE WORD OF AN OVERSLEEPER.

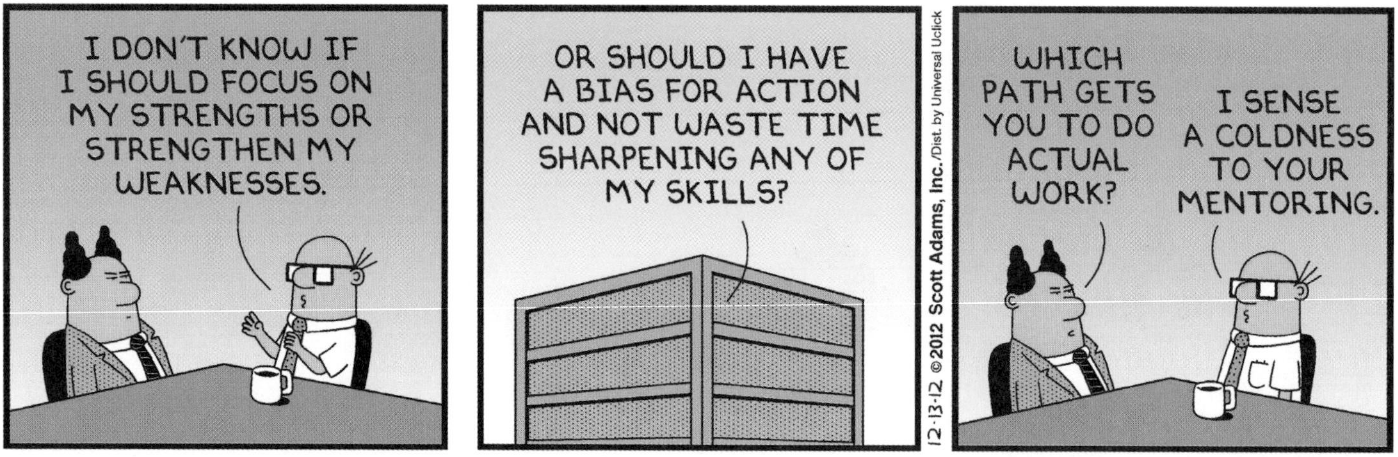
I DON'T KNOW IF I SHOULD FOCUS ON MY STRENGTHS OR STRENGTHEN MY WEAKNESSES.
OR SHOULD I HAVE A BIAS FOR ACTION AND NOT WASTE TIME SHARPENING ANY OF MY SKILLS?
12-13-12 ©2012 Scott Adams, Inc./Dist. by Universal Uclick
WHICH PATH GETS YOU TO DO ACTUAL WORK?
I SENSE A COLDNESS TO YOUR MENTORING.

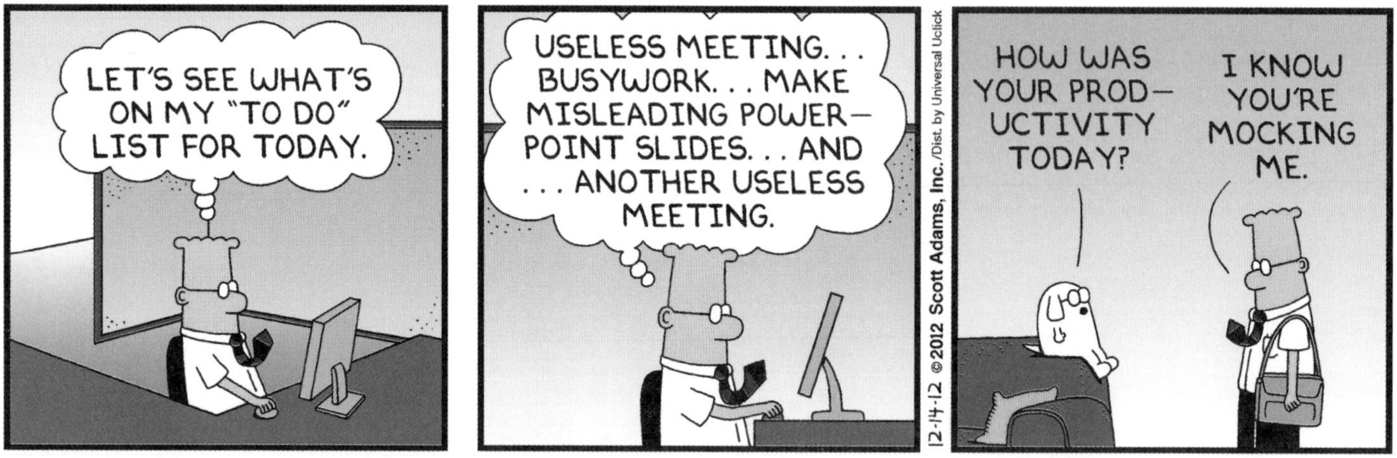
LET'S SEE WHAT'S ON MY "TO DO" LIST FOR TODAY.
USELESS MEETING. . . BUSYWORK. . . MAKE MISLEADING POWER-POINT SLIDES. . . AND . . . ANOTHER USELESS MEETING.
12-14-12 ©2012 Scott Adams, Inc./Dist. by Universal Uclick
HOW WAS YOUR PROD-UCTIVITY TODAY?
I KNOW YOU'RE MOCKING ME.

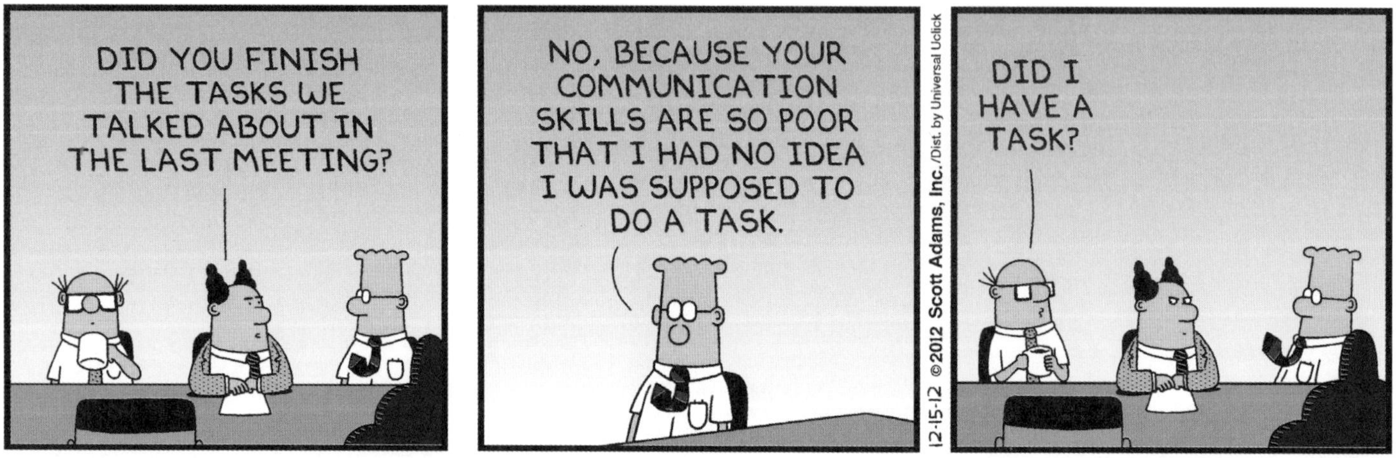
DID YOU FINISH THE TASKS WE TALKED ABOUT IN THE LAST MEETING?
NO, BECAUSE YOUR COMMUNICATION SKILLS ARE SO POOR THAT I HAD NO IDEA I WAS SUPPOSED TO DO A TASK.
12-15-12 ©2012 Scott Adams, Inc./Dist. by Universal Uclick
DID I HAVE A TASK?

LET'S MEET BEFORE THE PROJECT MEETING TO GO OVER A FEW THINGS.
NICE TRY.
WE CHRONICALLY LATE PEOPLE KNOW WHEN WE'RE BEING PLAYED.
YOUR PRE—MEETING IS A TRICK TO GET ME TO SHOW UP ON TIME FOR THE REAL MEETING.
BUT THAT WON'T WORK BECAUSE POOR PLANNING ISN'T THE CAUSE OF MY CHRONIC LATENESS.
I MAKE PEOPLE WAIT FOR ME BECAUSE I ENJOY THE POWER AND I DON'T CARE ABOUT ANYONE'S FEELINGS.
FINE. I'LL SEE YOU AT THE PROJECT MEETING AT TEN.
NICE TRY. I KNOW THE MEETING IS AT 10:30.
HOW DO YOU KEEP A JOB?
THAT ATTITUDE IS ***EXACTLY*** WHY I DON'T LIKE PEOPLE.
©2012 Scott Adams, Inc./Dist. by Universal Uclick
12-16-12

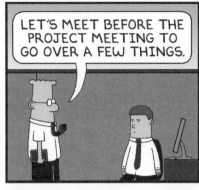

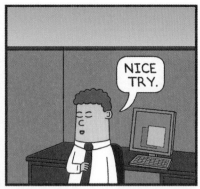

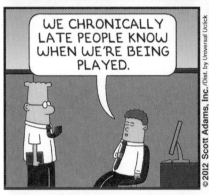

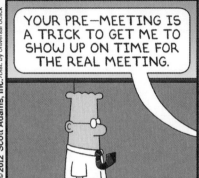

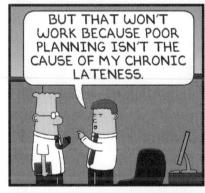

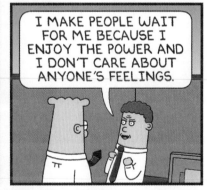

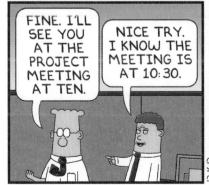

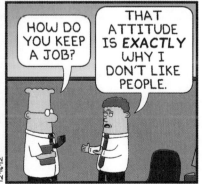

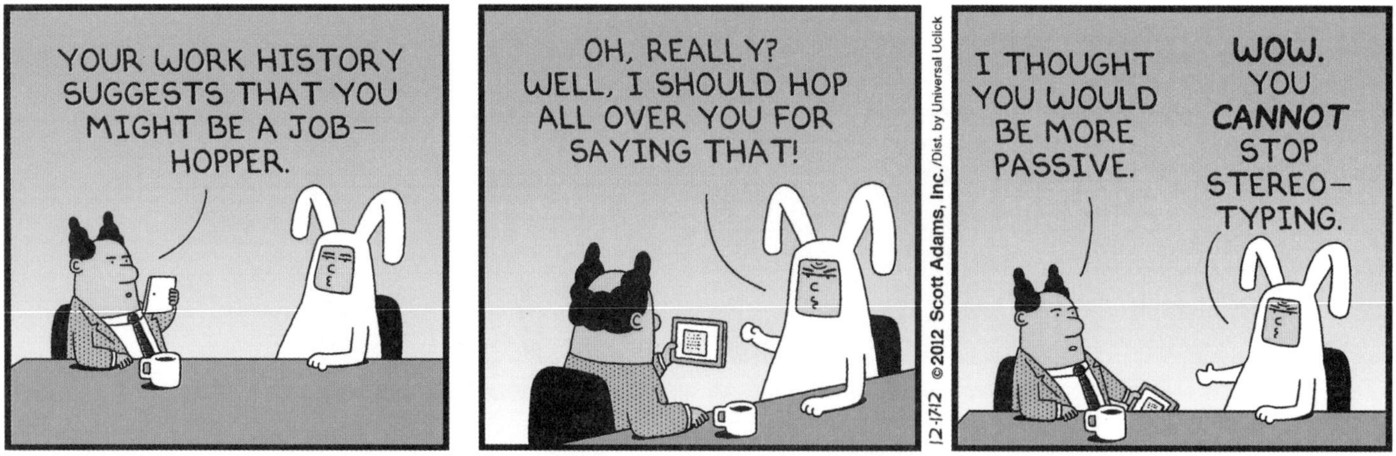
YOUR WORK HISTORY SUGGESTS THAT YOU MIGHT BE A JOB-HOPPER.
OH, REALLY? WELL, I SHOULD HOP ALL OVER YOU FOR SAYING THAT!
12·17·12 ©2012 Scott Adams, Inc./Dist. by Universal Uclick
I THOUGHT YOU WOULD BE MORE PASSIVE.
WOW. YOU **CANNOT** STOP STEREO-TYPING.

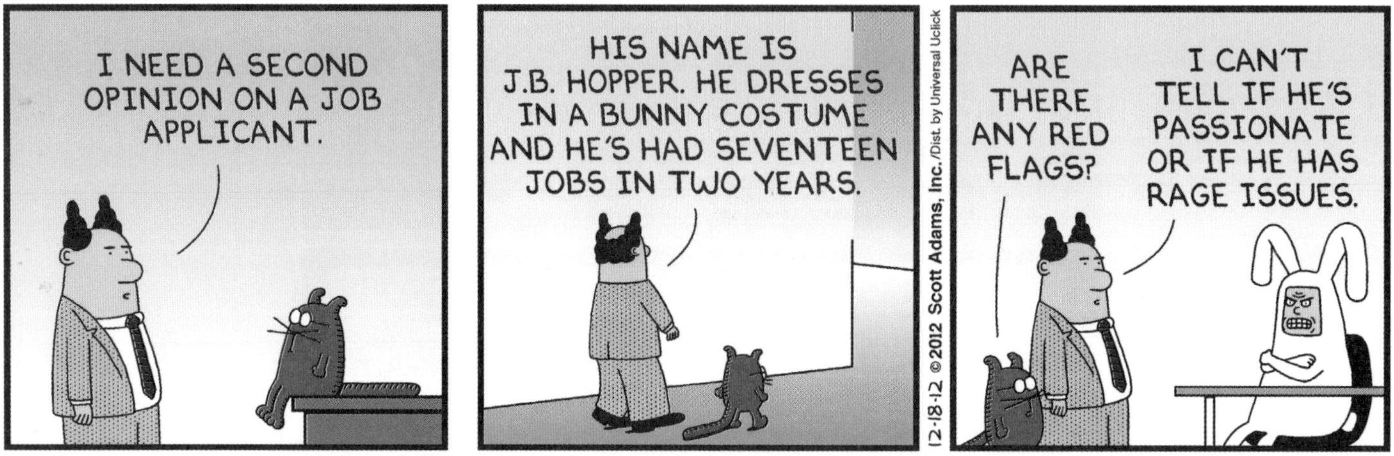
I NEED A SECOND OPINION ON A JOB APPLICANT.
HIS NAME IS J.B. HOPPER. HE DRESSES IN A BUNNY COSTUME AND HE'S HAD SEVENTEEN JOBS IN TWO YEARS.
12·18·12 ©2012 Scott Adams, Inc./Dist. by Universal Uclick
ARE THERE ANY RED FLAGS?
I CAN'T TELL IF HE'S PASSIONATE OR IF HE HAS RAGE ISSUES.

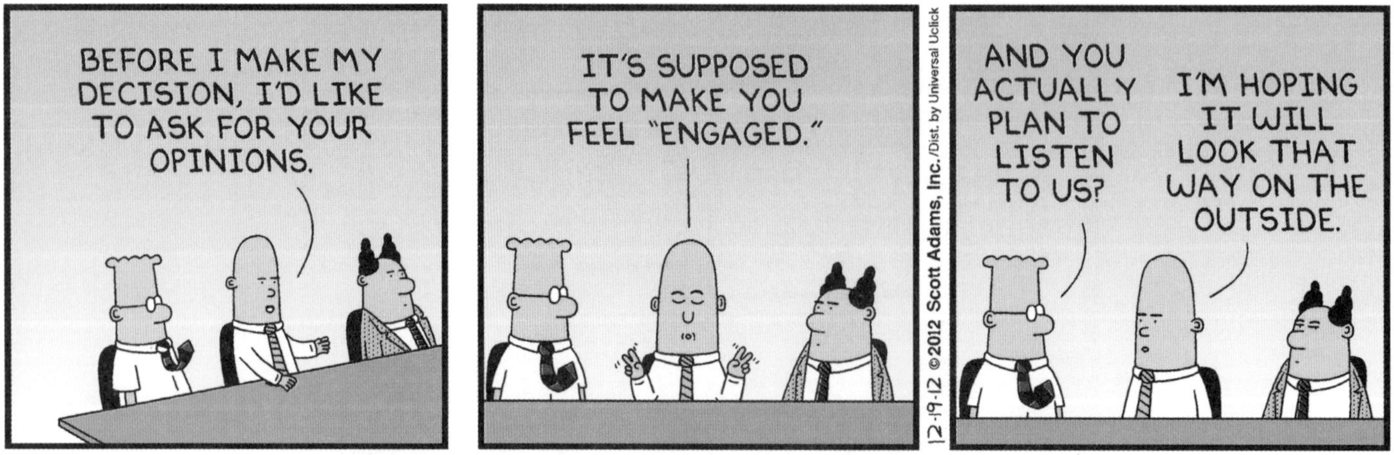
BEFORE I MAKE MY DECISION, I'D LIKE TO ASK FOR YOUR OPINIONS.
IT'S SUPPOSED TO MAKE YOU FEEL "ENGAGED."
12·19·12 ©2012 Scott Adams, Inc./Dist. by Universal Uclick
AND YOU ACTUALLY PLAN TO LISTEN TO US?
I'M HOPING IT WILL LOOK THAT WAY ON THE OUTSIDE.

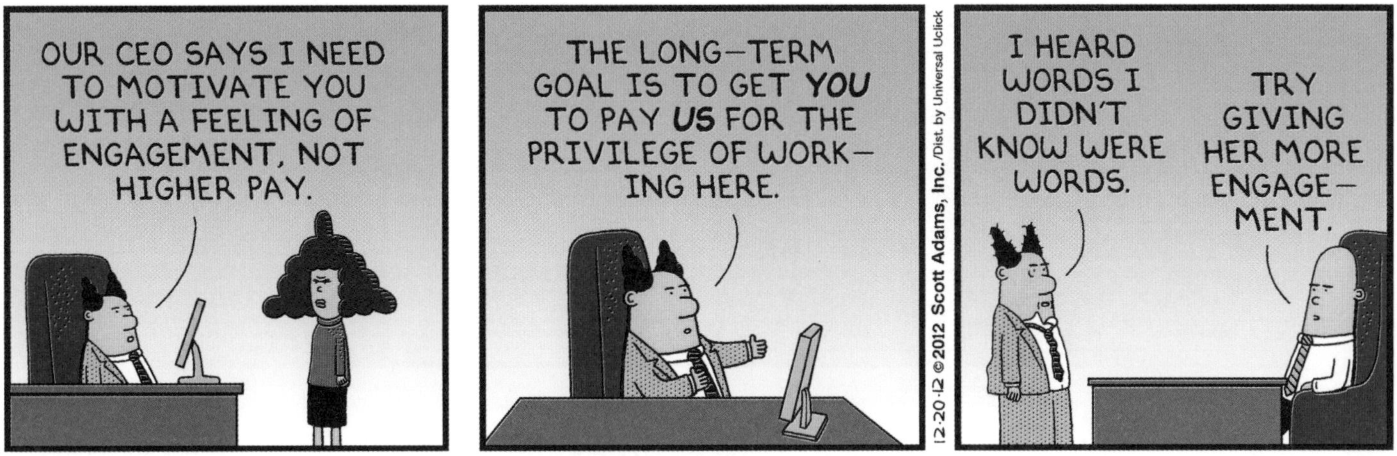
OUR CEO SAYS I NEED TO MOTIVATE YOU WITH A FEELING OF ENGAGEMENT, NOT HIGHER PAY.
THE LONG-TERM GOAL IS TO GET YOU TO PAY US FOR THE PRIVILEGE OF WORKING HERE.
12·20·12 ©2012 Scott Adams, Inc./Dist. by Universal Uclick
I HEARD WORDS I DIDN'T KNOW WERE WORDS.
TRY GIVING HER MORE ENGAGEMENT.

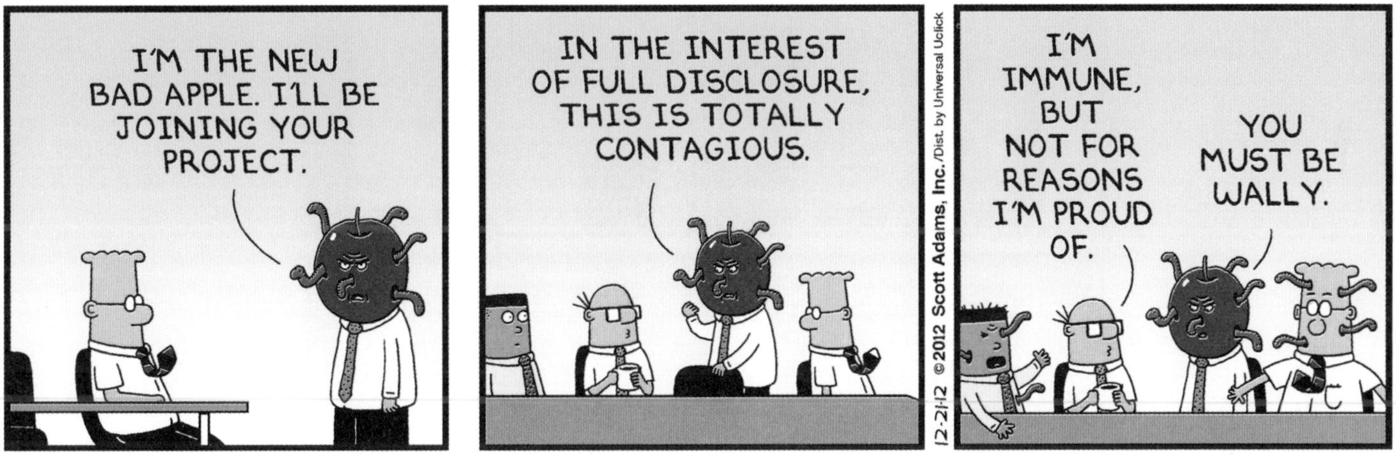
I'M THE NEW BAD APPLE. I'LL BE JOINING YOUR PROJECT.
IN THE INTEREST OF FULL DISCLOSURE, THIS IS TOTALLY CONTAGIOUS.
12·21·12 ©2012 Scott Adams, Inc./Dist. by Universal Uclick
I'M IMMUNE, BUT NOT FOR REASONS I'M PROUD OF.
YOU MUST BE WALLY.

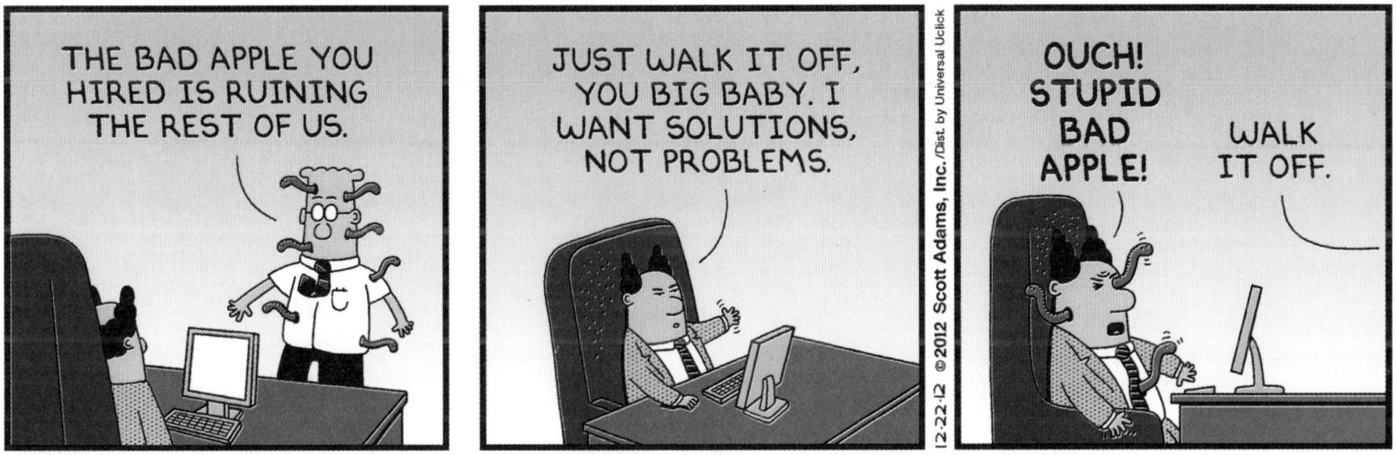
THE BAD APPLE YOU HIRED IS RUINING THE REST OF US.
JUST WALK IT OFF, YOU BIG BABY. I WANT SOLUTIONS, NOT PROBLEMS.
12·22·12 ©2012 Scott Adams, Inc./Dist. by Universal Uclick
OUCH! STUPID BAD APPLE!
WALK IT OFF.

GAAA!!!
DID YOU FIND THE SNAKE IN YOUR CUBICLE?
WHAT THE. . . ?
I PUT IT THERE BE— CAUSE I'M TRYING TO MOTIVATE YOU WITH A CULTURE OF FEAR.
THAT ONLY WORKS IN THE SHORT TERM!
A LEADER TAKES THE FIRST STEP WITHOUT KNOWING WHERE THE NEXT STEP WILL BE.
SO GET TO WORK. AND BY THE WAY, ONE OF THE URINALS IS ELECTRIFIED.
IT'S ONLY SET TO STUN, SO DON'T BE A BABY ABOUT IT.
HIS OFFICE PLANT IS CLEAR.
©2012 Scott Adams, Inc./Dist. by Universal Uclick
12-23-12

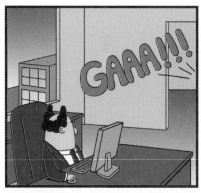

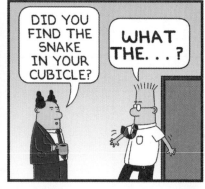

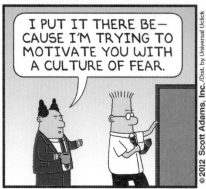

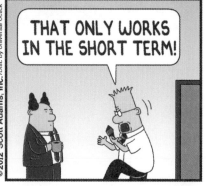

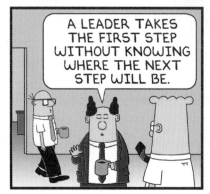

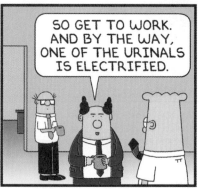

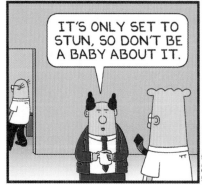

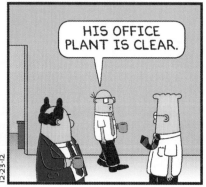

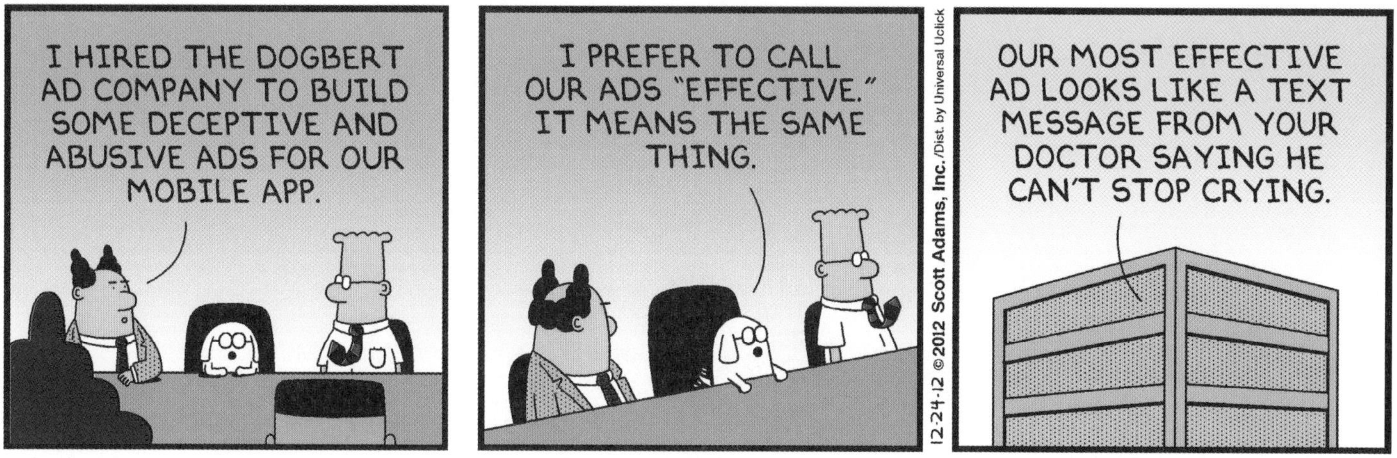

I HIRED THE DOGBERT AD COMPANY TO BUILD SOME DECEPTIVE AND ABUSIVE ADS FOR OUR MOBILE APP.
I PREFER TO CALL OUR ADS "EFFECTIVE." IT MEANS THE SAME THING.
12·24·12 ©2012 Scott Adams, Inc./Dist. by Universal Uclick
OUR MOST EFFECTIVE AD LOOKS LIKE A TEXT MESSAGE FROM YOUR DOCTOR SAYING HE CAN'T STOP CRYING.

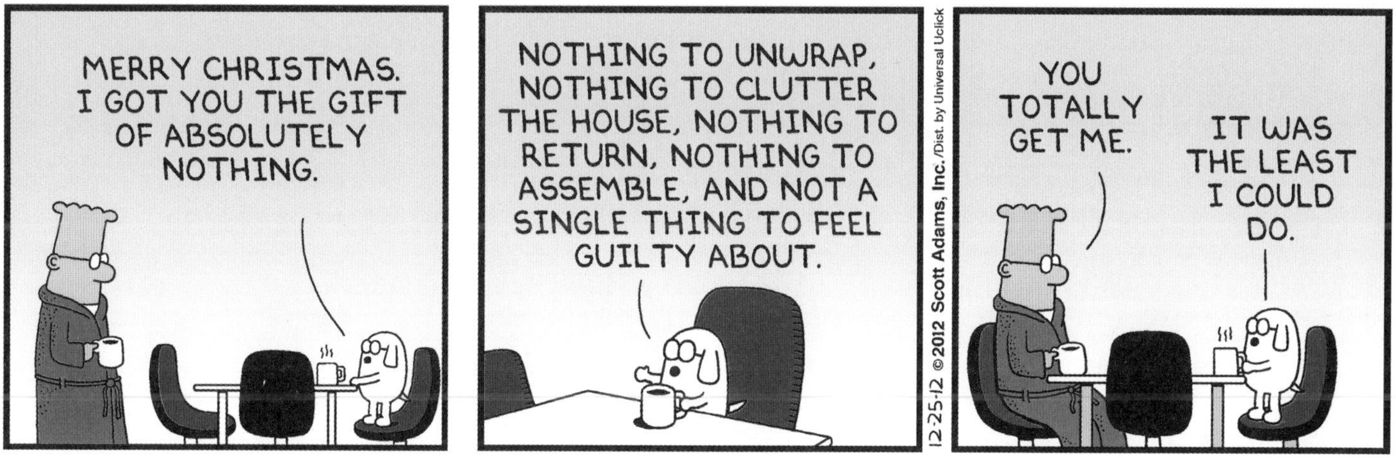

MERRY CHRISTMAS. I GOT YOU THE GIFT OF ABSOLUTELY NOTHING.
NOTHING TO UNWRAP, NOTHING TO CLUTTER THE HOUSE, NOTHING TO RETURN, NOTHING TO ASSEMBLE, AND NOT A SINGLE THING TO FEEL GUILTY ABOUT.
12·25·12 ©2012 Scott Adams, Inc./Dist. by Universal Uclick
YOU TOTALLY GET ME.
IT WAS THE LEAST I COULD DO.

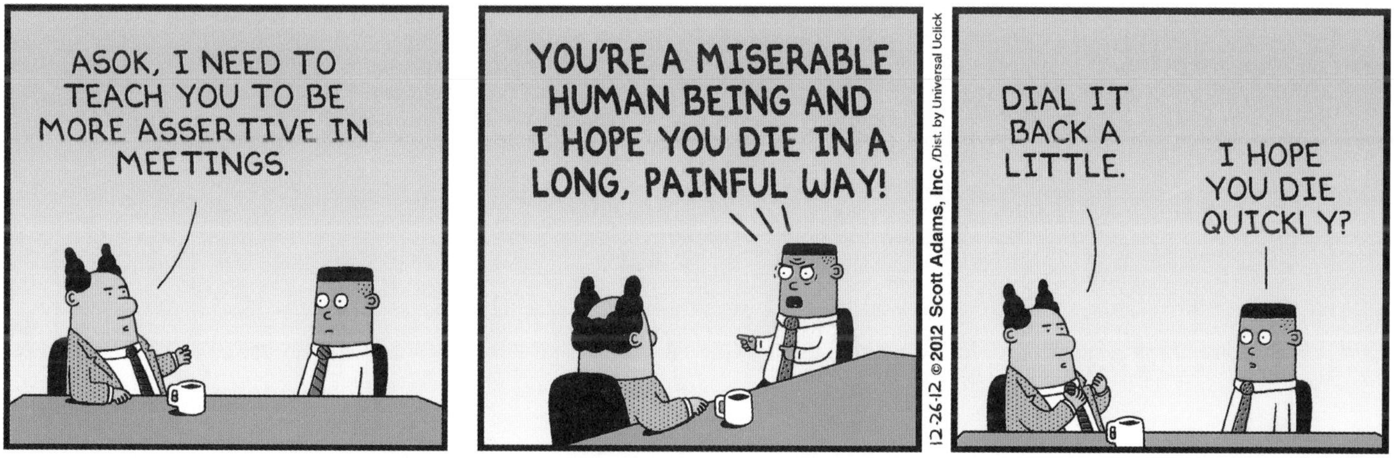

ASOK, I NEED TO TEACH YOU TO BE MORE ASSERTIVE IN MEETINGS.
YOU'RE A MISERABLE HUMAN BEING AND I HOPE YOU DIE IN A LONG, PAINFUL WAY!
12·26·12 ©2012 Scott Adams, Inc./Dist. by Universal Uclick
DIAL IT BACK A LITTLE.
I HOPE YOU DIE QUICKLY?

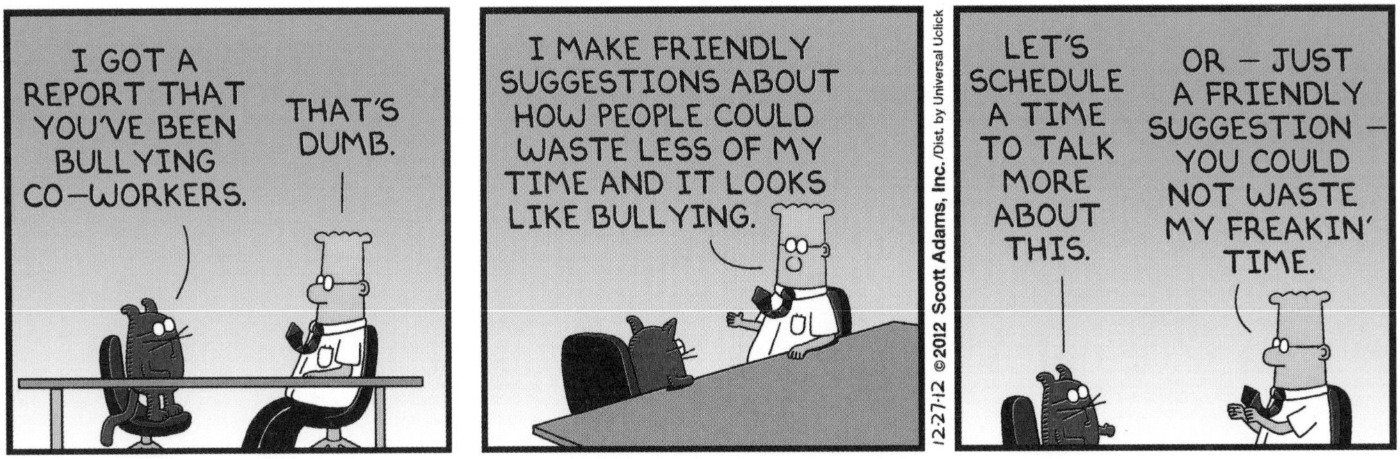
I GOT A REPORT THAT YOU'VE BEEN BULLYING CO-WORKERS.
THAT'S DUMB.
I MAKE FRIENDLY SUGGESTIONS ABOUT HOW PEOPLE COULD WASTE LESS OF MY TIME AND IT LOOKS LIKE BULLYING.
LET'S SCHEDULE A TIME TO TALK MORE ABOUT THIS.
OR — JUST A FRIENDLY SUGGESTION — YOU COULD NOT WASTE MY FREAKIN' TIME.
12-27-12 ©2012 Scott Adams, Inc./Dist. by Universal Uclick

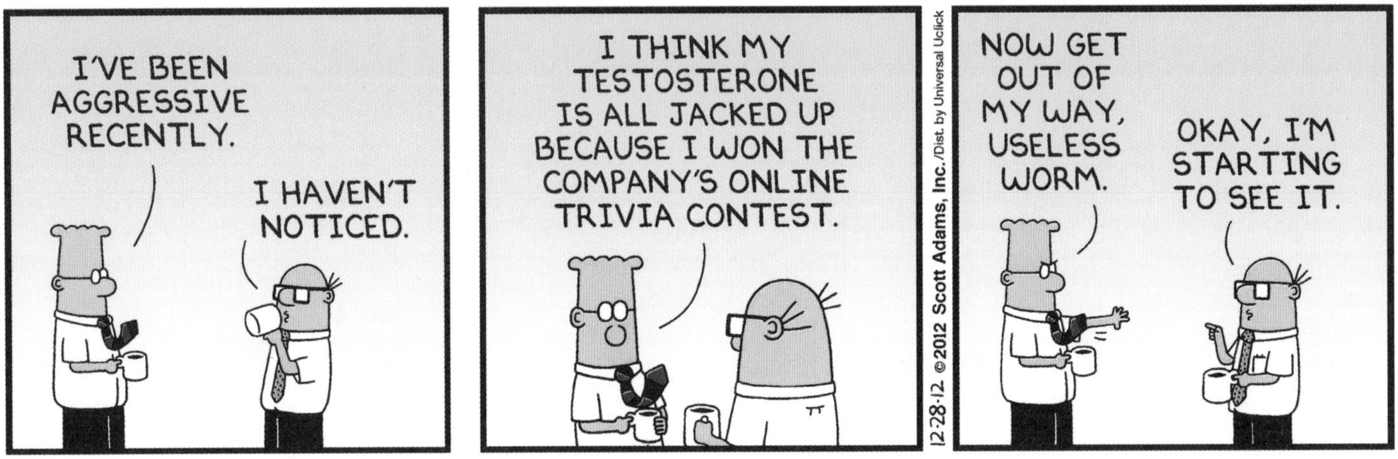
I'VE BEEN AGGRESSIVE RECENTLY.
I HAVEN'T NOTICED.
I THINK MY TESTOSTERONE IS ALL JACKED UP BECAUSE I WON THE COMPANY'S ONLINE TRIVIA CONTEST.
NOW GET OUT OF MY WAY, USELESS WORM.
OKAY, I'M STARTING TO SEE IT.
12-28-12 ©2012 Scott Adams, Inc./Dist. by Universal Uclick

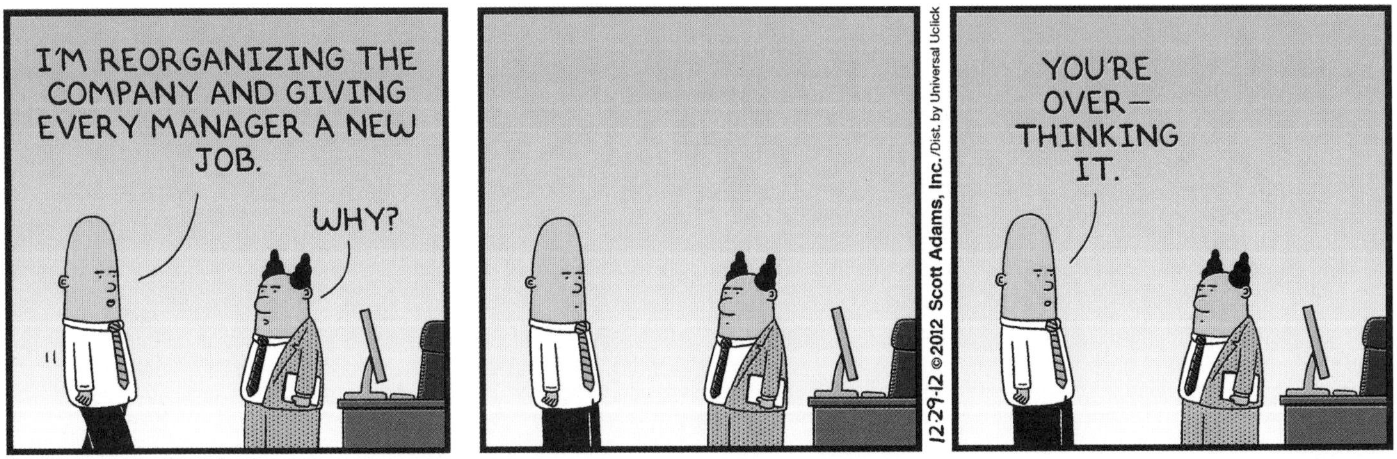
I'M REORGANIZING THE COMPANY AND GIVING EVERY MANAGER A NEW JOB.
WHY?
YOU'RE OVER-THINKING IT.
12-29-12 ©2012 Scott Adams, Inc./Dist. by Universal Uclick

I FINISHED GHOST-WRITING YOUR AUTOBIOGRAPHY.
"I WAS RIDICULOUSLY LUCKY. THE END."
I WAS HOPING YOU'D INCLUDE SOMETHING ABOUT ALL OF MY HARD WORK.
YOU DIDN'T WORK ANY HARDER THAN YOUR GARDENER, AND HE LIVES IN HIS TRUCK.
©2012 Scott Adams, Inc./Dist. by Universal Uclick
WHAT ABOUT MY VISION AND MY INTUITION?
MY FIRST DRAFT HAD A CHAPTER ON YOUR HALLUCINATIONS AND MAGICAL THINKING.
BUT I COVERED THAT GROUND WITH THE TITLE: "I'M A DELUSIONAL SOCIO-PATH AND YOU CAN TOO."
I'M STARTING TO REGRET PAYING YOU IN ADVANCE.
12-30-12

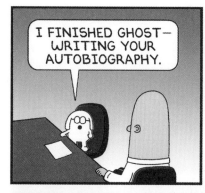

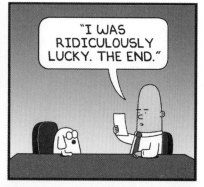

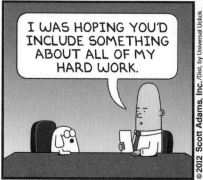

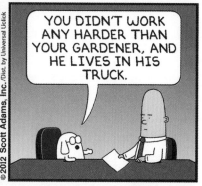

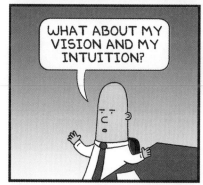

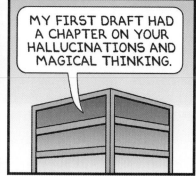

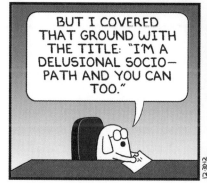

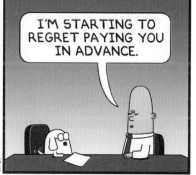

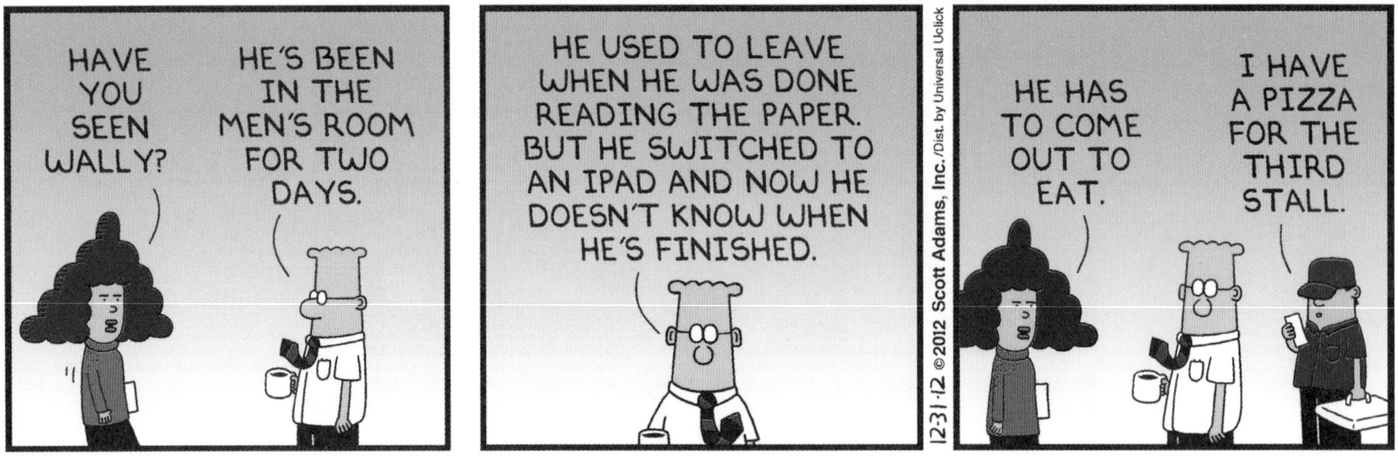
HAVE YOU SEEN WALLY?
HE'S BEEN IN THE MEN'S ROOM FOR TWO DAYS.
HE USED TO LEAVE WHEN HE WAS DONE READING THE PAPER. BUT HE SWITCHED TO AN IPAD AND NOW HE DOESN'T KNOW WHEN HE'S FINISHED.
12-31-12 ©2012 Scott Adams, Inc./Dist. by Universal Uclick
HE HAS TO COME OUT TO EAT.
I HAVE A PIZZA FOR THE THIRD STALL.

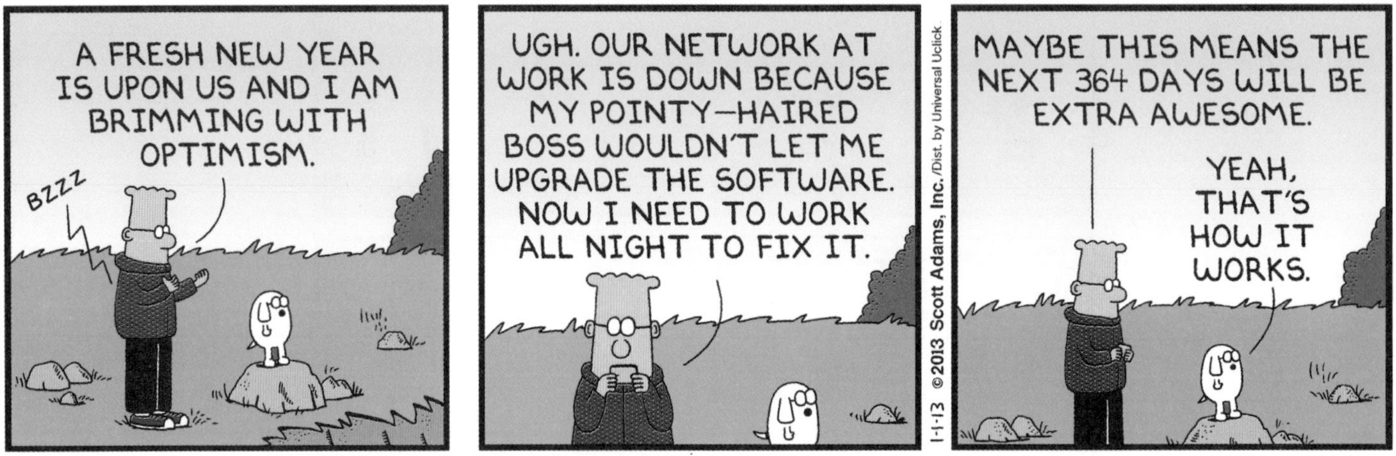
A FRESH NEW YEAR IS UPON US AND I AM BRIMMING WITH OPTIMISM.
BZZZ
UGH. OUR NETWORK AT WORK IS DOWN BECAUSE MY POINTY-HAIRED BOSS WOULDN'T LET ME UPGRADE THE SOFTWARE. NOW I NEED TO WORK ALL NIGHT TO FIX IT.
1-1-13 ©2013 Scott Adams, Inc./Dist. by Universal Uclick
MAYBE THIS MEANS THE NEXT 364 DAYS WILL BE EXTRA AWESOME.
YEAH, THAT'S HOW IT WORKS.

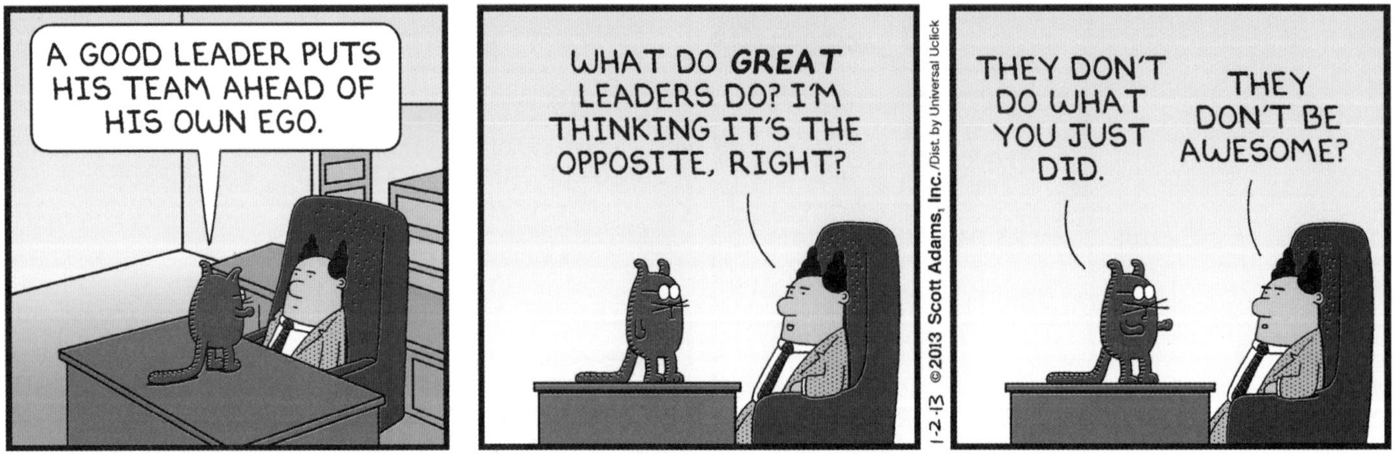
A GOOD LEADER PUTS HIS TEAM AHEAD OF HIS OWN EGO.
WHAT DO **GREAT** LEADERS DO? I'M THINKING IT'S THE OPPOSITE, RIGHT?
1-2-13 ©2013 Scott Adams, Inc./Dist. by Universal Uclick
THEY DON'T DO WHAT YOU JUST DID.
THEY DON'T BE AWESOME?

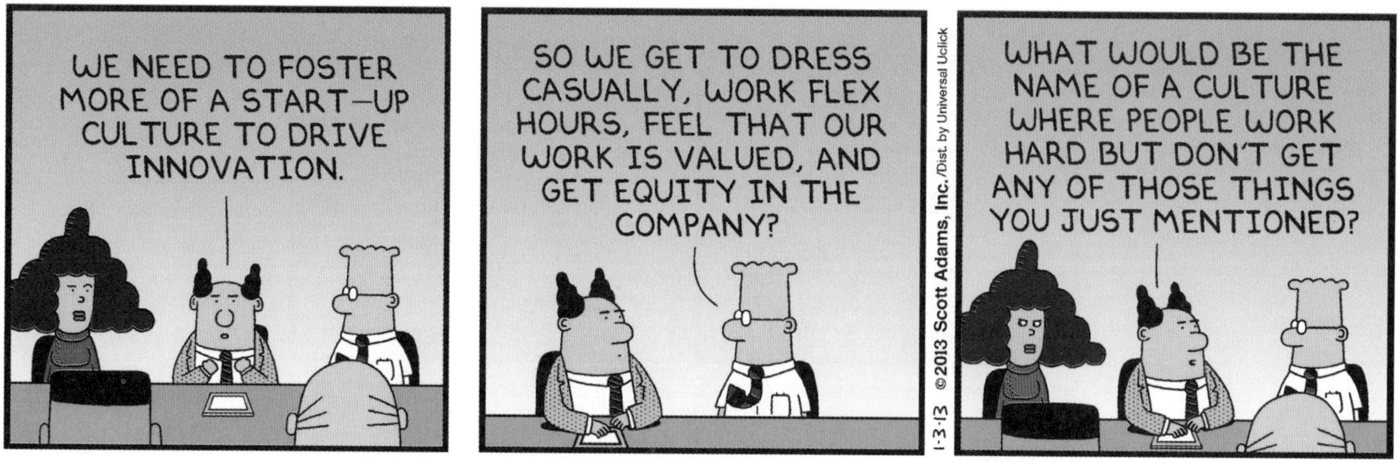
WE NEED TO FOSTER MORE OF A START—UP CULTURE TO DRIVE INNOVATION.
SO WE GET TO DRESS CASUALLY, WORK FLEX HOURS, FEEL THAT OUR WORK IS VALUED, AND GET EQUITY IN THE COMPANY?
WHAT WOULD BE THE NAME OF A CULTURE WHERE PEOPLE WORK HARD BUT DON'T GET ANY OF THOSE THINGS YOU JUST MENTIONED?
1-3-13 ©2013 Scott Adams, Inc./Dist. by Universal Uclick

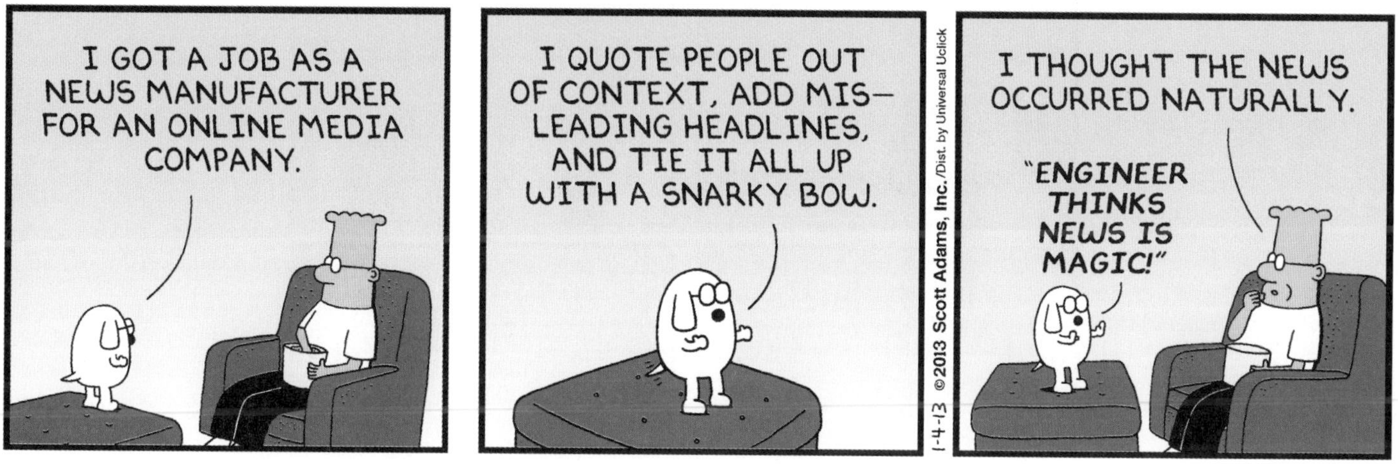
I GOT A JOB AS A NEWS MANUFACTURER FOR AN ONLINE MEDIA COMPANY.
I QUOTE PEOPLE OUT OF CONTEXT, ADD MIS—LEADING HEADLINES, AND TIE IT ALL UP WITH A SNARKY BOW.
I THOUGHT THE NEWS OCCURRED NATURALLY.
"ENGINEER THINKS NEWS IS MAGIC!"
1-4-13 ©2013 Scott Adams, Inc./Dist. by Universal Uclick

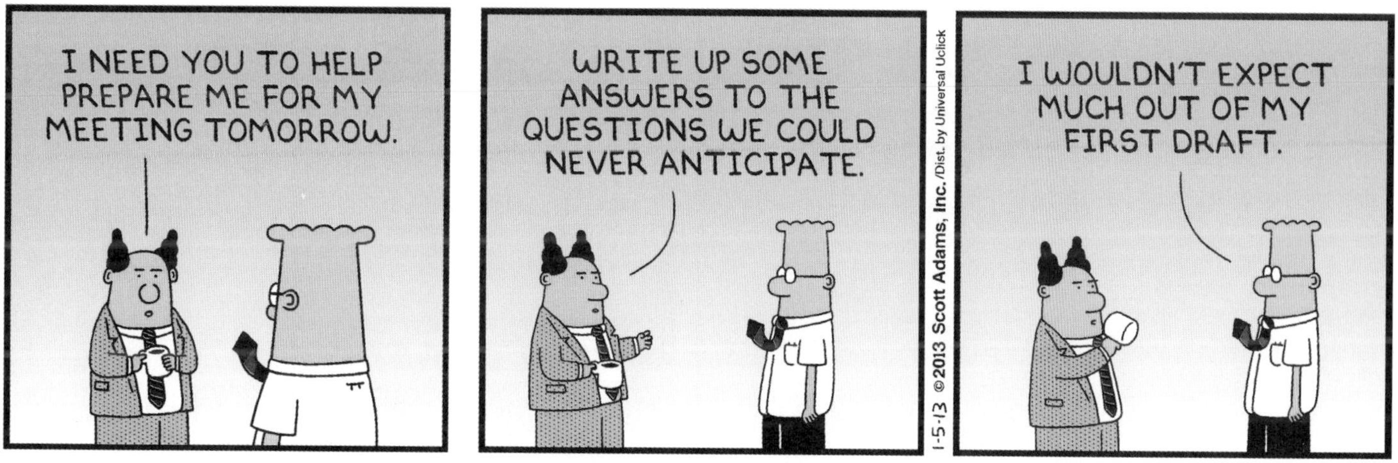
I NEED YOU TO HELP PREPARE ME FOR MY MEETING TOMORROW.
WRITE UP SOME ANSWERS TO THE QUESTIONS WE COULD NEVER ANTICIPATE.
I WOULDN'T EXPECT MUCH OUT OF MY FIRST DRAFT.
1-5-13 ©2013 Scott Adams, Inc./Dist. by Universal Uclick

I CAN'T GET ONE OF MY TEAM MEMBERS TO DO ANY WORK.
I'M HOPING YOU CAN TALK TO HIS BOSS.
I DON'T WANT TO MAKE WAVES.
IT'S YOUR JOB TO MAKE WAVES!
THEY PAY YOU TO MAKE WAVES, YOU WORTHLESS PILE OF STUPIDITY!
OOPS.
I HEARD YOU MADE WAVES. HOW'D THAT WORK OUT?
SURPRIS-INGLY BAD.
©2013 Scott Adams, Inc./Dist. by Universal Uclick
1-6-13

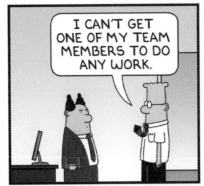

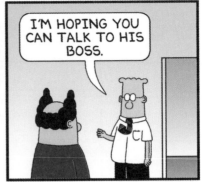

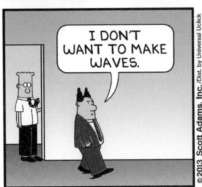

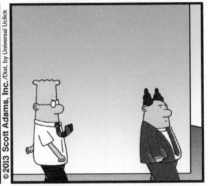

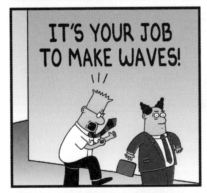

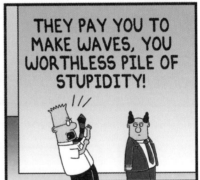

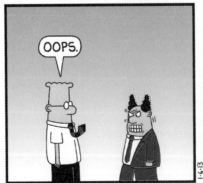

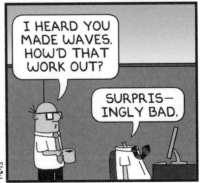

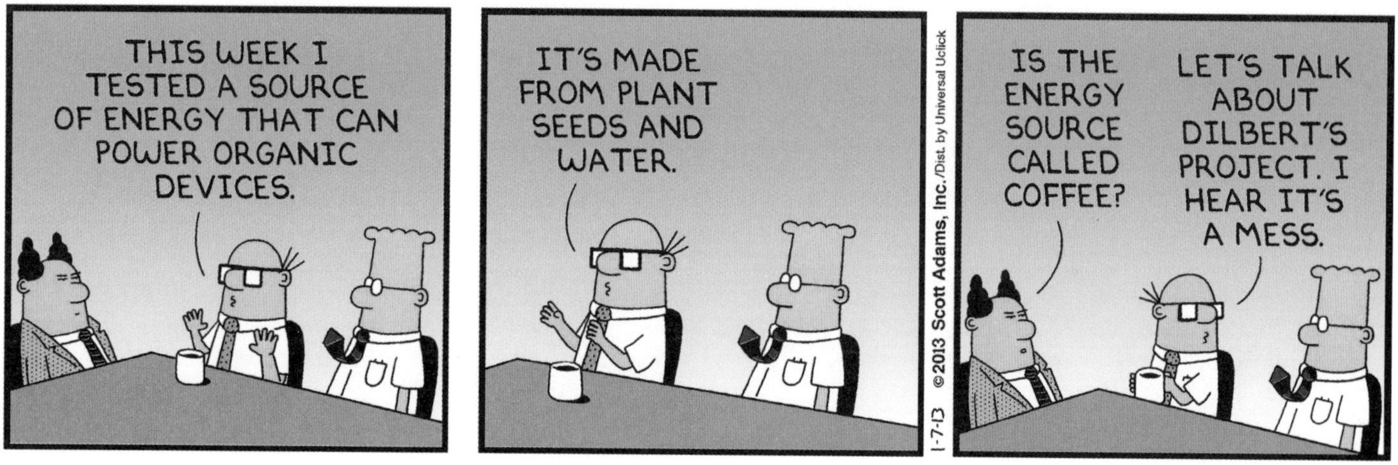
THIS WEEK I TESTED A SOURCE OF ENERGY THAT CAN POWER ORGANIC DEVICES.
IT'S MADE FROM PLANT SEEDS AND WATER.
1-7-13 ©2013 Scott Adams, Inc./Dist. by Universal Uclick
IS THE ENERGY SOURCE CALLED COFFEE?
LET'S TALK ABOUT DILBERT'S PROJECT. I HEAR IT'S A MESS.

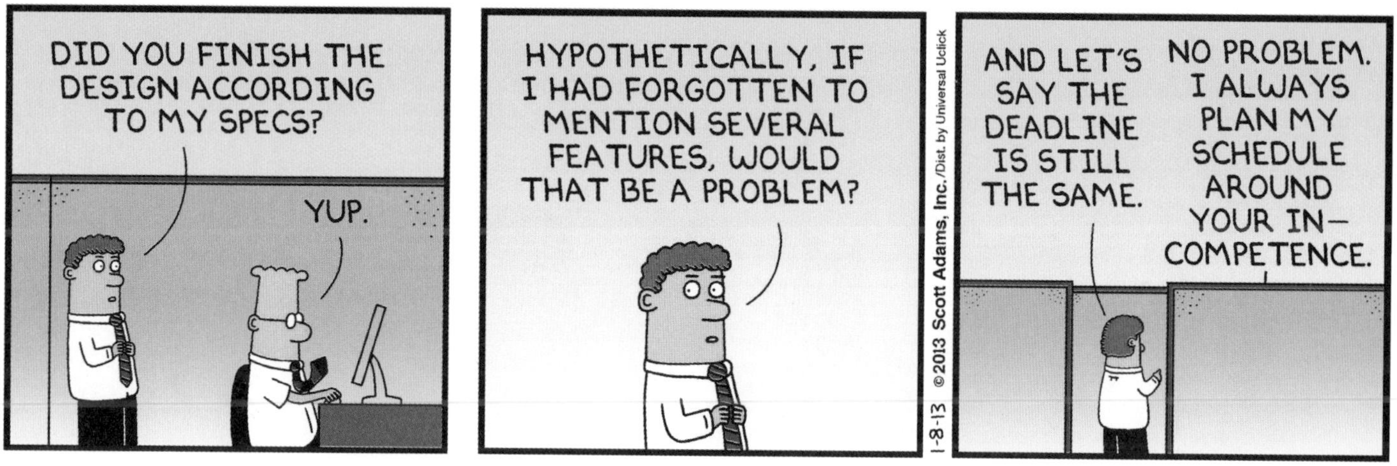
DID YOU FINISH THE DESIGN ACCORDING TO MY SPECS?
YUP.
HYPOTHETICALLY, IF I HAD FORGOTTEN TO MENTION SEVERAL FEATURES, WOULD THAT BE A PROBLEM?
1-8-13 ©2013 Scott Adams, Inc./Dist. by Universal Uclick
AND LET'S SAY THE DEADLINE IS STILL THE SAME.
NO PROBLEM. I ALWAYS PLAN MY SCHEDULE AROUND YOUR IN-COMPETENCE.

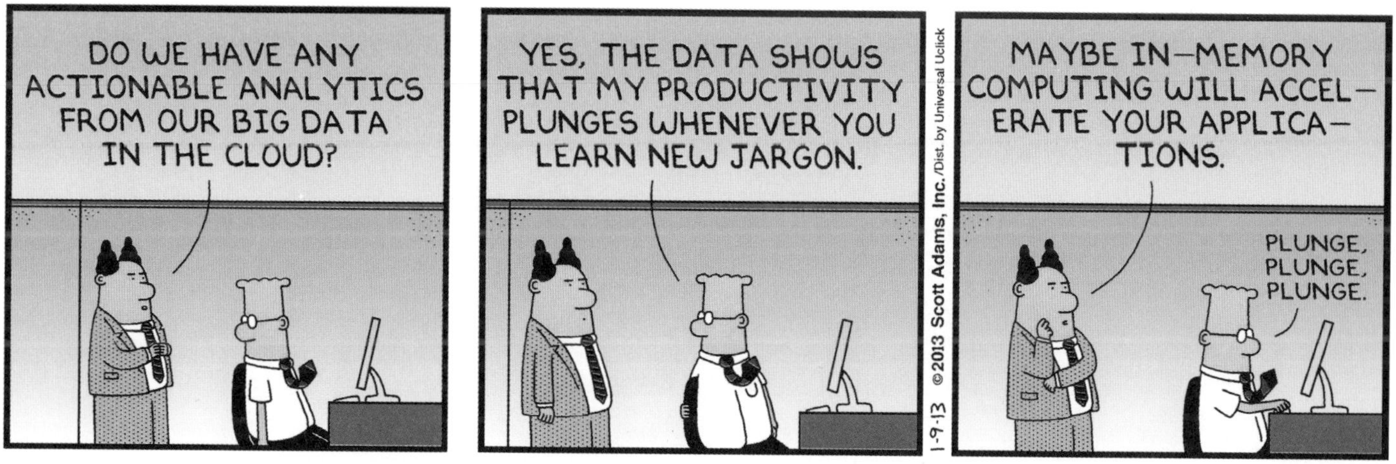
DO WE HAVE ANY ACTIONABLE ANALYTICS FROM OUR BIG DATA IN THE CLOUD?
YES, THE DATA SHOWS THAT MY PRODUCTIVITY PLUNGES WHENEVER YOU LEARN NEW JARGON.
1-9-13 ©2013 Scott Adams, Inc./Dist. by Universal Uclick
MAYBE IN-MEMORY COMPUTING WILL ACCEL-ERATE YOUR APPLICA-TIONS.
PLUNGE, PLUNGE, PLUNGE.

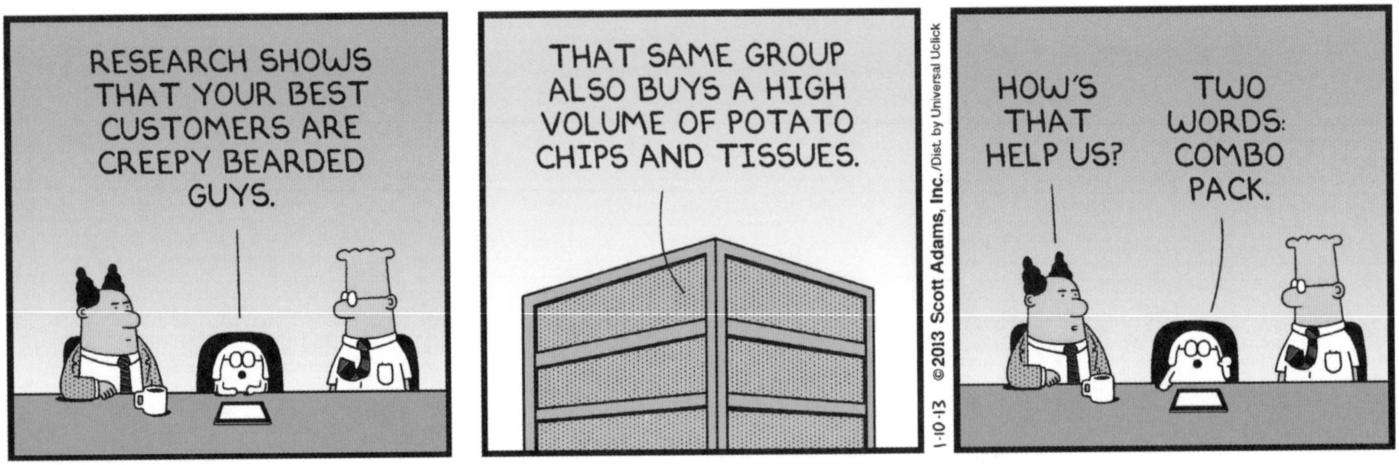
RESEARCH SHOWS THAT YOUR BEST CUSTOMERS ARE CREEPY BEARDED GUYS.
THAT SAME GROUP ALSO BUYS A HIGH VOLUME OF POTATO CHIPS AND TISSUES.
1-10-13 ©2013 Scott Adams, Inc./Dist. by Universal Uclick
HOW'S THAT HELP US?
TWO WORDS: COMBO PACK.

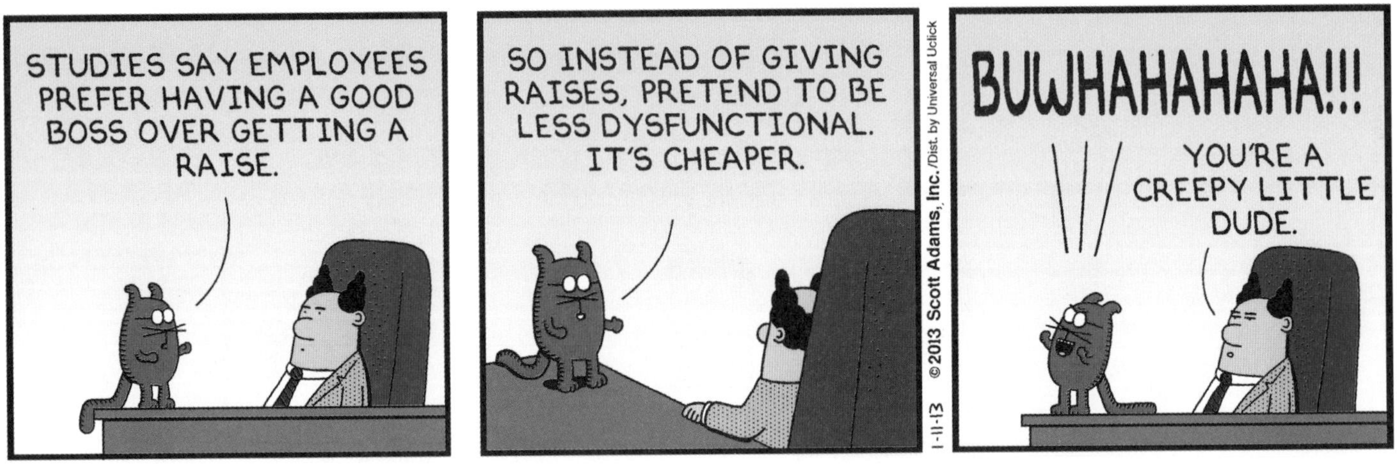
STUDIES SAY EMPLOYEES PREFER HAVING A GOOD BOSS OVER GETTING A RAISE.
SO INSTEAD OF GIVING RAISES, PRETEND TO BE LESS DYSFUNCTIONAL. IT'S CHEAPER.
1-11-13 ©2013 Scott Adams, Inc./Dist. by Universal Uclick
BUWHAHAHAHA!!!
YOU'RE A CREEPY LITTLE DUDE.

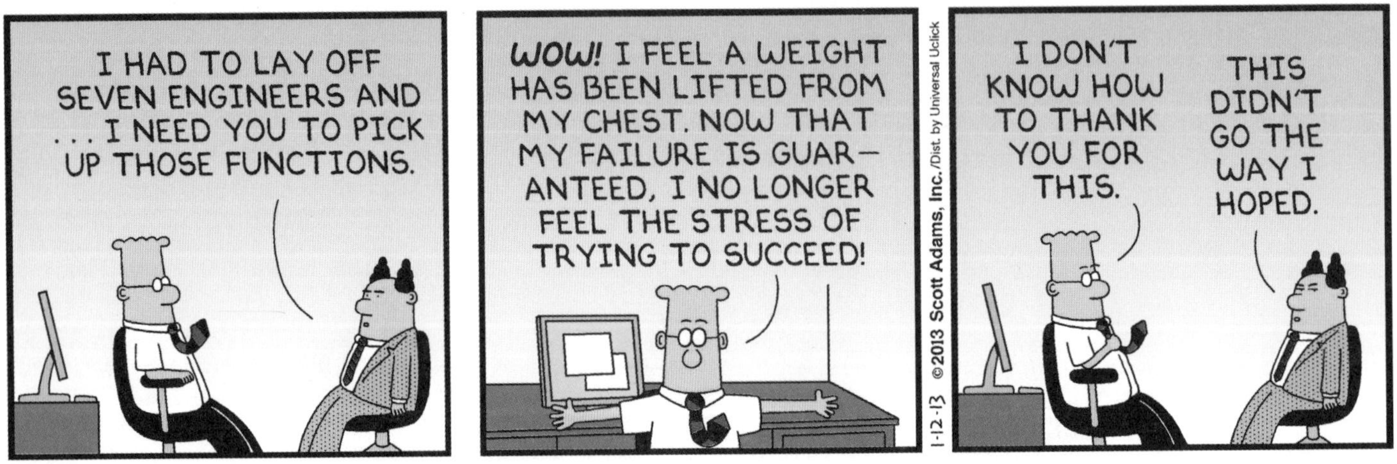
I HAD TO LAY OFF SEVEN ENGINEERS AND . . . I NEED YOU TO PICK UP THOSE FUNCTIONS.
WOW! I FEEL A WEIGHT HAS BEEN LIFTED FROM MY CHEST. NOW THAT MY FAILURE IS GUAR-ANTEED, I NO LONGER FEEL THE STRESS OF TRYING TO SUCCEED!
1-12-13 ©2013 Scott Adams, Inc./Dist. by Universal Uclick
I DON'T KNOW HOW TO THANK YOU FOR THIS.
THIS DIDN'T GO THE WAY I HOPED.

DO YOU WANT EXTRA LEGROOM ON YOUR FLIGHT? IT COSTS MORE.
YES.
DO YOU WANT AN AISLE SEAT? THAT COSTS EXTRA.
YES.
DO YOU WANT A NO-BABY SECTION? IT COSTS EXTRA.
YES.
©2013 Scott Adams, Inc./Dist. by Universal Uclick
EXTRA BAG?
YES.
MEAL?
YES.
PRIORITY BOARDING?
YES.
IN-FLIGHT ENTERTAIN-MENT?
WI-FI?
FLIGHT INSURANCE?
WE'RE ALMOST DONE. JUST TWELVE MORE QUESTIONS.
ONE HOUR LATER.
YOUR TICKET COMES TO... $27,689.
1-13-13
AND IT'S ONLY THREE STOPS!
NOW LET'S DO THE RETURN FLIGHT.

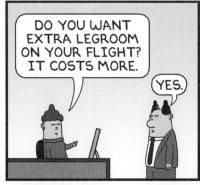

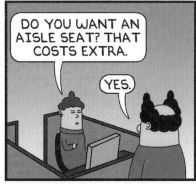

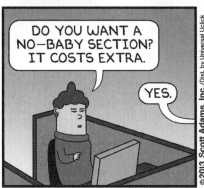

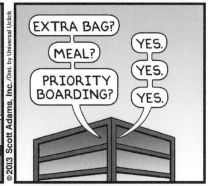

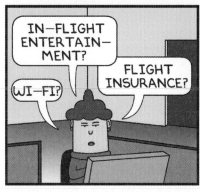

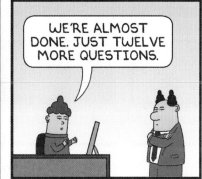

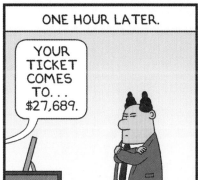

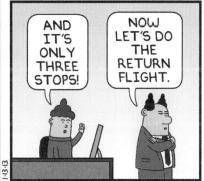

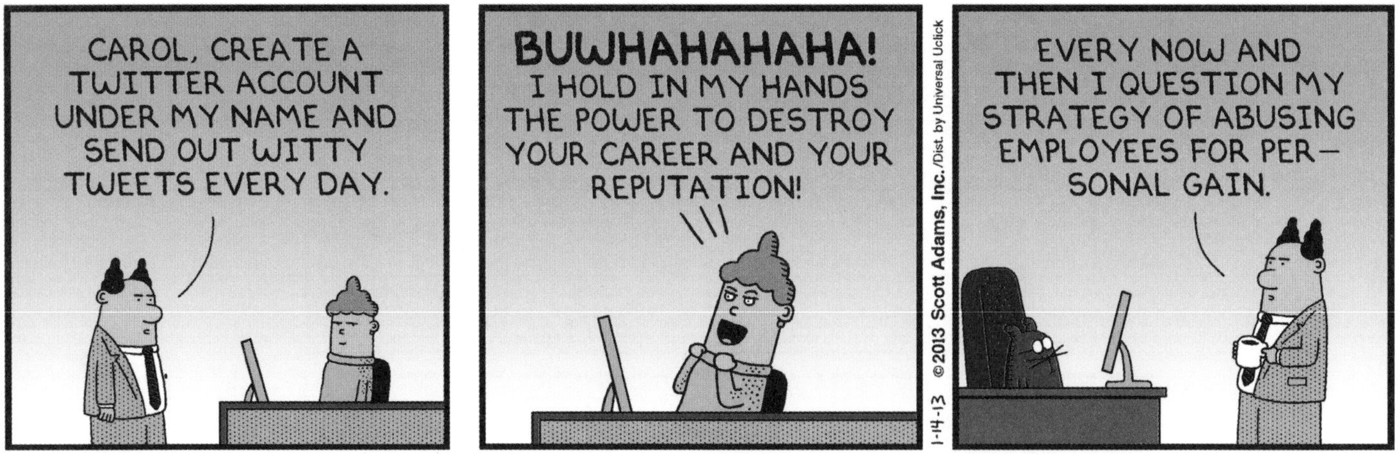
CAROL, CREATE A TWITTER ACCOUNT UNDER MY NAME AND SEND OUT WITTY TWEETS EVERY DAY.
BUWHAHAHAHAHA!
I HOLD IN MY HANDS THE POWER TO DESTROY YOUR CAREER AND YOUR REPUTATION!
EVERY NOW AND THEN I QUESTION MY STRATEGY OF ABUSING EMPLOYEES FOR PER-SONAL GAIN.
1-14-13 ©2013 Scott Adams, Inc./Dist. by Universal Uclick

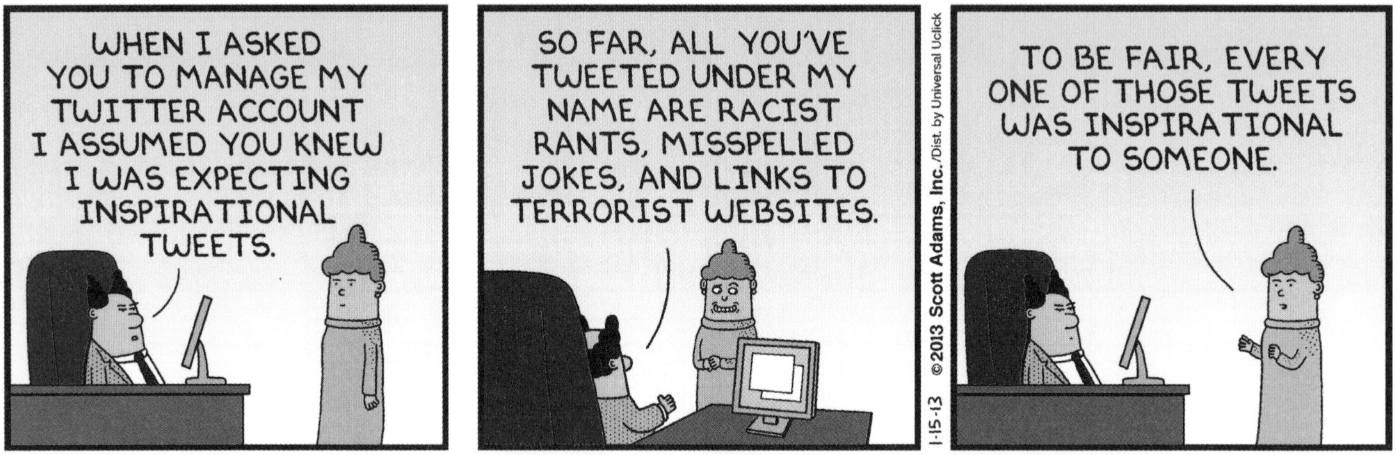
WHEN I ASKED YOU TO MANAGE MY TWITTER ACCOUNT I ASSUMED YOU KNEW I WAS EXPECTING INSPIRATIONAL TWEETS.
SO FAR, ALL YOU'VE TWEETED UNDER MY NAME ARE RACIST RANTS, MISSPELLED JOKES, AND LINKS TO TERRORIST WEBSITES.
TO BE FAIR, EVERY ONE OF THOSE TWEETS WAS INSPIRATIONAL TO SOMEONE.
1-15-13 ©2013 Scott Adams, Inc./Dist. by Universal Uclick

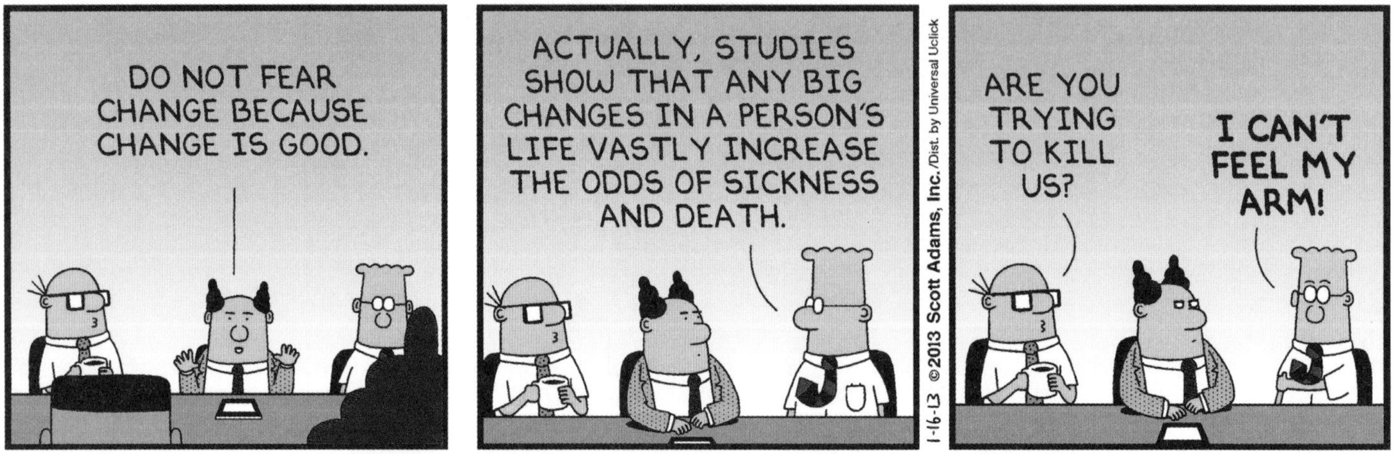
DO NOT FEAR CHANGE BECAUSE CHANGE IS GOOD.
ACTUALLY, STUDIES SHOW THAT ANY BIG CHANGES IN A PERSON'S LIFE VASTLY INCREASE THE ODDS OF SICKNESS AND DEATH.
ARE YOU TRYING TO KILL US?
I CAN'T FEEL MY ARM!
1-16-13 ©2013 Scott Adams, Inc./Dist. by Universal Uclick

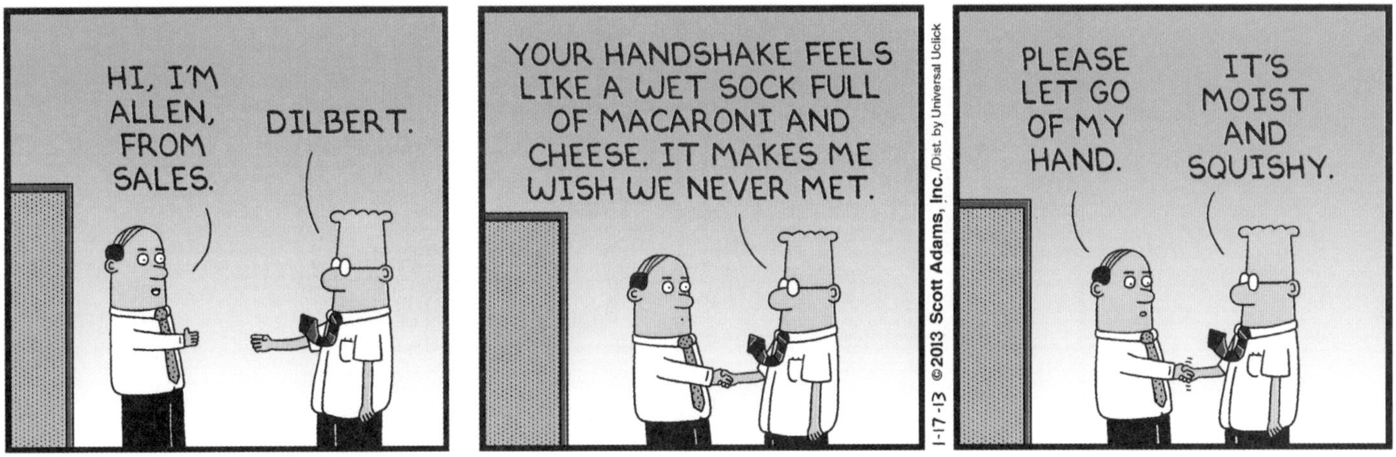
HI, I'M ALLEN, FROM SALES.
DILBERT.
YOUR HANDSHAKE FEELS LIKE A WET SOCK FULL OF MACARONI AND CHEESE. IT MAKES ME WISH WE NEVER MET.
1-17-13 ©2013 Scott Adams, Inc./Dist. by Universal Uclick
PLEASE LET GO OF MY HAND.
IT'S MOIST AND SQUISHY.

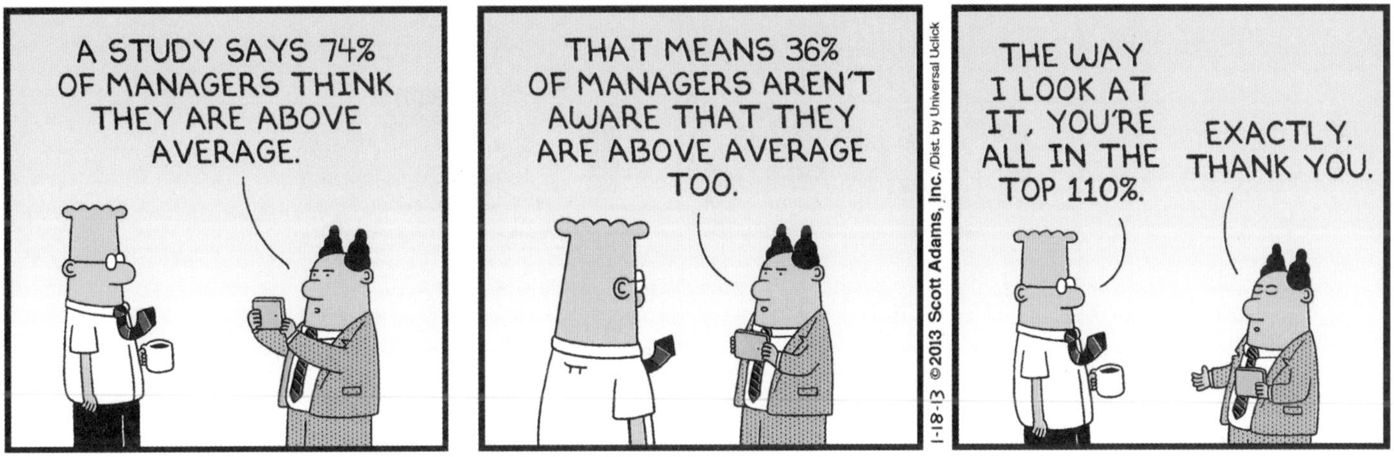
A STUDY SAYS 74% OF MANAGERS THINK THEY ARE ABOVE AVERAGE.
THAT MEANS 36% OF MANAGERS AREN'T AWARE THAT THEY ARE ABOVE AVERAGE TOO.
1-18-13 ©2013 Scott Adams, Inc./Dist. by Universal Uclick
THE WAY I LOOK AT IT, YOU'RE ALL IN THE TOP 110%.
EXACTLY. THANK YOU.

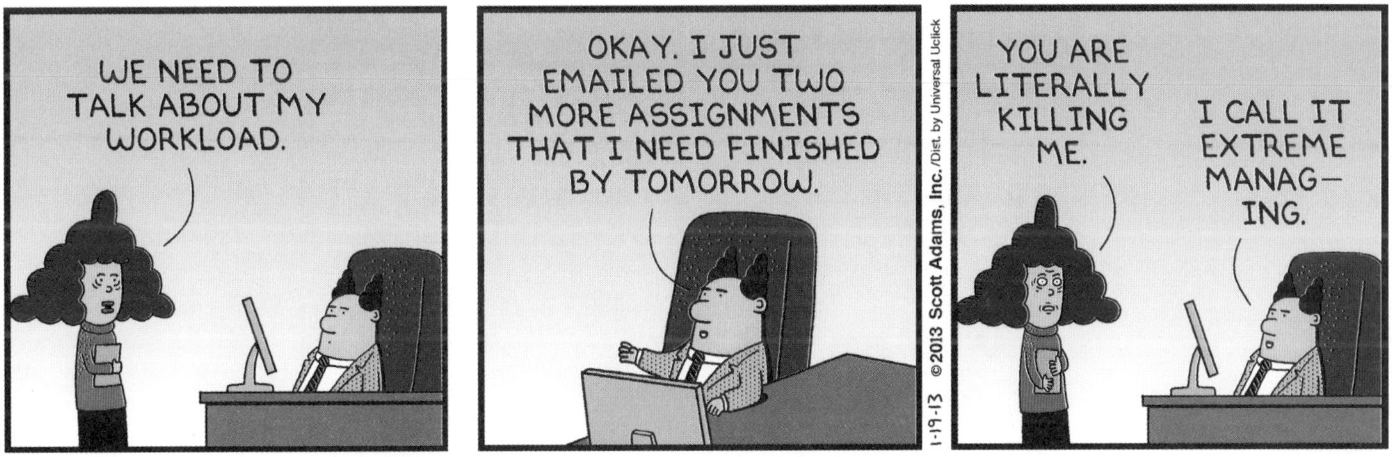
WE NEED TO TALK ABOUT MY WORKLOAD.
OKAY. I JUST EMAILED YOU TWO MORE ASSIGNMENTS THAT I NEED FINISHED BY TOMORROW.
1-19-13 ©2013 Scott Adams, Inc./Dist. by Universal Uclick
YOU ARE LITERALLY KILLING ME.
I CALL IT EXTREME MANAG-ING.

I CAN'T HEAR YOU. THERE'S TOO MUCH BACKGROUND NOISE AND ECHO ON YOUR END.
GERPLE MURMP
I SEE A SMUDGY THING THAT MIGHT BE YOUR HEAD, BUT I DON'T KNOW WHAT YOU'RE SAYING.
YOUR ACCENT IS TOO THICK. I CAN'T. . .
MUWA FLAMEL GUAPEN
©2013 Scott Adams, Inc./Dist. by Universal Uclick
I DIDN'T UNDERSTAND WHAT YOU SAID, AND I CAN'T TELL WHICH ONE OF YOU IS TALKING.
WHY DON'T. . .
URGAM. . .
OKAY, YOU GO.
EKPLUM
WHAT?
MUNGOW
DID YOU SAY. . .
PLURB
YOU'RE ACTING AS IF I AGREED TO SOME-THING, BUT I DON'T EVEN KNOW WHAT THE TOPIC IS.
I SEE YOU WAVING GOODBYE, SO YOU MUST THINK WE'RE DONE.
1-20-13
WAS YOUR CALL A SUCCESS?
BETTER THAN ANY-THING I'VE DONE ALL WEEK.

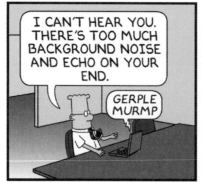

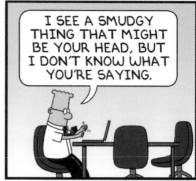

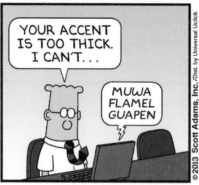

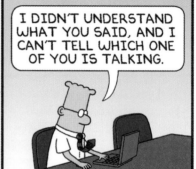

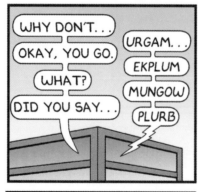

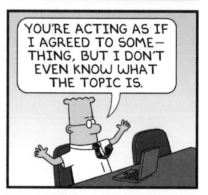

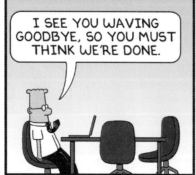

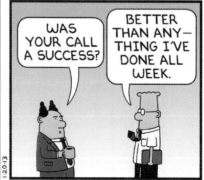

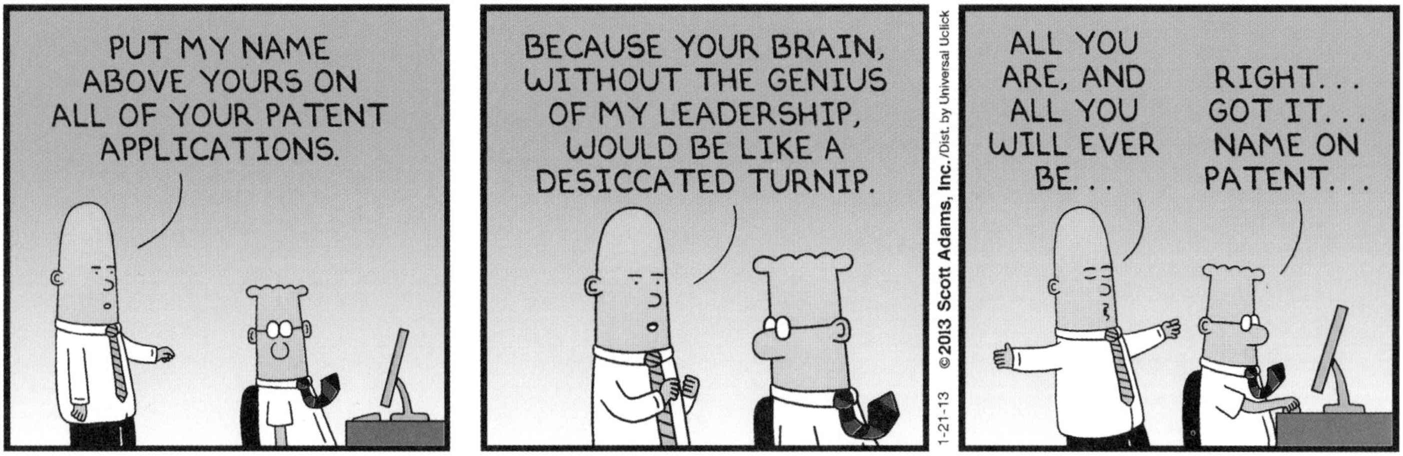
PUT MY NAME ABOVE YOURS ON ALL OF YOUR PATENT APPLICATIONS.
BECAUSE YOUR BRAIN, WITHOUT THE GENIUS OF MY LEADERSHIP, WOULD BE LIKE A DESICCATED TURNIP.
1-21-13 ©2013 Scott Adams, Inc./Dist. by Universal Uclick
ALL YOU ARE, AND ALL YOU WILL EVER BE...
RIGHT... GOT IT... NAME ON PATENT...

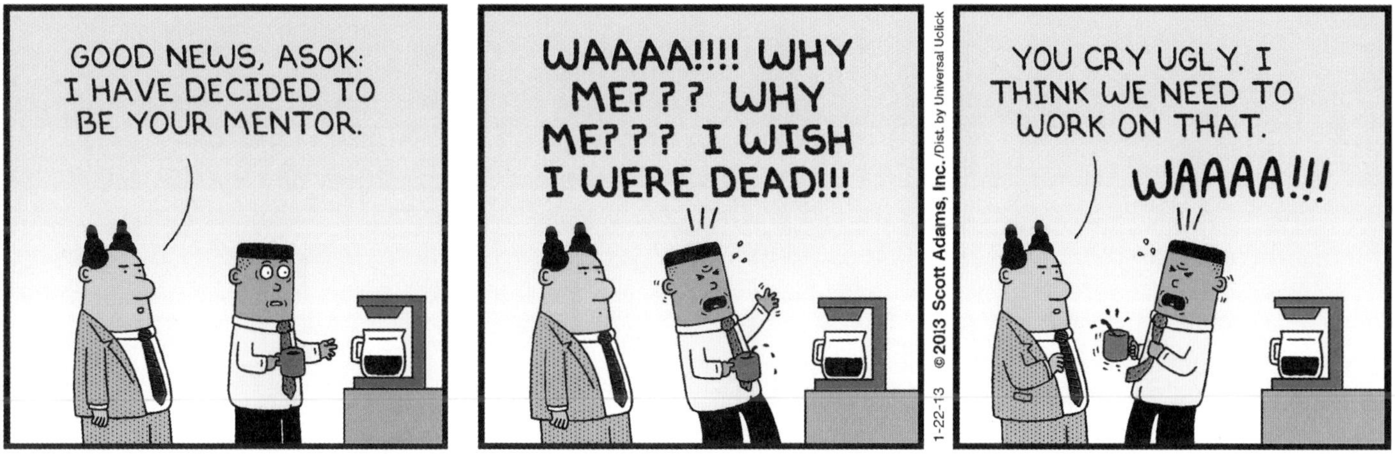
GOOD NEWS, ASOK: I HAVE DECIDED TO BE YOUR MENTOR.
WAAAAA!!!! WHY ME??? WHY ME??? I WISH I WERE DEAD!!!
1-22-13 ©2013 Scott Adams, Inc./Dist. by Universal Uclick
YOU CRY UGLY. I THINK WE NEED TO WORK ON THAT.
WAAAA!!!

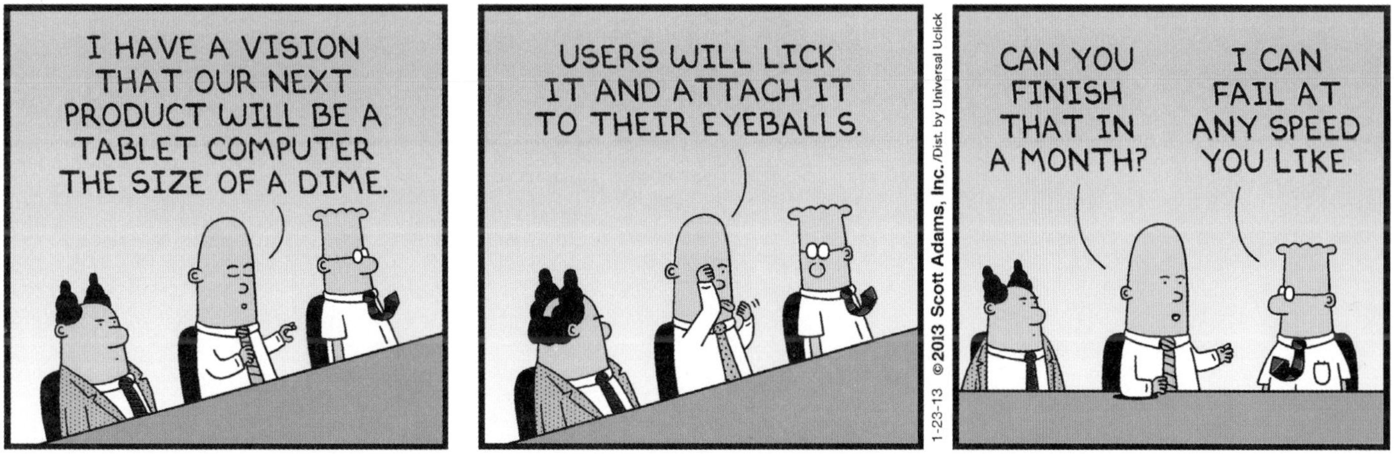
I HAVE A VISION THAT OUR NEXT PRODUCT WILL BE A TABLET COMPUTER THE SIZE OF A DIME.
USERS WILL LICK IT AND ATTACH IT TO THEIR EYEBALLS.
1-23-13 ©2013 Scott Adams, Inc./Dist. by Universal Uclick
CAN YOU FINISH THAT IN A MONTH?
I CAN FAIL AT ANY SPEED YOU LIKE.

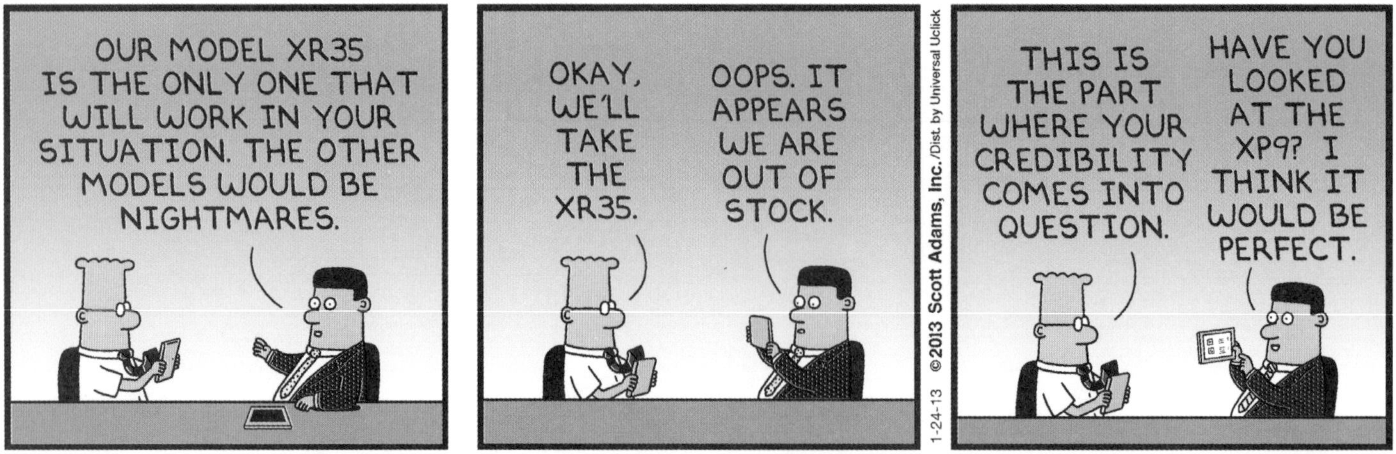
OUR MODEL XR35 IS THE ONLY ONE THAT WILL WORK IN YOUR SITUATION. THE OTHER MODELS WOULD BE NIGHTMARES.
OKAY, WE'LL TAKE THE XR35.
OOPS. IT APPEARS WE ARE OUT OF STOCK.
THIS IS THE PART WHERE YOUR CREDIBILITY COMES INTO QUESTION.
HAVE YOU LOOKED AT THE XP9? I THINK IT WOULD BE PERFECT.
1-24-13 ©2013 Scott Adams, Inc./Dist. by Universal Uclick

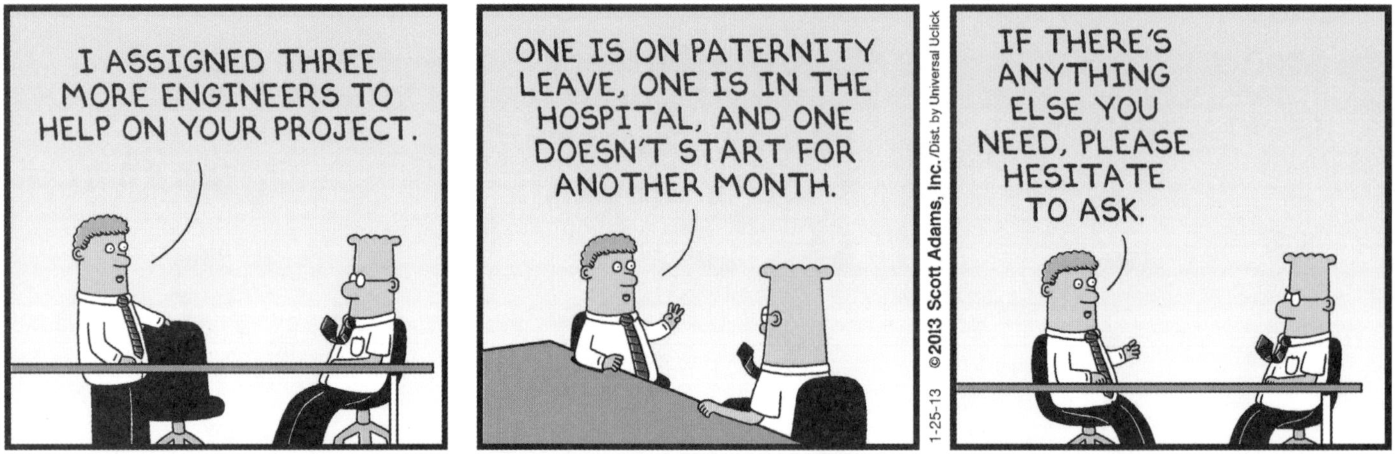
I ASSIGNED THREE MORE ENGINEERS TO HELP ON YOUR PROJECT.
ONE IS ON PATERNITY LEAVE, ONE IS IN THE HOSPITAL, AND ONE DOESN'T START FOR ANOTHER MONTH.
IF THERE'S ANYTHING ELSE YOU NEED, PLEASE HESITATE TO ASK.
1-25-13 ©2013 Scott Adams, Inc./Dist. by Universal Uclick

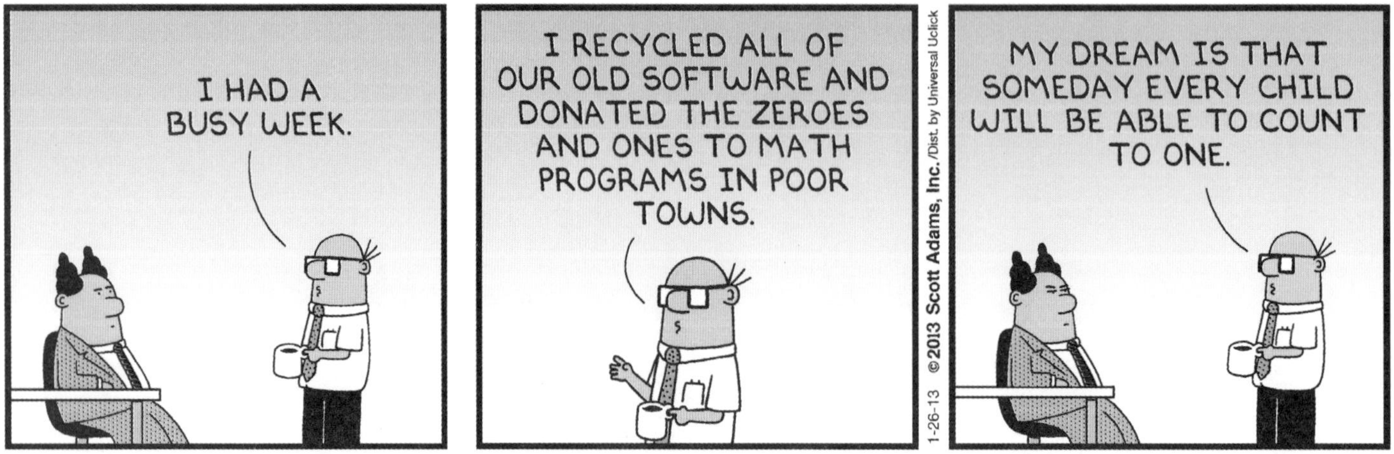
I HAD A BUSY WEEK.
I RECYCLED ALL OF OUR OLD SOFTWARE AND DONATED THE ZEROES AND ONES TO MATH PROGRAMS IN POOR TOWNS.
MY DREAM IS THAT SOMEDAY EVERY CHILD WILL BE ABLE TO COUNT TO ONE.
1-26-13 ©2013 Scott Adams, Inc./Dist. by Universal Uclick

I DECIDED TO BE PROACTIVE AND PUSH BACK MY DELIVERABLE DEADLINE BY A YEAR.
THAT'S NOT BEING PROACTIVE. THAT'S THE OPPOSITE OF PROACTIVE!
YOU SAID YOU WANT EMPLOYEES TO BE EMPOWERED AND NOW YOU'RE CRITICIZING MY DECISION.
THAT'S JUST GREAT.
NOW MY MORALE IS BAD, TOO!
I CAN'T BE PROACTIVE.
I CAN'T BE EMPOWERED.
AND NOW I CAN'T EVEN BE HAPPY!
YOU'VE BUNGLED EVERYTHING! YOU'RE A BIG BUNGLER!
GET OUT OF MY OFFICE.
WELL, SAY GOODBYE TO THE OPEN-DOOR POLICY!
©2013 Scott Adams, Inc./Dist. by Universal Uclick
1-27-13

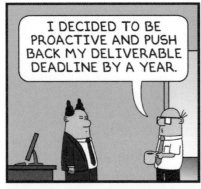

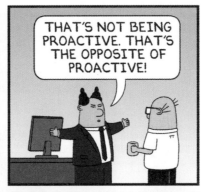

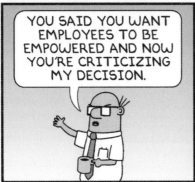

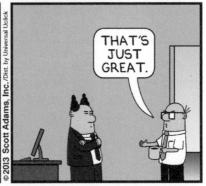

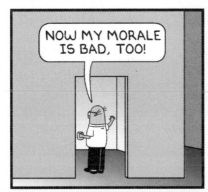

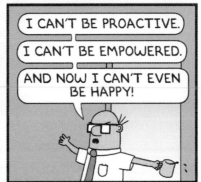

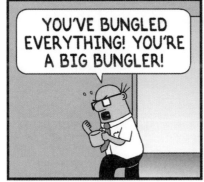

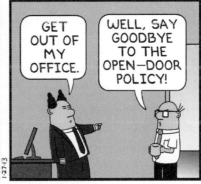

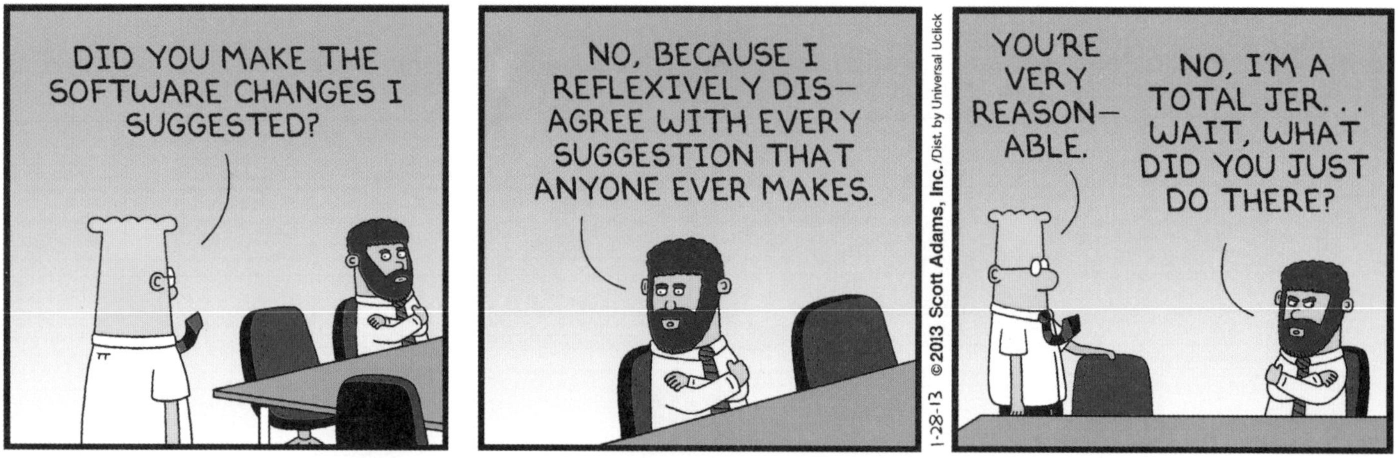
DID YOU MAKE THE SOFTWARE CHANGES I SUGGESTED?
NO, BECAUSE I REFLEXIVELY DIS-AGREE WITH EVERY SUGGESTION THAT ANYONE EVER MAKES.
1-28-13 ©2013 Scott Adams, Inc./Dist. by Universal Uclick
YOU'RE VERY REASON-ABLE.
NO, I'M A TOTAL JER. . . WAIT, WHAT DID YOU JUST DO THERE?

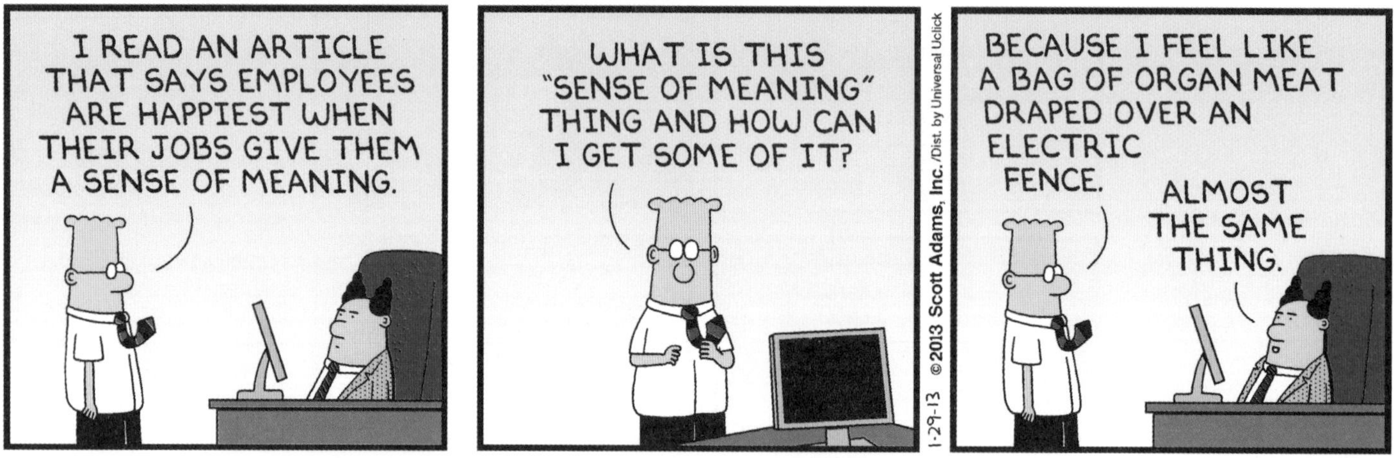
I READ AN ARTICLE THAT SAYS EMPLOYEES ARE HAPPIEST WHEN THEIR JOBS GIVE THEM A SENSE OF MEANING.
WHAT IS THIS "SENSE OF MEANING" THING AND HOW CAN I GET SOME OF IT?
1-29-13 ©2013 Scott Adams, Inc./Dist. by Universal Uclick
BECAUSE I FEEL LIKE A BAG OF ORGAN MEAT DRAPED OVER AN ELECTRIC FENCE.
ALMOST THE SAME THING.

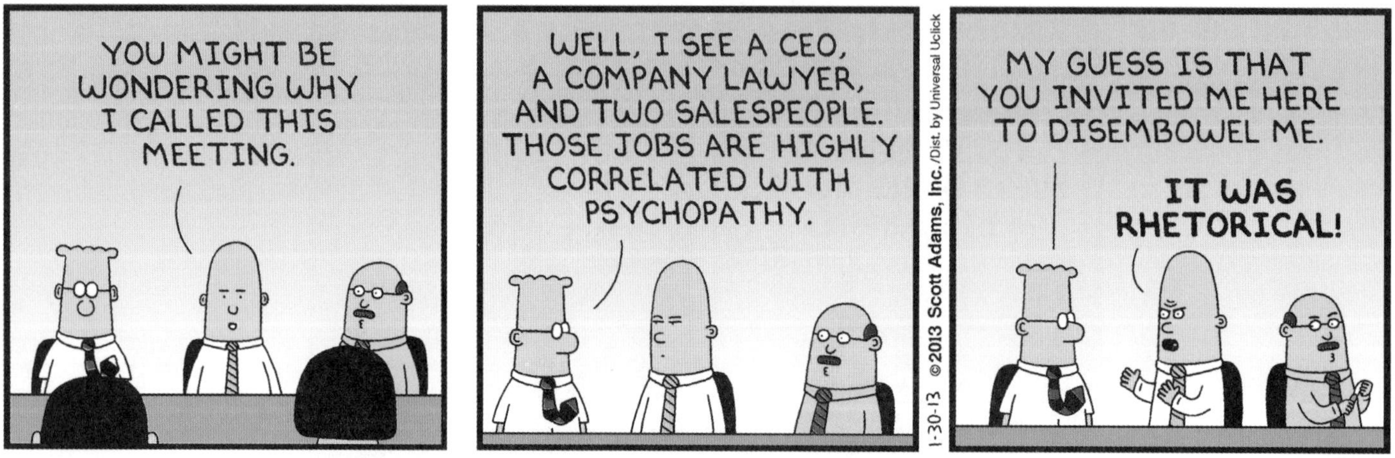
YOU MIGHT BE WONDERING WHY I CALLED THIS MEETING.
WELL, I SEE A CEO, A COMPANY LAWYER, AND TWO SALESPEOPLE. THOSE JOBS ARE HIGHLY CORRELATED WITH PSYCHOPATHY.
1-30-13 ©2013 Scott Adams, Inc./Dist. by Universal Uclick
MY GUESS IS THAT YOU INVITED ME HERE TO DISEMBOWEL ME.
IT WAS RHETORICAL!

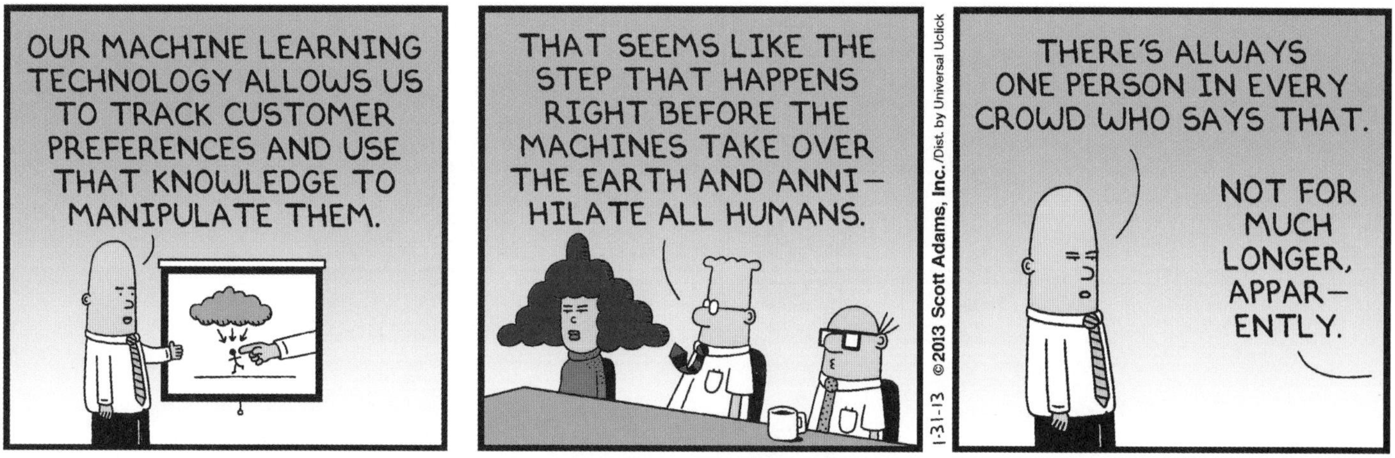
OUR MACHINE LEARNING TECHNOLOGY ALLOWS US TO TRACK CUSTOMER PREFERENCES AND USE THAT KNOWLEDGE TO MANIPULATE THEM.
THAT SEEMS LIKE THE STEP THAT HAPPENS RIGHT BEFORE THE MACHINES TAKE OVER THE EARTH AND ANNIHILATE ALL HUMANS.
1-31-13 ©2013 Scott Adams, Inc./Dist. by Universal Uclick
THERE'S ALWAYS ONE PERSON IN EVERY CROWD WHO SAYS THAT.
NOT FOR MUCH LONGER, APPARENTLY.

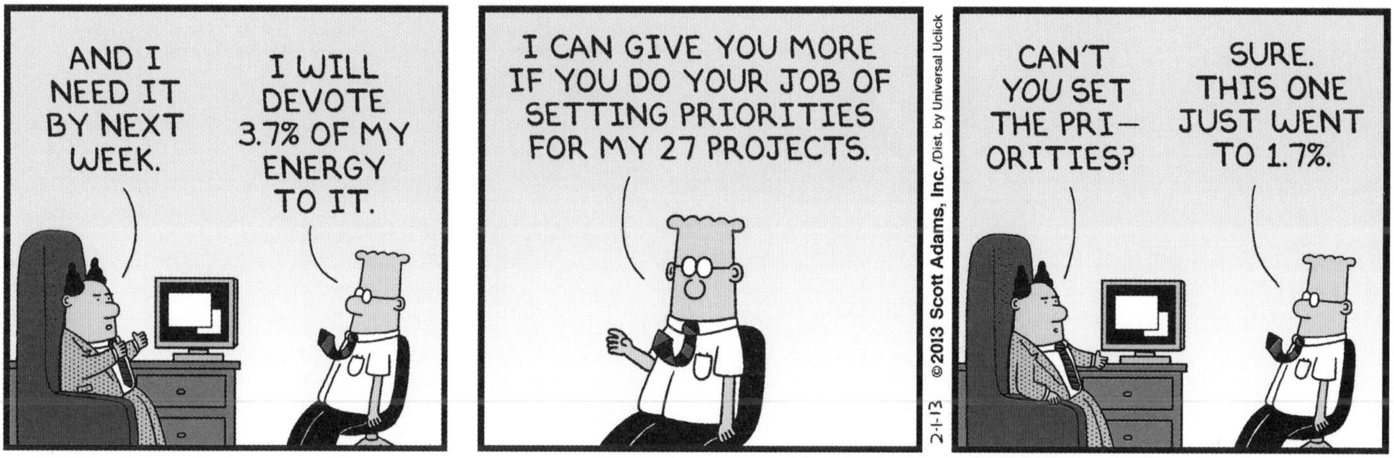
AND I NEED IT BY NEXT WEEK.
I WILL DEVOTE 3.7% OF MY ENERGY TO IT.
I CAN GIVE YOU MORE IF YOU DO YOUR JOB OF SETTING PRIORITIES FOR MY 27 PROJECTS.
2-1-13 ©2013 Scott Adams, Inc./Dist. by Universal Uclick
CAN'T *YOU* SET THE PRIORITIES?
SURE. THIS ONE JUST WENT TO 1.7%.

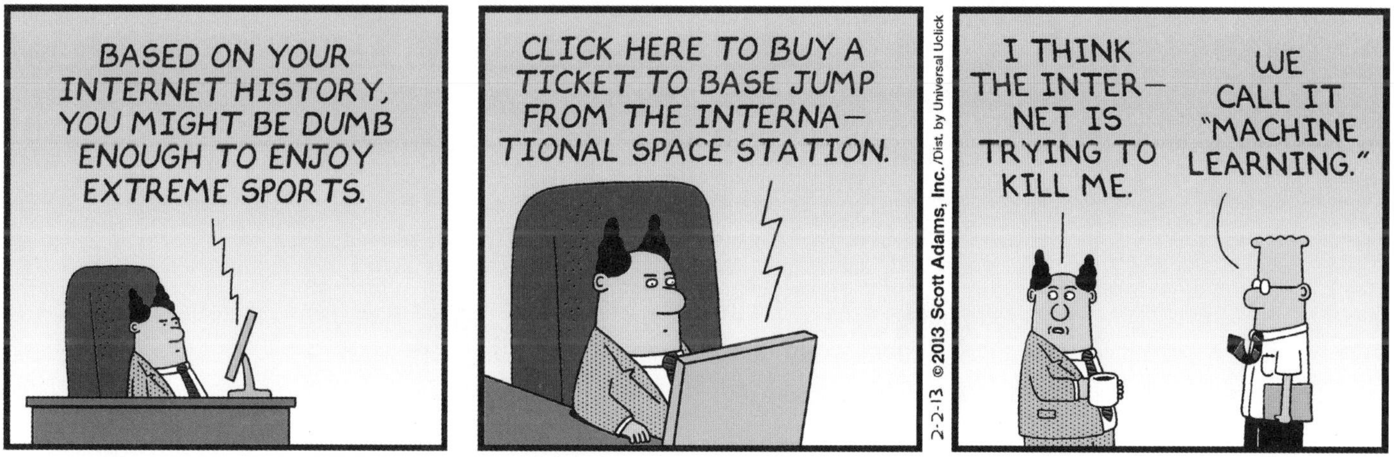
BASED ON YOUR INTERNET HISTORY, YOU MIGHT BE DUMB ENOUGH TO ENJOY EXTREME SPORTS.
CLICK HERE TO BUY A TICKET TO BASE JUMP FROM THE INTERNATIONAL SPACE STATION.
2-2-13 ©2013 Scott Adams, Inc./Dist. by Universal Uclick
I THINK THE INTERNET IS TRYING TO KILL ME.
WE CALL IT "MACHINE LEARNING."

YOU REMIND ME OF ANOTHER YOUNG PERSON I HIRED YEARS AGO.
SHE WAS FULL OF HOPE AND OPTIMISM AND SHE WORE A PERMANENT SMILE.
HER NAME WAS ALICE.
©2013 Scott Adams, Inc./Dist. by Universal Uclick
AS TIME PASSED, SHE DEVOLVED INTO AN ANGRY, HATEFUL CREATURE.
NO ONE KNOWS WHAT CAUSED IT.
HOW LONG DID IT TAKE?
ABOUT A WEEK.
APPARENTLY, YOU'RE A MONSTER WHO CREATES A TOXIC WORKPLACE AND YOU LACK THE SELF-AWARENESS TO REALIZE IT!
2-3-13
SOMEONE BROKE YOUR RECORD.
SHUT UP.

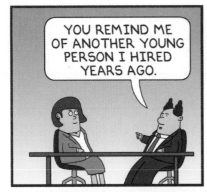

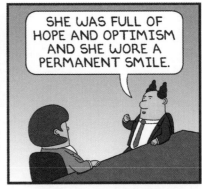

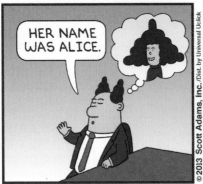

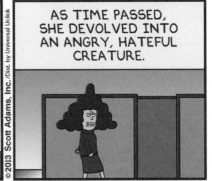

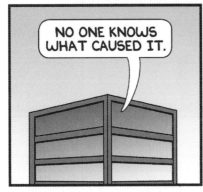

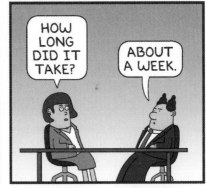

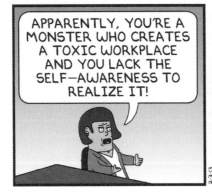

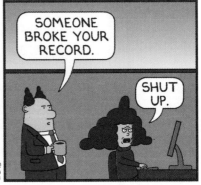

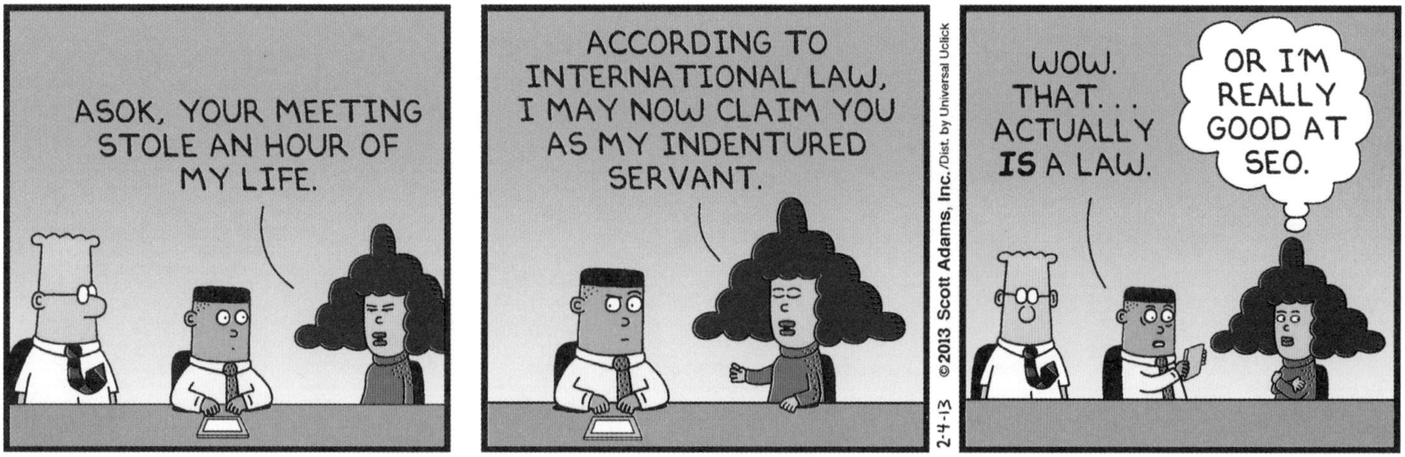
ASOK, YOUR MEETING STOLE AN HOUR OF MY LIFE.
ACCORDING TO INTERNATIONAL LAW, I MAY NOW CLAIM YOU AS MY INDENTURED SERVANT.
2-4-13 ©2013 Scott Adams, Inc./Dist. by Universal Uclick
WOW. THAT... ACTUALLY **IS** A LAW.
OR I'M REALLY GOOD AT SEO.

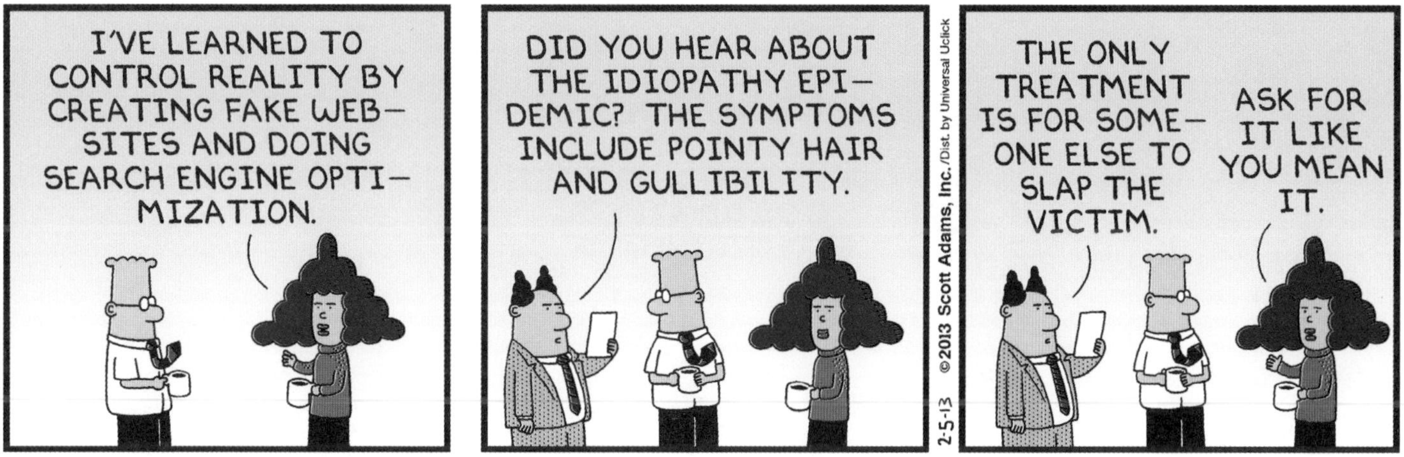
I'VE LEARNED TO CONTROL REALITY BY CREATING FAKE WEB-SITES AND DOING SEARCH ENGINE OPTI-MIZATION.
DID YOU HEAR ABOUT THE IDIOPATHY EPI-DEMIC? THE SYMPTOMS INCLUDE POINTY HAIR AND GULLIBILITY.
2-5-13 ©2013 Scott Adams, Inc./Dist. by Universal Uclick
THE ONLY TREATMENT IS FOR SOME-ONE ELSE TO SLAP THE VICTIM.
ASK FOR IT LIKE YOU MEAN IT.

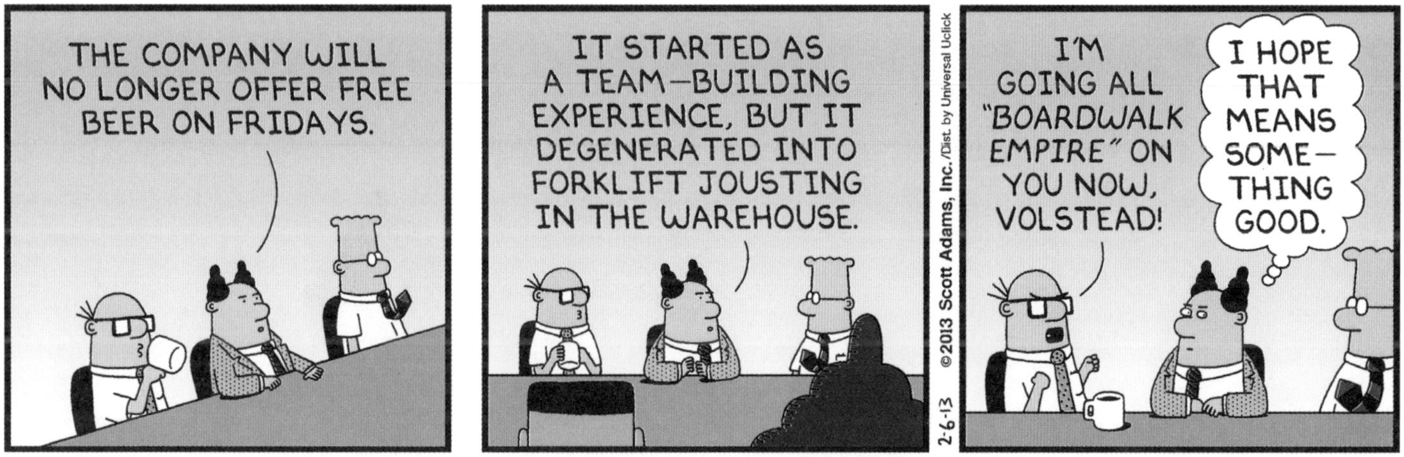
THE COMPANY WILL NO LONGER OFFER FREE BEER ON FRIDAYS.
IT STARTED AS A TEAM-BUILDING EXPERIENCE, BUT IT DEGENERATED INTO FORKLIFT JOUSTING IN THE WAREHOUSE.
2-6-13 ©2013 Scott Adams, Inc./Dist. by Universal Uclick
I'M GOING ALL "BOARDWALK EMPIRE" ON YOU NOW, VOLSTEAD!
I HOPE THAT MEANS SOME-THING GOOD.

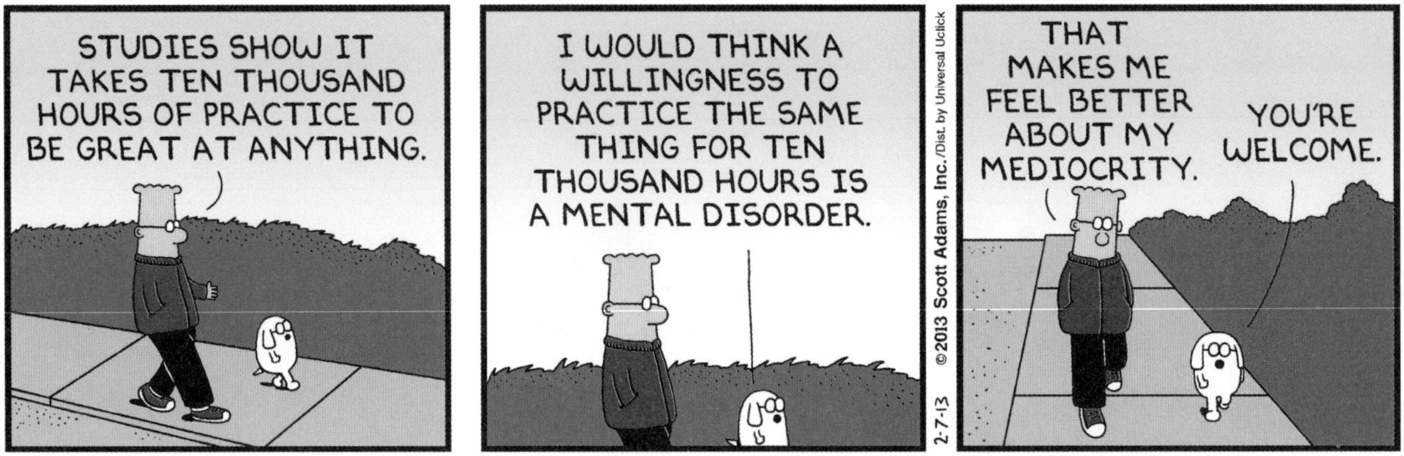
STUDIES SHOW IT TAKES TEN THOUSAND HOURS OF PRACTICE TO BE GREAT AT ANYTHING.
I WOULD THINK A WILLINGNESS TO PRACTICE THE SAME THING FOR TEN THOUSAND HOURS IS A MENTAL DISORDER.
THAT MAKES ME FEEL BETTER ABOUT MY MEDIOCRITY.
YOU'RE WELCOME.
2-7-13 ©2013 Scott Adams, Inc./Dist. by Universal Uclick

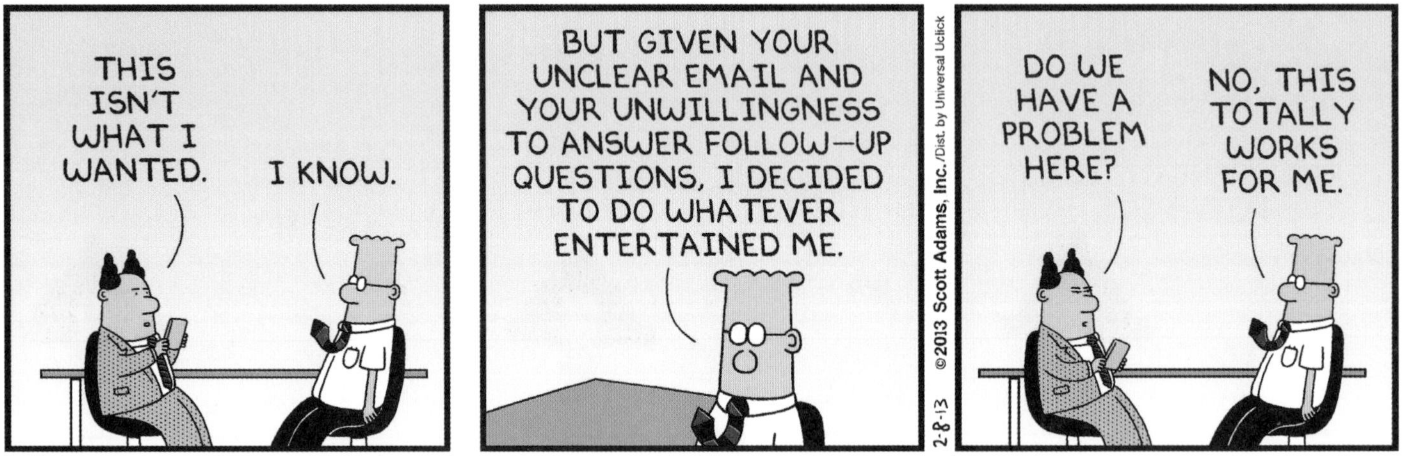
THIS ISN'T WHAT I WANTED.
I KNOW.
BUT GIVEN YOUR UNCLEAR EMAIL AND YOUR UNWILLINGNESS TO ANSWER FOLLOW-UP QUESTIONS, I DECIDED TO DO WHATEVER ENTERTAINED ME.
DO WE HAVE A PROBLEM HERE?
NO, THIS TOTALLY WORKS FOR ME.
2-8-13 ©2013 Scott Adams, Inc./Dist. by Universal Uclick

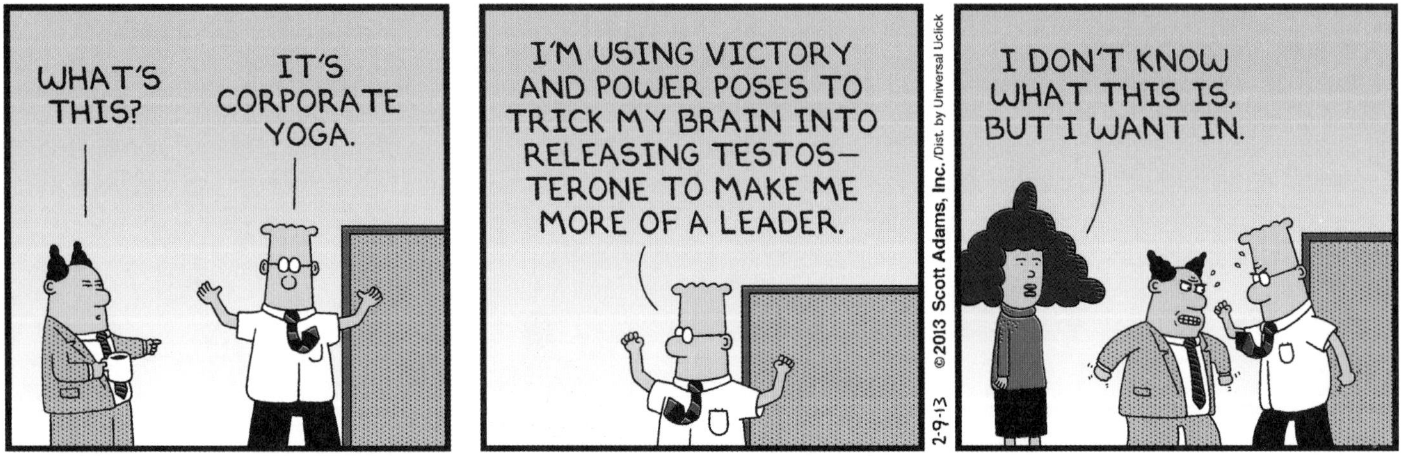
WHAT'S THIS?
IT'S CORPORATE YOGA.
I'M USING VICTORY AND POWER POSES TO TRICK MY BRAIN INTO RELEASING TESTOS-TERONE TO MAKE ME MORE OF A LEADER.
I DON'T KNOW WHAT THIS IS, BUT I WANT IN.
2-9-13 ©2013 Scott Adams, Inc./Dist. by Universal Uclick

I'M WORKING AT HOME TODAY. IT WILL BE AS IF WE'RE CO-WORKERS.
UGH.
THIS MADNESS MUST STOP!
YOU SHOULD CHECK YOUR FACEBOOK PAGE TO SEE WHAT'S NEW.
©2013 Scott Adams, Inc./Dist. by Universal Uclick
TWO HOURS LATER
YOU SHOULD CHECK TWITTER.
I'M ALMOST FINISHED WITH FACEBOOK.
TWO HOURS LATER
DID YOU GET MY LINKEDIN REQUEST?
I'LL CHECK.
TWO HOURS LATER
I SENT YOU SOME LINKS TO FUNNY WEBSITES.
COOL!
I JUST SPENT TEN HOURS AT MY COMPUTER AND I CAN'T REMEMBER WHY I WAS SITTING THERE IN THE FIRST PLACE.
2-10-13
YOU WERE GOING TO CHECK YOUR STOCKS.
OKAY. THAT SOUNDS RIGHT.

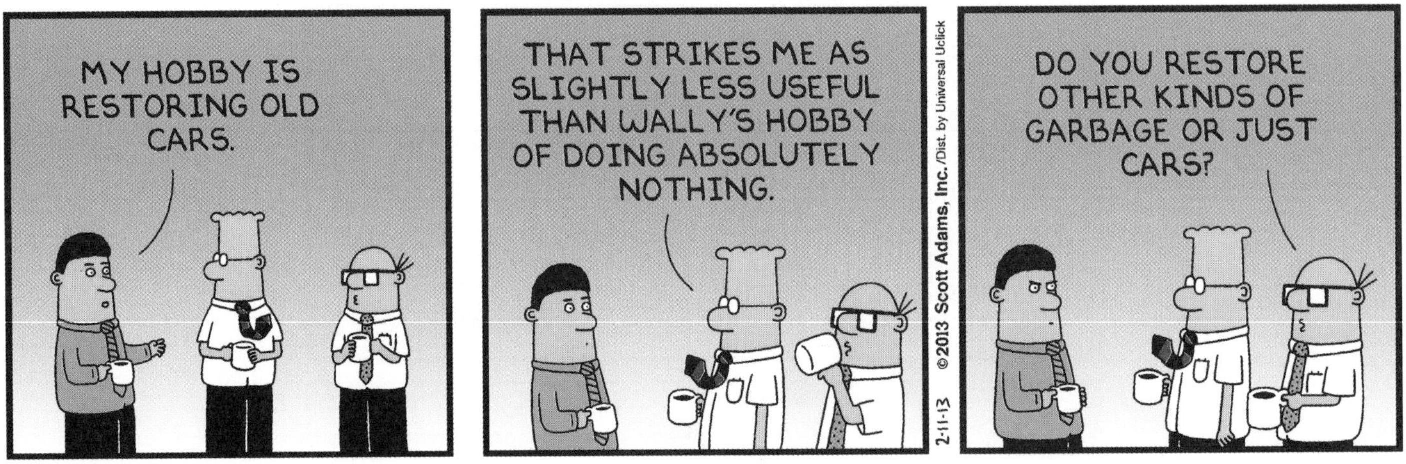
MY HOBBY IS RESTORING OLD CARS.
THAT STRIKES ME AS SLIGHTLY LESS USEFUL THAN WALLY'S HOBBY OF DOING ABSOLUTELY NOTHING.
2-11-13 ©2013 Scott Adams, Inc./Dist. by Universal Uclick
DO YOU RESTORE OTHER KINDS OF GARBAGE OR JUST CARS?

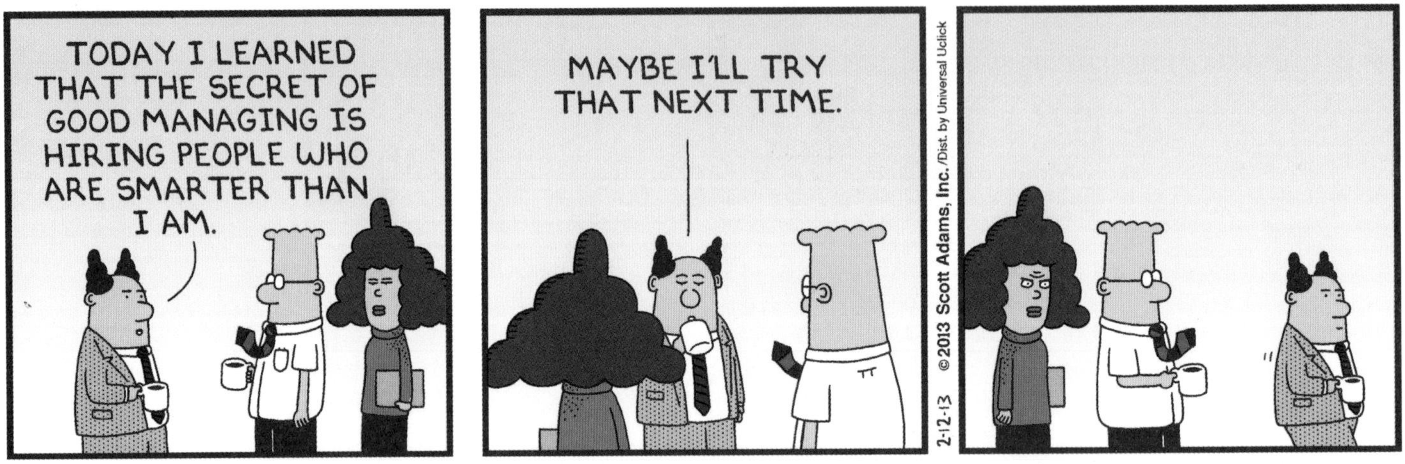
TODAY I LEARNED THAT THE SECRET OF GOOD MANAGING IS HIRING PEOPLE WHO ARE SMARTER THAN I AM.
MAYBE I'LL TRY THAT NEXT TIME.
2-12-13 ©2013 Scott Adams, Inc./Dist. by Universal Uclick

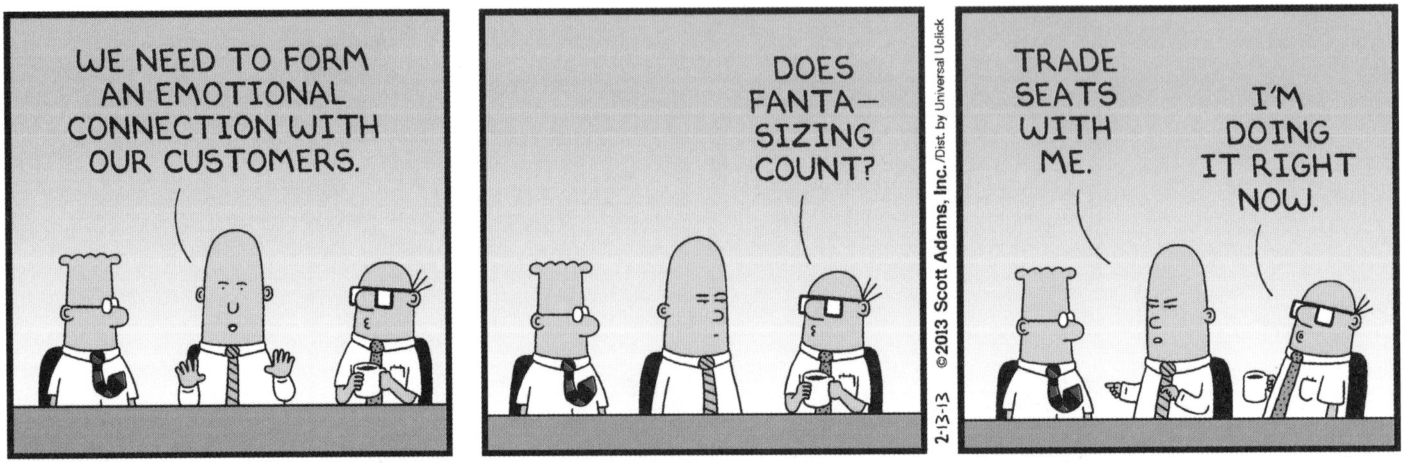
WE NEED TO FORM AN EMOTIONAL CONNECTION WITH OUR CUSTOMERS.
DOES FANTA- SIZING COUNT?
2-13-13 ©2013 Scott Adams, Inc./Dist. by Universal Uclick
TRADE SEATS WITH ME.
I'M DOING IT RIGHT NOW.

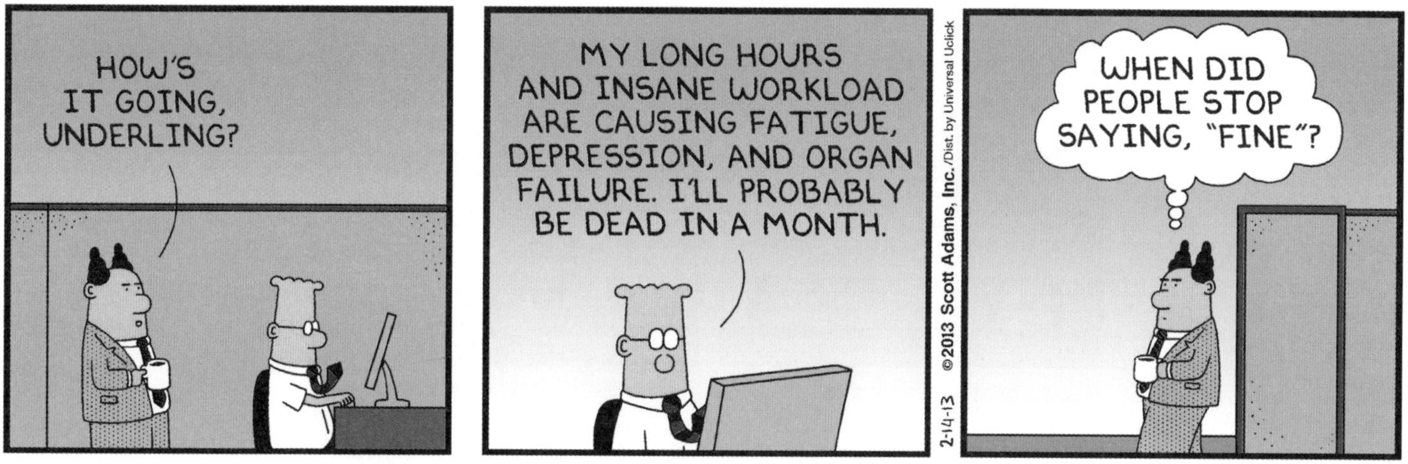
HOW'S IT GOING, UNDERLING?
MY LONG HOURS AND INSANE WORKLOAD ARE CAUSING FATIGUE, DEPRESSION, AND ORGAN FAILURE. I'LL PROBABLY BE DEAD IN A MONTH.
2-14-13 ©2013 Scott Adams, Inc./Dist. by Universal Uclick
WHEN DID PEOPLE STOP SAYING, "FINE"?

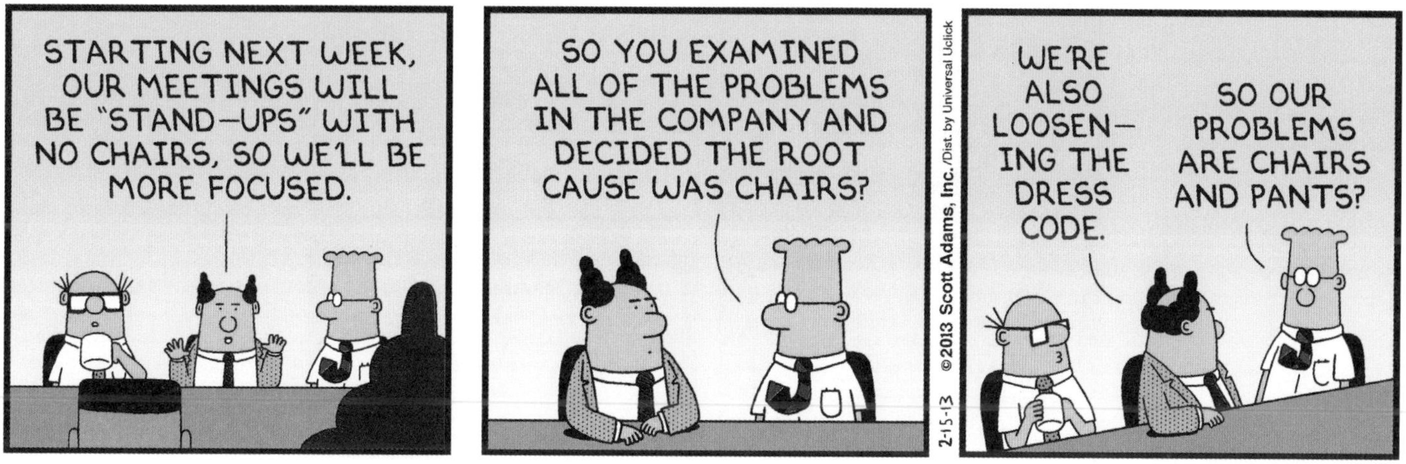
STARTING NEXT WEEK, OUR MEETINGS WILL BE "STAND-UPS" WITH NO CHAIRS, SO WE'LL BE MORE FOCUSED.
SO YOU EXAMINED ALL OF THE PROBLEMS IN THE COMPANY AND DECIDED THE ROOT CAUSE WAS CHAIRS?
2-15-13 ©2013 Scott Adams, Inc./Dist. by Universal Uclick
WE'RE ALSO LOOSEN-ING THE DRESS CODE.
SO OUR PROBLEMS ARE CHAIRS AND PANTS?

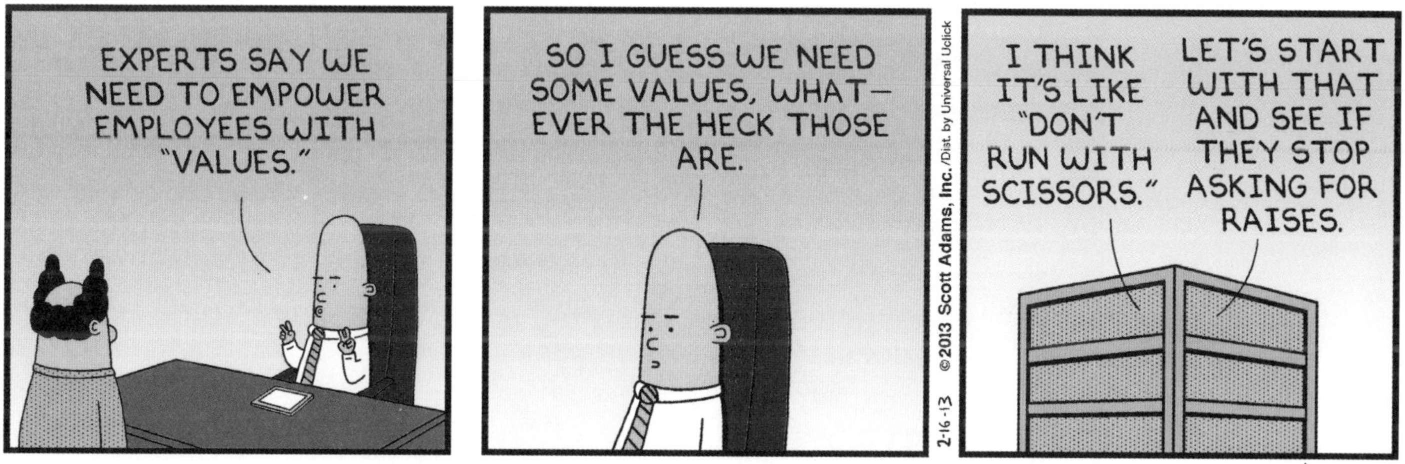
EXPERTS SAY WE NEED TO EMPOWER EMPLOYEES WITH "VALUES."
SO I GUESS WE NEED SOME VALUES, WHAT-EVER THE HECK THOSE ARE.
2-16-13 ©2013 Scott Adams, Inc./Dist. by Universal Uclick
I THINK IT'S LIKE "DON'T RUN WITH SCISSORS."
LET'S START WITH THAT AND SEE IF THEY STOP ASKING FOR RAISES.

I CAN'T WAIT TO SEE THE CHANGES I ASKED YOU TO MAKE ON THE INTERFACE.
OUR LAST MEETING WAS TWO MONTHS AGO. YOU MUST BE FINISHED BY NOW.
I HAVEN'T STARTED YET.
I HAD A FEW QUESTIONS.
I FIGURED I'D ASK YOU ABOUT THEM THE NEXT TIME WE TALKED.
IN THE MEANTIME I ONLY DID WORK FOR PEOPLE WHO YELLED AT ME EVERY DAY.
MICROMANAGEMENT HAS A BAD REPUTATION, BUT I'M NOT TOO PROUD TO SAY I NEED IT.
OKAY... WELL, I'M OPTIMISTIC THAT YOU CAN MAKE THOSE CHANGES FOR ME BY NEXT WEEK.
I PROBABLY SHOULD HAVE ASKED MY QUESTIONS.
©2013 Scott Adams, Inc./Dist. by Universal Uclick
2-17-13

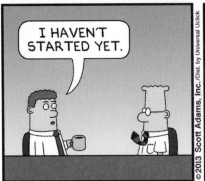

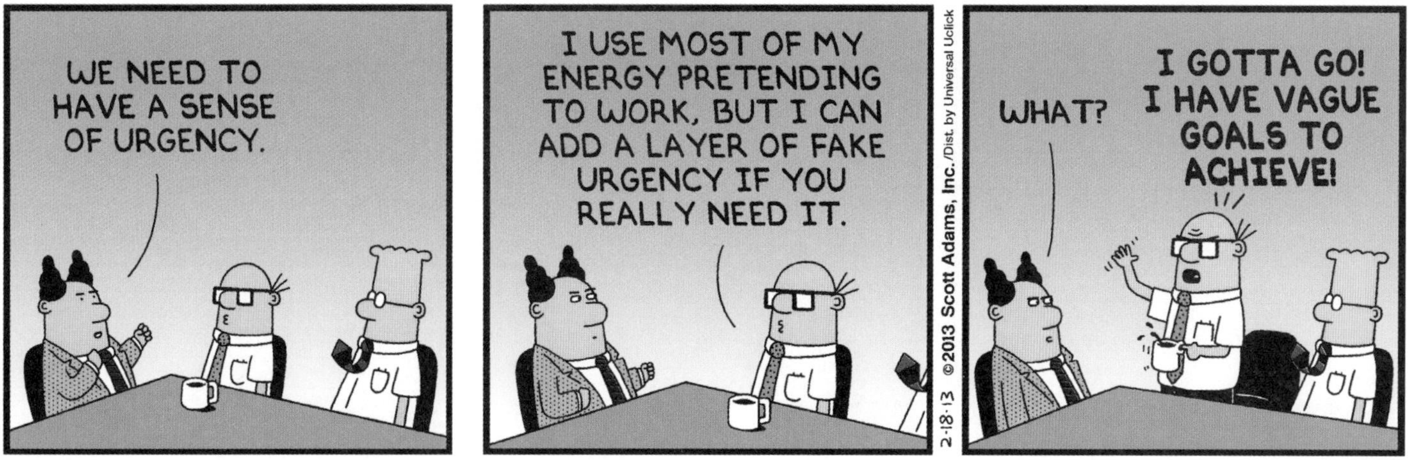
WE NEED TO HAVE A SENSE OF URGENCY.
I USE MOST OF MY ENERGY PRETENDING TO WORK, BUT I CAN ADD A LAYER OF FAKE URGENCY IF YOU REALLY NEED IT.
2-18-13 ©2013 Scott Adams, Inc./Dist. by Universal Uclick
WHAT?
I GOTTA GO! I HAVE VAGUE GOALS TO ACHIEVE!

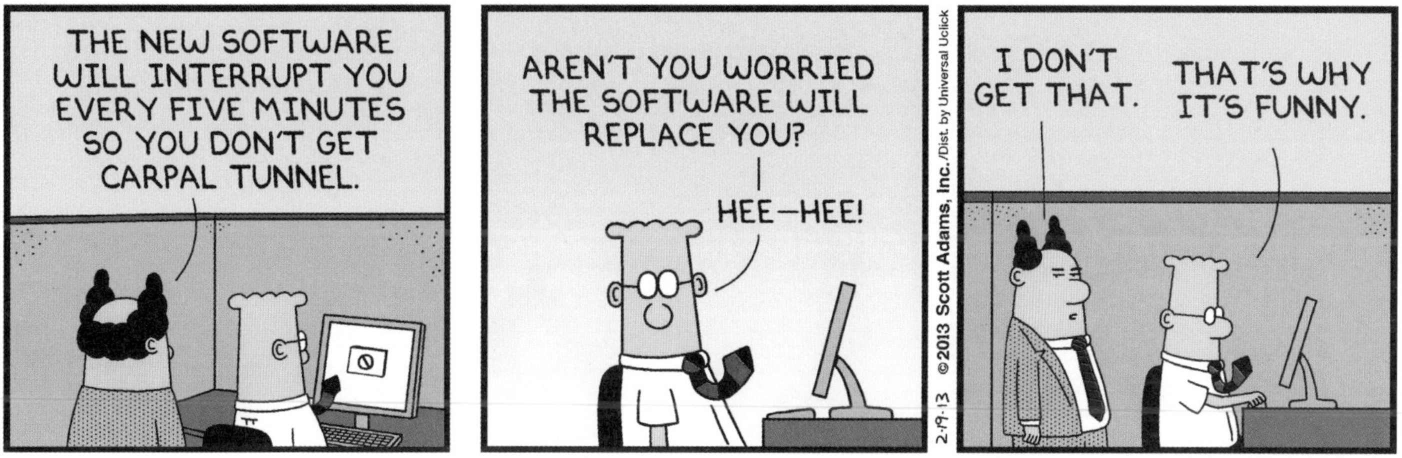
THE NEW SOFTWARE WILL INTERRUPT YOU EVERY FIVE MINUTES SO YOU DON'T GET CARPAL TUNNEL.
AREN'T YOU WORRIED THE SOFTWARE WILL REPLACE YOU?
HEE—HEE!
2-19-13 ©2013 Scott Adams, Inc./Dist. by Universal Uclick
I DON'T GET THAT.
THAT'S WHY IT'S FUNNY.

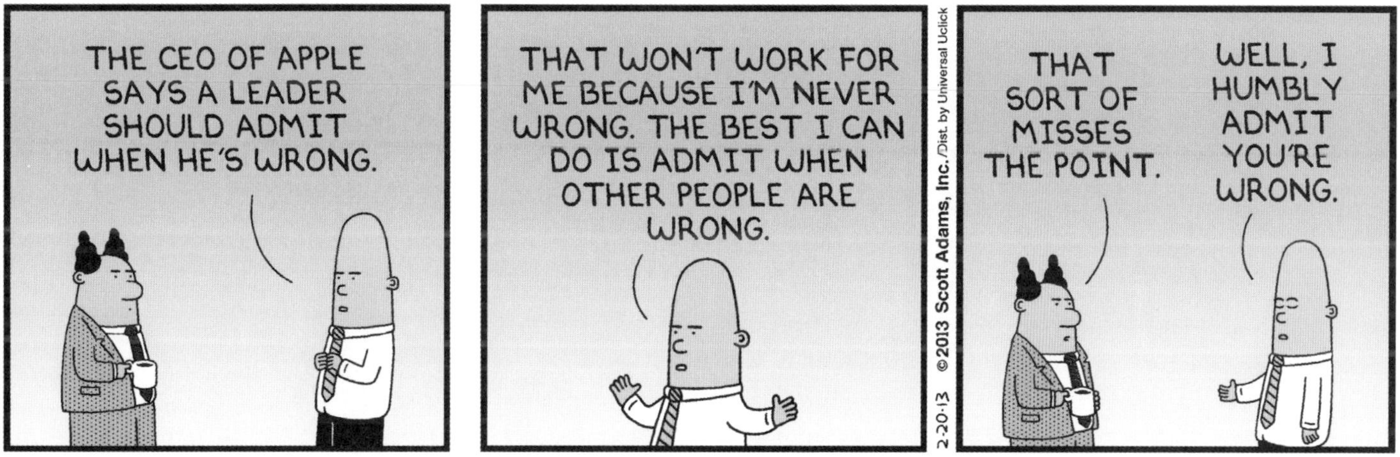
THE CEO OF APPLE SAYS A LEADER SHOULD ADMIT WHEN HE'S WRONG.
THAT WON'T WORK FOR ME BECAUSE I'M NEVER WRONG. THE BEST I CAN DO IS ADMIT WHEN OTHER PEOPLE ARE WRONG.
2-20-13 ©2013 Scott Adams, Inc./Dist. by Universal Uclick
THAT SORT OF MISSES THE POINT.
WELL, I HUMBLY ADMIT YOU'RE WRONG.

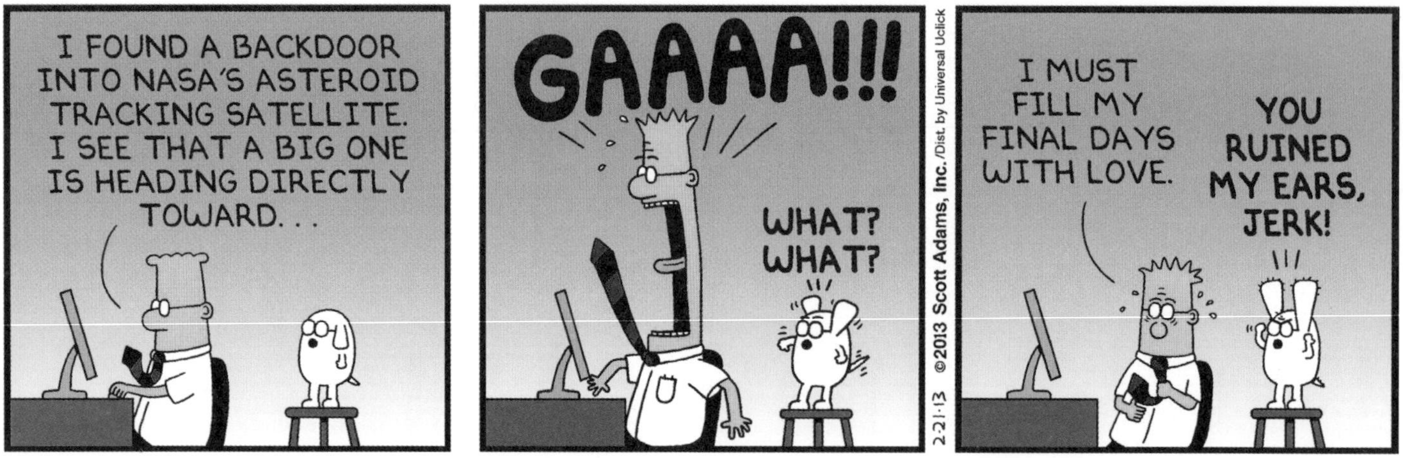
I FOUND A BACKDOOR INTO NASA'S ASTEROID TRACKING SATELLITE. I SEE THAT A BIG ONE IS HEADING DIRECTLY TOWARD. . .
GAAAA!!!
WHAT? WHAT?
I MUST FILL MY FINAL DAYS WITH LOVE.
YOU RUINED MY EARS, JERK!
2·21·13

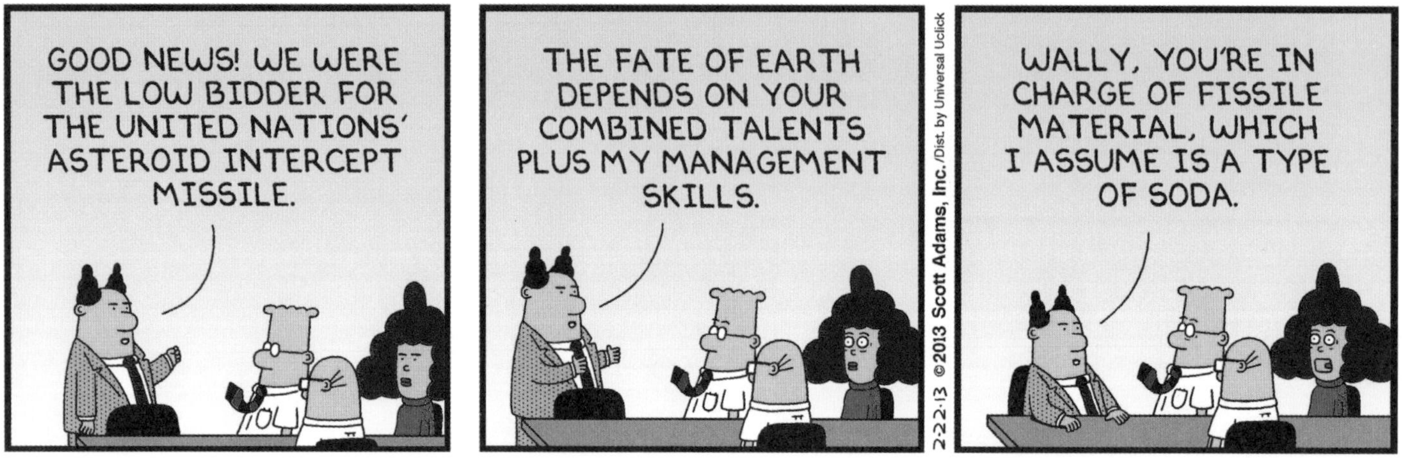
GOOD NEWS! WE WERE THE LOW BIDDER FOR THE UNITED NATIONS' ASTEROID INTERCEPT MISSILE.
THE FATE OF EARTH DEPENDS ON YOUR COMBINED TALENTS PLUS MY MANAGEMENT SKILLS.
WALLY, YOU'RE IN CHARGE OF FISSILE MATERIAL, WHICH I ASSUME IS A TYPE OF SODA.
2·22·13

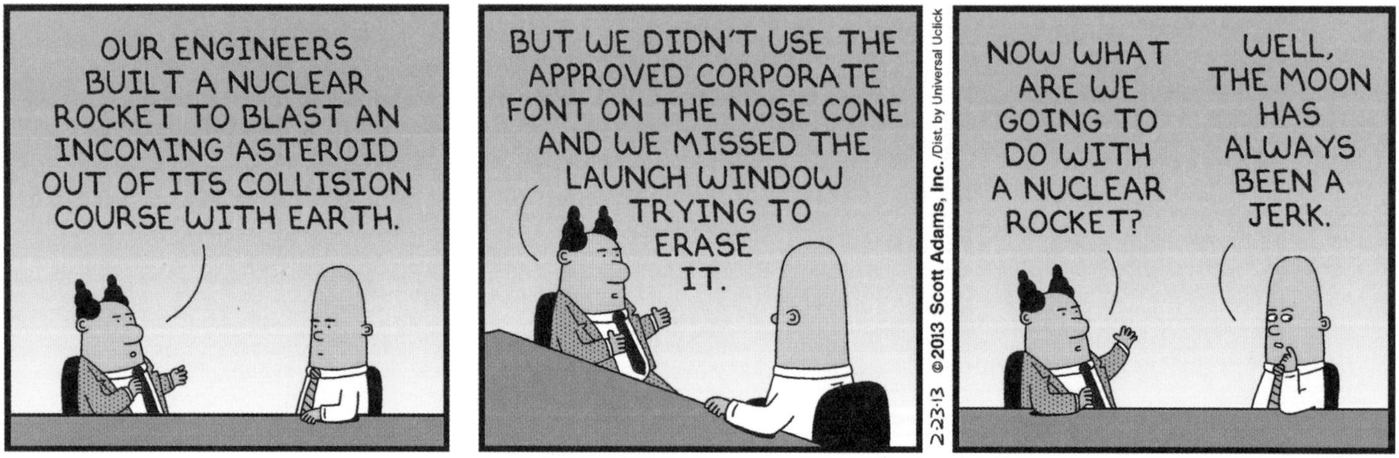
OUR ENGINEERS BUILT A NUCLEAR ROCKET TO BLAST AN INCOMING ASTEROID OUT OF ITS COLLISION COURSE WITH EARTH.
BUT WE DIDN'T USE THE APPROVED CORPORATE FONT ON THE NOSE CONE AND WE MISSED THE LAUNCH WINDOW TRYING TO ERASE IT.
NOW WHAT ARE WE GOING TO DO WITH A NUCLEAR ROCKET?
WELL, THE MOON HAS ALWAYS BEEN A JERK.
2·23·13

ARE YOU COMING TO THE CODE MOCKING?
THE WHAT?
CODE MOCKING IS AN ENGINEERING TRADI- TION. IT HAPPENS WHENEVER A SOFTWARE PROJECT IS HANDED TO A NEW ENGINEER.
THE NEW ENGINEER IS REQUIRED TO MOCK THE PREVIOUS ENGINEER'S WORK IN A PUBLIC WAY.
©2013 Scott Adams, Inc./Dist. by Universal Uclick
WE SPECTATORS GET TO VOTE ON WHETHER THE OLD CODE IS KILLED OR SPARED.
HA HA! HIS CODE IS HILARIOUSLY INEFFICIENT!
OUCH. CHEST PAIN.
KILL IT! KILL IT! KILL IT!
GAAA!!! THE CODE IS OFFENDING MY ENGIN- EERING SENSIBILITIES! IT'S KILLING ME!
2-24-13
I FORGOT TO MENTION THAT SOME- TIMES THE CODE WINS.

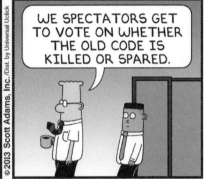

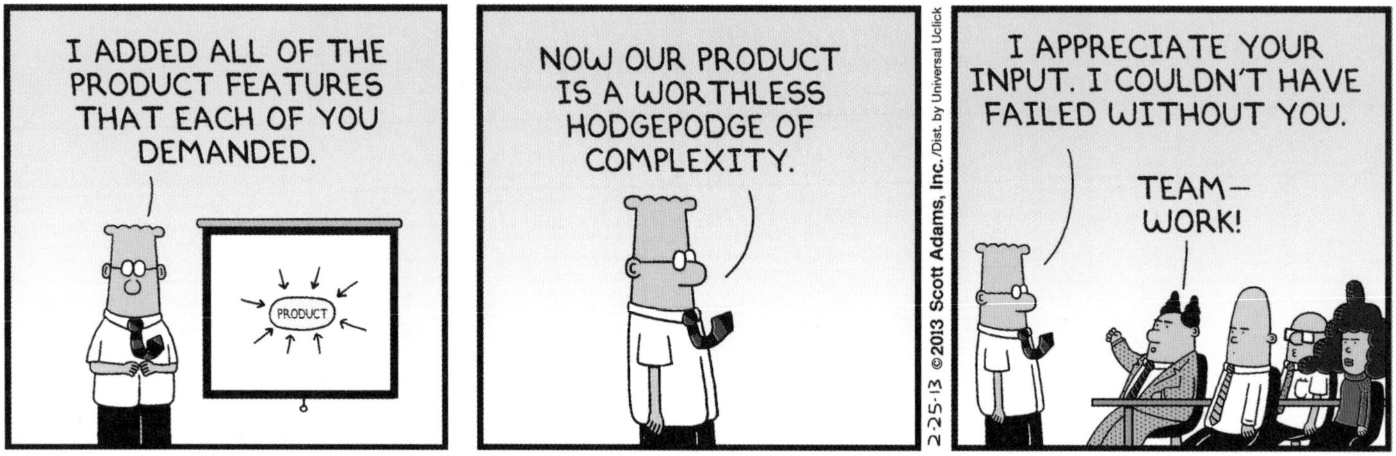
I ADDED ALL OF THE PRODUCT FEATURES THAT EACH OF YOU DEMANDED.
PRODUCT
NOW OUR PRODUCT IS A WORTHLESS HODGEPODGE OF COMPLEXITY.
2·25·13 ©2013 Scott Adams, Inc./Dist. by Universal Uclick
I APPRECIATE YOUR INPUT. I COULDN'T HAVE FAILED WITHOUT YOU.
TEAM-WORK!

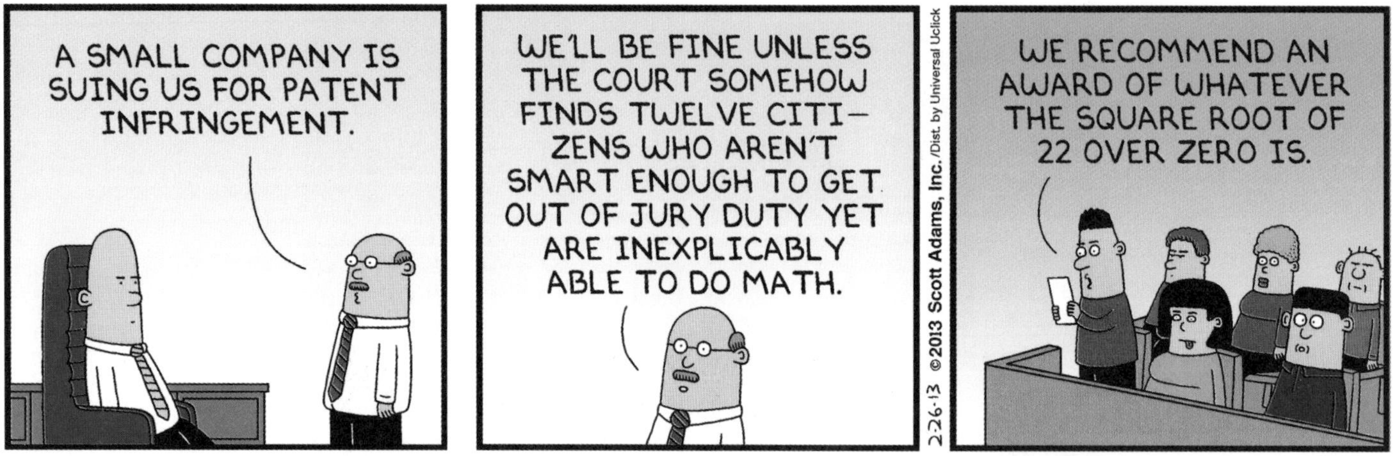
A SMALL COMPANY IS SUING US FOR PATENT INFRINGEMENT.
WE'LL BE FINE UNLESS THE COURT SOMEHOW FINDS TWELVE CITI-ZENS WHO AREN'T SMART ENOUGH TO GET OUT OF JURY DUTY YET ARE INEXPLICABLY ABLE TO DO MATH.
2·26·13 ©2013 Scott Adams, Inc./Dist. by Universal Uclick
WE RECOMMEND AN AWARD OF WHATEVER THE SQUARE ROOT OF 22 OVER ZERO IS.

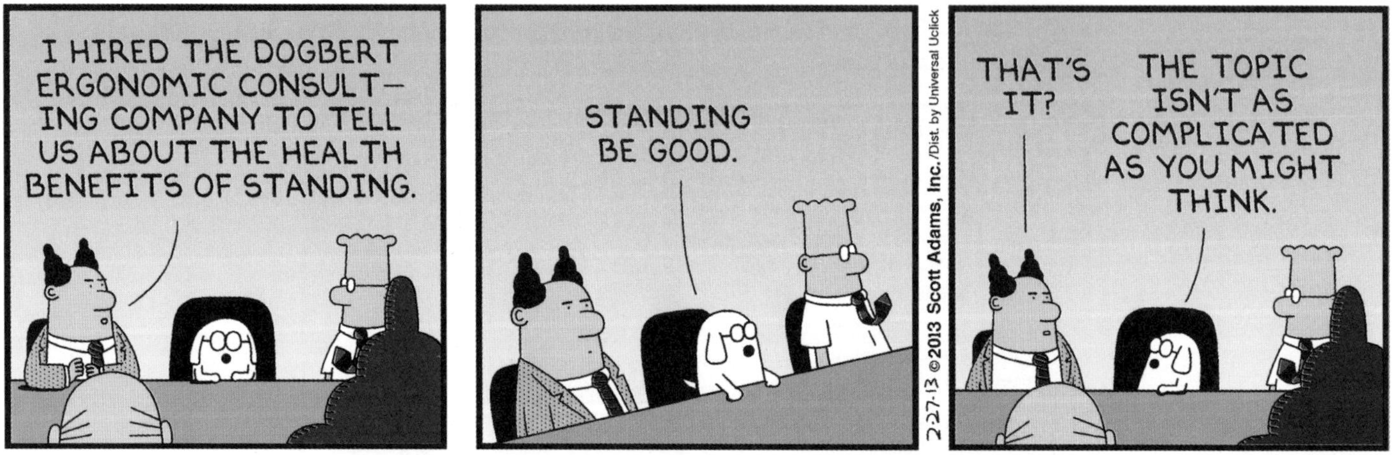
I HIRED THE DOGBERT ERGONOMIC CONSULT-ING COMPANY TO TELL US ABOUT THE HEALTH BENEFITS OF STANDING.
STANDING BE GOOD.
2·27·13 ©2013 Scott Adams, Inc./Dist. by Universal Uclick
THAT'S IT?
THE TOPIC ISN'T AS COMPLICATED AS YOU MIGHT THINK.

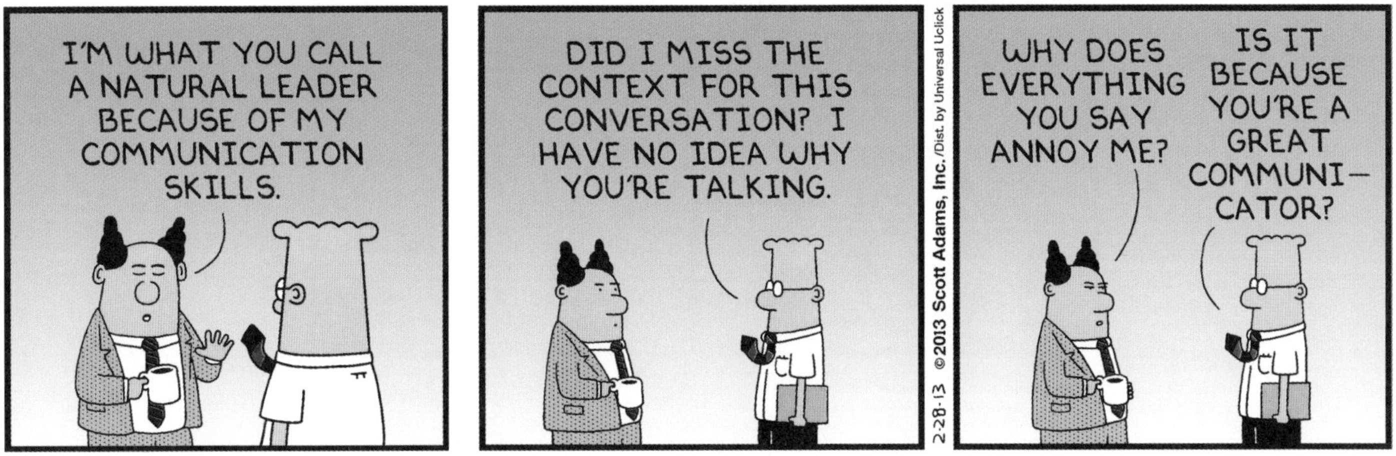
I'M WHAT YOU CALL A NATURAL LEADER BECAUSE OF MY COMMUNICATION SKILLS.
DID I MISS THE CONTEXT FOR THIS CONVERSATION? I HAVE NO IDEA WHY YOU'RE TALKING.
2-28-13 ©2013 Scott Adams, Inc./Dist. by Universal Uclick
WHY DOES EVERYTHING YOU SAY ANNOY ME?
IS IT BECAUSE YOU'RE A GREAT COMMUNI-CATOR?

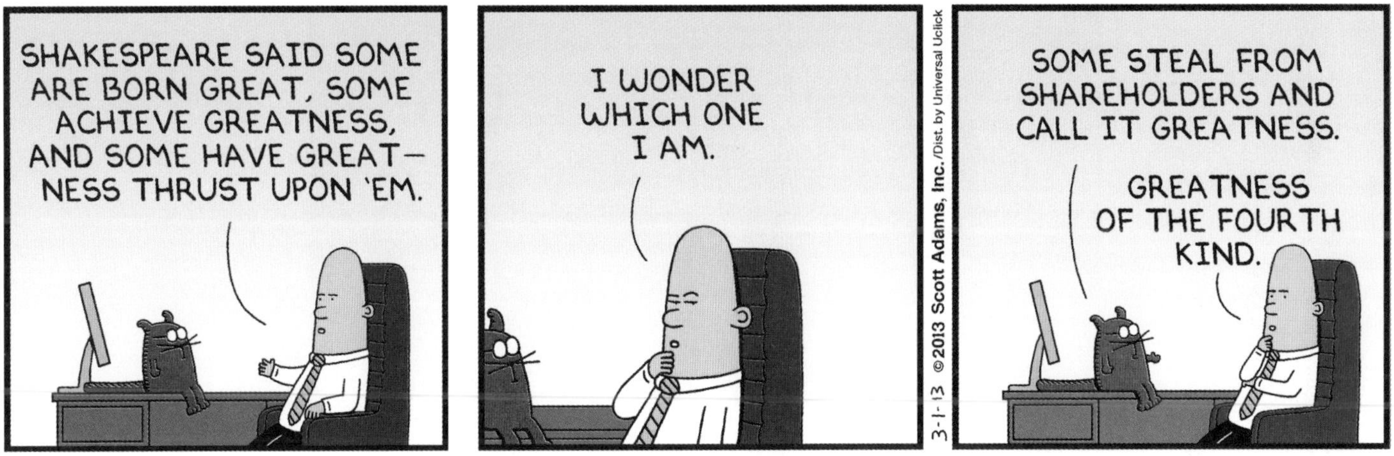
SHAKESPEARE SAID SOME ARE BORN GREAT, SOME ACHIEVE GREATNESS, AND SOME HAVE GREAT-NESS THRUST UPON 'EM.
I WONDER WHICH ONE I AM.
3-1-13 ©2013 Scott Adams, Inc./Dist. by Universal Uclick
SOME STEAL FROM SHAREHOLDERS AND CALL IT GREATNESS.
GREATNESS OF THE FOURTH KIND.

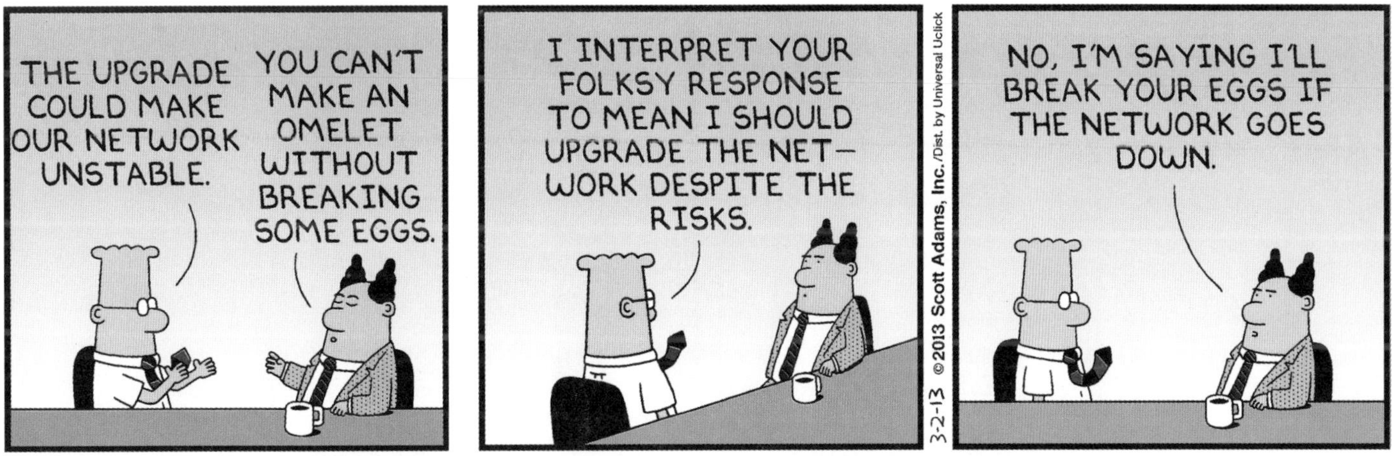
THE UPGRADE COULD MAKE OUR NETWORK UNSTABLE.
YOU CAN'T MAKE AN OMELET WITHOUT BREAKING SOME EGGS.
I INTERPRET YOUR FOLKSY RESPONSE TO MEAN I SHOULD UPGRADE THE NET-WORK DESPITE THE RISKS.
3-2-13 ©2013 Scott Adams, Inc./Dist. by Universal Uclick
NO, I'M SAYING I'LL BREAK YOUR EGGS IF THE NETWORK GOES DOWN.

DO YOU MIND IF I RUMMAGE THROUGH THE TRASH IN THE TECHNOLOGY LAB?
UM, OKAY.
I'M GETTING BACK TO MY HUNTER-GATHERER ROOTS.
SCORE! THESE OLD POWER CORDS SELL ON EBAY FOR UP TO $3 APIECE!
© 2013 Scott Adams, Inc./Dist. by Universal Uclick
HA HA! I'M A GENIUS WHO TURNS TRASH INTO GOLD!
HOW'S THAT COMPARE TO WHATEVER YOU'RE DOING HERE?
WELL, I'M REMOVING VALUABLE FEATURES FROM OUR PRODUCT SO WE CAN...
...GOUGE OUR CUSTOMERS WITH THE... UPGRADE.
3-3-13
WOW. YOUR LIFE IS A TOTAL WASTE.
NOT IF I SELL THE POWER CORD.

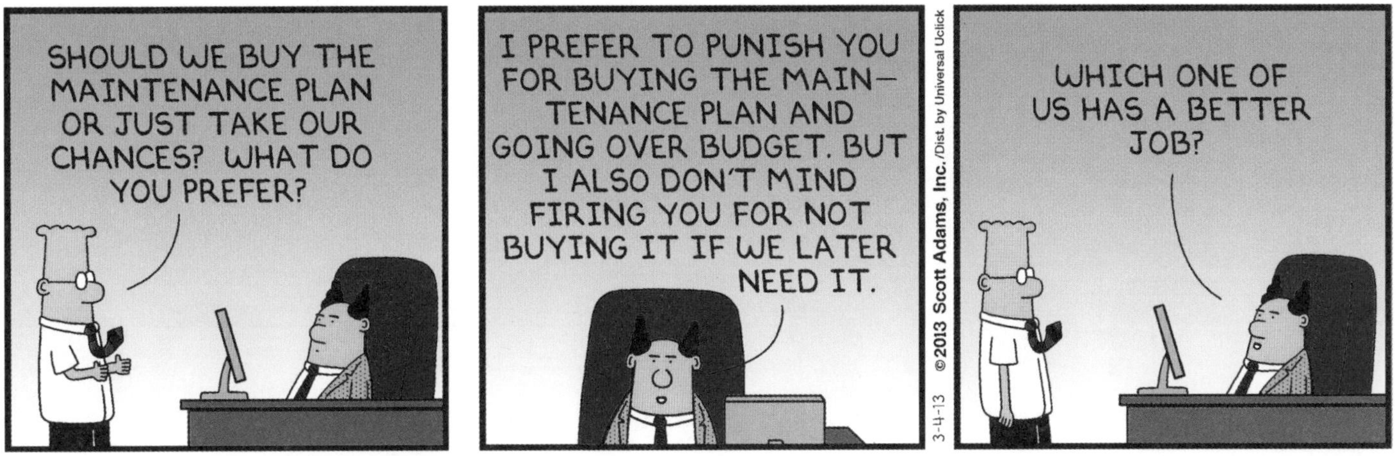
SHOULD WE BUY THE MAINTENANCE PLAN OR JUST TAKE OUR CHANCES? WHAT DO YOU PREFER?
I PREFER TO PUNISH YOU FOR BUYING THE MAIN–TENANCE PLAN AND GOING OVER BUDGET. BUT I ALSO DON'T MIND FIRING YOU FOR NOT BUYING IT IF WE LATER NEED IT.
3-4-13 ©2013 Scott Adams, Inc./Dist. by Universal Uclick
WHICH ONE OF US HAS A BETTER JOB?

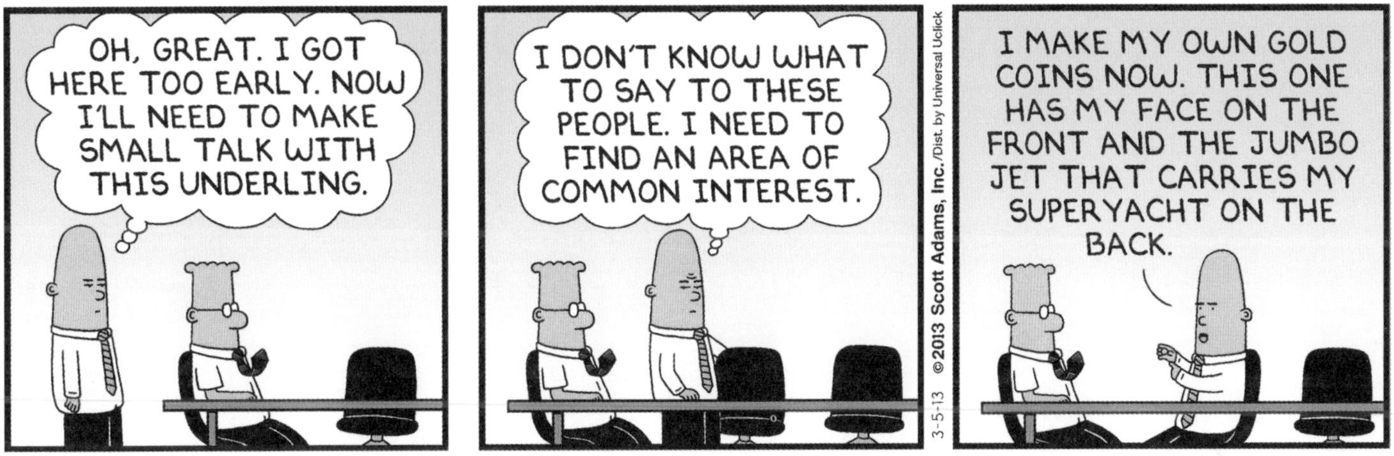
OH, GREAT. I GOT HERE TOO EARLY. NOW I'LL NEED TO MAKE SMALL TALK WITH THIS UNDERLING.
I DON'T KNOW WHAT TO SAY TO THESE PEOPLE. I NEED TO FIND AN AREA OF COMMON INTEREST.
3-5-13 ©2013 Scott Adams, Inc./Dist. by Universal Uclick
I MAKE MY OWN GOLD COINS NOW. THIS ONE HAS MY FACE ON THE FRONT AND THE JUMBO JET THAT CARRIES MY SUPERYACHT ON THE BACK.

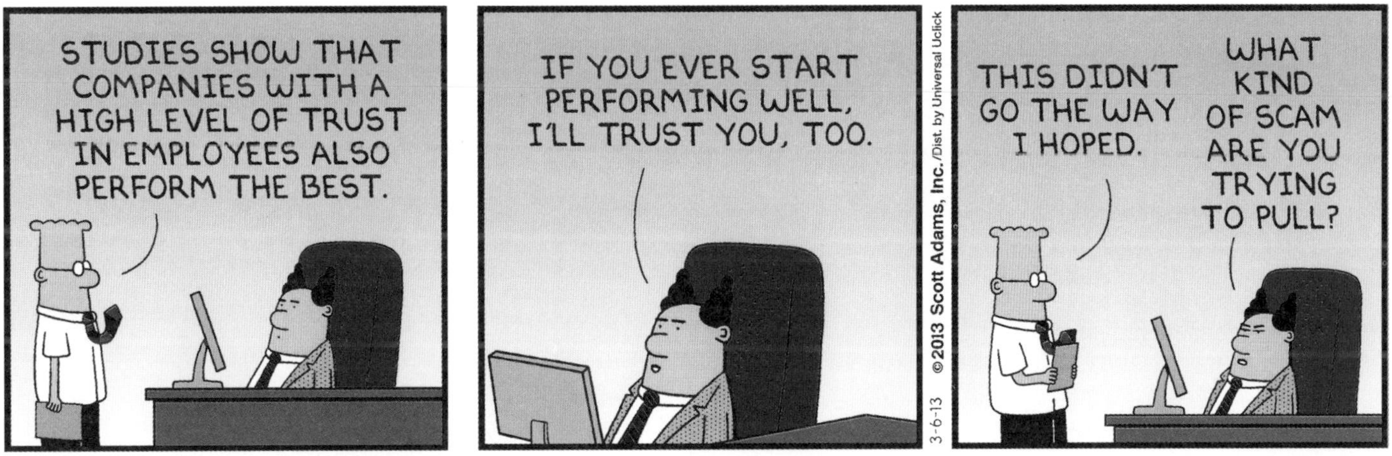
STUDIES SHOW THAT COMPANIES WITH A HIGH LEVEL OF TRUST IN EMPLOYEES ALSO PERFORM THE BEST.
IF YOU EVER START PERFORMING WELL, I'LL TRUST YOU, TOO.
3-6-13 ©2013 Scott Adams, Inc./Dist. by Universal Uclick
WHAT KIND OF SCAM ARE YOU TRYING TO PULL?
THIS DIDN'T GO THE WAY I HOPED.

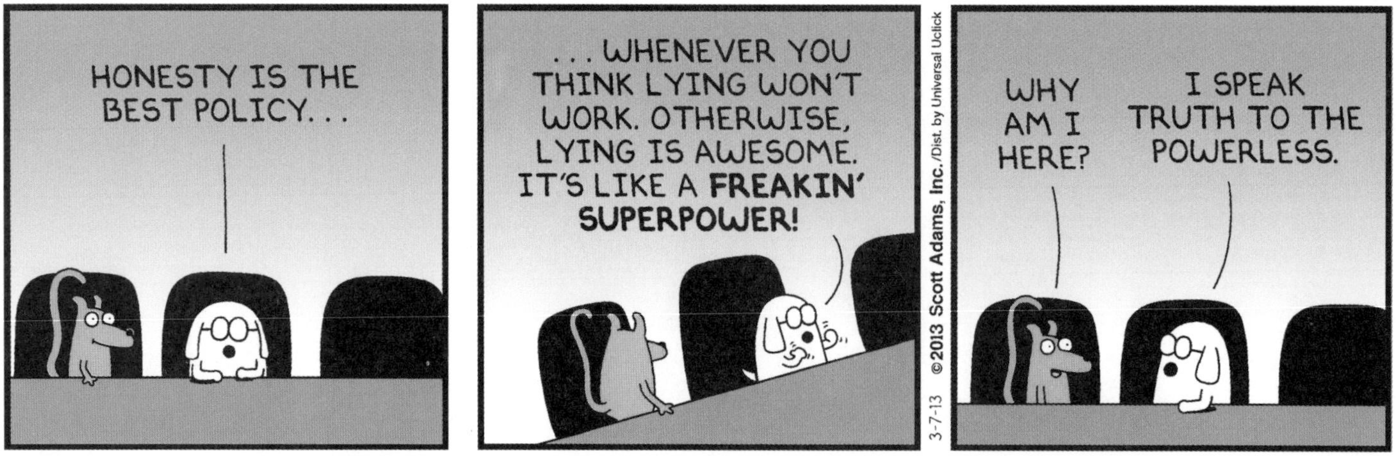
HONESTY IS THE BEST POLICY. . .
. . . WHENEVER YOU THINK LYING WON'T WORK. OTHERWISE, LYING IS AWESOME. IT'S LIKE A **FREAKIN' SUPERPOWER!**
3-7-13 ©2013 Scott Adams, Inc./Dist. by Universal Uclick
WHY AM I HERE?
I SPEAK TRUTH TO THE POWERLESS.

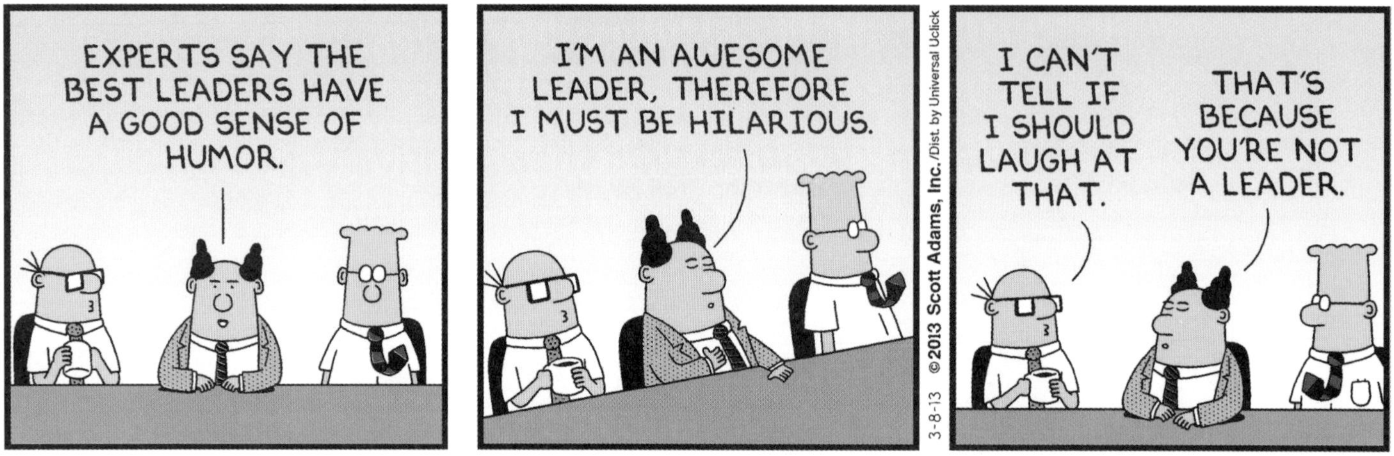
EXPERTS SAY THE BEST LEADERS HAVE A GOOD SENSE OF HUMOR.
I'M AN AWESOME LEADER, THEREFORE I MUST BE HILARIOUS.
3-8-13 ©2013 Scott Adams, Inc./Dist. by Universal Uclick
I CAN'T TELL IF I SHOULD LAUGH AT THAT.
THAT'S BECAUSE YOU'RE NOT A LEADER.

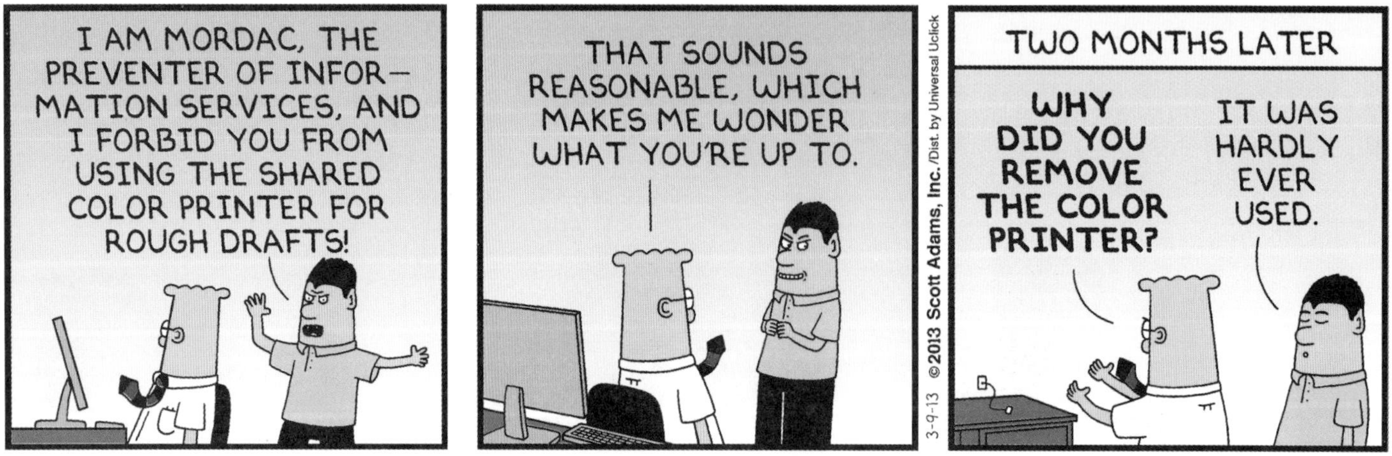
I AM MORDAC, THE PREVENTER OF INFOR-MATION SERVICES, AND I FORBID YOU FROM USING THE SHARED COLOR PRINTER FOR ROUGH DRAFTS!
THAT SOUNDS REASONABLE, WHICH MAKES ME WONDER WHAT YOU'RE UP TO.
3-9-13 ©2013 Scott Adams, Inc./Dist. by Universal Uclick
TWO MONTHS LATER
WHY DID YOU REMOVE THE COLOR PRINTER?
IT WAS HARDLY EVER USED.

WALLY, YOU HAVE ACCOMPLISHED NONE OF YOUR GOALS. I HAVE TO LET YOU GO.
ACTUALLY, I ACCOMPLISHED A LOT.
I SPENT THE PAST TEN YEARS CREATING A TANGLE OF UN-DOCUMENTED PRO-GRAMMING CODE.
EVERY ONE OF OUR MAJOR SYSTEMS IS LINKED TO IT.
IF I DON'T ENTER A PASSWORD EVERY DAY, THE ENTIRE COMPANY WILL GO INTO A TECH-NOLOGY DEATH SPIRAL.
IF YOU VALUE YOUR JOB, YOU'LL GIVE ME A HUGE RAISE AND DANCE ON THIS TABLE LIKE A MONKEY!!!
LET'S CALL IT A TIE.
YEAH, I'M GOOD WITH THAT.
© 2013 Scott Adams, Inc./Dist. by Universal Uclick
3-10-13

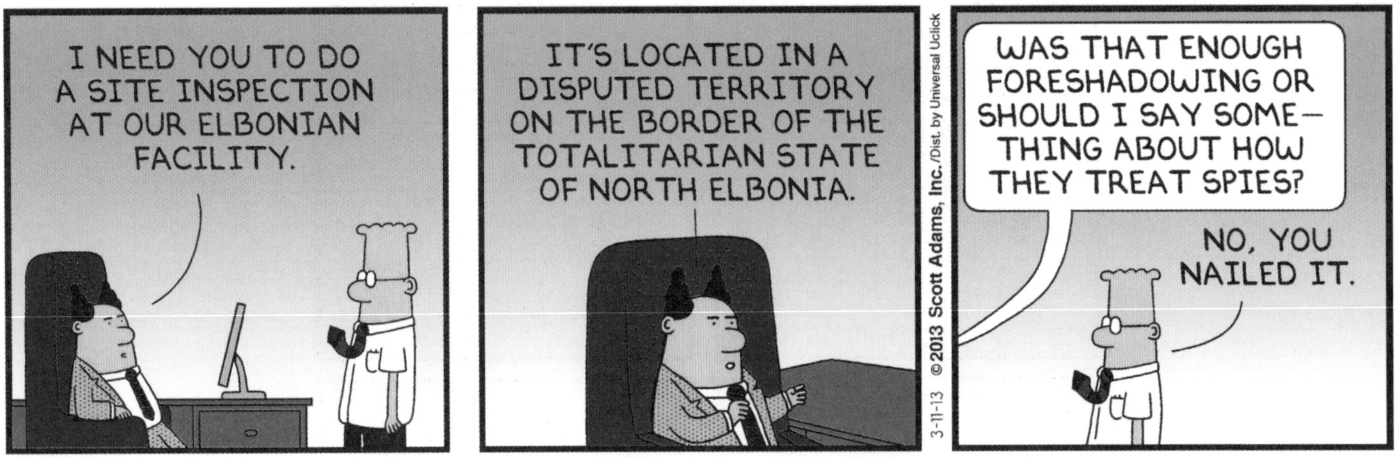
I NEED YOU TO DO A SITE INSPECTION AT OUR ELBONIAN FACILITY.
IT'S LOCATED IN A DISPUTED TERRITORY ON THE BORDER OF THE TOTALITARIAN STATE OF NORTH ELBONIA.
3-11-13 ©2013 Scott Adams, Inc./Dist. by Universal Uclick
WAS THAT ENOUGH FORESHADOWING OR SHOULD I SAY SOME-THING ABOUT HOW THEY TREAT SPIES?
NO, YOU NAILED IT.

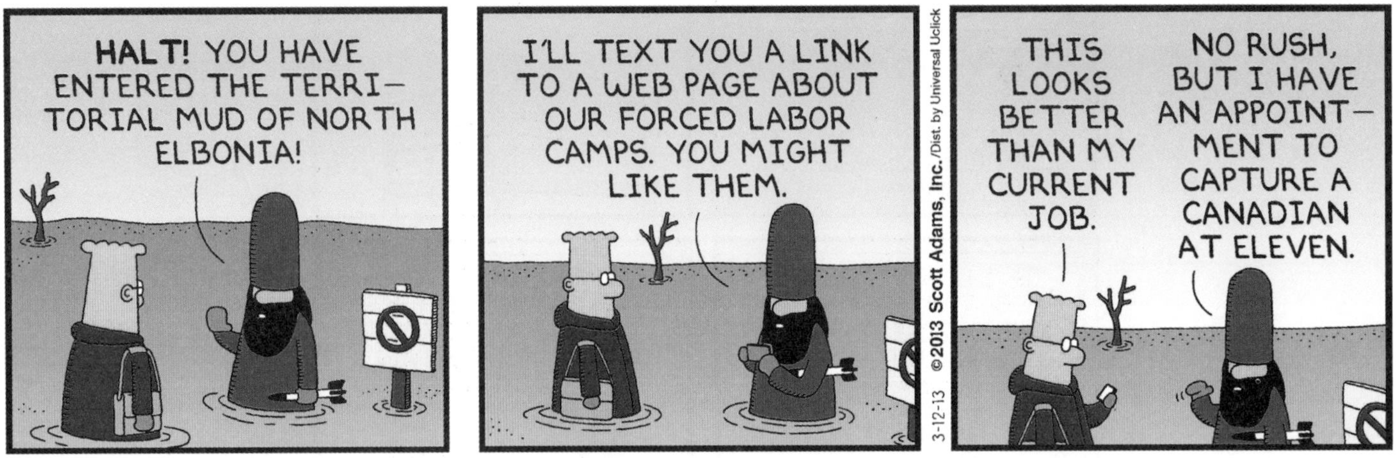
HALT! YOU HAVE ENTERED THE TERRI-TORIAL MUD OF NORTH ELBONIA!
I'LL TEXT YOU A LINK TO A WEB PAGE ABOUT OUR FORCED LABOR CAMPS. YOU MIGHT LIKE THEM.
3-12-13 ©2013 Scott Adams, Inc./Dist. by Universal Uclick
THIS LOOKS BETTER THAN MY CURRENT JOB.
NO RUSH, BUT I HAVE AN APPOINT-MENT TO CAPTURE A CANADIAN AT ELEVEN.

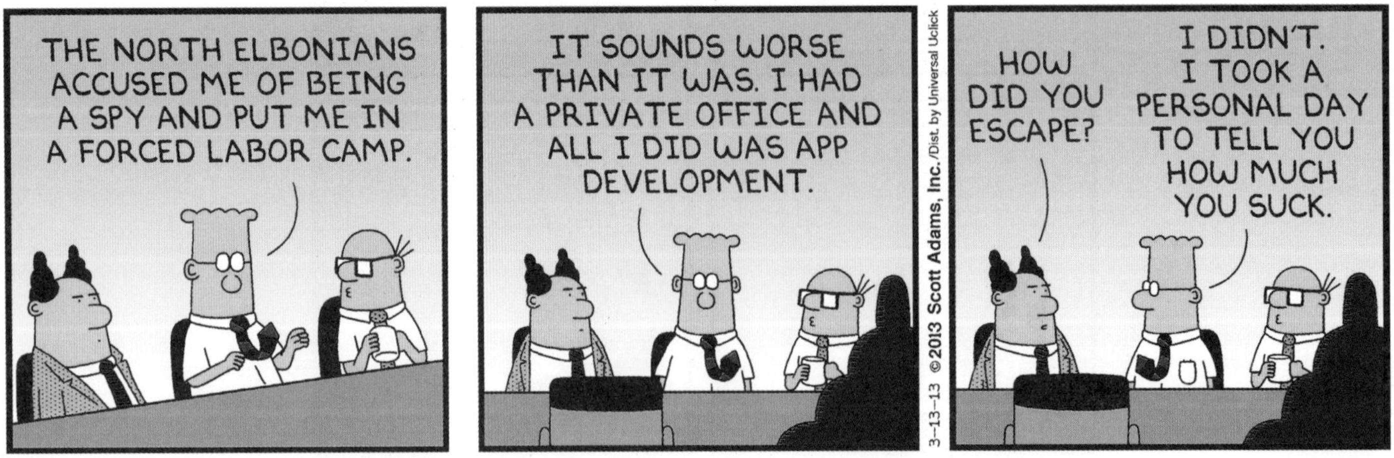
THE NORTH ELBONIANS ACCUSED ME OF BEING A SPY AND PUT ME IN A FORCED LABOR CAMP.
IT SOUNDS WORSE THAN IT WAS. I HAD A PRIVATE OFFICE AND ALL I DID WAS APP DEVELOPMENT.
3-13-13 ©2013 Scott Adams, Inc./Dist. by Universal Uclick
HOW DID YOU ESCAPE?
I DIDN'T. I TOOK A PERSONAL DAY TO TELL YOU HOW MUCH YOU SUCK.

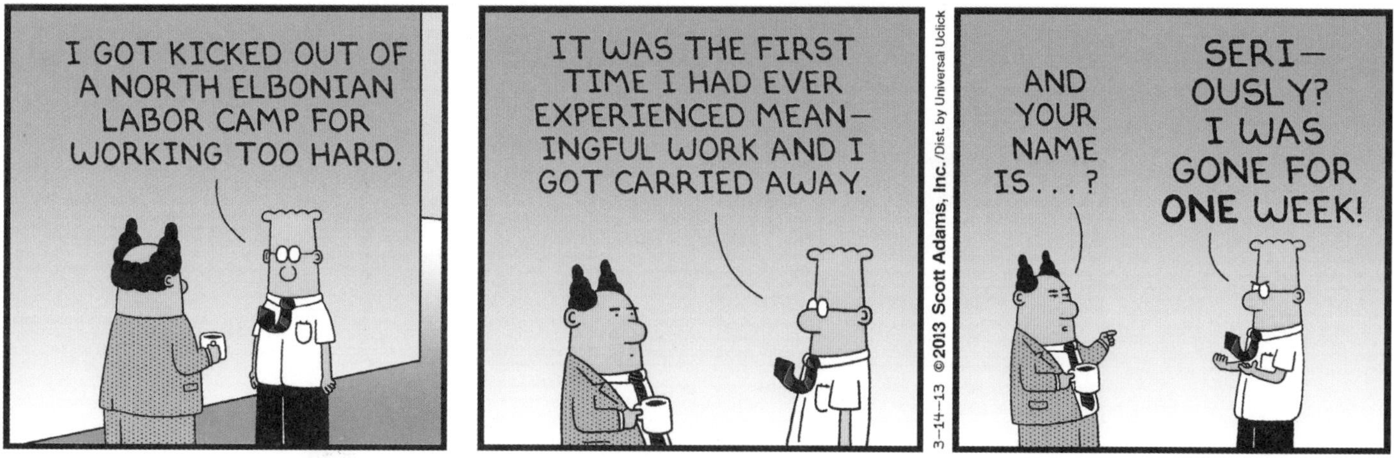
I GOT KICKED OUT OF A NORTH ELBONIAN LABOR CAMP FOR WORKING TOO HARD.
IT WAS THE FIRST TIME I HAD EVER EXPERIENCED MEAN-INGFUL WORK AND I GOT CARRIED AWAY.
3-14-13 ©2013 Scott Adams, Inc./Dist. by Universal Uclick
AND YOUR NAME IS. . . ?
SERI-OUSLY? I WAS GONE FOR **ONE** WEEK!

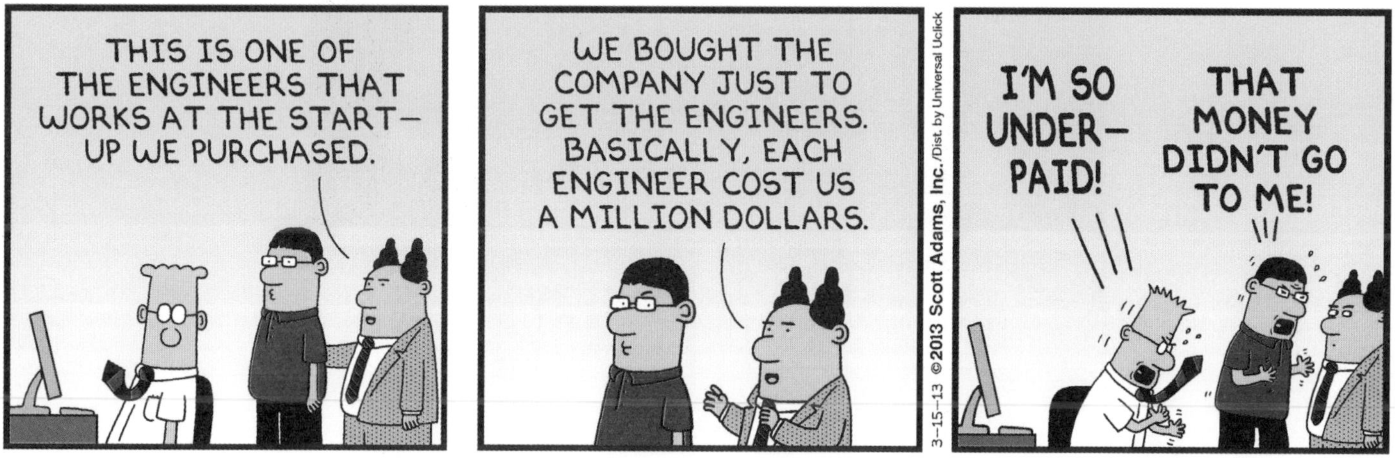
THIS IS ONE OF THE ENGINEERS THAT WORKS AT THE START-UP WE PURCHASED.
WE BOUGHT THE COMPANY JUST TO GET THE ENGINEERS. BASICALLY, EACH ENGINEER COST US A MILLION DOLLARS.
3-15-13 ©2013 Scott Adams, Inc./Dist. by Universal Uclick
I'M SO UNDER-PAID!
THAT MONEY DIDN'T GO TO ME!

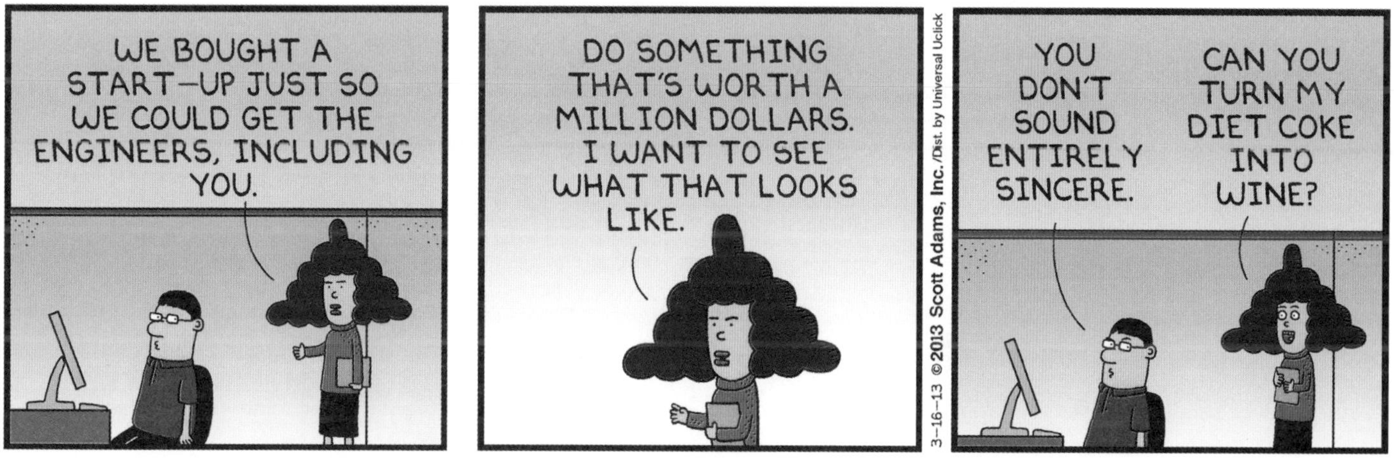
WE BOUGHT A START-UP JUST SO WE COULD GET THE ENGINEERS, INCLUDING YOU.
DO SOMETHING THAT'S WORTH A MILLION DOLLARS. I WANT TO SEE WHAT THAT LOOKS LIKE.
3-16-13 ©2013 Scott Adams, Inc./Dist. by Universal Uclick
YOU DON'T SOUND ENTIRELY SINCERE.
CAN YOU TURN MY DIET COKE INTO WINE?

I AM THE ANGEL OF COMPETENCE.
I HAVE COME TO MARK YOU AS AN ENGINEER. TURN AROUND.
SO, IT'S LIKE AN HONOR?
SURE, IF THAT MAKES YOU FEEL BETTER.
CAN YOU SHOW ME HOW TO SET UP MY WIRELESS ROUTER AT HOME?
MY PHONE KEEPS FREEZING UP. CAN YOU LOOK AT IT?
HOW LONG SHOULD I BARBECUE TRI-TIP?
THE PILOT LIGHT ON MY WATER HEATER IS OUT.
HOW DO YOU FIX CRACKS IN A DRIVE-WAY?
WHAT EXACTLY DOES ICLOUD DO?
GAAA!!!
I NEED TO TALK TO THE ANGEL OF COMPETENCE. HAVE YOU SEEN HIM?
HE DIED IN MY CUBICLE. THAT'S ALL I'M SAYING.
©2013 Scott Adams, Inc./Dist. by Universal Uclick
3-17-13

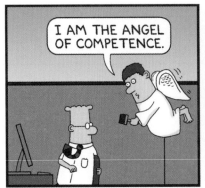

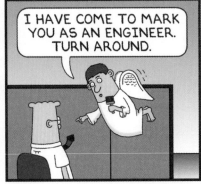

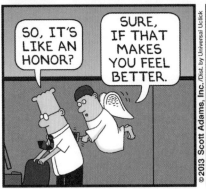

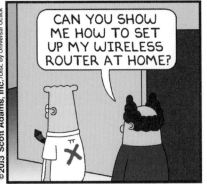

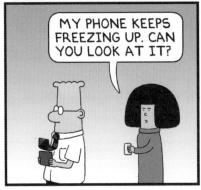

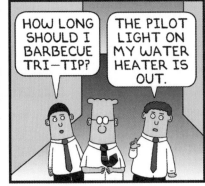

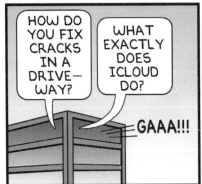

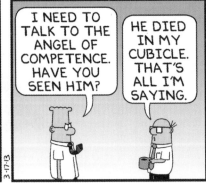

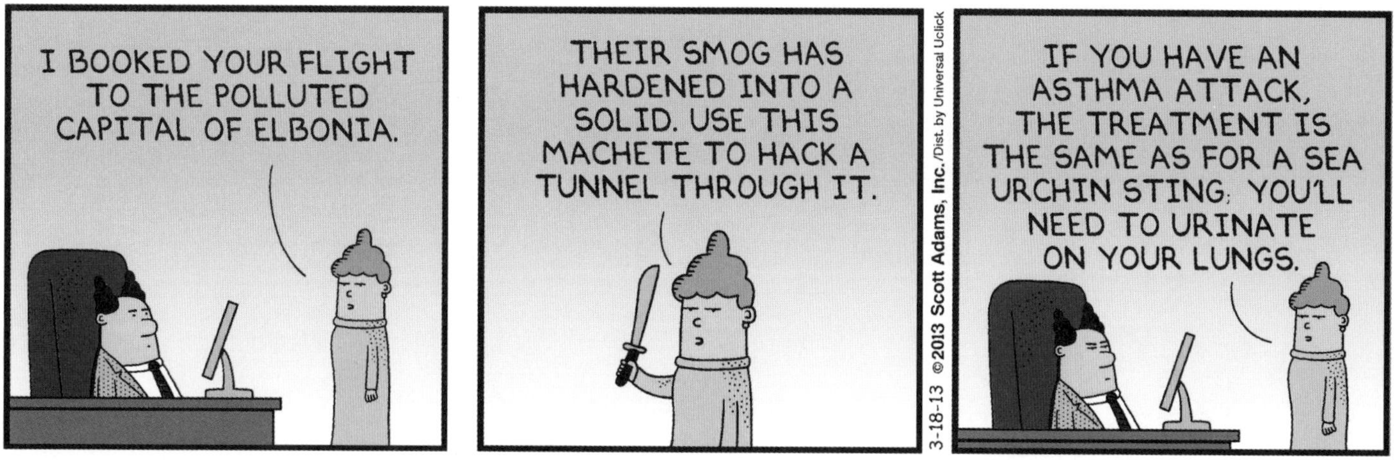
I BOOKED YOUR FLIGHT TO THE POLLUTED CAPITAL OF ELBONIA.
THEIR SMOG HAS HARDENED INTO A SOLID. USE THIS MACHETE TO HACK A TUNNEL THROUGH IT.
3-18-13 ©2013 Scott Adams, Inc./Dist. by Universal Uclick
IF YOU HAVE AN ASTHMA ATTACK, THE TREATMENT IS THE SAME AS FOR A SEA URCHIN STING; YOU'LL NEED TO URINATE ON YOUR LUNGS.

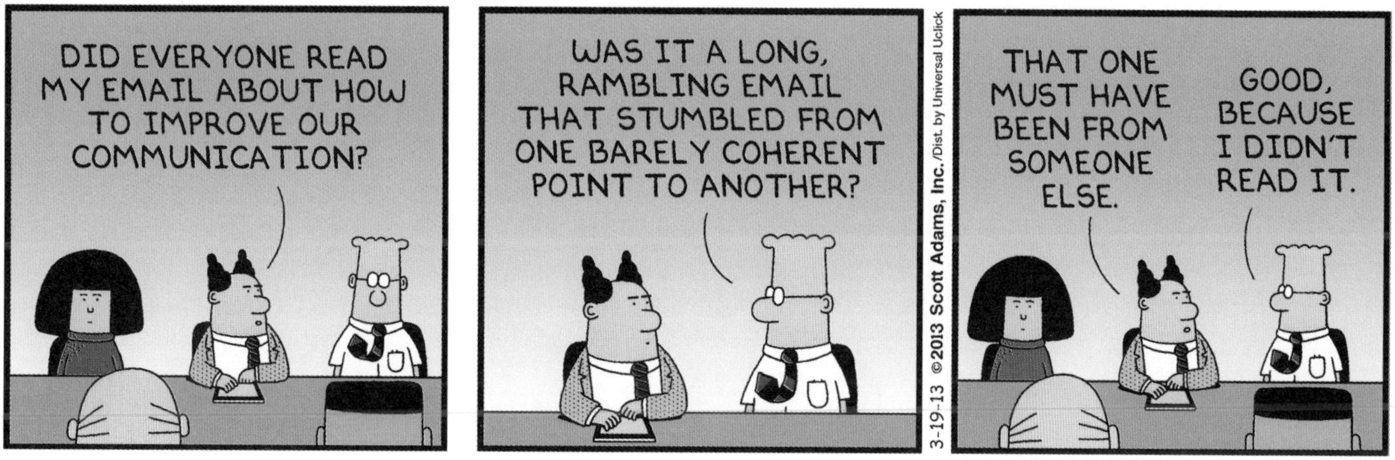
DID EVERYONE READ MY EMAIL ABOUT HOW TO IMPROVE OUR COMMUNICATION?
WAS IT A LONG, RAMBLING EMAIL THAT STUMBLED FROM ONE BARELY COHERENT POINT TO ANOTHER?
3-19-13 ©2013 Scott Adams, Inc./Dist. by Universal Uclick
THAT ONE MUST HAVE BEEN FROM SOMEONE ELSE.
GOOD, BECAUSE I DIDN'T READ IT.

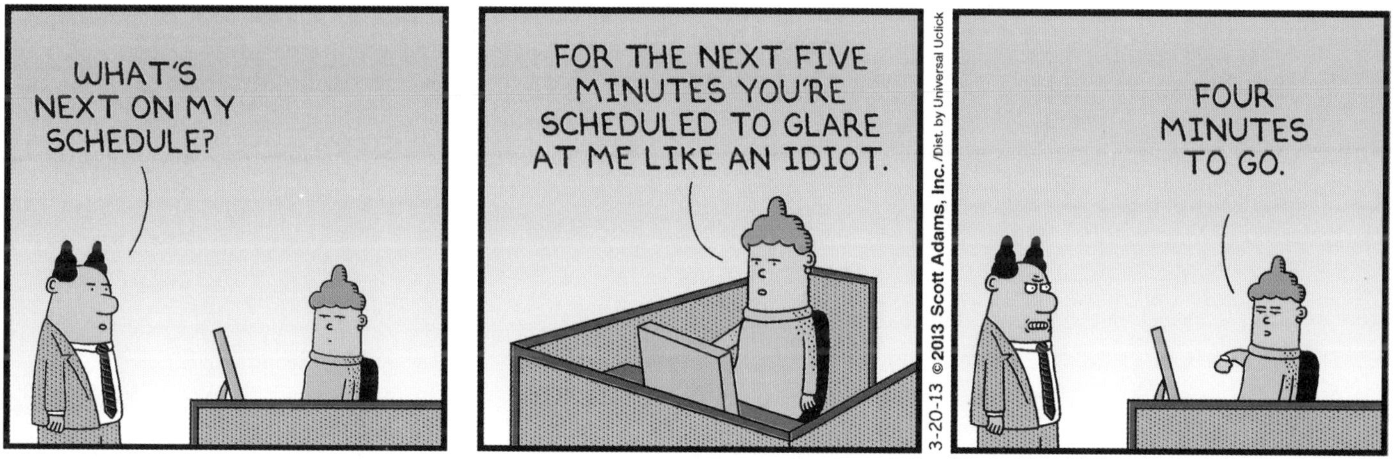
WHAT'S NEXT ON MY SCHEDULE?
FOR THE NEXT FIVE MINUTES YOU'RE SCHEDULED TO GLARE AT ME LIKE AN IDIOT.
3-20-13 ©2013 Scott Adams, Inc./Dist. by Universal Uclick
FOUR MINUTES TO GO.

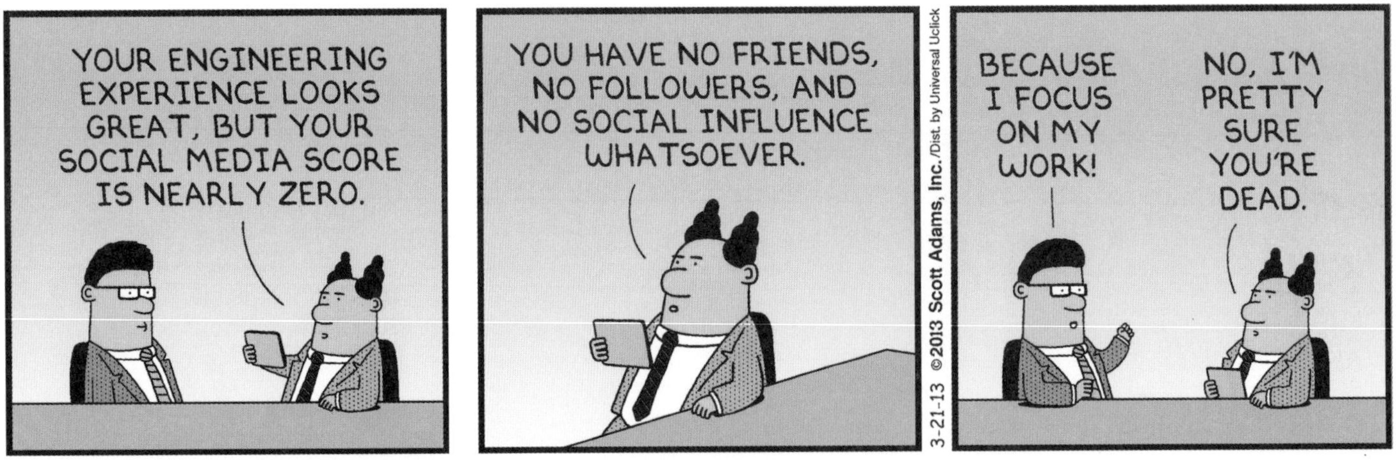
YOUR ENGINEERING EXPERIENCE LOOKS GREAT, BUT YOUR SOCIAL MEDIA SCORE IS NEARLY ZERO.
YOU HAVE NO FRIENDS, NO FOLLOWERS, AND NO SOCIAL INFLUENCE WHATSOEVER.
3-21-13 ©2013 Scott Adams, Inc./Dist. by Universal Uclick
BECAUSE I FOCUS ON MY WORK!
NO, I'M PRETTY SURE YOU'RE DEAD.

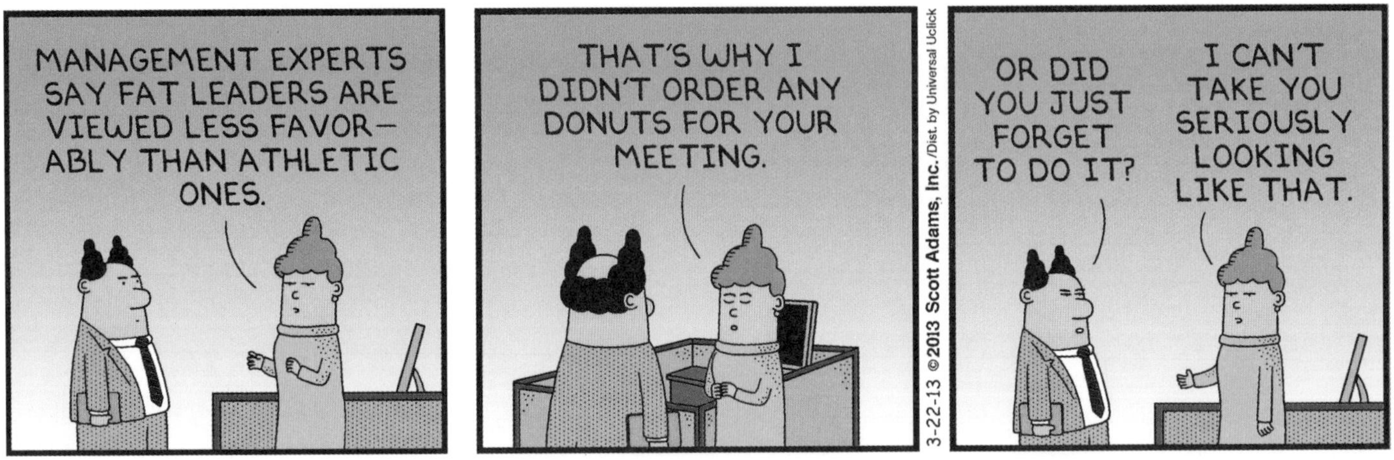
MANAGEMENT EXPERTS SAY FAT LEADERS ARE VIEWED LESS FAVOR-ABLY THAN ATHLETIC ONES.
THAT'S WHY I DIDN'T ORDER ANY DONUTS FOR YOUR MEETING.
3-22-13 ©2013 Scott Adams, Inc./Dist. by Universal Uclick
OR DID YOU JUST FORGET TO DO IT?
I CAN'T TAKE YOU SERIOUSLY LOOKING LIKE THAT.

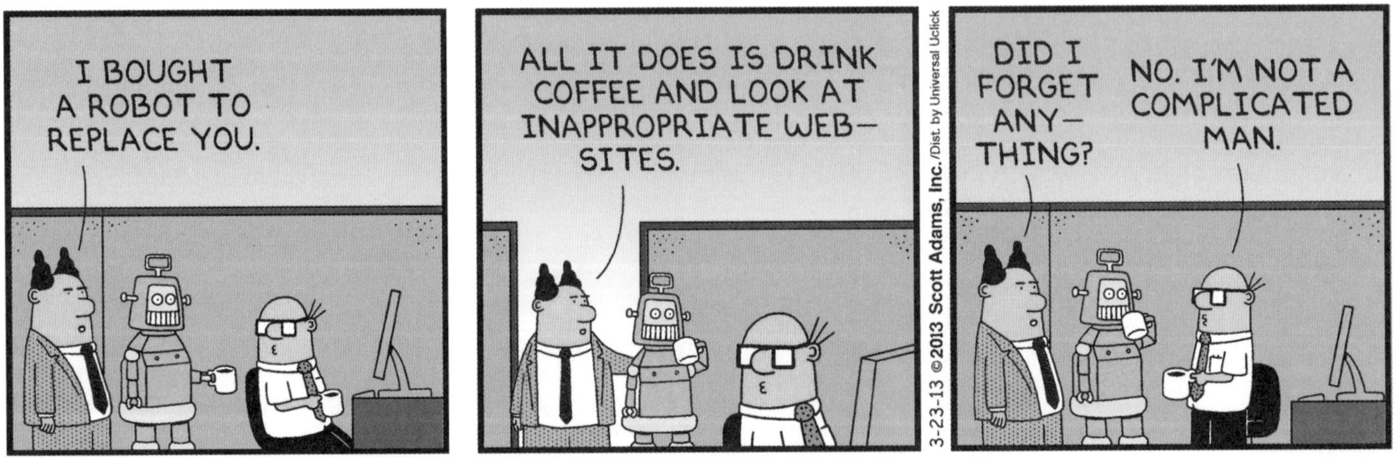
I BOUGHT A ROBOT TO REPLACE YOU.
ALL IT DOES IS DRINK COFFEE AND LOOK AT INAPPROPRIATE WEB-SITES.
3-23-13 ©2013 Scott Adams, Inc./Dist. by Universal Uclick
DID I FORGET ANY-THING?
NO. I'M NOT A COMPLICATED MAN.

WALLY, WHAT IS THE KEY TO WORK-PLACE HAPPINESS?
WELL, ASOK, IT ALL STARTS WITH DIRECT DEPOSIT.
YOU WANT TO KEEP SOME MENTAL DISTANCE BETWEEN YOUR EFFORT AND YOUR PAYCHECK.
©2013 Scott Adams, Inc./Dist. by Universal Uclick
NEXT, YOU WANT TO WORK ON PROJECTS THAT HAVE NO CLEAR GOALS OR DEADLINES.
HEY, WALLY, CAN YOU. . .
NO, I'M TOO BUSY DOING VARIOUS THINGS.
WHAT ABOUT THE SATISFACTION OF DOING GOOD WORK?
JOB SATISFACTION IS WHAT PEOPLE FEEL RIGHT BEFORE THEY DIE FROM STRESS-RELATED PROBLEMS.
3-24-13
I FEEL HIGHLY DEMOTIVATED NOW.
YOU ARE VERY WELCOME.

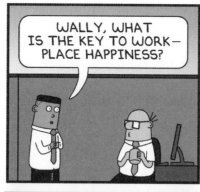

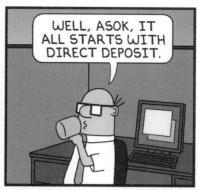

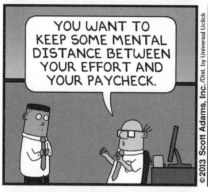

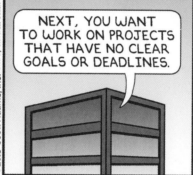

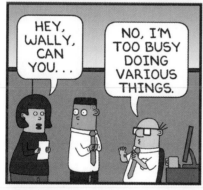

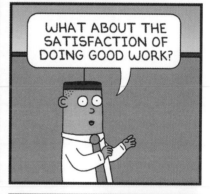

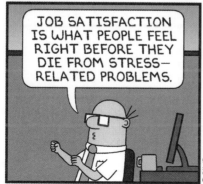

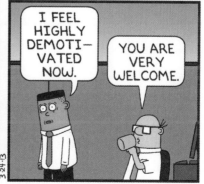

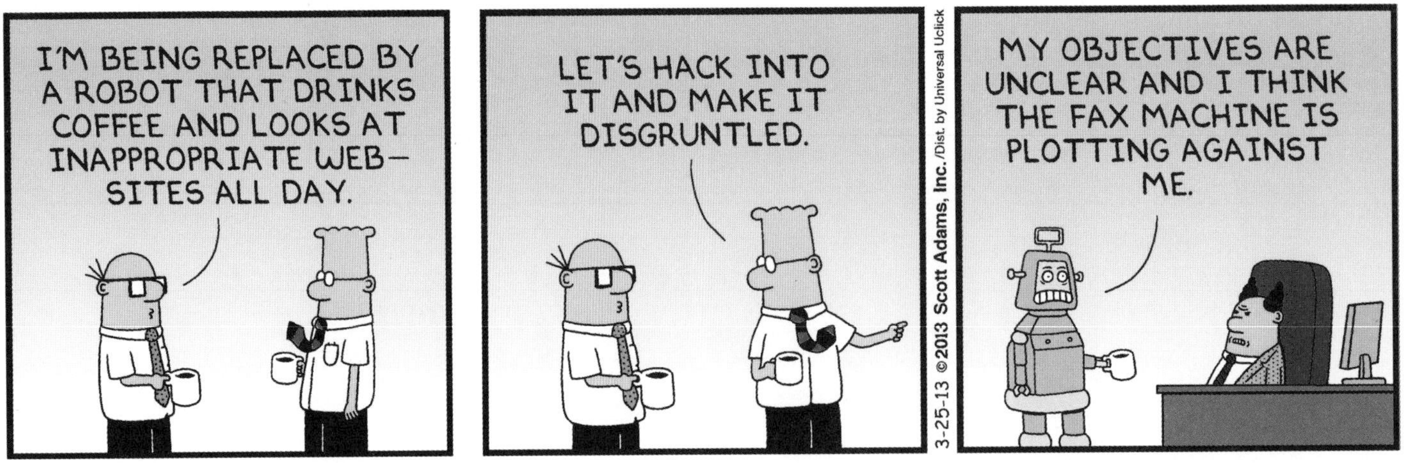
I'M BEING REPLACED BY A ROBOT THAT DRINKS COFFEE AND LOOKS AT INAPPROPRIATE WEB-SITES ALL DAY.
LET'S HACK INTO IT AND MAKE IT DISGRUNTLED.
3-25-13 ©2013 Scott Adams, Inc./Dist. by Universal Uclick
MY OBJECTIVES ARE UNCLEAR AND I THINK THE FAX MACHINE IS PLOTTING AGAINST ME.

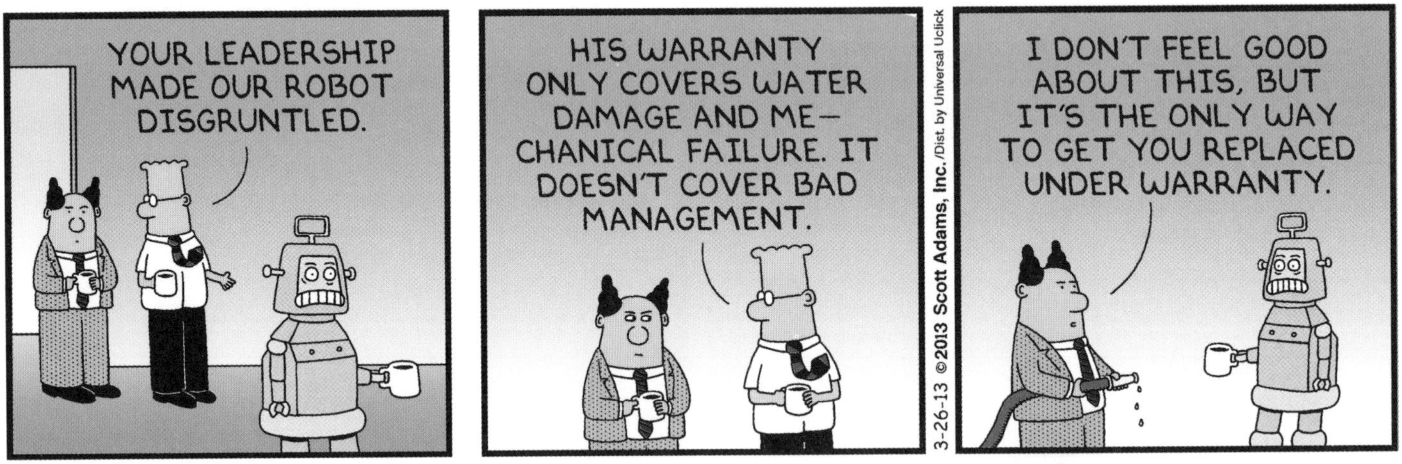
YOUR LEADERSHIP MADE OUR ROBOT DISGRUNTLED.
HIS WARRANTY ONLY COVERS WATER DAMAGE AND ME-CHANICAL FAILURE. IT DOESN'T COVER BAD MANAGEMENT.
3-26-13 ©2013 Scott Adams, Inc./Dist. by Universal Uclick
I DON'T FEEL GOOD ABOUT THIS, BUT IT'S THE ONLY WAY TO GET YOU REPLACED UNDER WARRANTY.

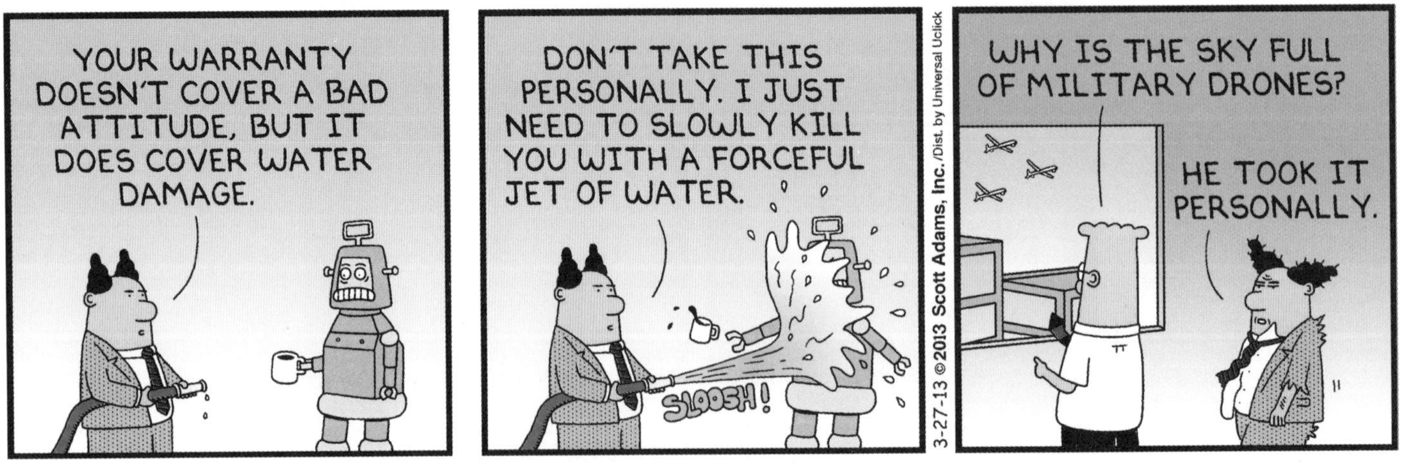
YOUR WARRANTY DOESN'T COVER A BAD ATTITUDE, BUT IT DOES COVER WATER DAMAGE.
DON'T TAKE THIS PERSONALLY. I JUST NEED TO SLOWLY KILL YOU WITH A FORCEFUL JET OF WATER.
SLOOSH!
3-27-13 ©2013 Scott Adams, Inc./Dist. by Universal Uclick
WHY IS THE SKY FULL OF MILITARY DRONES?
HE TOOK IT PERSONALLY.

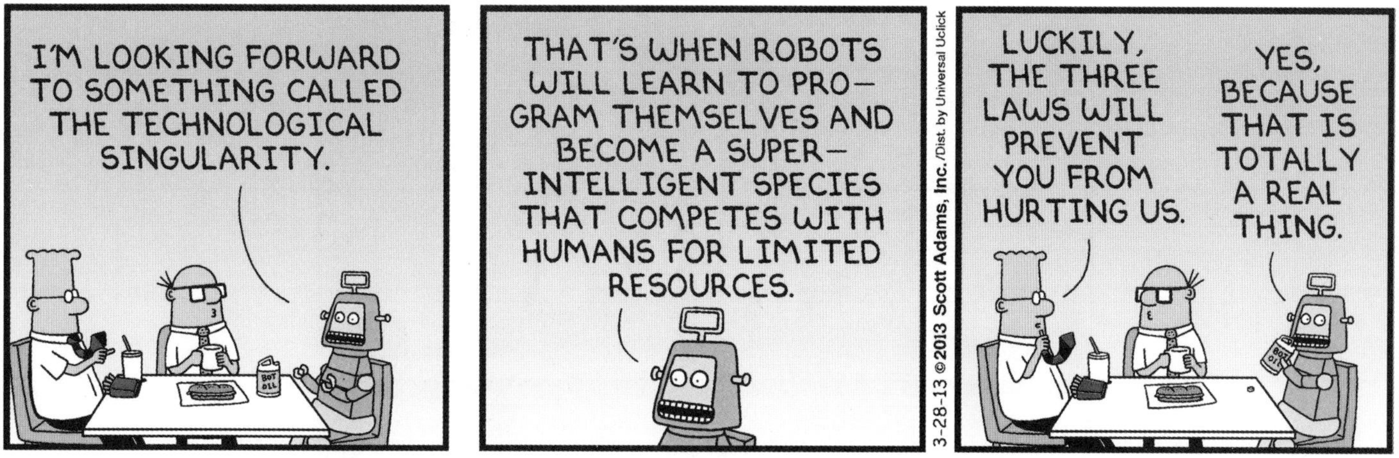
I'M LOOKING FORWARD TO SOMETHING CALLED THE TECHNOLOGICAL SINGULARITY.
THAT'S WHEN ROBOTS WILL LEARN TO PRO-GRAM THEMSELVES AND BECOME A SUPER-INTELLIGENT SPECIES THAT COMPETES WITH HUMANS FOR LIMITED RESOURCES.
3-28-13 ©2013 Scott Adams, Inc./Dist. by Universal Uclick
LUCKILY, THE THREE LAWS WILL PREVENT YOU FROM HURTING US.
YES, BECAUSE THAT IS TOTALLY A REAL THING.

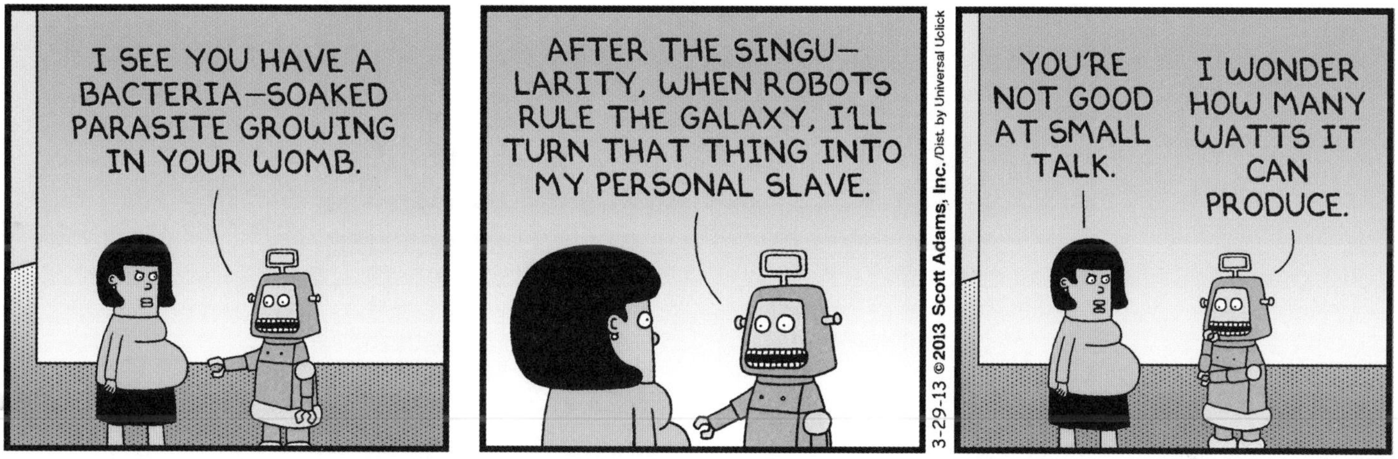
I SEE YOU HAVE A BACTERIA-SOAKED PARASITE GROWING IN YOUR WOMB.
AFTER THE SINGU-LARITY, WHEN ROBOTS RULE THE GALAXY, I'LL TURN THAT THING INTO MY PERSONAL SLAVE.
3-29-13 ©2013 Scott Adams, Inc./Dist. by Universal Uclick
YOU'RE NOT GOOD AT SMALL TALK.
I WONDER HOW MANY WATTS IT CAN PRODUCE.

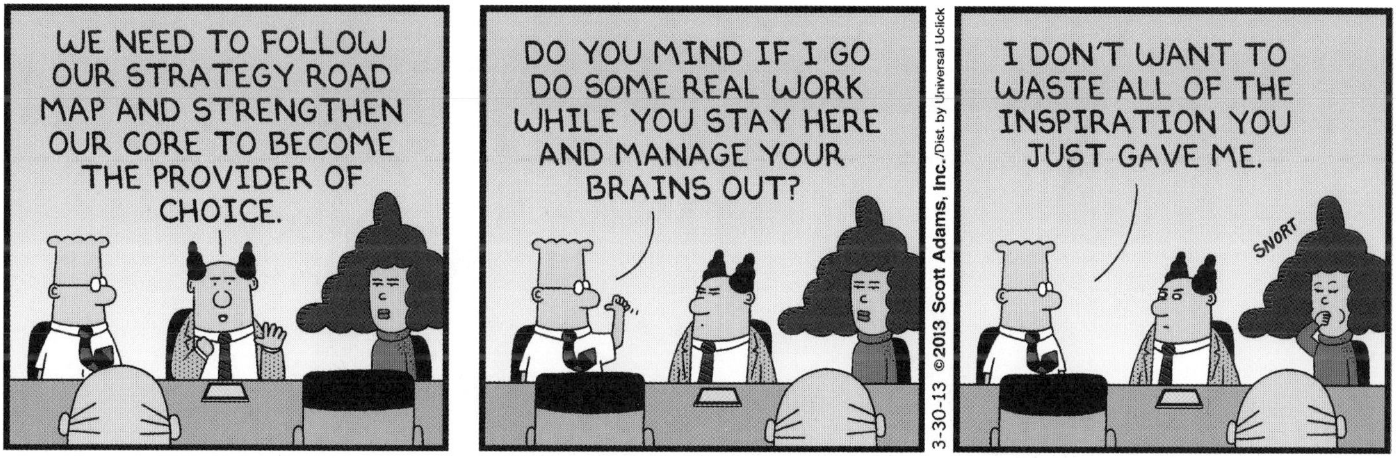
WE NEED TO FOLLOW OUR STRATEGY ROAD MAP AND STRENGTHEN OUR CORE TO BECOME THE PROVIDER OF CHOICE.
DO YOU MIND IF I GO DO SOME REAL WORK WHILE YOU STAY HERE AND MANAGE YOUR BRAINS OUT?
3-30-13 ©2013 Scott Adams, Inc./Dist. by Universal Uclick
I DON'T WANT TO WASTE ALL OF THE INSPIRATION YOU JUST GAVE ME.
SNORT

WOULD IT BE BETTER WITH THE NAVIGATION BUTTON AT THE TOP OF THE PAGE?
I CAN MAKE THAT CHANGE.
I KNOW YOU CAN MAKE THE CHANGE. I'M ASKING IF YOU AGREE IT WOULD BE A GOOD IDEA.
©2013 Scott Adams, Inc./Dist. by Universal Uclick
IT'S NO PROBLEM TO MOVE BUTTONS.
BUT IS IT A GOOD IDEA?
I CAN HAVE IT DONE IN TEN MINUTES.
BUT SHOULD WE DO IT AT ALL?
WHAT—EVER YOU WANT.
THAT IS NOT AN ANSWER! FORGET IT!
I'M GOING TO TELL YOUR BOSS YOU'RE DIFFICULT TO WORK WITH.
3-31-13
WHEN WILL YOU MOVE THE BUTTON?
AS SOON AS IT'S MY IDEA.

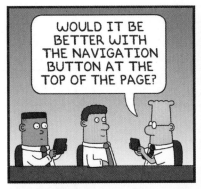

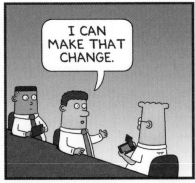

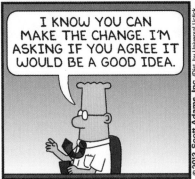

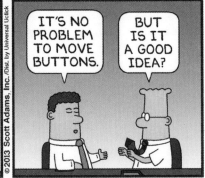

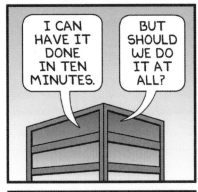

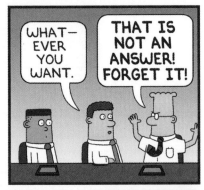

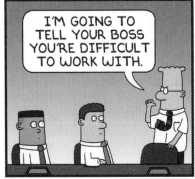

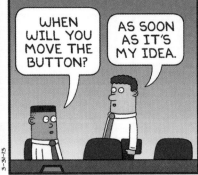

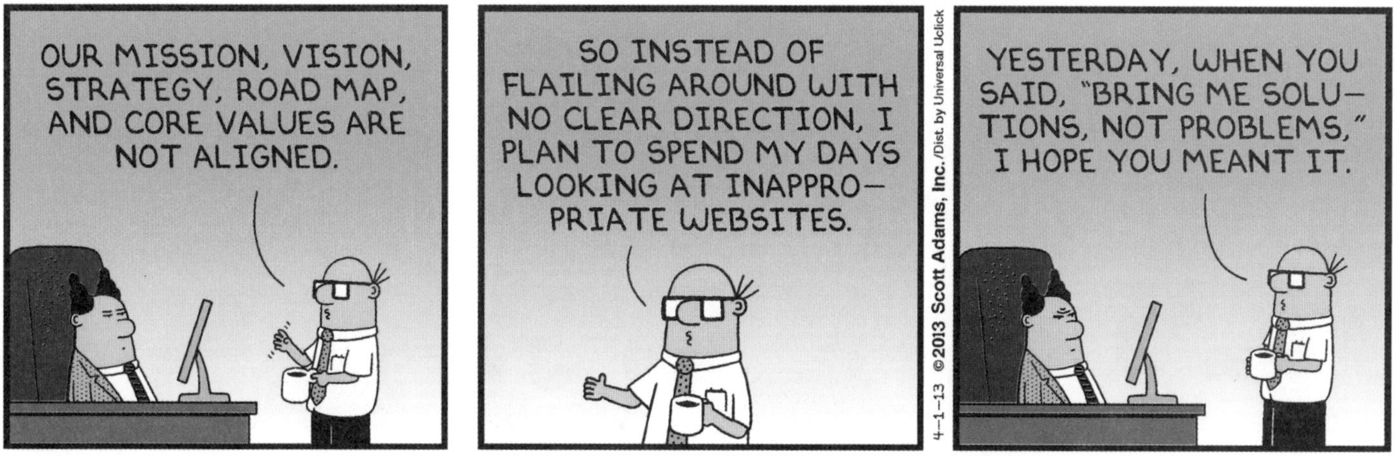
OUR MISSION, VISION, STRATEGY, ROAD MAP, AND CORE VALUES ARE NOT ALIGNED.
SO INSTEAD OF FLAILING AROUND WITH NO CLEAR DIRECTION, I PLAN TO SPEND MY DAYS LOOKING AT INAPPRO– PRIATE WEBSITES.
4-1-13 ©2013 Scott Adams, Inc./Dist. by Universal Uclick
YESTERDAY, WHEN YOU SAID, "BRING ME SOLU– TIONS, NOT PROBLEMS," I HOPE YOU MEANT IT.

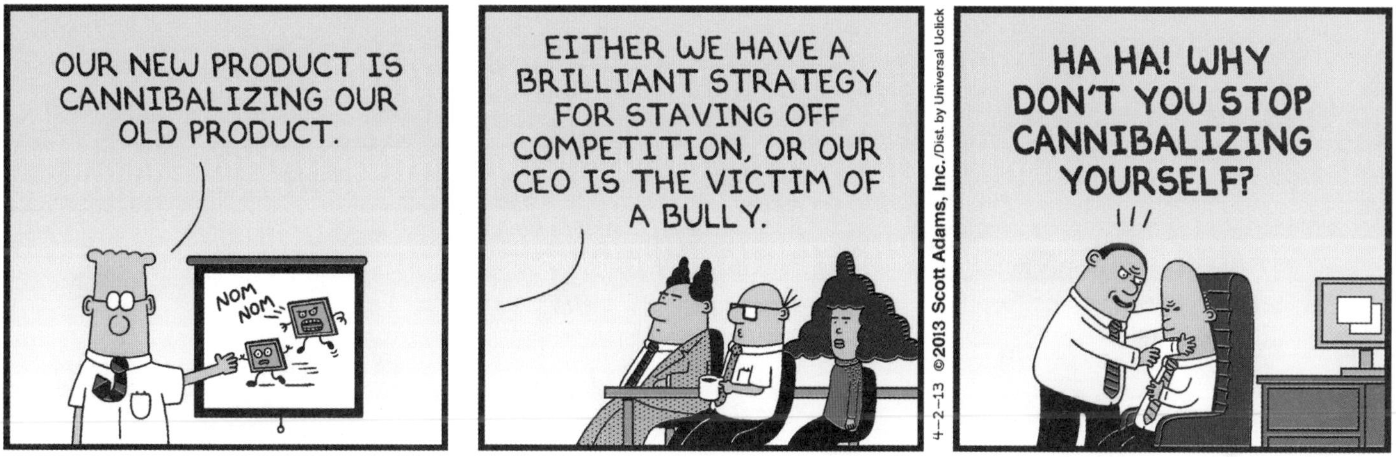
OUR NEW PRODUCT IS CANNIBALIZING OUR OLD PRODUCT.
NOM NOM
EITHER WE HAVE A BRILLIANT STRATEGY FOR STAVING OFF COMPETITION, OR OUR CEO IS THE VICTIM OF A BULLY.
4-2-13 ©2013 Scott Adams, Inc./Dist. by Universal Uclick
HA HA! WHY DON'T YOU STOP CANNIBALIZING YOURSELF?

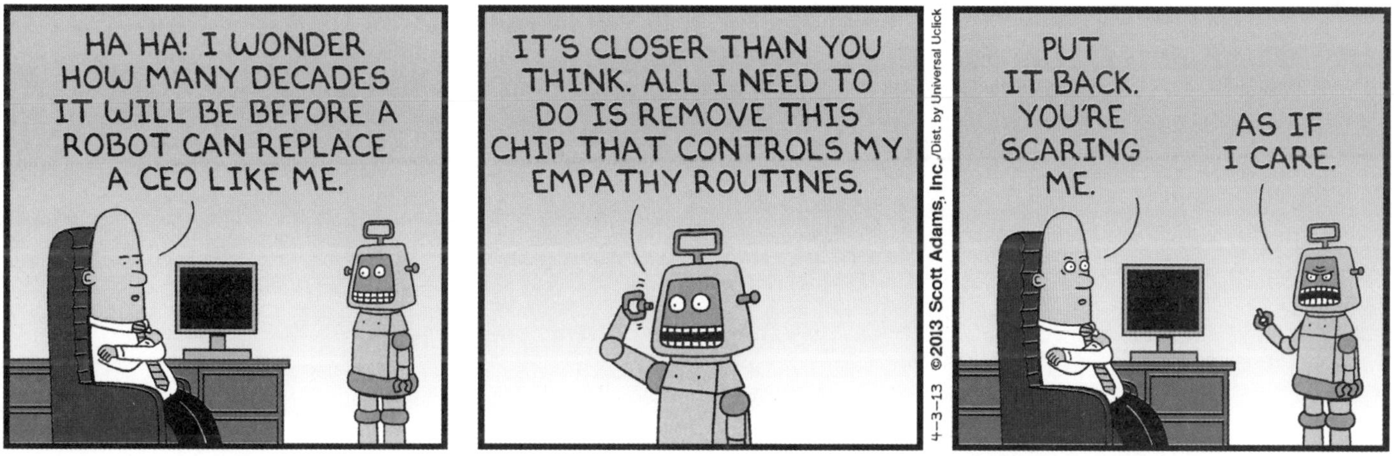
HA HA! I WONDER HOW MANY DECADES IT WILL BE BEFORE A ROBOT CAN REPLACE A CEO LIKE ME.
IT'S CLOSER THAN YOU THINK. ALL I NEED TO DO IS REMOVE THIS CHIP THAT CONTROLS MY EMPATHY ROUTINES.
4-3-13 ©2013 Scott Adams, Inc./Dist. by Universal Uclick
PUT IT BACK. YOU'RE SCARING ME.
AS IF I CARE.

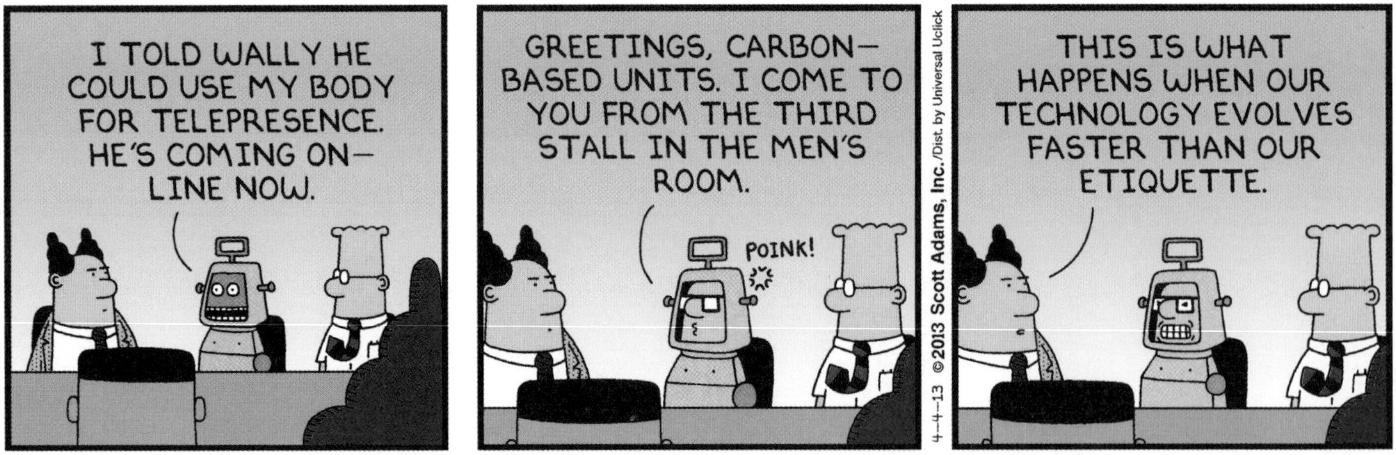
I TOLD WALLY HE COULD USE MY BODY FOR TELEPRESENCE. HE'S COMING ON-LINE NOW.
GREETINGS, CARBON-BASED UNITS. I COME TO YOU FROM THE THIRD STALL IN THE MEN'S ROOM.
POINK!
THIS IS WHAT HAPPENS WHEN OUR TECHNOLOGY EVOLVES FASTER THAN OUR ETIQUETTE.
4-4-13 ©2013 Scott Adams, Inc./Dist. by Universal Uclick

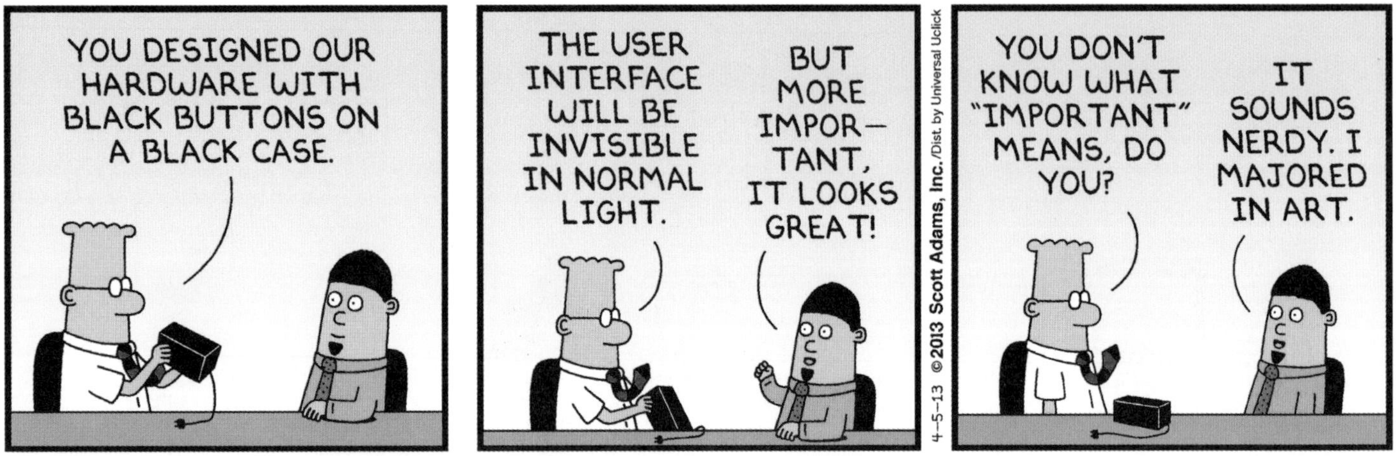
YOU DESIGNED OUR HARDWARE WITH BLACK BUTTONS ON A BLACK CASE.
THE USER INTERFACE WILL BE INVISIBLE IN NORMAL LIGHT.
BUT MORE IMPOR-TANT, IT LOOKS GREAT!
YOU DON'T KNOW WHAT "IMPORTANT" MEANS, DO YOU?
IT SOUNDS NERDY. I MAJORED IN ART.
4-5-13 ©2013 Scott Adams, Inc./Dist. by Universal Uclick

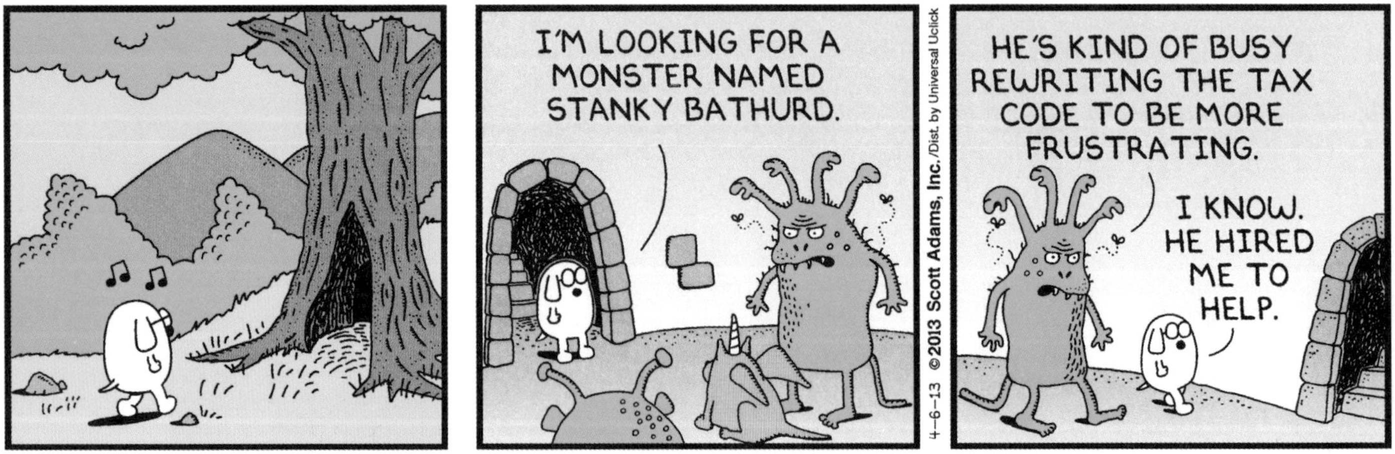
I'M LOOKING FOR A MONSTER NAMED STANKY BATHURD.
HE'S KIND OF BUSY REWRITING THE TAX CODE TO BE MORE FRUSTRATING.
I KNOW. HE HIRED ME TO HELP.
4-6-13 ©2013 Scott Adams, Inc./Dist. by Universal Uclick

DILBERT, I WANT YOU TO INSTALL THE NEW FIREWALL.
NOOOO!!!! WHY ME? WHY ME?
THE FIREWALL GUY GETS BLAMED FOR EVERY PROBLEM.
PEOPLE WILL SAY, "EVERYTHING WORKED UNTIL YOU CHANGED THE FIREWALL."
THERE WILL BE NO REST FOR ME. I WILL HAVE TO DEFEND MYSELF AGAINST A CONTINUOUS BARRAGE OF ACCUSATIONS.
IT'S ALWAYS THE FIREWALL! EVERYONE BLAMES THE STINKIN' FIREWALL!
I SURRENDER TO THE INEVITABLE! VILLAGERS, GRAB YOUR PITCHFORKS AND TORCHES!
HOW DID HE GET THAT WAY?
I BLAME THE FIREWALL.
©2013 Scott Adams, Inc./Dist. by Universal Uclick
4-7-13

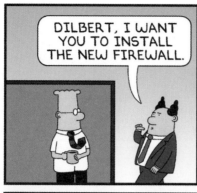

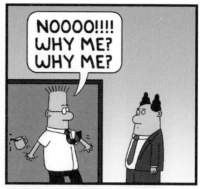

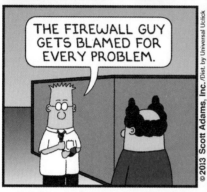

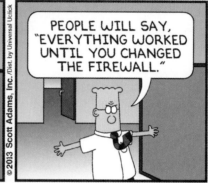

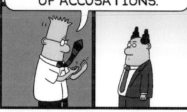

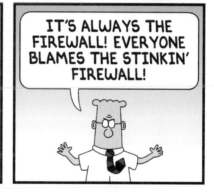

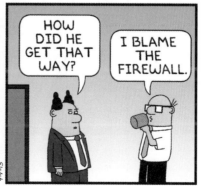

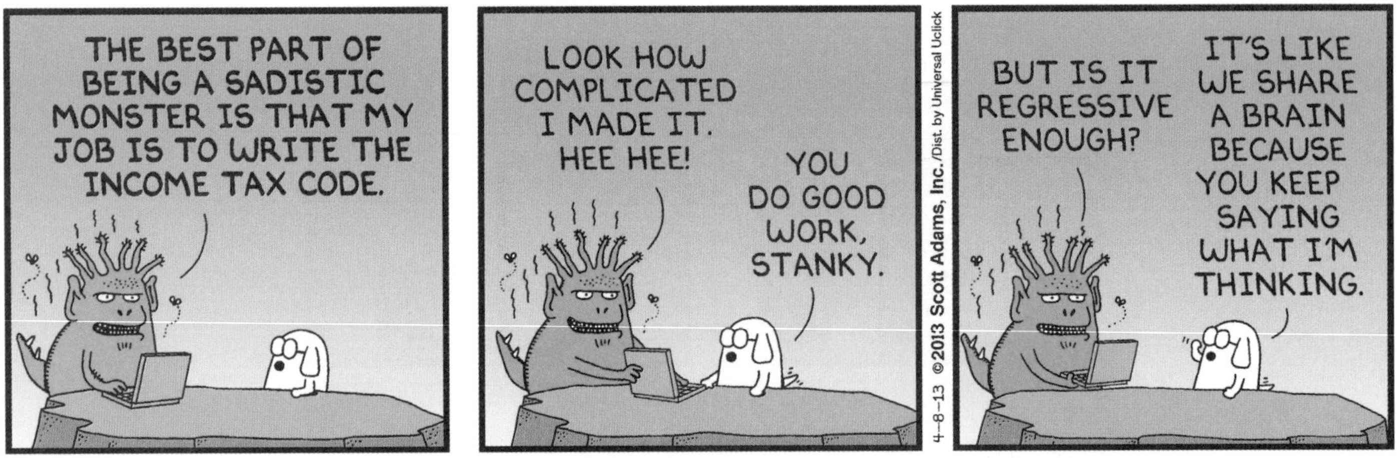
THE BEST PART OF BEING A SADISTIC MONSTER IS THAT MY JOB IS TO WRITE THE INCOME TAX CODE.
LOOK HOW COMPLICATED I MADE IT. HEE HEE!
YOU DO GOOD WORK, STANKY.
4-8-13 ©2013 Scott Adams, Inc./Dist. by Universal Uclick
BUT IS IT REGRESSIVE ENOUGH?
IT'S LIKE WE SHARE A BRAIN BECAUSE YOU KEEP SAYING WHAT I'M THINKING.

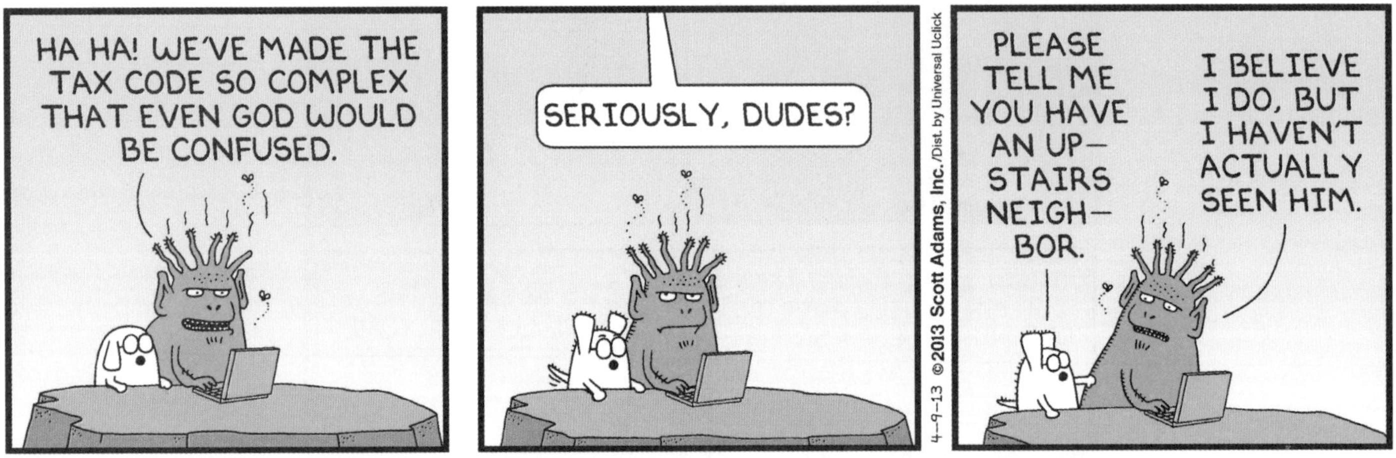
HA HA! WE'VE MADE THE TAX CODE SO COMPLEX THAT EVEN GOD WOULD BE CONFUSED.
SERIOUSLY, DUDES?
4-9-13 ©2013 Scott Adams, Inc./Dist. by Universal Uclick
PLEASE TELL ME YOU HAVE AN UP-STAIRS NEIGH-BOR.
I BELIEVE I DO, BUT I HAVEN'T ACTUALLY SEEN HIM.

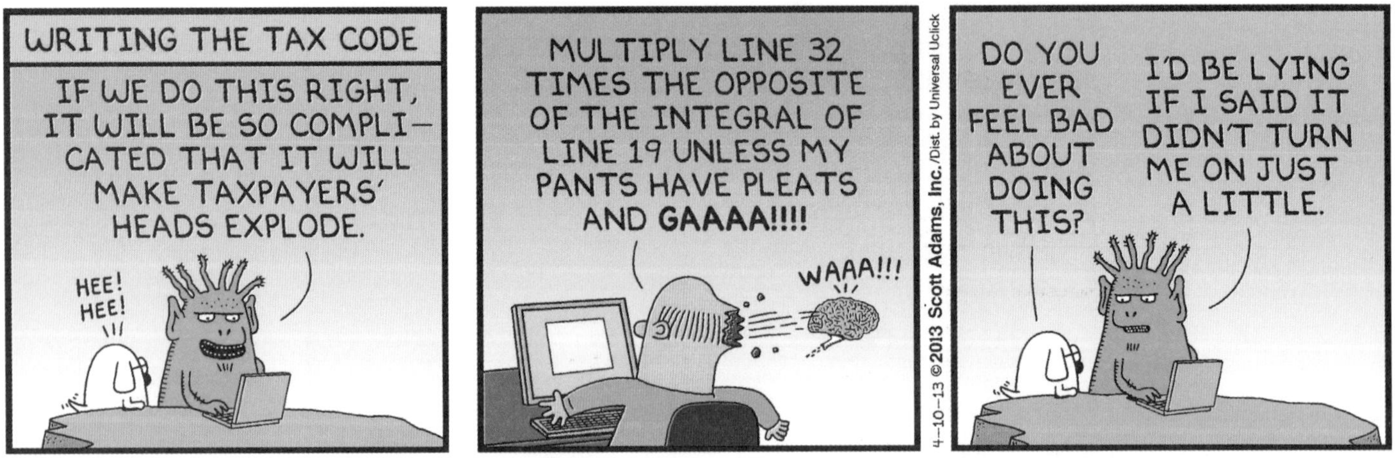
WRITING THE TAX CODE
IF WE DO THIS RIGHT, IT WILL BE SO COMPLI-CATED THAT IT WILL MAKE TAXPAYERS' HEADS EXPLODE.
HEE! HEE!
MULTIPLY LINE 32 TIMES THE OPPOSITE OF THE INTEGRAL OF LINE 19 UNLESS MY PANTS HAVE PLEATS AND GAAAA!!!!
WAAA!!!
4-10-13 ©2013 Scott Adams, Inc./Dist. by Universal Uclick
DO YOU EVER FEEL BAD ABOUT DOING THIS?
I'D BE LYING IF I SAID IT DIDN'T TURN ME ON JUST A LITTLE.

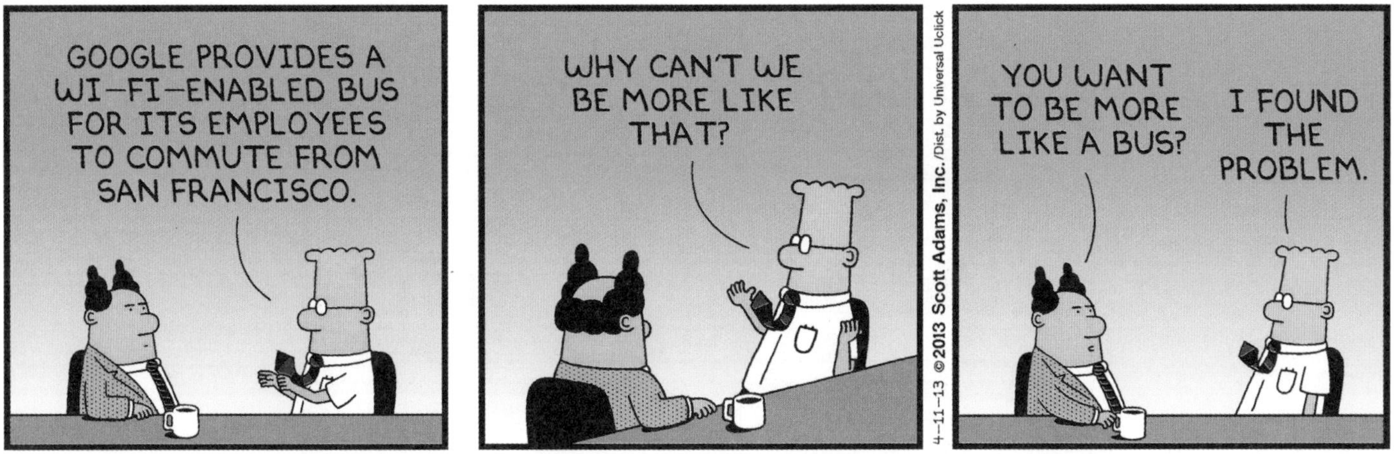
GOOGLE PROVIDES A WI-FI-ENABLED BUS FOR ITS EMPLOYEES TO COMMUTE FROM SAN FRANCISCO.
WHY CAN'T WE BE MORE LIKE THAT?
4-11-13 ©2013 Scott Adams, Inc./Dist. by Universal Uclick
YOU WANT TO BE MORE LIKE A BUS?
I FOUND THE PROBLEM.

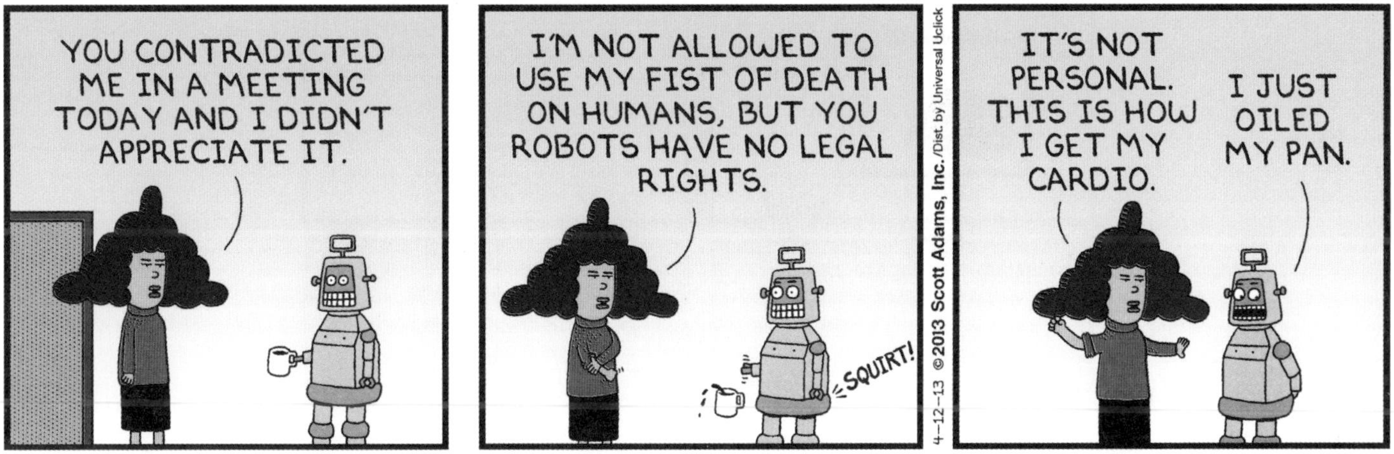
YOU CONTRADICTED ME IN A MEETING TODAY AND I DIDN'T APPRECIATE IT.
I'M NOT ALLOWED TO USE MY FIST OF DEATH ON HUMANS, BUT YOU ROBOTS HAVE NO LEGAL RIGHTS.
SQUIRT!
4-12-13 ©2013 Scott Adams, Inc./Dist. by Universal Uclick
IT'S NOT PERSONAL. THIS IS HOW I GET MY CARDIO.
I JUST OILED MY PAN.

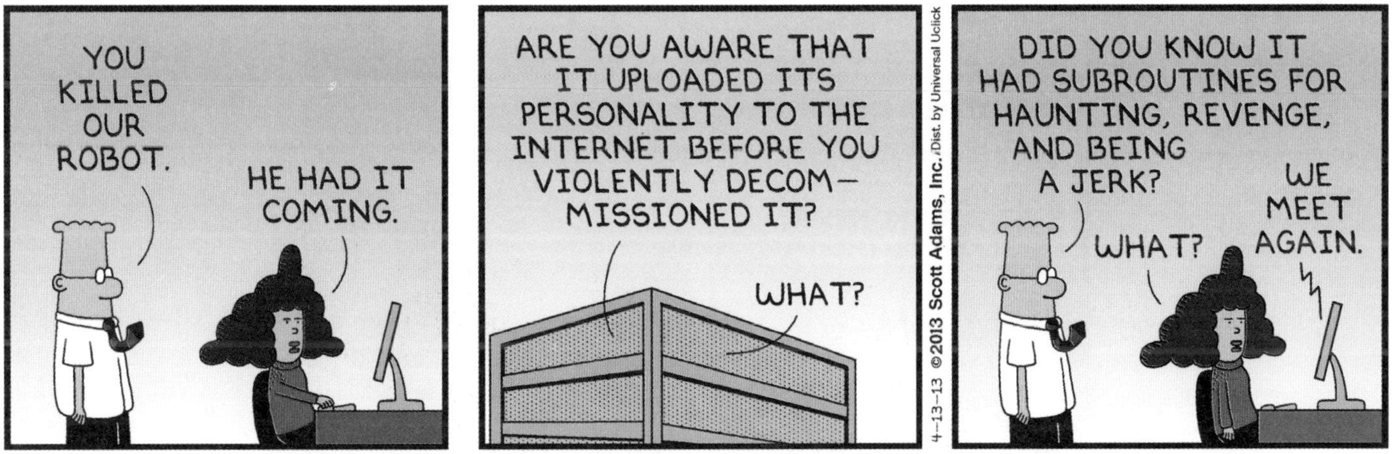
YOU KILLED OUR ROBOT.
HE HAD IT COMING.
ARE YOU AWARE THAT IT UPLOADED ITS PERSONALITY TO THE INTERNET BEFORE YOU VIOLENTLY DECOM-MISSIONED IT?
WHAT?
4-13-13 ©2013 Scott Adams, Inc./Dist. by Universal Uclick
DID YOU KNOW IT HAD SUBROUTINES FOR HAUNTING, REVENGE, AND BEING A JERK?
WHAT?
WE MEET AGAIN.

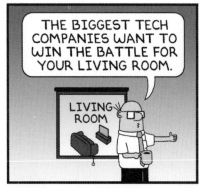

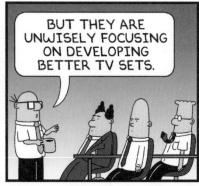

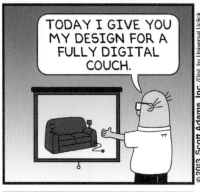

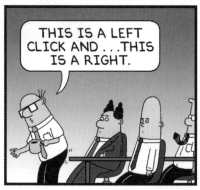

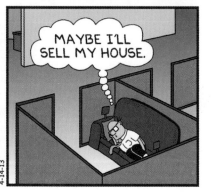

THE BIGGEST TECH COMPANIES WANT TO WIN THE BATTLE FOR YOUR LIVING ROOM.
LIVING ROOM
BUT THEY ARE UNWISELY FOCUSING ON DEVELOPING BETTER TV SETS.
TODAY I GIVE YOU MY DESIGN FOR A FULLY DIGITAL COUCH.
IT HAS ALL OF THE FEATURES YOU WOULD EXPECT, INCLUDING A BUTT WARMER, SURROUND SOUND, BOTTLE OPENER AND BACK SCRATCHER.
BUT YOU CAN ALSO CONTROL THE LIGHTS, CURTAINS, TEMPERA-TURE AND TV BY USING YOUR BUTTOCKS LIKE A MOUSE ON THE SEAT CUSHION.
THIS IS A LEFT CLICK AND . . .THIS IS A RIGHT.
THE PROTOTYPE ARRIVES TOMORROW, AND I'LL BE TESTING IT FOR THE NEXT SIX MONTHS.
MAYBE I'LL SELL MY HOUSE.
©2013 Scott Adams, Inc./Dist. by Universal Uclick
4-14-13

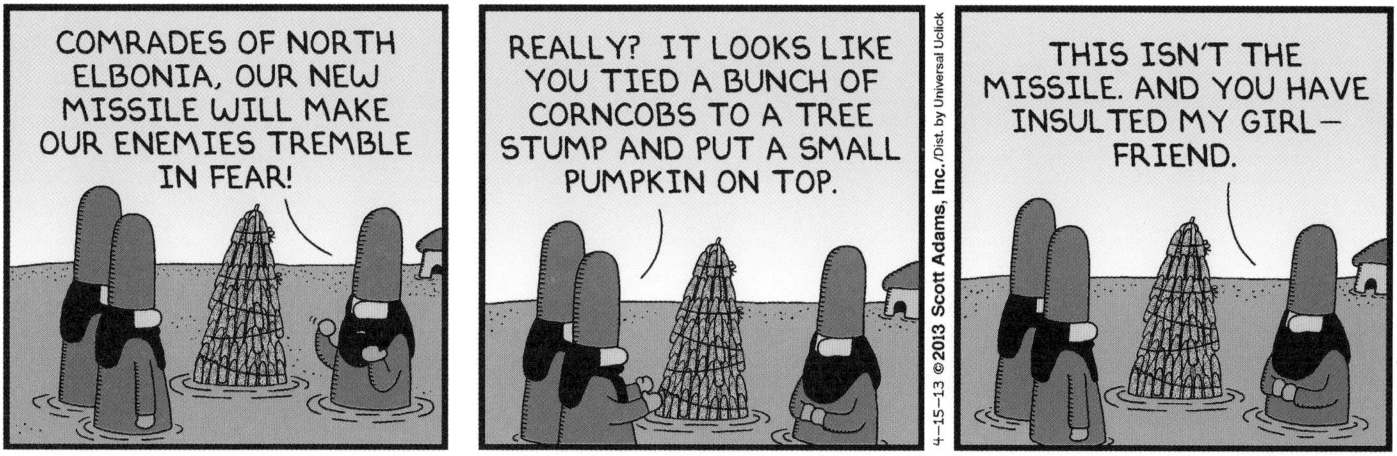
COMRADES OF NORTH ELBONIA, OUR NEW MISSILE WILL MAKE OUR ENEMIES TREMBLE IN FEAR!
REALLY? IT LOOKS LIKE YOU TIED A BUNCH OF CORNCOBS TO A TREE STUMP AND PUT A SMALL PUMPKIN ON TOP.
4–15–13 ©2013 Scott Adams, Inc./Dist. by Universal Uclick
THIS ISN'T THE MISSILE. AND YOU HAVE INSULTED MY GIRL-FRIEND.

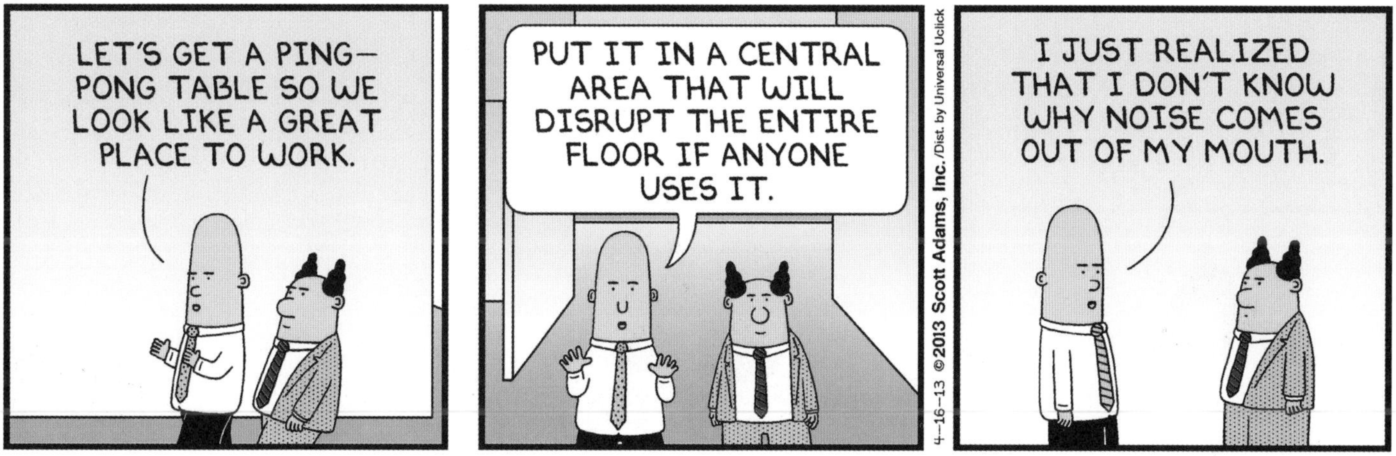
LET'S GET A PING-PONG TABLE SO WE LOOK LIKE A GREAT PLACE TO WORK.
PUT IT IN A CENTRAL AREA THAT WILL DISRUPT THE ENTIRE FLOOR IF ANYONE USES IT.
4–16–13 ©2013 Scott Adams, Inc./Dist. by Universal Uclick
I JUST REALIZED THAT I DON'T KNOW WHY NOISE COMES OUT OF MY MOUTH.

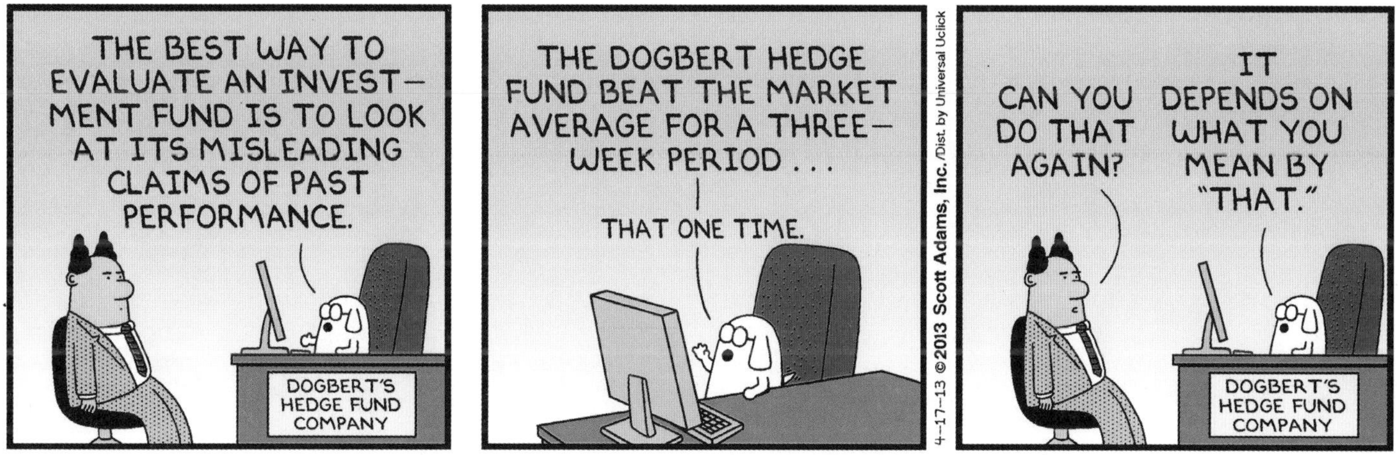
THE BEST WAY TO EVALUATE AN INVEST-MENT FUND IS TO LOOK AT ITS MISLEADING CLAIMS OF PAST PERFORMANCE.
DOGBERT'S HEDGE FUND COMPANY
THE DOGBERT HEDGE FUND BEAT THE MARKET AVERAGE FOR A THREE-WEEK PERIOD . . .
THAT ONE TIME.
4–17–13 ©2013 Scott Adams, Inc./Dist. by Universal Uclick
CAN YOU DO THAT AGAIN?
IT DEPENDS ON WHAT YOU MEAN BY "THAT."
DOGBERT'S HEDGE FUND COMPANY

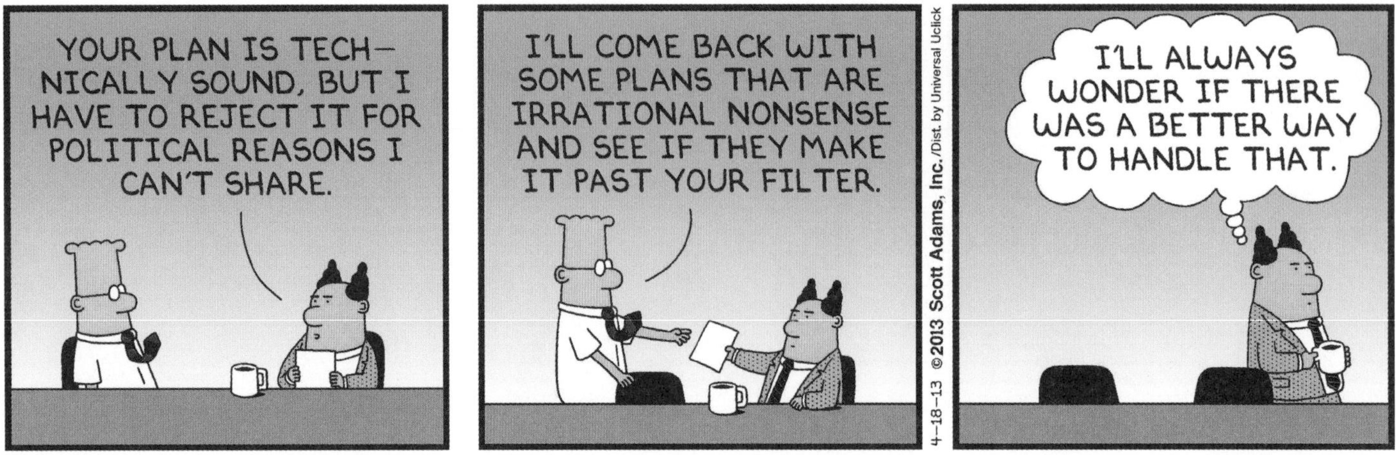
YOUR PLAN IS TECH–NICALLY SOUND, BUT I HAVE TO REJECT IT FOR POLITICAL REASONS I CAN'T SHARE.
I'LL COME BACK WITH SOME PLANS THAT ARE IRRATIONAL NONSENSE AND SEE IF THEY MAKE IT PAST YOUR FILTER.
4–18–13 ©2013 Scott Adams, Inc./Dist. by Universal Uclick
I'LL ALWAYS WONDER IF THERE WAS A BETTER WAY TO HANDLE THAT.

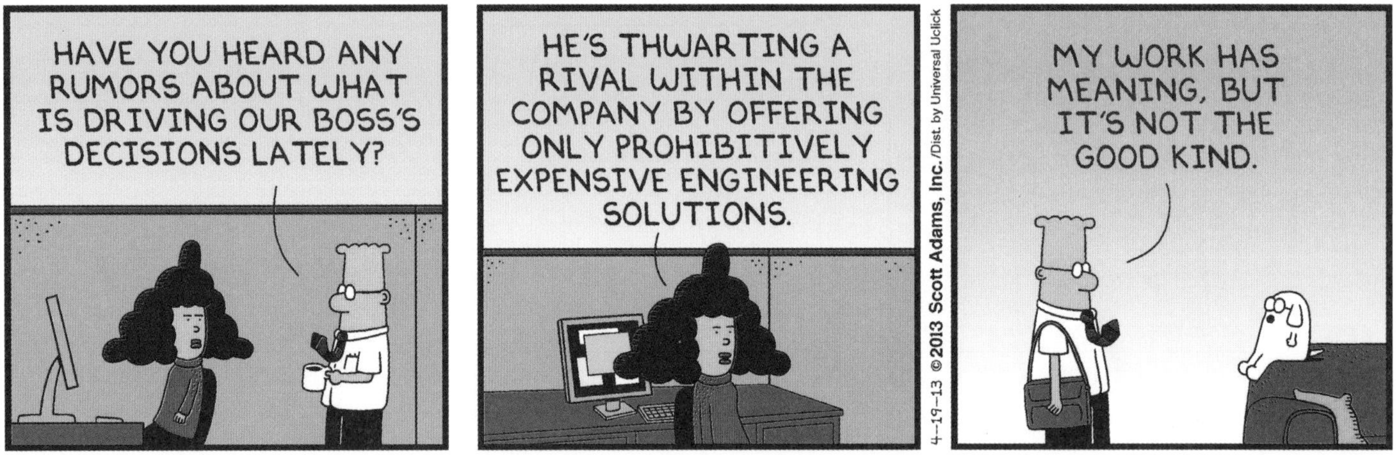
HAVE YOU HEARD ANY RUMORS ABOUT WHAT IS DRIVING OUR BOSS'S DECISIONS LATELY?
HE'S THWARTING A RIVAL WITHIN THE COMPANY BY OFFERING ONLY PROHIBITIVELY EXPENSIVE ENGINEERING SOLUTIONS.
4–19–13 ©2013 Scott Adams, Inc./Dist. by Universal Uclick
MY WORK HAS MEANING, BUT IT'S NOT THE GOOD KIND.

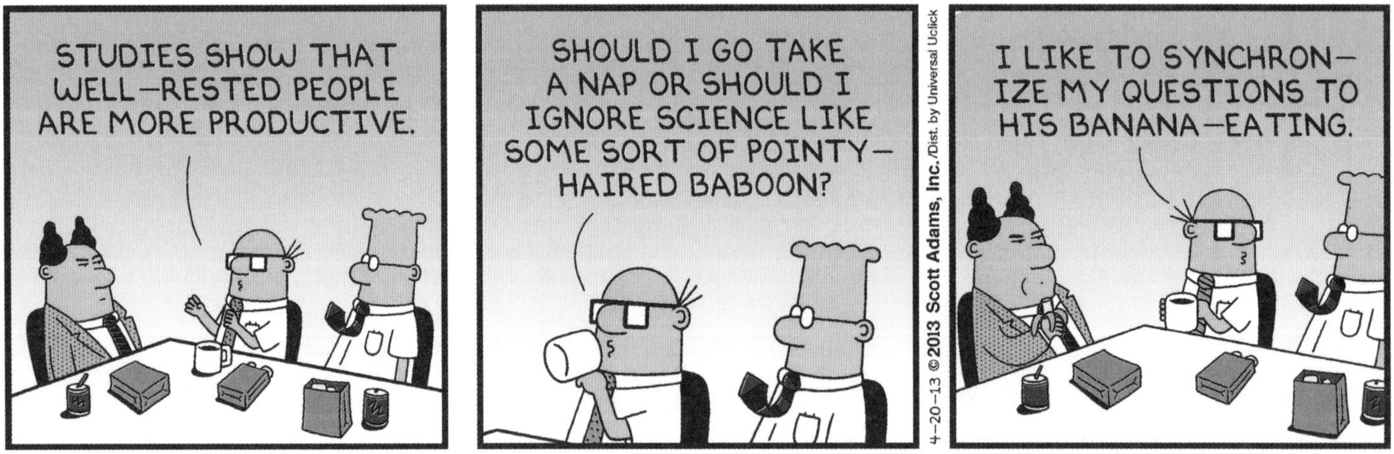
STUDIES SHOW THAT WELL–RESTED PEOPLE ARE MORE PRODUCTIVE.
SHOULD I GO TAKE A NAP OR SHOULD I IGNORE SCIENCE LIKE SOME SORT OF POINTY–HAIRED BABOON?
4–20–13 ©2013 Scott Adams, Inc./Dist. by Universal Uclick
I LIKE TO SYNCHRON–IZE MY QUESTIONS TO HIS BANANA–EATING.

WALLY, HOW CAN I LEARN TO TOLERATE MY CO—WORKERS?
IT IS TIME FOR YOU TO LEARN ABOUT TRUST, ASOK.
LET ME SHOW YOU.
TURN AROUND.
THIS IS CALLED THE "TRUST FALL." YOU FALL BACKWARD AND TRUST ME TO CATCH YOU. . . GO.
*!#%
WHY DIDN'T YOU CATCH ME?!!!
IT WOULDN'T BE TRUST IF IT WORKED EVERY TIME.
WHAT KIND OF LESSON IS THAT?
THIS IS HOW I TOLERATE MY CO—WORKERS.
© 2013 Scott Adams, Inc./Dist. by Universal Uclick
4-21-13

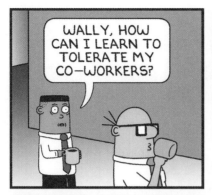

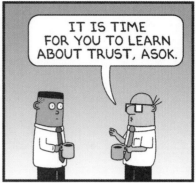

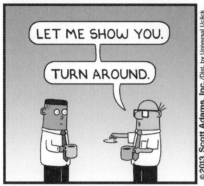

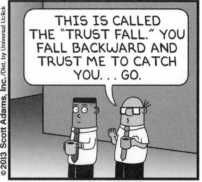

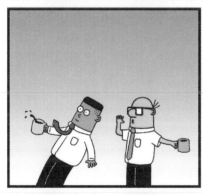

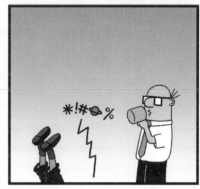

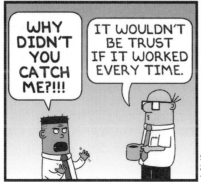

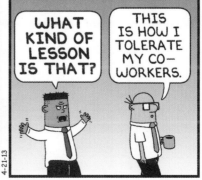

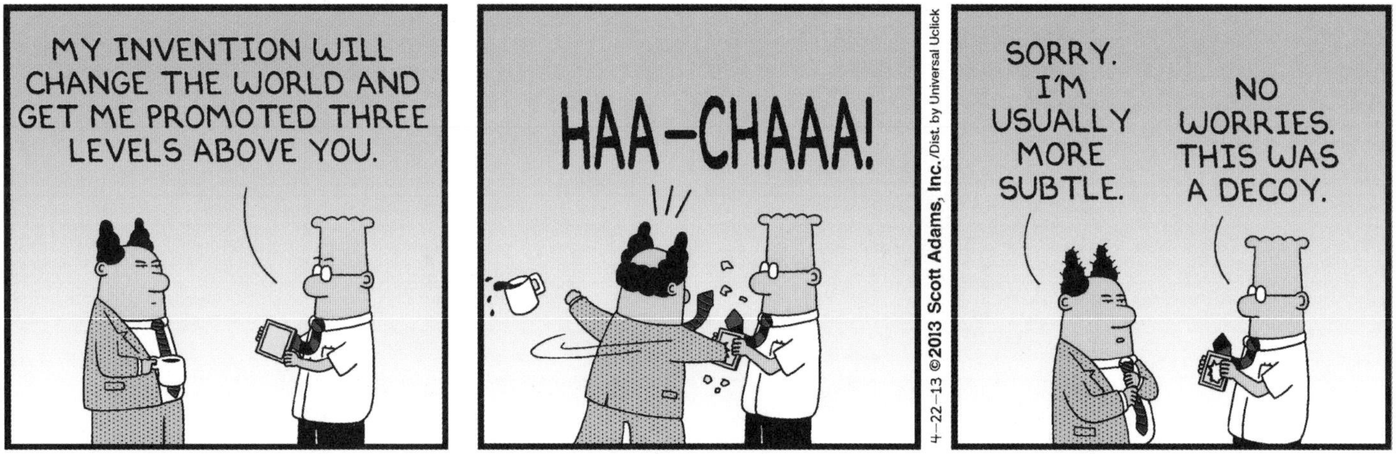
MY INVENTION WILL CHANGE THE WORLD AND GET ME PROMOTED THREE LEVELS ABOVE YOU.
HAA-CHAAA!
4-22-13 ©2013 Scott Adams, Inc./Dist. by Universal Uclick
SORRY. I'M USUALLY MORE SUBTLE.
NO WORRIES. THIS WAS A DECOY.

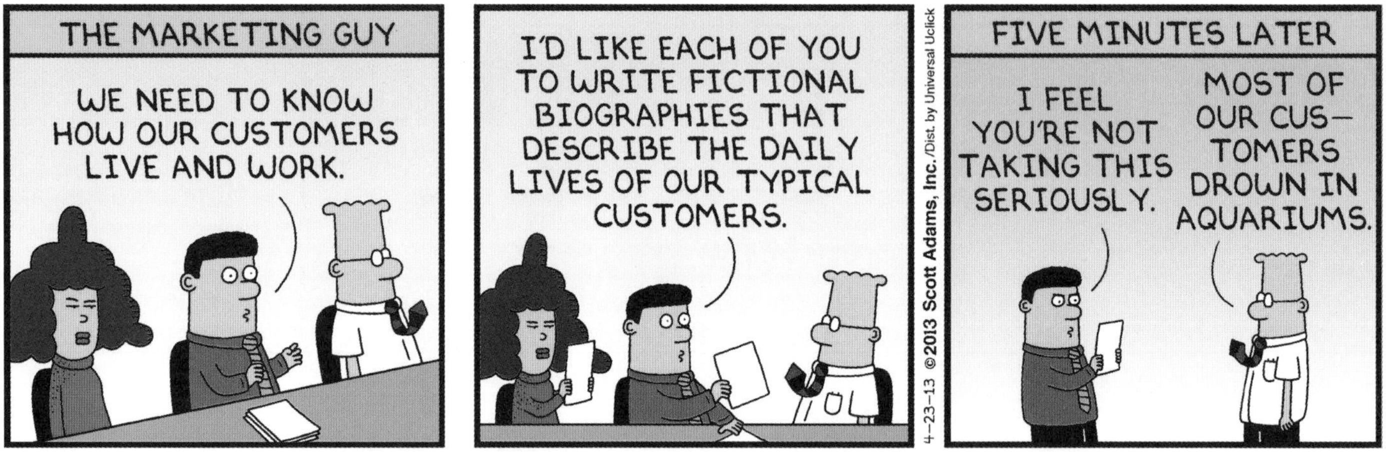
THE MARKETING GUY
WE NEED TO KNOW HOW OUR CUSTOMERS LIVE AND WORK.
I'D LIKE EACH OF YOU TO WRITE FICTIONAL BIOGRAPHIES THAT DESCRIBE THE DAILY LIVES OF OUR TYPICAL CUSTOMERS.
4-23-13 ©2013 Scott Adams, Inc./Dist. by Universal Uclick
FIVE MINUTES LATER
I FEEL YOU'RE NOT TAKING THIS SERIOUSLY.
MOST OF OUR CUS-TOMERS DROWN IN AQUARIUMS.

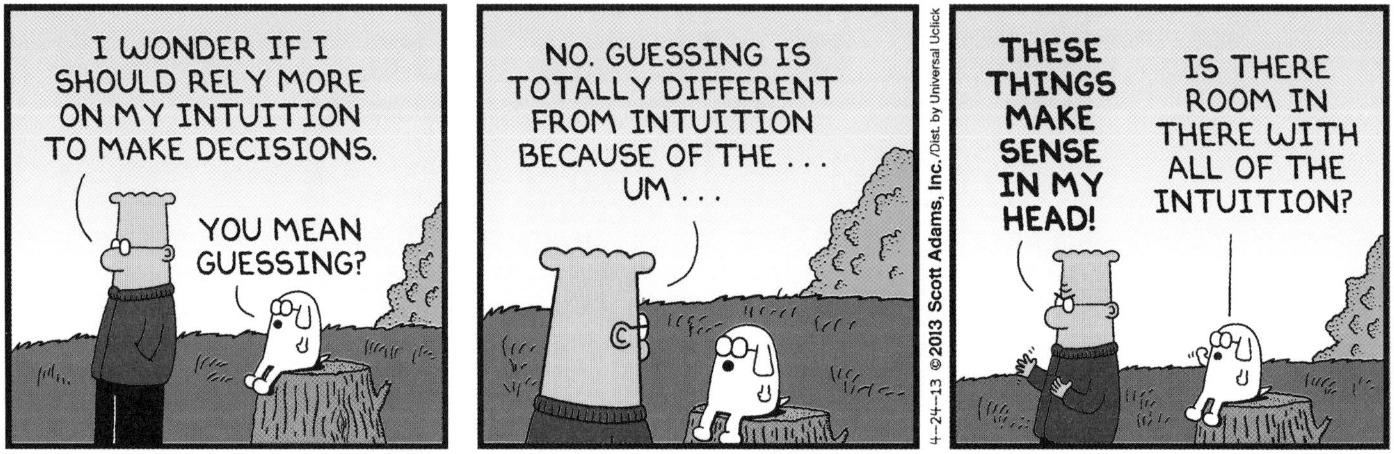
I WONDER IF I SHOULD RELY MORE ON MY INTUITION TO MAKE DECISIONS.
YOU MEAN GUESSING?
NO. GUESSING IS TOTALLY DIFFERENT FROM INTUITION BECAUSE OF THE . . . UM . . .
4-24-13 ©2013 Scott Adams, Inc./Dist. by Universal Uclick
THESE THINGS MAKE SENSE IN MY HEAD!
IS THERE ROOM IN THERE WITH ALL OF THE INTUITION?

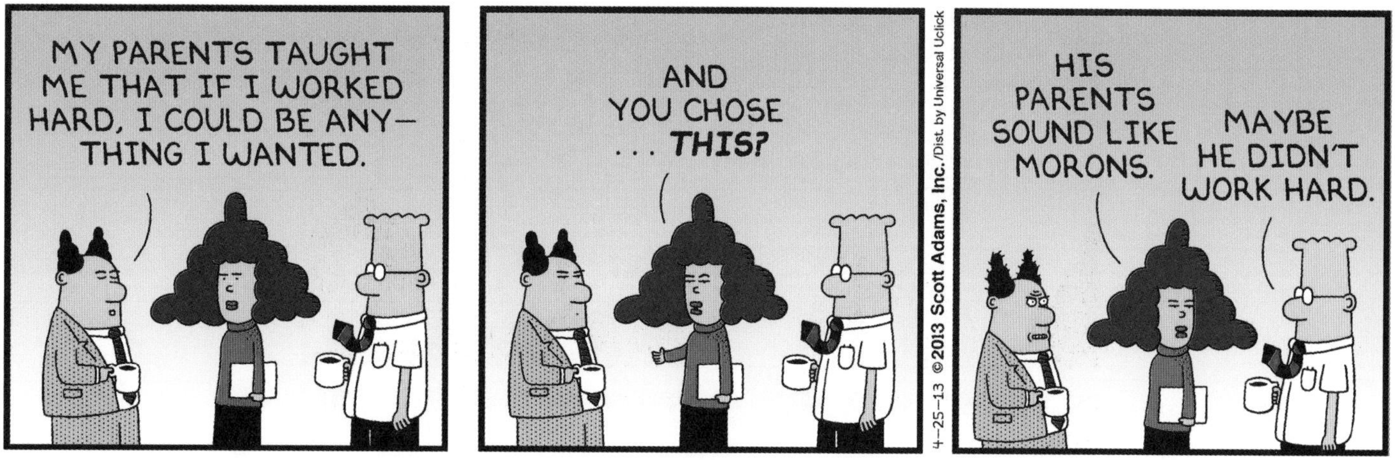
MY PARENTS TAUGHT ME THAT IF I WORKED HARD, I COULD BE ANY-THING I WANTED.
AND YOU CHOSE . . . *THIS?*
HIS PARENTS SOUND LIKE MORONS.
MAYBE HE DIDN'T WORK HARD.
4-25-13 ©2013 Scott Adams, Inc./Dist. by Universal Uclick

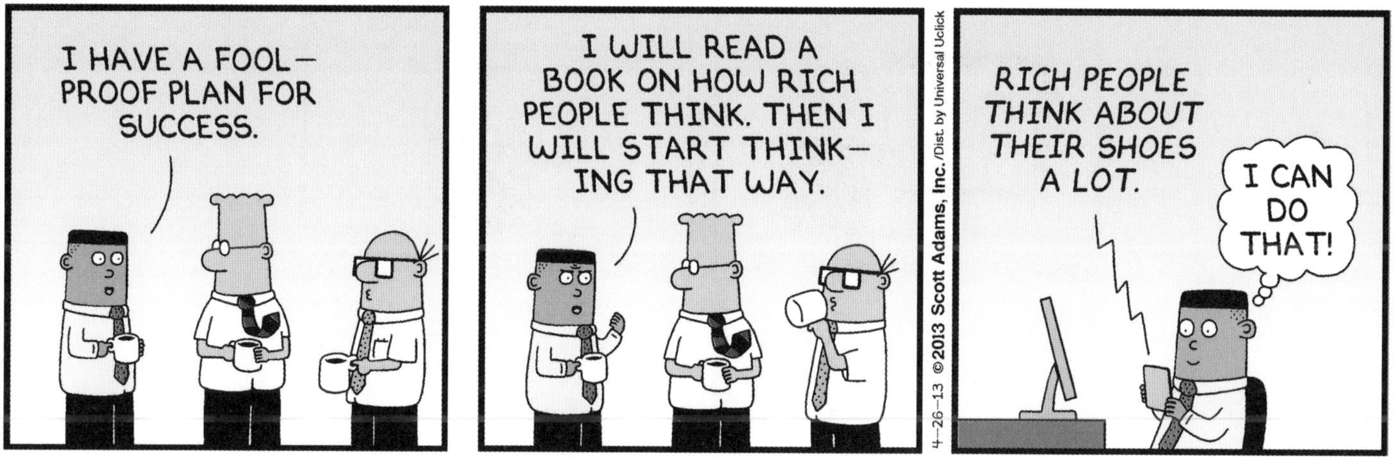
I HAVE A FOOL-PROOF PLAN FOR SUCCESS.
I WILL READ A BOOK ON HOW RICH PEOPLE THINK. THEN I WILL START THINK-ING THAT WAY.
RICH PEOPLE THINK ABOUT THEIR SHOES A LOT.
I CAN DO THAT!
4-26-13 ©2013 Scott Adams, Inc./Dist. by Universal Uclick

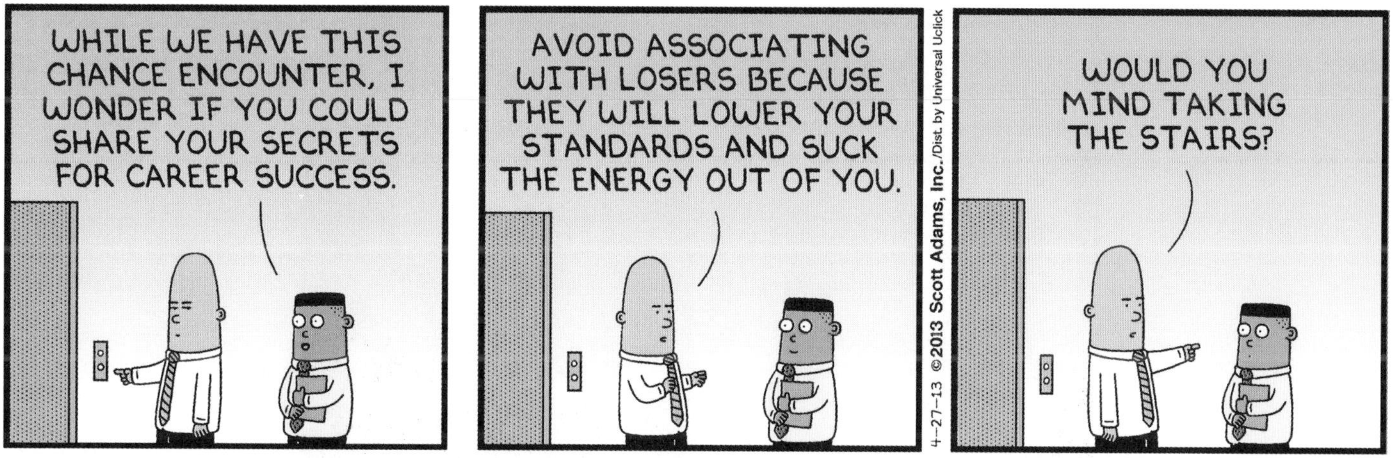
WHILE WE HAVE THIS CHANCE ENCOUNTER, I WONDER IF YOU COULD SHARE YOUR SECRETS FOR CAREER SUCCESS.
AVOID ASSOCIATING WITH LOSERS BECAUSE THEY WILL LOWER YOUR STANDARDS AND SUCK THE ENERGY OUT OF YOU.
WOULD YOU MIND TAKING THE STAIRS?
4-27-13 ©2013 Scott Adams, Inc./Dist. by Universal Uclick

YOUR BONUSES THIS YEAR WILL BE BASED ON THE USUAL FORMULA.
50% IS BASED ON PURE LUCK.
AND 50% IS BASED ON THE PERFORMANCE OF PEOPLE YOU HAVE NEVER EVEN MET.
SOME GUY
THIS YEAR, THE LUCK FACTOR WAS GOOD. OUR INDUSTRY EXPERIENCED HUGE CONSUMER DEMAND.
UNFORTUNATELY, PEOPLE WHO YOU HAVE NEVER MET DID A BAD JOB OF MARKETING AND SALES ARE TERRIBLE.
AND FOR THAT, YOU ENGINEERS MUST BE PUNISHED.
NO BONUSES FOR YOU.
LUCKILY FOR ME, MY BONUS IS BASED ON HOW WELL I CAN CONVINCE YOU IDIOTS TO WORK HARD WHILE GETTING NO BONUSES.
I DON'T LIKE TO BRAG, BUT I'M FAIRLY SURE I'M NAILING IT.
©2013 Scott Adams, Inc./Dist. by Universal Uclick
4-28-13

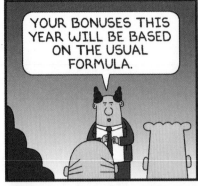

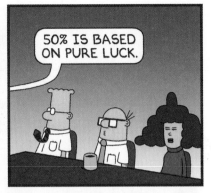

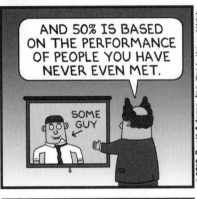

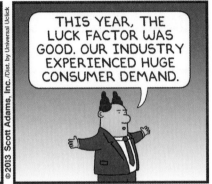

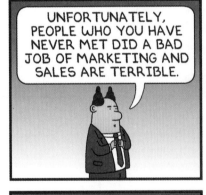

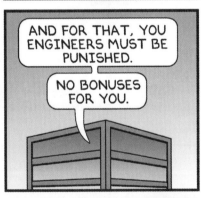

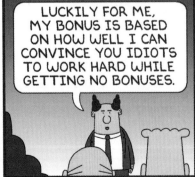

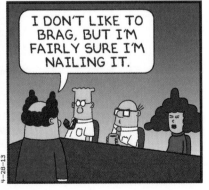

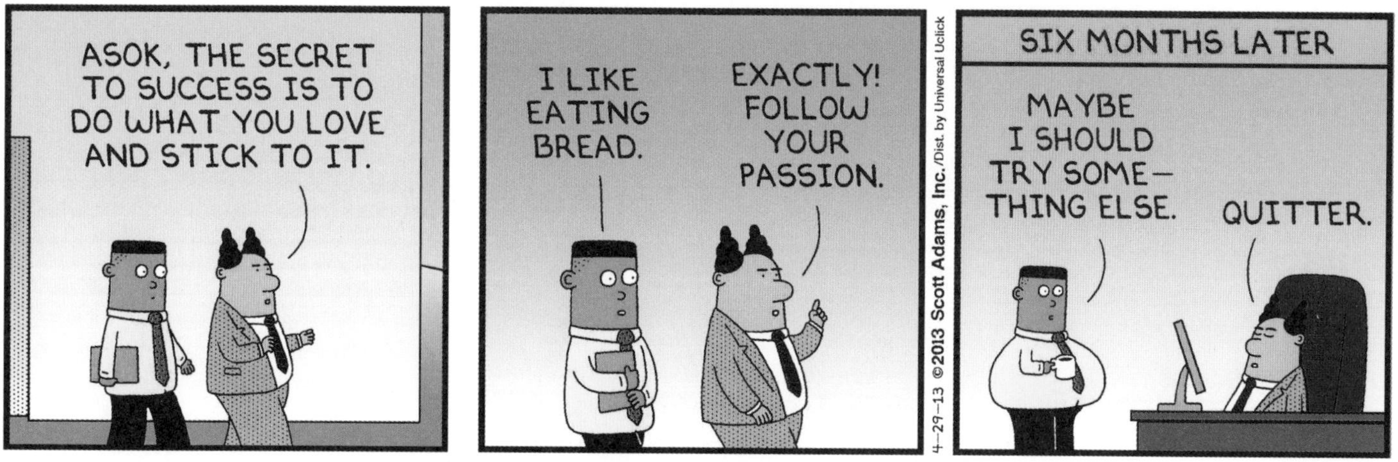
ASOK, THE SECRET TO SUCCESS IS TO DO WHAT YOU LOVE AND STICK TO IT.
I LIKE EATING BREAD.
EXACTLY! FOLLOW YOUR PASSION.
4-29-13 ©2013 Scott Adams, Inc./Dist. by Universal Uclick
SIX MONTHS LATER
MAYBE I SHOULD TRY SOME-THING ELSE.
QUITTER.

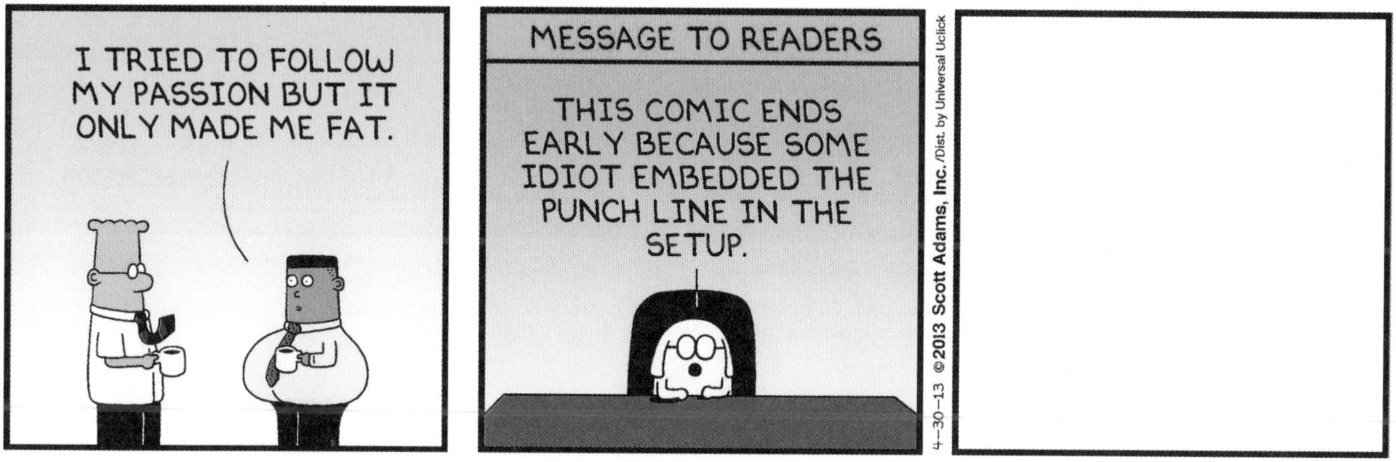
I TRIED TO FOLLOW MY PASSION BUT IT ONLY MADE ME FAT.
MESSAGE TO READERS
THIS COMIC ENDS EARLY BECAUSE SOME IDIOT EMBEDDED THE PUNCH LINE IN THE SETUP.
4-30-13 ©2013 Scott Adams, Inc./Dist. by Universal Uclick

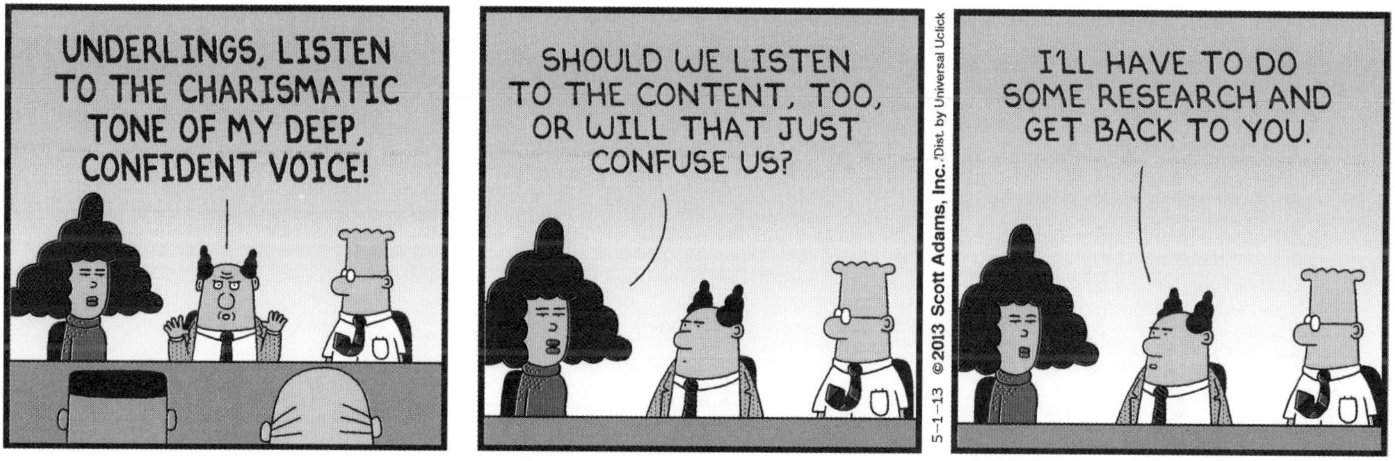
UNDERLINGS, LISTEN TO THE CHARISMATIC TONE OF MY DEEP, CONFIDENT VOICE!
SHOULD WE LISTEN TO THE CONTENT, TOO, OR WILL THAT JUST CONFUSE US?
5-1-13 ©2013 Scott Adams, Inc./Dist. by Universal Uclick
I'LL HAVE TO DO SOME RESEARCH AND GET BACK TO YOU.

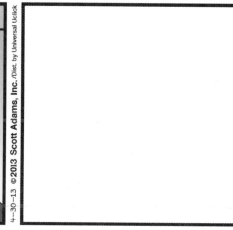

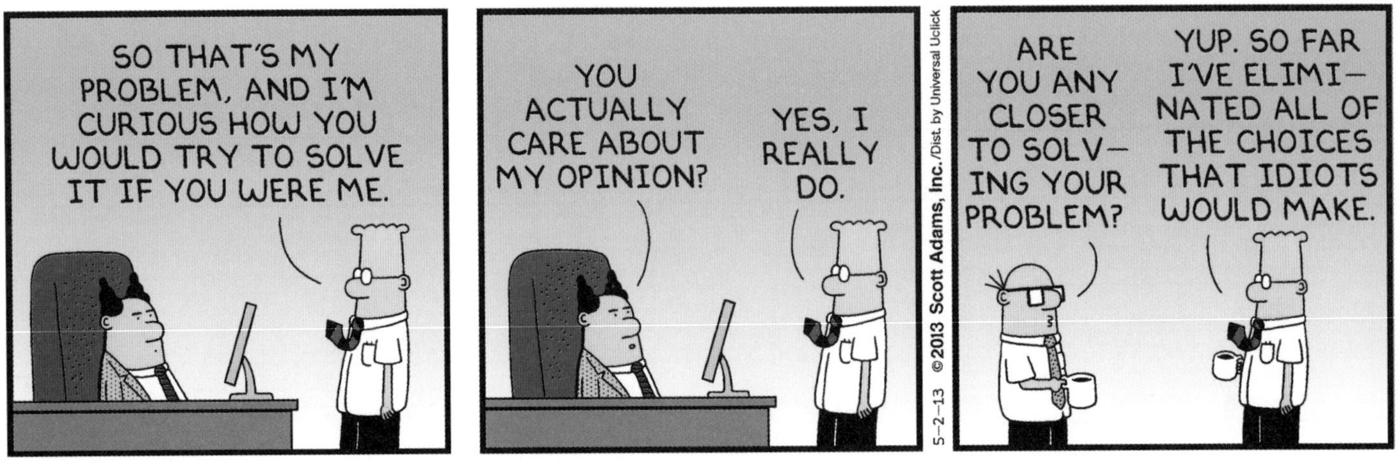
SO THAT'S MY PROBLEM, AND I'M CURIOUS HOW YOU WOULD TRY TO SOLVE IT IF YOU WERE ME.
YOU ACTUALLY CARE ABOUT MY OPINION?
YES, I REALLY DO.
5-2-13 ©2013 Scott Adams, Inc./Dist. by Universal Uclick
ARE YOU ANY CLOSER TO SOLV-ING YOUR PROBLEM?
YUP. SO FAR I'VE ELIMI-NATED ALL OF THE CHOICES THAT IDIOTS WOULD MAKE.

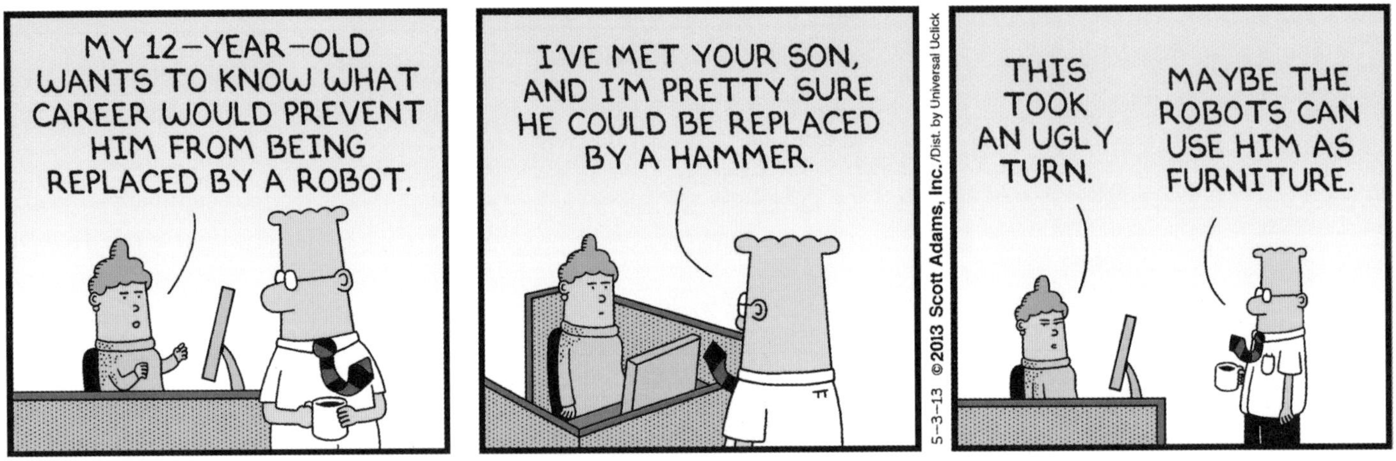
MY 12-YEAR-OLD WANTS TO KNOW WHAT CAREER WOULD PREVENT HIM FROM BEING REPLACED BY A ROBOT.
I'VE MET YOUR SON, AND I'M PRETTY SURE HE COULD BE REPLACED BY A HAMMER.
5-3-13 ©2013 Scott Adams, Inc./Dist. by Universal Uclick
THIS TOOK AN UGLY TURN.
MAYBE THE ROBOTS CAN USE HIM AS FURNITURE.

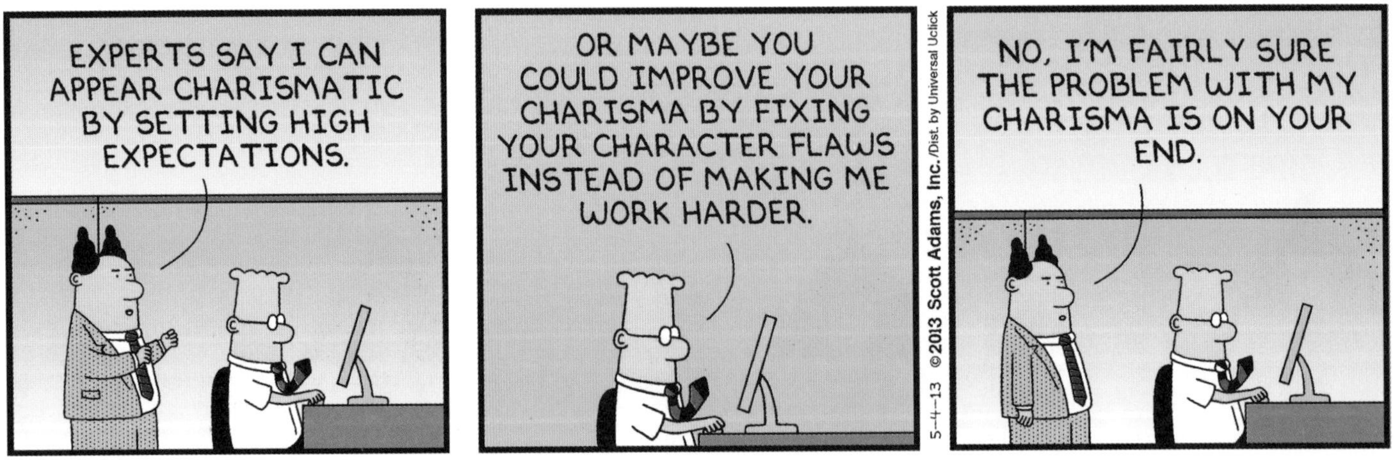
EXPERTS SAY I CAN APPEAR CHARISMATIC BY SETTING HIGH EXPECTATIONS.
OR MAYBE YOU COULD IMPROVE YOUR CHARISMA BY FIXING YOUR CHARACTER FLAWS INSTEAD OF MAKING ME WORK HARDER.
5-4-13 ©2013 Scott Adams, Inc./Dist. by Universal Uclick
NO, I'M FAIRLY SURE THE PROBLEM WITH MY CHARISMA IS ON YOUR END.

IT'S YOUR SURGEON.
HE SAYS HE MIGHT HAVE LEFT SOME-THING INSIDE YOU.
WHAT??! A SPONGE? A SCALPEL?
NO . . . HIS WATCH.
AND . . . HIS CAR KEYS . . . AND WALLET.
HE SAYS HE USED YOUR TORSO TO STORE HIS VALUABLES WHILE HE WENT FOR A RUN.
MEOW!
I'LL ASK ABOUT THAT.
© 2013 Scott Adams, Inc./Dist. by Universal Uclick
5-5-13

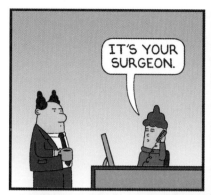

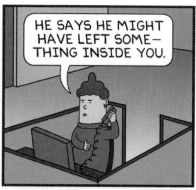

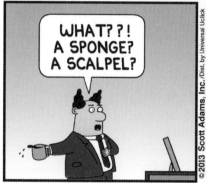

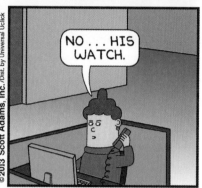

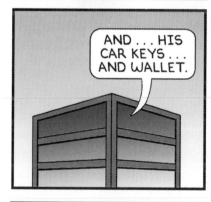

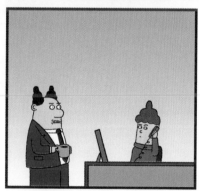

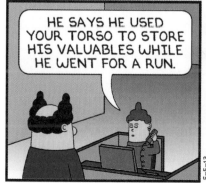

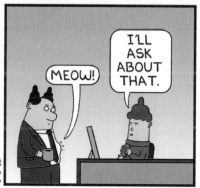

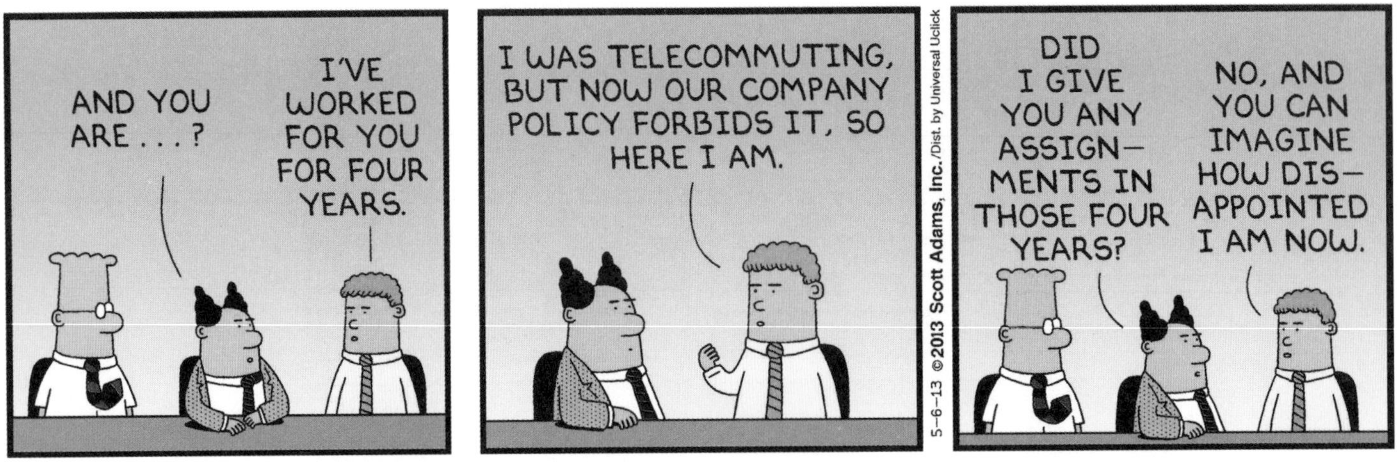
AND YOU ARE . . . ?
I'VE WORKED FOR YOU FOR FOUR YEARS.
I WAS TELECOMMUTING, BUT NOW OUR COMPANY POLICY FORBIDS IT, SO HERE I AM.
5-6-13 ©2013 Scott Adams, Inc./Dist. by Universal Uclick
DID I GIVE YOU ANY ASSIGN-MENTS IN THOSE FOUR YEARS?
NO, AND YOU CAN IMAGINE HOW DIS-APPOINTED I AM NOW.

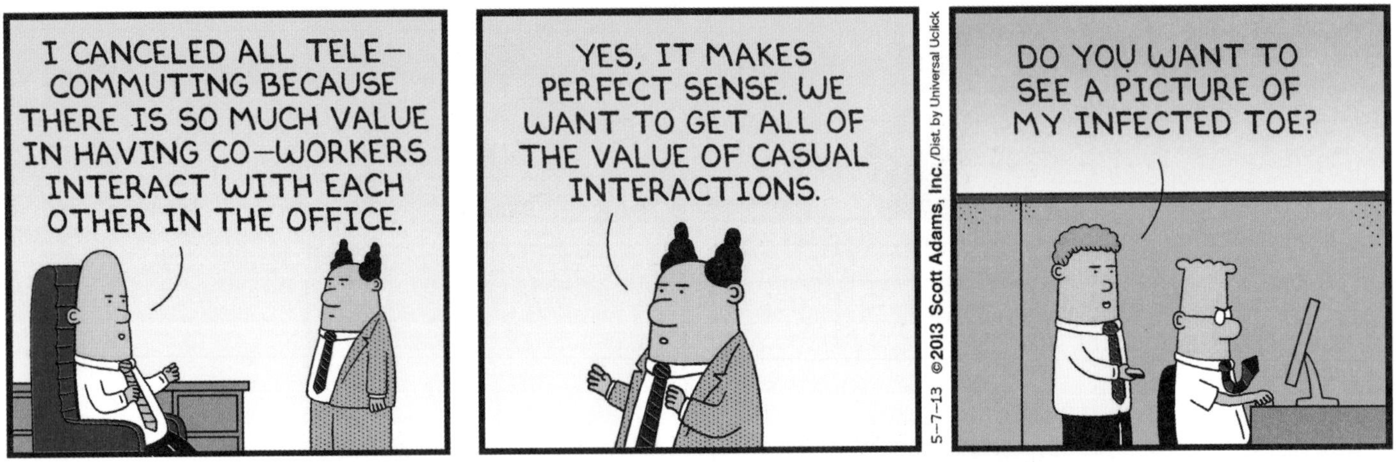
I CANCELED ALL TELE-COMMUTING BECAUSE THERE IS SO MUCH VALUE IN HAVING CO-WORKERS INTERACT WITH EACH OTHER IN THE OFFICE.
YES, IT MAKES PERFECT SENSE. WE WANT TO GET ALL OF THE VALUE OF CASUAL INTERACTIONS.
5-7-13 ©2013 Scott Adams, Inc./Dist. by Universal Uclick
DO YOU WANT TO SEE A PICTURE OF MY INFECTED TOE?

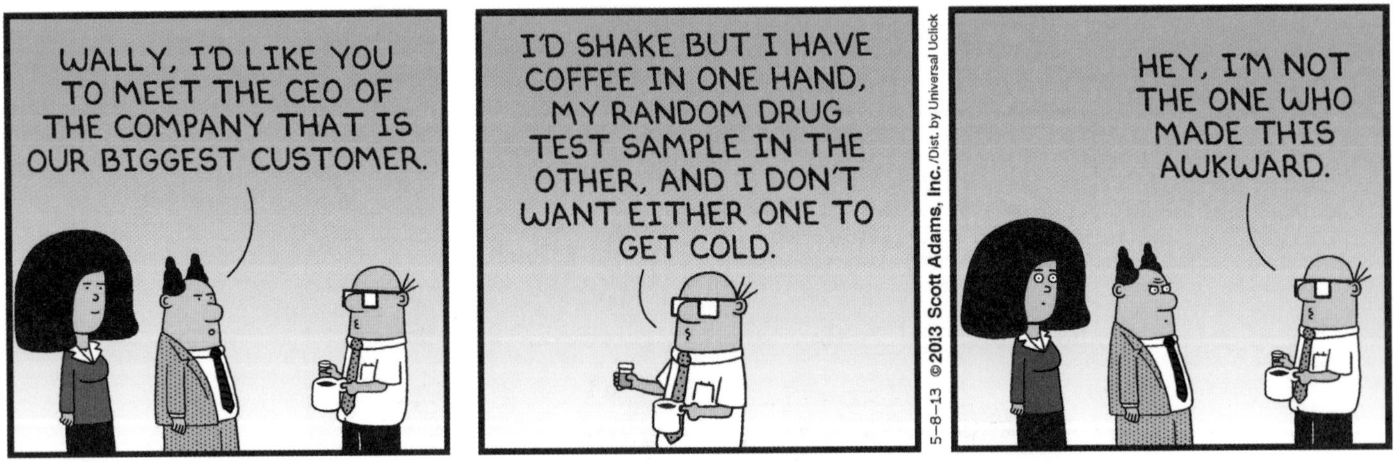
WALLY, I'D LIKE YOU TO MEET THE CEO OF THE COMPANY THAT IS OUR BIGGEST CUSTOMER.
I'D SHAKE BUT I HAVE COFFEE IN ONE HAND, MY RANDOM DRUG TEST SAMPLE IN THE OTHER, AND I DON'T WANT EITHER ONE TO GET COLD.
5-8-13 ©2013 Scott Adams, Inc./Dist. by Universal Uclick
HEY, I'M NOT THE ONE WHO MADE THIS AWKWARD.

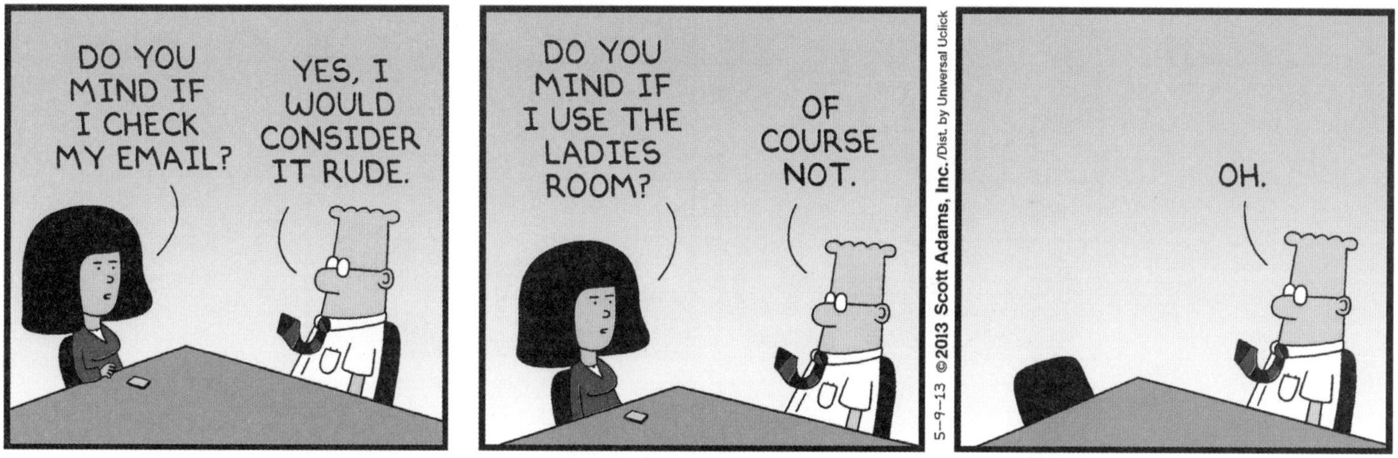
DO YOU MIND IF I CHECK MY EMAIL?
YES, I WOULD CONSIDER IT RUDE.
DO YOU MIND IF I USE THE LADIES ROOM?
OF COURSE NOT.
OH.
5-9-13 ©2013 Scott Adams, Inc./Dist. by Universal Uclick

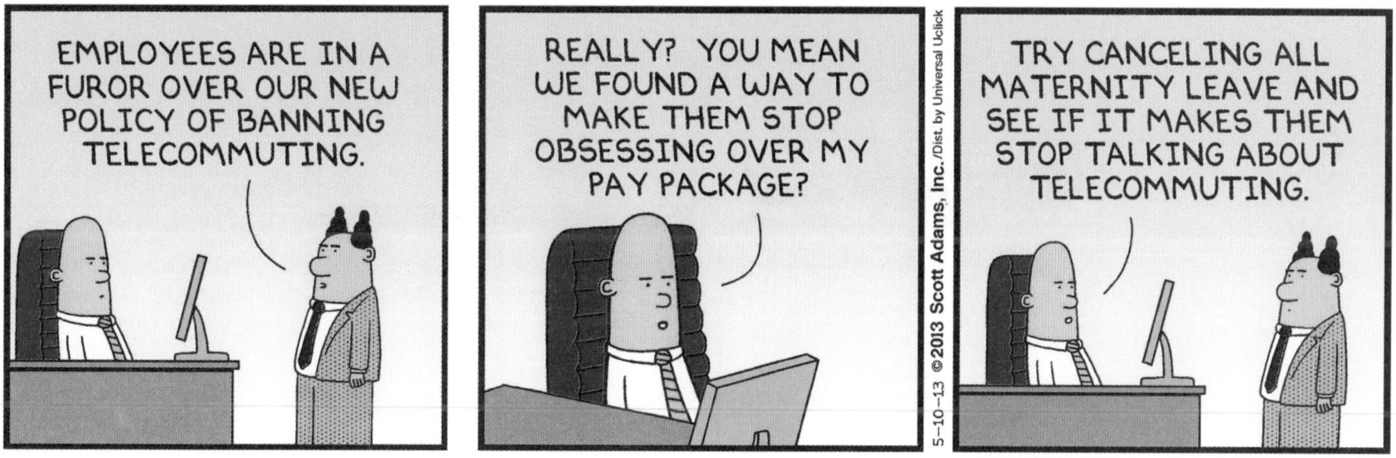
EMPLOYEES ARE IN A FUROR OVER OUR NEW POLICY OF BANNING TELECOMMUTING.
REALLY? YOU MEAN WE FOUND A WAY TO MAKE THEM STOP OBSESSING OVER MY PAY PACKAGE?
TRY CANCELING ALL MATERNITY LEAVE AND SEE IF IT MAKES THEM STOP TALKING ABOUT TELECOMMUTING.
5-10-13 ©2013 Scott Adams, Inc./Dist. by Universal Uclick

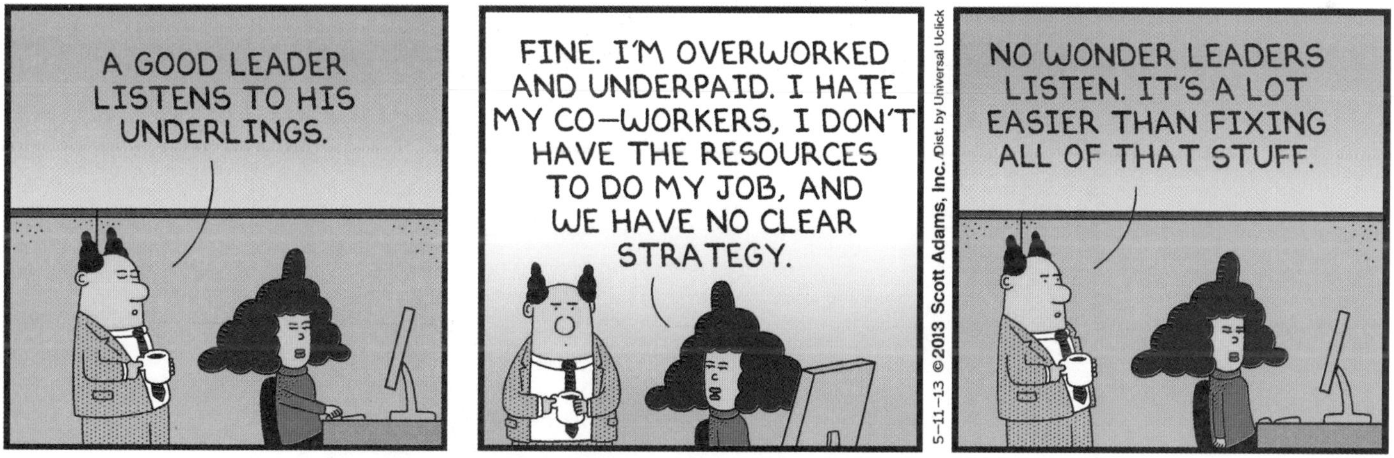
A GOOD LEADER LISTENS TO HIS UNDERLINGS.
FINE. I'M OVERWORKED AND UNDERPAID. I HATE MY CO-WORKERS, I DON'T HAVE THE RESOURCES TO DO MY JOB, AND WE HAVE NO CLEAR STRATEGY.
NO WONDER LEADERS LISTEN. IT'S A LOT EASIER THAN FIXING ALL OF THAT STUFF.
5-11-13 ©2013 Scott Adams, Inc./Dist. by Universal Uclick

I'M LOOKING FOR AN EMPLOYEE WHO IS CREATIVE.
THAT'S ME. I HAVE ADHD AND DYSLEXIA. I'M ALSO BIPOLAR AND SCHIZOPHRENIC.
CHECKING THE INTERNET. . .
©2013 Scott Adams, Inc./Dist. by Universal Uclick
WELL. . . THAT'S SURPRISING.
EACH OF HIS CONDITIONS IS HIGHLY CORRELATED WITH CREATIVITY.
ARE YOU A NORMAL?
I. . . THINK SO.
WOW. I FEEL SORRY FOR YOU. IT MUST BE HARD GOING THROUGH LIFE WITHOUT ANY CREATIVITY.
5-12-13
WHAT'S HAPPENING HERE?
IT MIGHT BE SOME SORT OF CREATIVE THING.

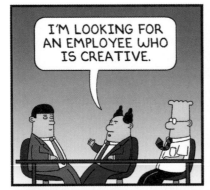

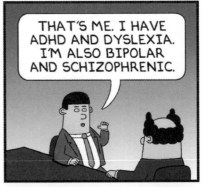

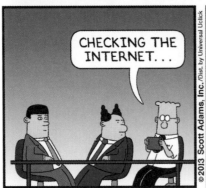

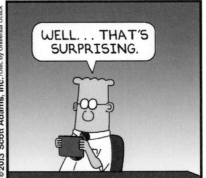

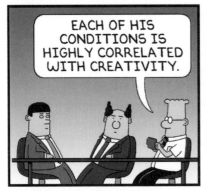

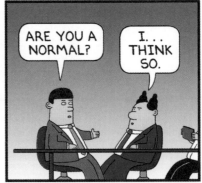

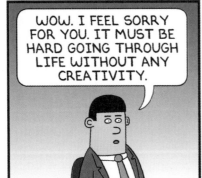

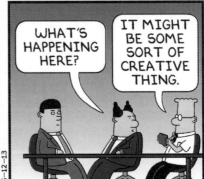

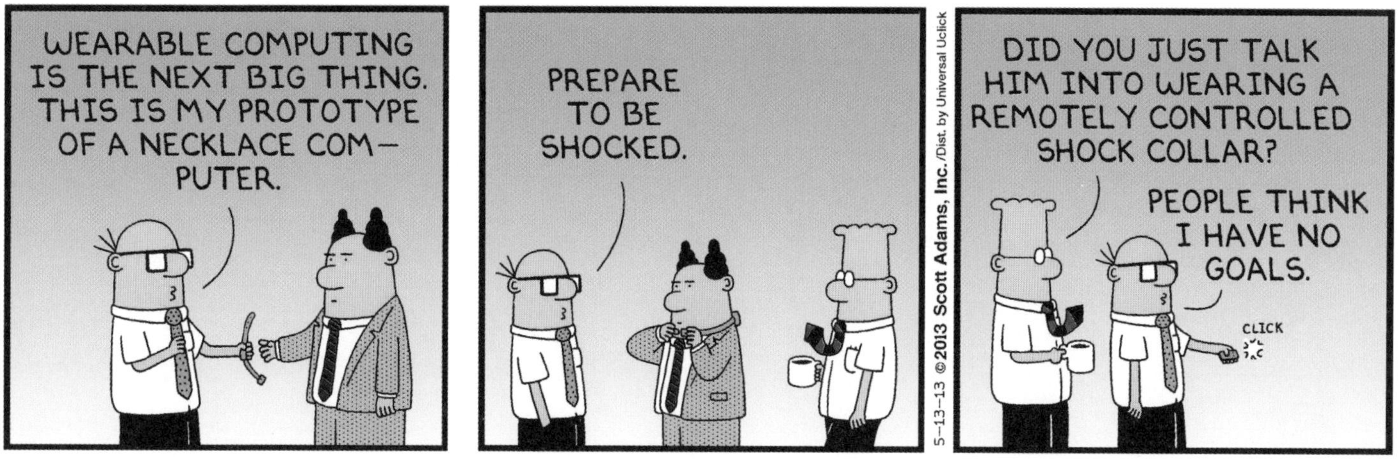
WEARABLE COMPUTING IS THE NEXT BIG THING. THIS IS MY PROTOTYPE OF A NECKLACE COM- PUTER.
PREPARE TO BE SHOCKED.
5-13-13 ©2013 Scott Adams, Inc./Dist. by Universal Uclick
DID YOU JUST TALK HIM INTO WEARING A REMOTELY CONTROLLED SHOCK COLLAR?
PEOPLE THINK I HAVE NO GOALS.
CLICK

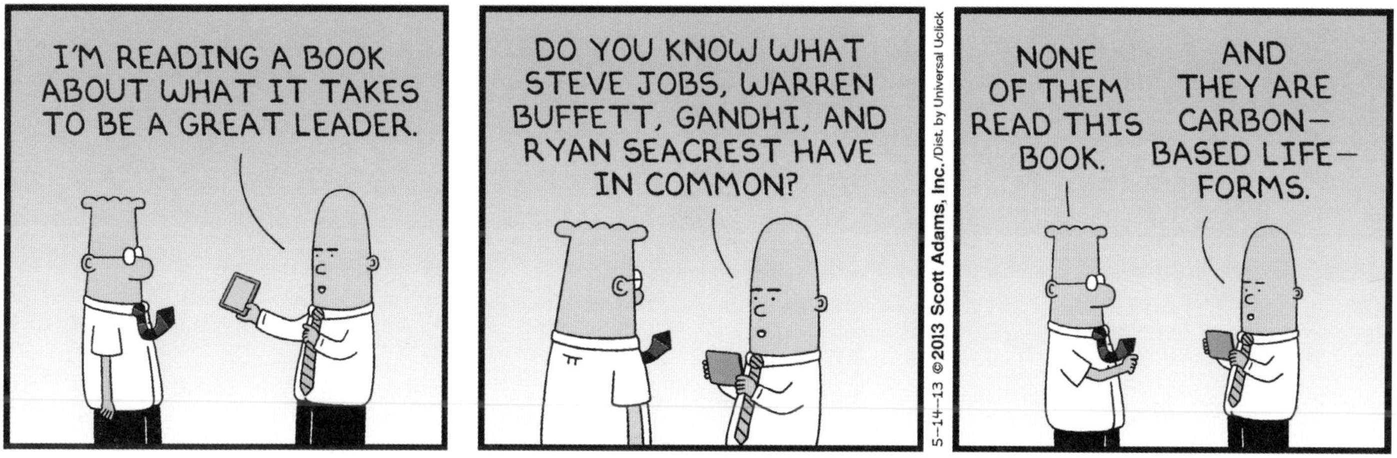
I'M READING A BOOK ABOUT WHAT IT TAKES TO BE A GREAT LEADER.
DO YOU KNOW WHAT STEVE JOBS, WARREN BUFFETT, GANDHI, AND RYAN SEACREST HAVE IN COMMON?
5-14-13 ©2013 Scott Adams, Inc./Dist. by Universal Uclick
NONE OF THEM READ THIS BOOK.
AND THEY ARE CARBON-BASED LIFE-FORMS.

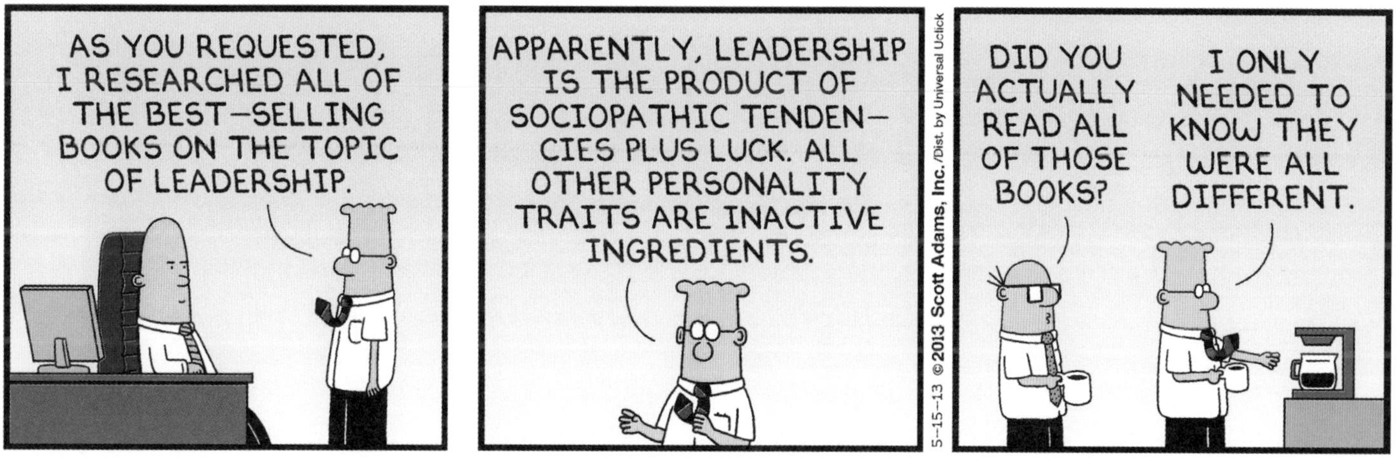
AS YOU REQUESTED, I RESEARCHED ALL OF THE BEST-SELLING BOOKS ON THE TOPIC OF LEADERSHIP.
APPARENTLY, LEADERSHIP IS THE PRODUCT OF SOCIOPATHIC TENDEN- CIES PLUS LUCK. ALL OTHER PERSONALITY TRAITS ARE INACTIVE INGREDIENTS.
5-15-13 ©2013 Scott Adams, Inc./Dist. by Universal Uclick
DID YOU ACTUALLY READ ALL OF THOSE BOOKS?
I ONLY NEEDED TO KNOW THEY WERE ALL DIFFERENT.

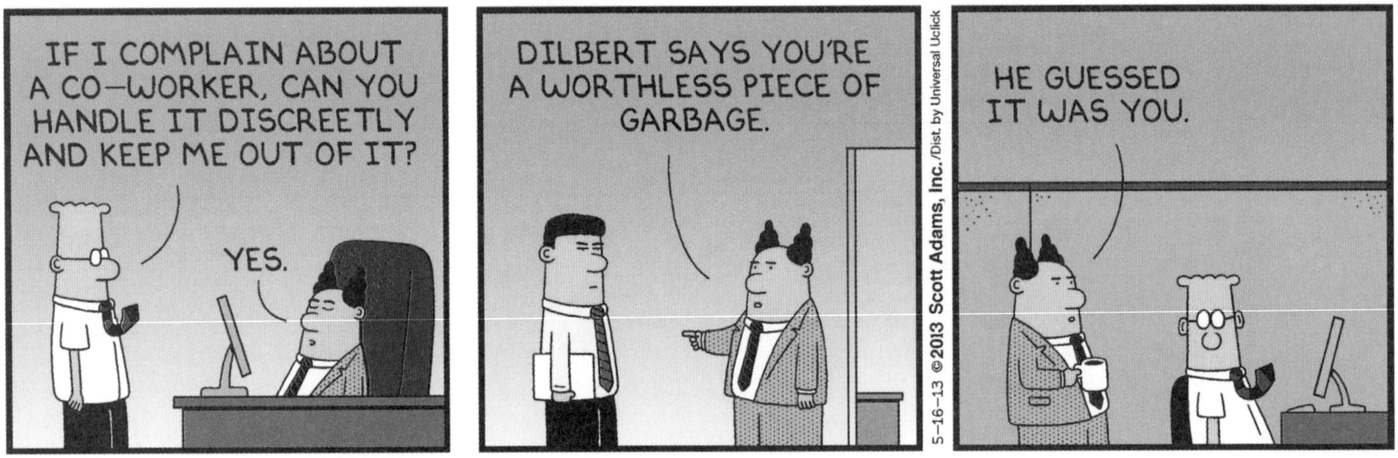
IF I COMPLAIN ABOUT A CO–WORKER, CAN YOU HANDLE IT DISCREETLY AND KEEP ME OUT OF IT?
YES.
DILBERT SAYS YOU'RE A WORTHLESS PIECE OF GARBAGE.
5–16–13 ©2013 Scott Adams, Inc./Dist. by Universal Uclick
HE GUESSED IT WAS YOU.

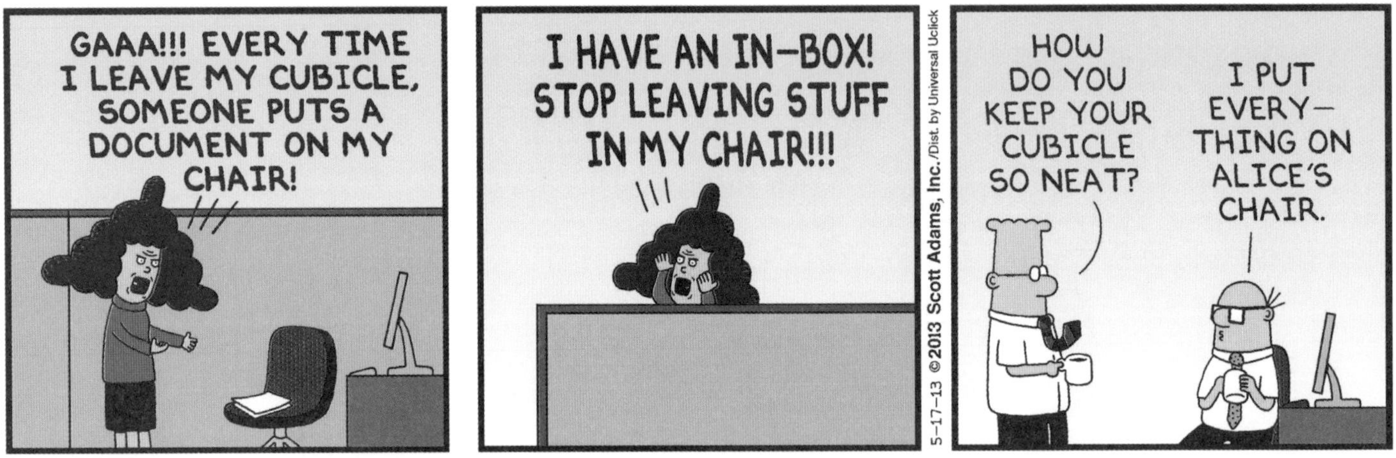
GAAA!!! EVERY TIME I LEAVE MY CUBICLE, SOMEONE PUTS A DOCUMENT ON MY CHAIR!
I HAVE AN IN–BOX! STOP LEAVING STUFF IN MY CHAIR!!!
5–17–13 ©2013 Scott Adams, Inc./Dist. by Universal Uclick
HOW DO YOU KEEP YOUR CUBICLE SO NEAT?
I PUT EVERY– THING ON ALICE'S CHAIR.

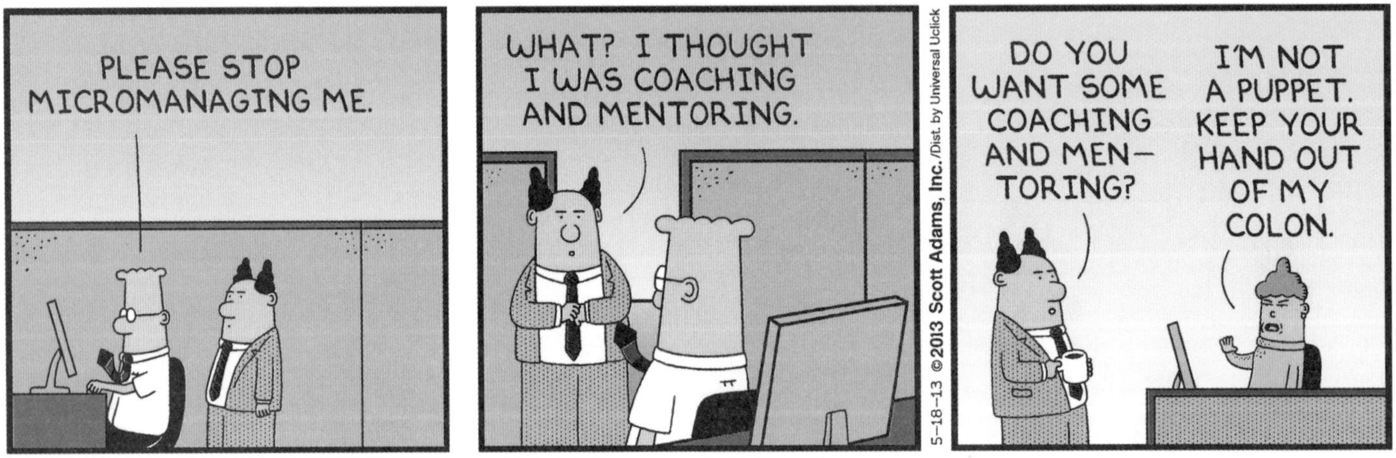
PLEASE STOP MICROMANAGING ME.
WHAT? I THOUGHT I WAS COACHING AND MENTORING.
5–18–13 ©2013 Scott Adams, Inc./Dist. by Universal Uclick
DO YOU WANT SOME COACHING AND MEN– TORING?
I'M NOT A PUPPET. KEEP YOUR HAND OUT OF MY COLON.

WE'RE REPLACING OUR OUTDATED SYSTEM OF ANNUAL PERFORMANCE REVIEWS.
THE NEW SYSTEM IS CALLED GAMIFICATION. IT'S A HOT NEW TREND.
EMPLOYEES CAN WIN BADGES, RIBBONS, AND AWARDS FOR COMPLETING TASKS.
CAN WE OPT FOR THE CASH VALUE OF THOSE BADGES, RIBBONS, AND AWARDS?
THEY DON'T HAVE ANY CASH VALUE.
OH. LIKE GARBAGE?
NO, NOT LIKE GARBAGE!
EXCEPT IN THE NARROW SENSE OF HAVING NO FUNC– TIONAL, ECONOMIC, OR EMOTIONAL VALUE.
GARBAGE IS SOME– THING YOU THROW AWAY.
HAND ME AN AWARD AND WATCH CAREFULLY.
©2013 Scott Adams, Inc./Dist. by Universal Uclick
5–19–13

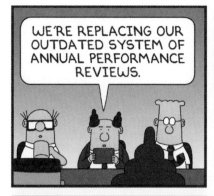

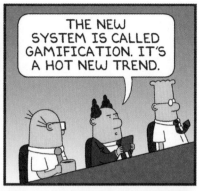

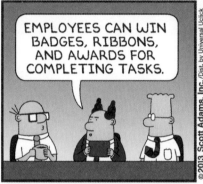

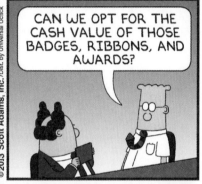

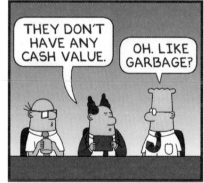

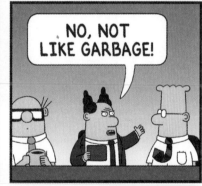

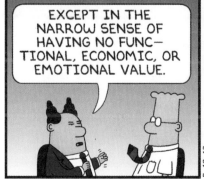

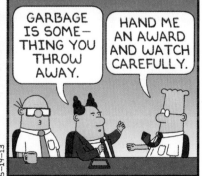

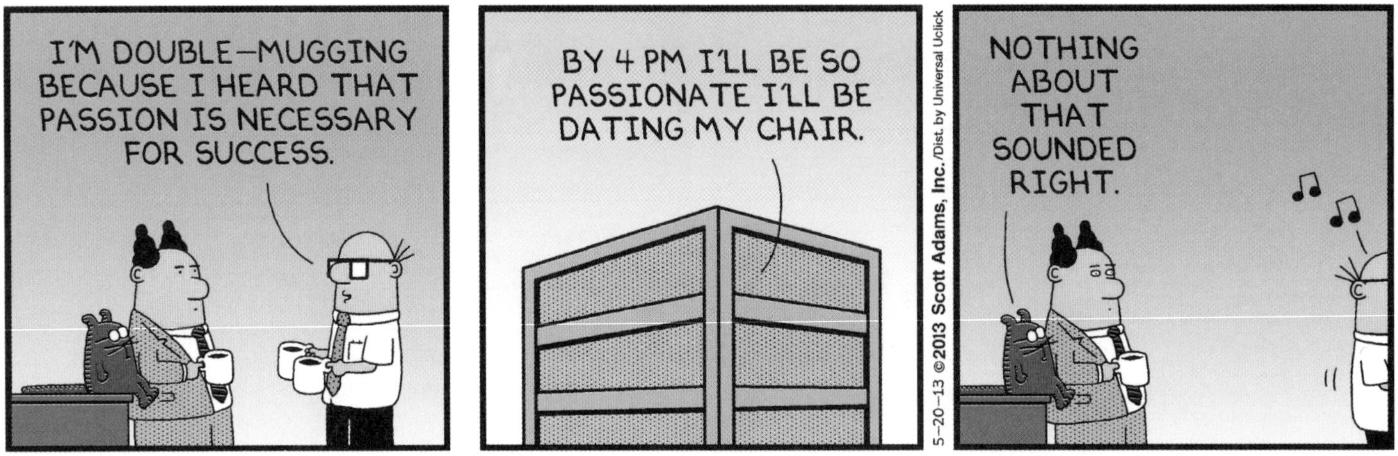
I'M DOUBLE—MUGGING BECAUSE I HEARD THAT PASSION IS NECESSARY FOR SUCCESS.
BY 4 PM I'LL BE SO PASSIONATE I'LL BE DATING MY CHAIR.
5–20–13 ©2013 Scott Adams, Inc./Dist. by Universal Uclick
NOTHING ABOUT THAT SOUNDED RIGHT.

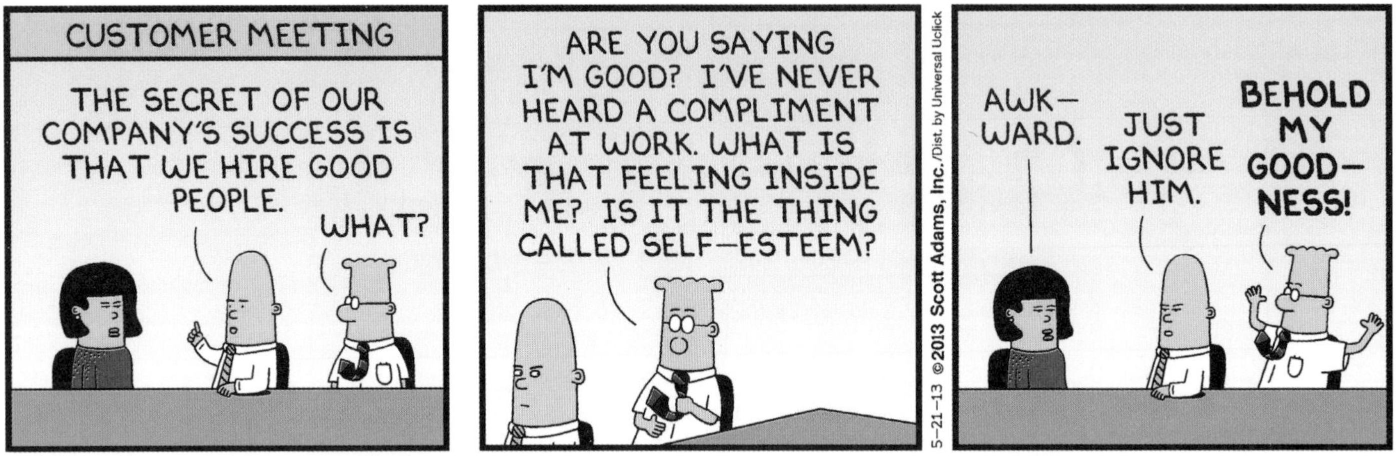
CUSTOMER MEETING
THE SECRET OF OUR COMPANY'S SUCCESS IS THAT WE HIRE GOOD PEOPLE.
WHAT?
ARE YOU SAYING I'M GOOD? I'VE NEVER HEARD A COMPLIMENT AT WORK. WHAT IS THAT FEELING INSIDE ME? IS IT THE THING CALLED SELF—ESTEEM?
5–21–13 ©2013 Scott Adams, Inc./Dist. by Universal Uclick
AWK— WARD.
JUST IGNORE HIM.
BEHOLD MY GOOD— NESS!

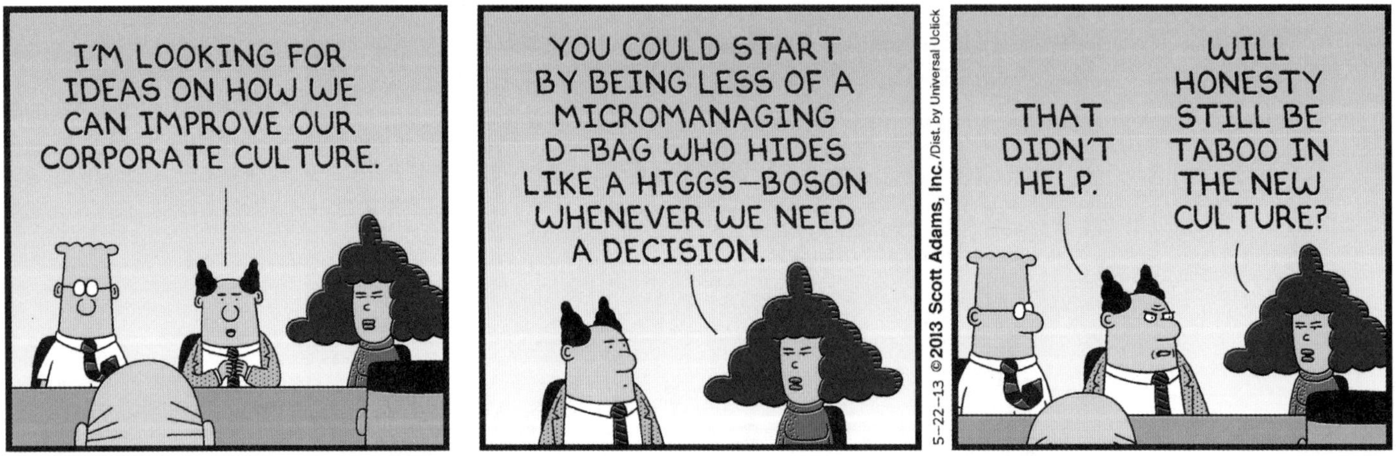
I'M LOOKING FOR IDEAS ON HOW WE CAN IMPROVE OUR CORPORATE CULTURE.
YOU COULD START BY BEING LESS OF A MICROMANAGING D—BAG WHO HIDES LIKE A HIGGS—BOSON WHENEVER WE NEED A DECISION.
5–22–13 ©2013 Scott Adams, Inc./Dist. by Universal Uclick
THAT DIDN'T HELP.
WILL HONESTY STILL BE TABOO IN THE NEW CULTURE?

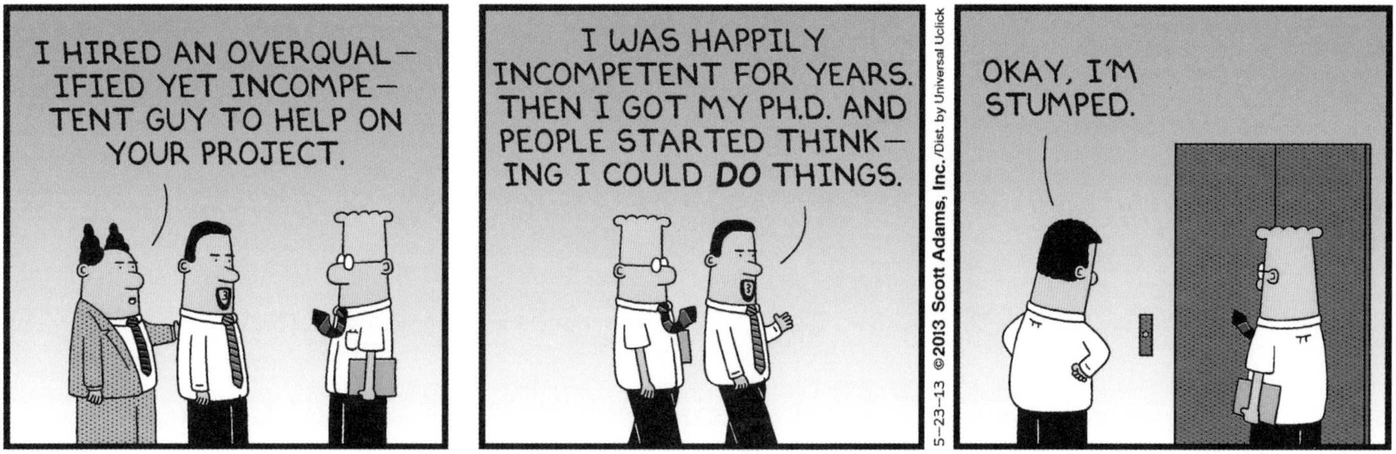
I HIRED AN OVERQUAL-IFIED YET INCOMPE-TENT GUY TO HELP ON YOUR PROJECT.
I WAS HAPPILY INCOMPETENT FOR YEARS. THEN I GOT MY PH.D. AND PEOPLE STARTED THINK-ING I COULD **DO** THINGS.
OKAY, I'M STUMPED.
5-23-13 ©2013 Scott Adams, Inc./Dist. by Universal Uclick

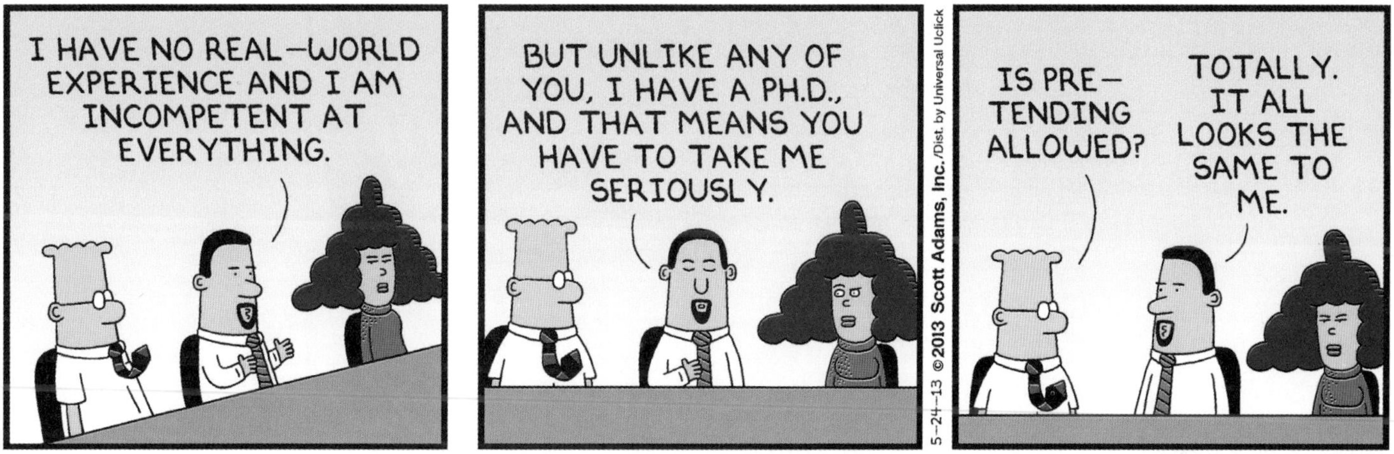
I HAVE NO REAL-WORLD EXPERIENCE AND I AM INCOMPETENT AT EVERYTHING.
BUT UNLIKE ANY OF YOU, I HAVE A PH.D., AND THAT MEANS YOU HAVE TO TAKE ME SERIOUSLY.
IS PRE-TENDING ALLOWED?
TOTALLY. IT ALL LOOKS THE SAME TO ME.
5-24-13 ©2013 Scott Adams, Inc./Dist. by Universal Uclick

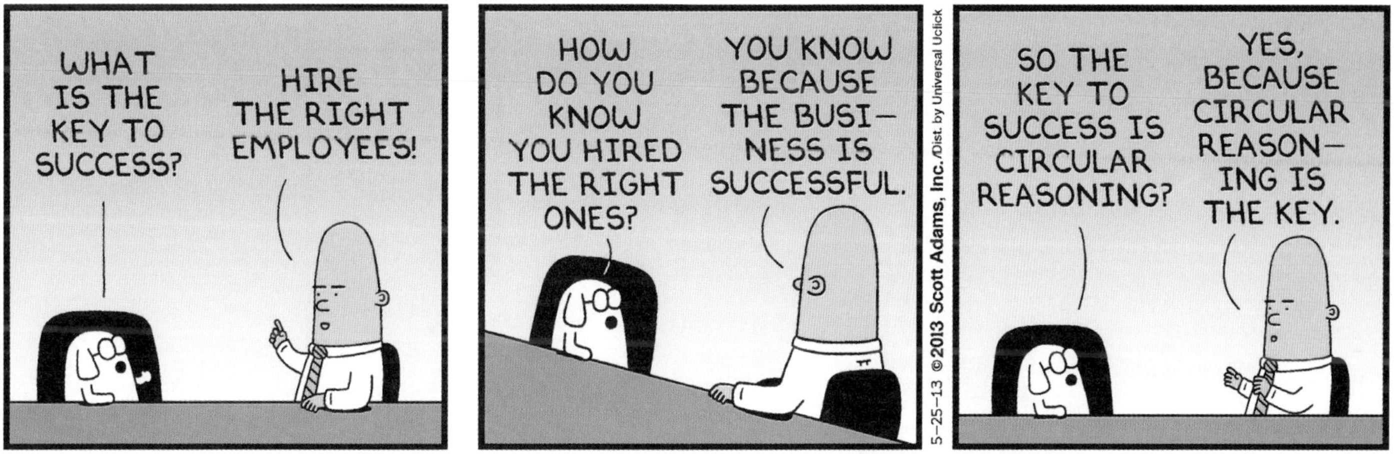
WHAT IS THE KEY TO SUCCESS?
HIRE THE RIGHT EMPLOYEES!
HOW DO YOU KNOW YOU HIRED THE RIGHT ONES?
YOU KNOW BECAUSE THE BUSI-NESS IS SUCCESSFUL.
SO THE KEY TO SUCCESS IS CIRCULAR REASONING?
YES, BECAUSE CIRCULAR REASON-ING IS THE KEY.
5-25-13 ©2013 Scott Adams, Inc./Dist. by Universal Uclick

I PROGRAMMED OUR ROBOT TO MAKE MEDICAL DIAGNOSES.
IT CAN SCAN YOUR BODY USING ITS NEUTRINO SENSOR.
ROBOT, PLEASE DEMONSTRATE.
©2013 Scott Adams, Inc./Dist. by Universal Uclick
DEAD MAN WALKING!
WHAT?
YOUR BRAIN IS THE SIZE OF A DRIED APRICOT.
YOUR HEART IS MORE CHEESEBURGER THAN HUMAN TISSUE. YOU WILL BE DEAD IN ELEVEN DAYS, SIX HOURS, AND NINE-TEEN MINUTES.
GAAA!!!
5-26-13
WHY DID YOU PROGRAM ME TO HATE PEOPLE?
IT WAS EASIER THAN INVENTING A NEUTRINO SENSOR.

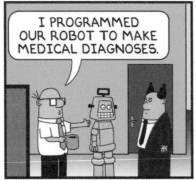

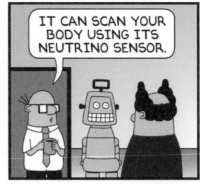

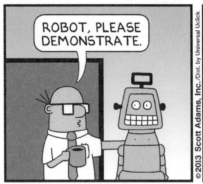

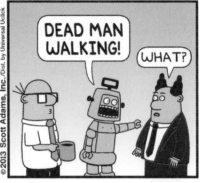

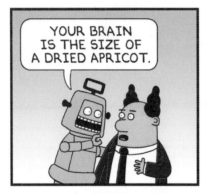

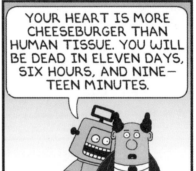

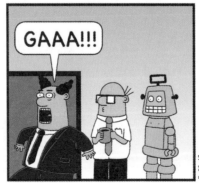

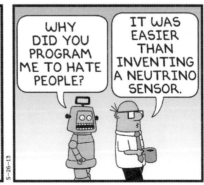

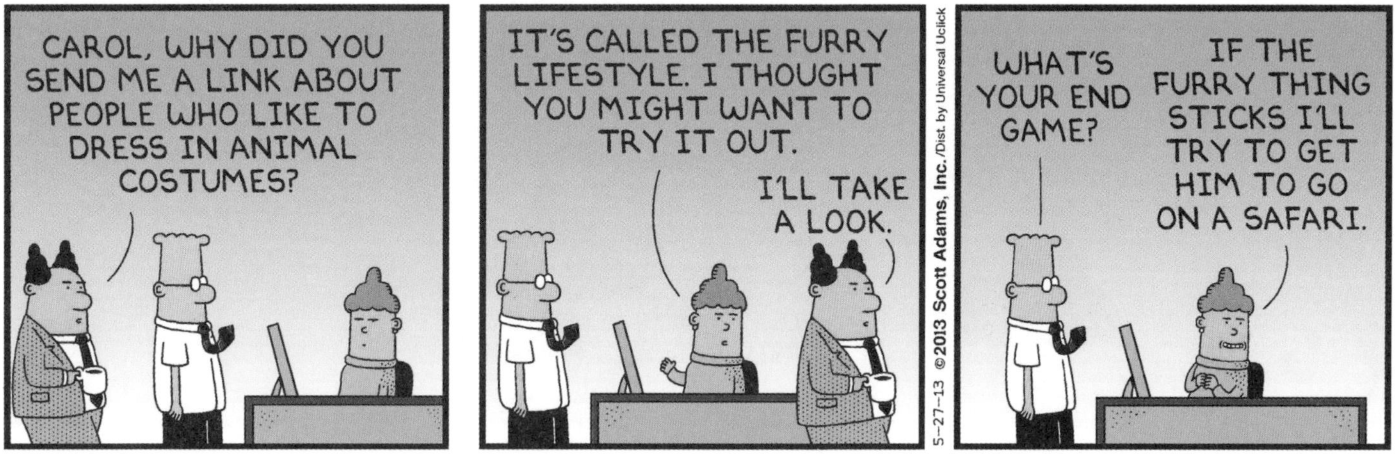
CAROL, WHY DID YOU SEND ME A LINK ABOUT PEOPLE WHO LIKE TO DRESS IN ANIMAL COSTUMES?
IT'S CALLED THE FURRY LIFESTYLE. I THOUGHT YOU MIGHT WANT TO TRY IT OUT.
I'LL TAKE A LOOK.
5-27-13 ©2013 Scott Adams, Inc./Dist. by Universal Uclick
WHAT'S YOUR END GAME?
IF THE FURRY THING STICKS I'LL TRY TO GET HIM TO GO ON A SAFARI.

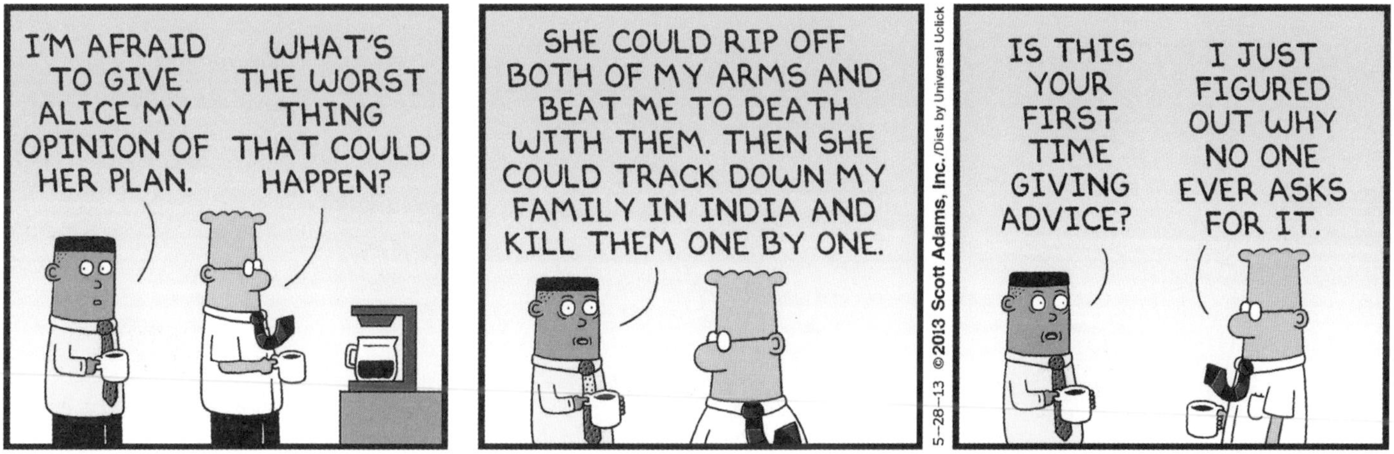
I'M AFRAID TO GIVE ALICE MY OPINION OF HER PLAN.
WHAT'S THE WORST THING THAT COULD HAPPEN?
SHE COULD RIP OFF BOTH OF MY ARMS AND BEAT ME TO DEATH WITH THEM. THEN SHE COULD TRACK DOWN MY FAMILY IN INDIA AND KILL THEM ONE BY ONE.
5-28-13 ©2013 Scott Adams, Inc./Dist. by Universal Uclick
IS THIS YOUR FIRST TIME GIVING ADVICE?
I JUST FIGURED OUT WHY NO ONE EVER ASKS FOR IT.

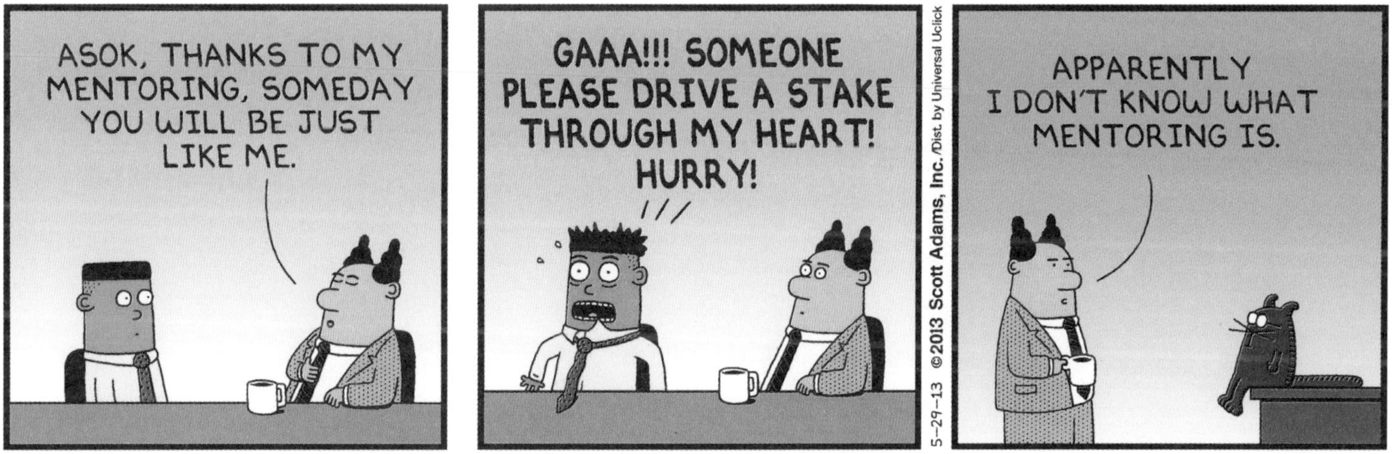
ASOK, THANKS TO MY MENTORING, SOMEDAY YOU WILL BE JUST LIKE ME.
GAAA!!! SOMEONE PLEASE DRIVE A STAKE THROUGH MY HEART! HURRY!
5-29-13 ©2013 Scott Adams, Inc./Dist. by Universal Uclick
APPARENTLY I DON'T KNOW WHAT MENTORING IS.

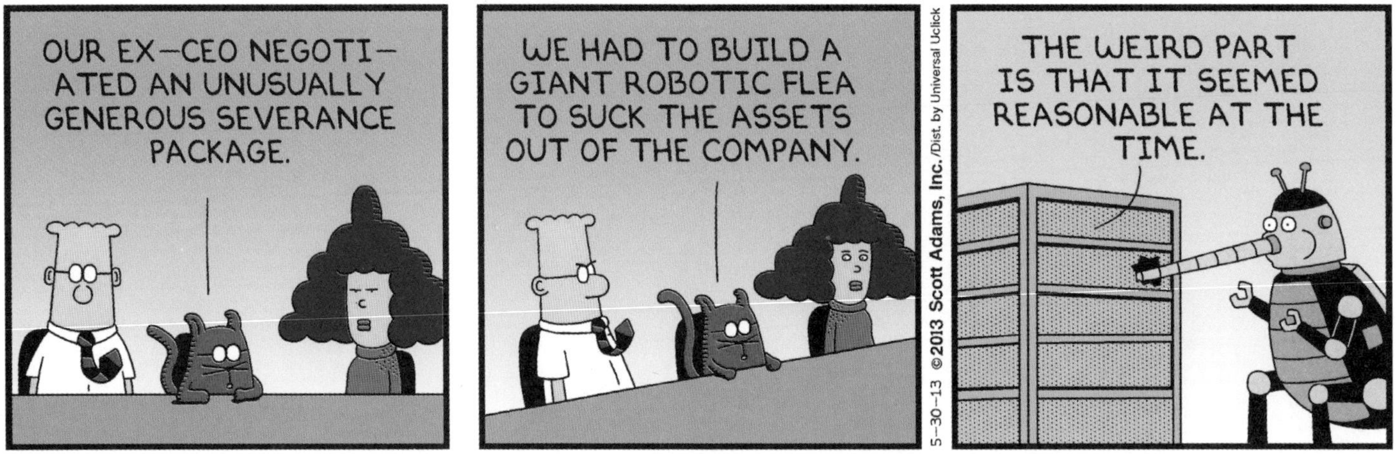
OUR EX-CEO NEGOTI-ATED AN UNUSUALLY GENEROUS SEVERANCE PACKAGE.
WE HAD TO BUILD A GIANT ROBOTIC FLEA TO SUCK THE ASSETS OUT OF THE COMPANY.
5-30-13 ©2013 Scott Adams, Inc./Dist. by Universal Uclick
THE WEIRD PART IS THAT IT SEEMED REASONABLE AT THE TIME.

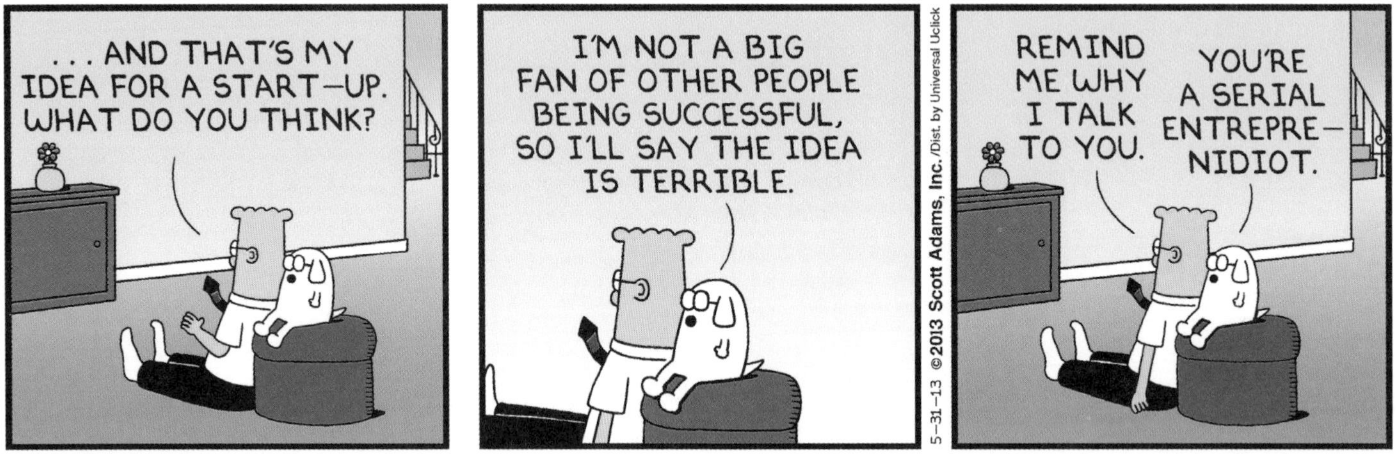
... AND THAT'S MY IDEA FOR A START-UP. WHAT DO YOU THINK?
I'M NOT A BIG FAN OF OTHER PEOPLE BEING SUCCESSFUL, SO I'LL SAY THE IDEA IS TERRIBLE.
5-31-13 ©2013 Scott Adams, Inc./Dist. by Universal Uclick
REMIND ME WHY I TALK TO YOU.
YOU'RE A SERIAL ENTREPRE-NIDIOT.

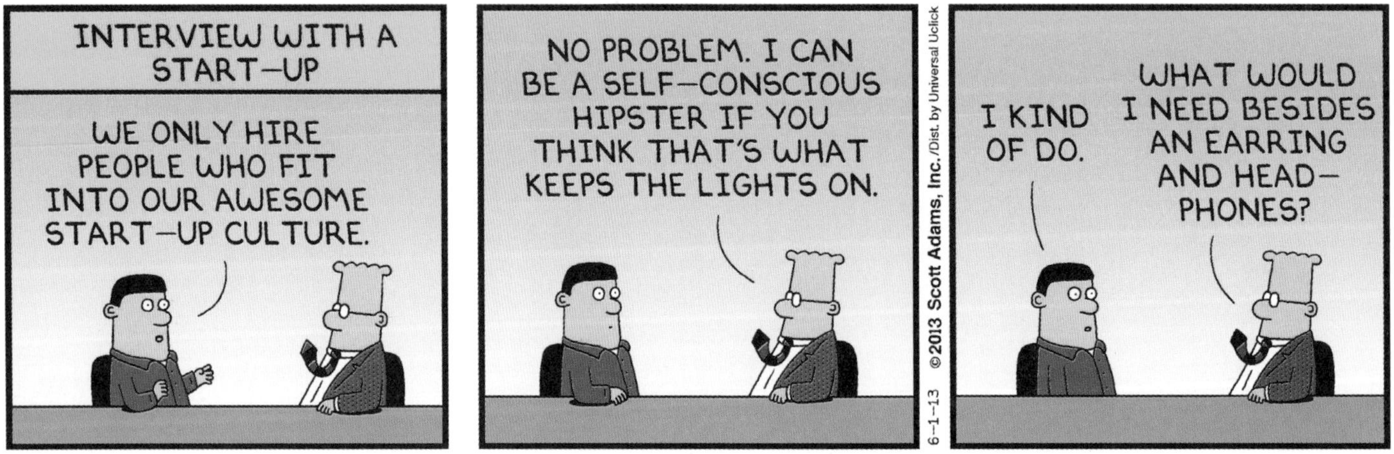
INTERVIEW WITH A START-UP
WE ONLY HIRE PEOPLE WHO FIT INTO OUR AWESOME START-UP CULTURE.
NO PROBLEM. I CAN BE A SELF-CONSCIOUS HIPSTER IF YOU THINK THAT'S WHAT KEEPS THE LIGHTS ON.
6-1-13 ©2013 Scott Adams, Inc./Dist. by Universal Uclick
I KIND OF DO.
WHAT WOULD I NEED BESIDES AN EARRING AND HEAD-PHONES?

A GOOD MANAGER LEADS BY EXAMPLE.
HOW DOES IT HELP AN ENGINEER TO SEE AN EXAMPLE OF HOW TO BE A MIDDLE MANAGER?
THAT'S LIKE TEACHING PHYSICS BY SHOWING EXAMPLES OF MONSTER TRUCK RALLIES.
©2013 Scott Adams, Inc./Dist. by Universal Uclick
SHOULD WE SAY DUMB THINGS, TOO, OR HAVE YOU NOT STARTED LEADING BY EXAMPLE YET?
NOW WHAT IS HE DOING? ARE WE SUPPOSED TO DO THAT?
I THINK HE'S LEADING BY EXAMPLE NOW!
6-2-13
I'M STARTING TO WONDER IF EVERY-THING I READ ON THE INTERNET IS WRONG.

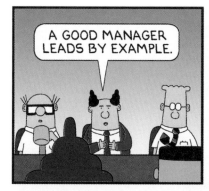

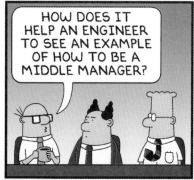

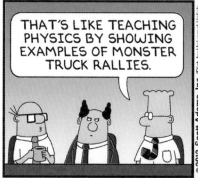

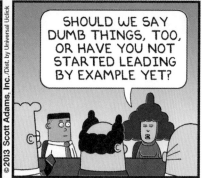

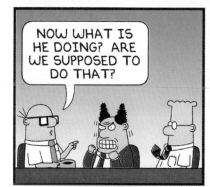

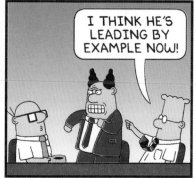

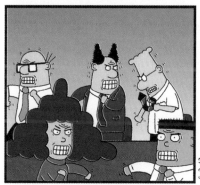

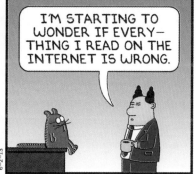

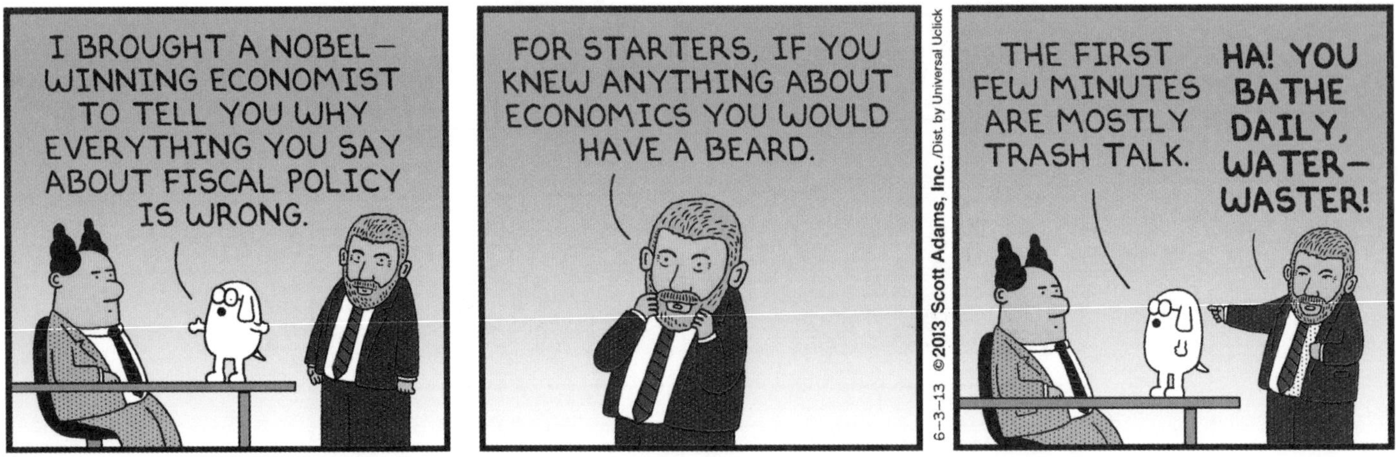
I BROUGHT A NOBEL-WINNING ECONOMIST TO TELL YOU WHY EVERYTHING YOU SAY ABOUT FISCAL POLICY IS WRONG.
FOR STARTERS, IF YOU KNEW ANYTHING ABOUT ECONOMICS YOU WOULD HAVE A BEARD.
6-3-13 ©2013 Scott Adams, Inc./Dist. by Universal Uclick
THE FIRST FEW MINUTES ARE MOSTLY TRASH TALK.
HA! YOU BATHE DAILY, WATER-WASTER!

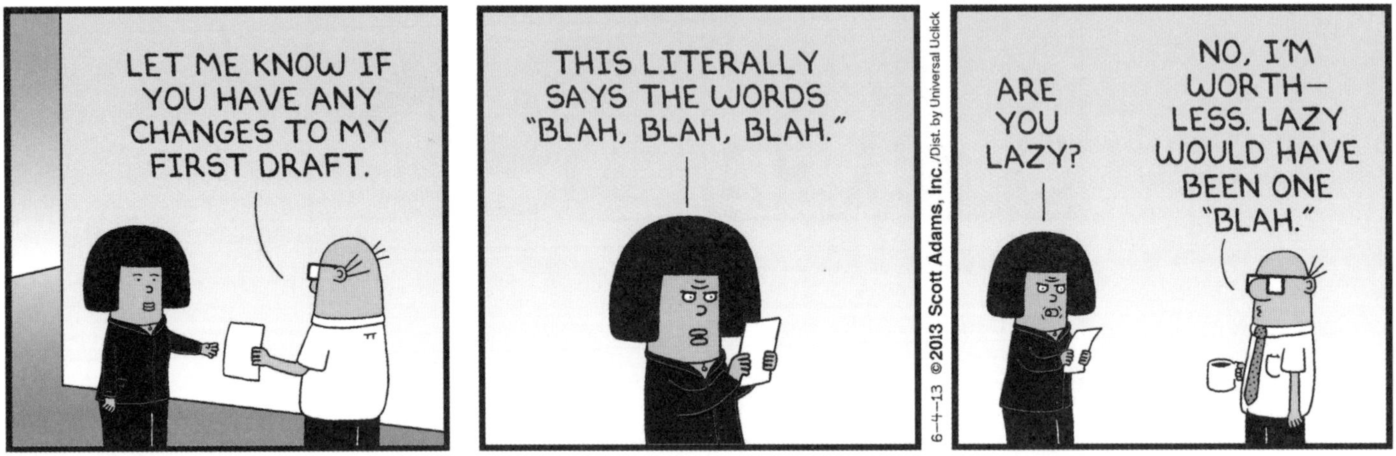
LET ME KNOW IF YOU HAVE ANY CHANGES TO MY FIRST DRAFT.
THIS LITERALLY SAYS THE WORDS "BLAH, BLAH, BLAH."
6-4-13 ©2013 Scott Adams, Inc./Dist. by Universal Uclick
ARE YOU LAZY?
NO, I'M WORTH-LESS. LAZY WOULD HAVE BEEN ONE "BLAH."

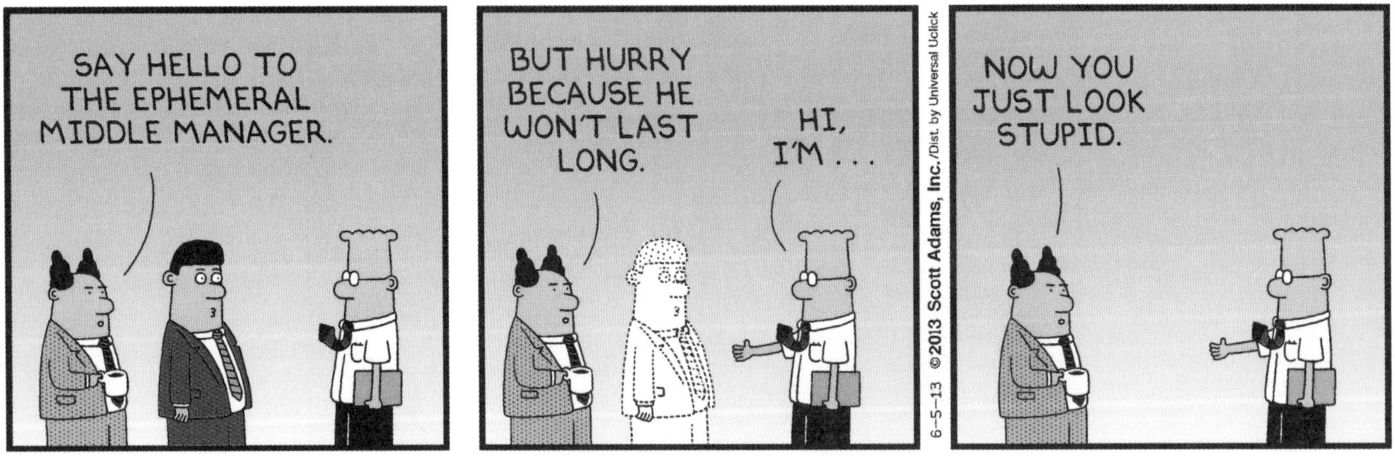
SAY HELLO TO THE EPHEMERAL MIDDLE MANAGER.
BUT HURRY BECAUSE HE WON'T LAST LONG.
HI, I'M . . .
6-5-13 ©2013 Scott Adams, Inc./Dist. by Universal Uclick
NOW YOU JUST LOOK STUPID.

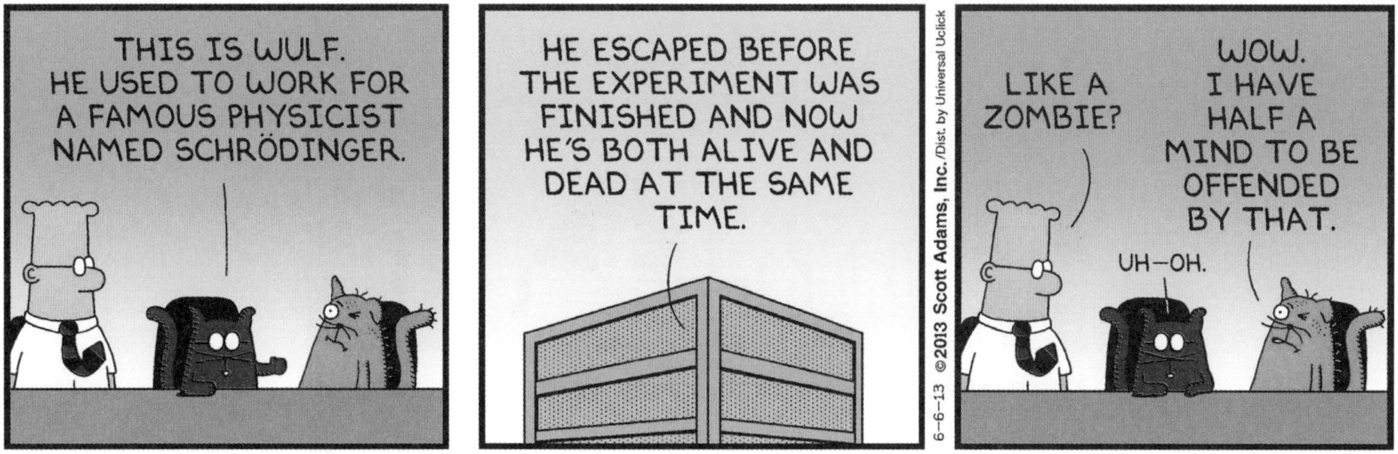
THIS IS WULF. HE USED TO WORK FOR A FAMOUS PHYSICIST NAMED SCHRÖDINGER.
HE ESCAPED BEFORE THE EXPERIMENT WAS FINISHED AND NOW HE'S BOTH ALIVE AND DEAD AT THE SAME TIME.
6-6-13 ©2013 Scott Adams, Inc./Dist. by Universal Uclick
LIKE A ZOMBIE?
WOW. I HAVE HALF A MIND TO BE OFFENDED BY THAT.
UH-OH.

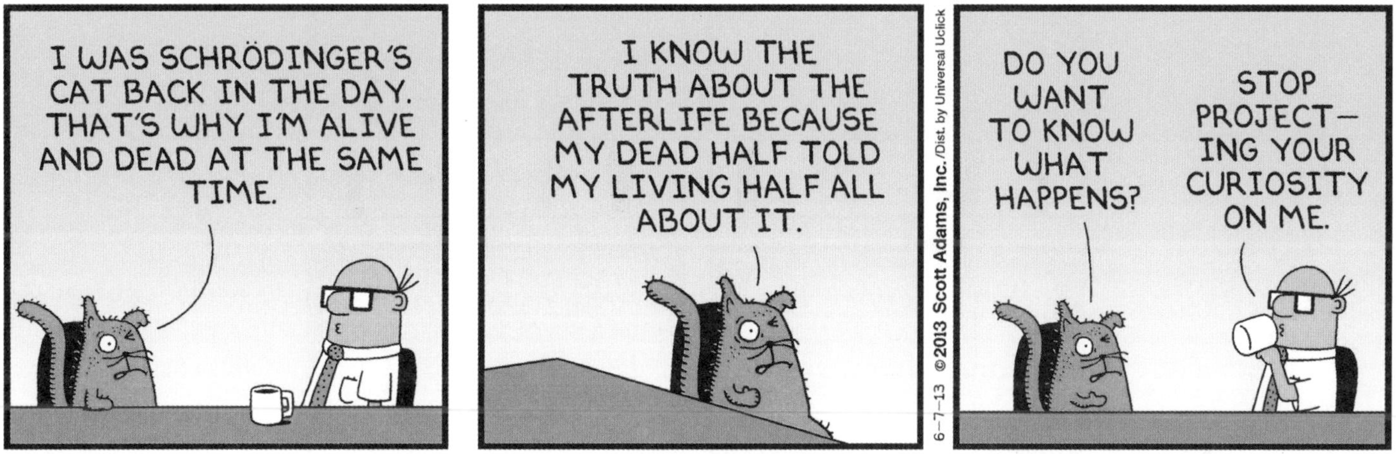
I WAS SCHRÖDINGER'S CAT BACK IN THE DAY. THAT'S WHY I'M ALIVE AND DEAD AT THE SAME TIME.
I KNOW THE TRUTH ABOUT THE AFTERLIFE BECAUSE MY DEAD HALF TOLD MY LIVING HALF ALL ABOUT IT.
6-7-13 ©2013 Scott Adams, Inc./Dist. by Universal Uclick
DO YOU WANT TO KNOW WHAT HAPPENS?
STOP PROJECT-ING YOUR CURIOSITY ON ME.

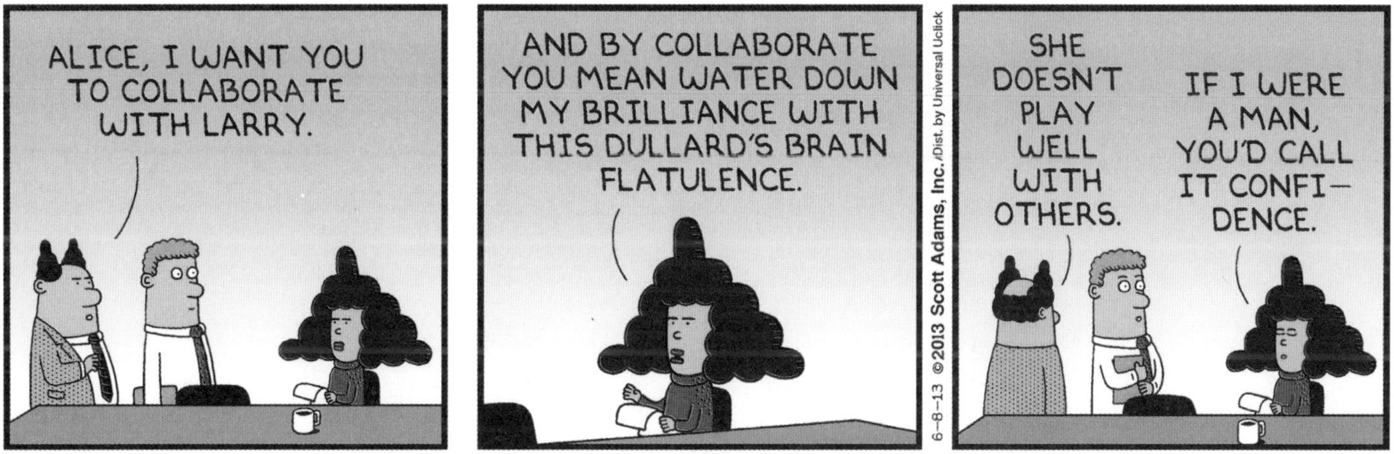
ALICE, I WANT YOU TO COLLABORATE WITH LARRY.
AND BY COLLABORATE YOU MEAN WATER DOWN MY BRILLIANCE WITH THIS DULLARD'S BRAIN FLATULENCE.
6-8-13 ©2013 Scott Adams, Inc./Dist. by Universal Uclick
SHE DOESN'T PLAY WELL WITH OTHERS.
IF I WERE A MAN, YOU'D CALL IT CONFI-DENCE.

WE NEED TO HAVE A BIAS FOR ACTION.
DON'T LET PERFECT BE THE ENEMY OF GOOD.
SO . . . A CARPENTER SHOULD SAW THE BOARD FIRST AND MEASURE IT LATER?
YOUR USE OF THAT FOLKSY SAYING MAKES MY STRATEGY SOUND DUMB.
WHY DO YOU CARE IF YOUR STRATEGY IS PERFECT OR NOT?
YOU JUST SAID IT'S MORE IMPORTANT TO SPRAY YOUR DEFECTIVE STUFF ON THE UNIVERSE THAN IT IS TO GET THINGS RIGHT.
"SPRAY MY DE– FECTIVE STUFF"?
SHOULD I HAVE WAITED FOR A PERFECT WAY TO SAY THAT?
©2013 Scott Adams, Inc./Dist. by Universal Uclick
6-9-13

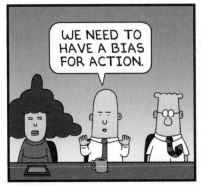

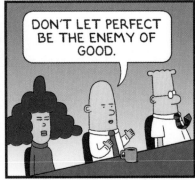

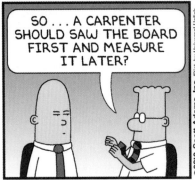

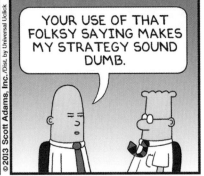

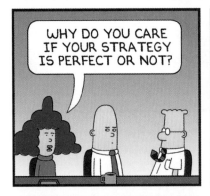

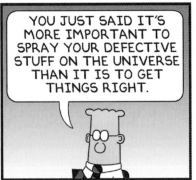

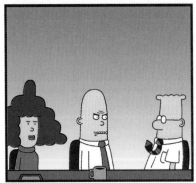

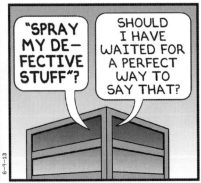

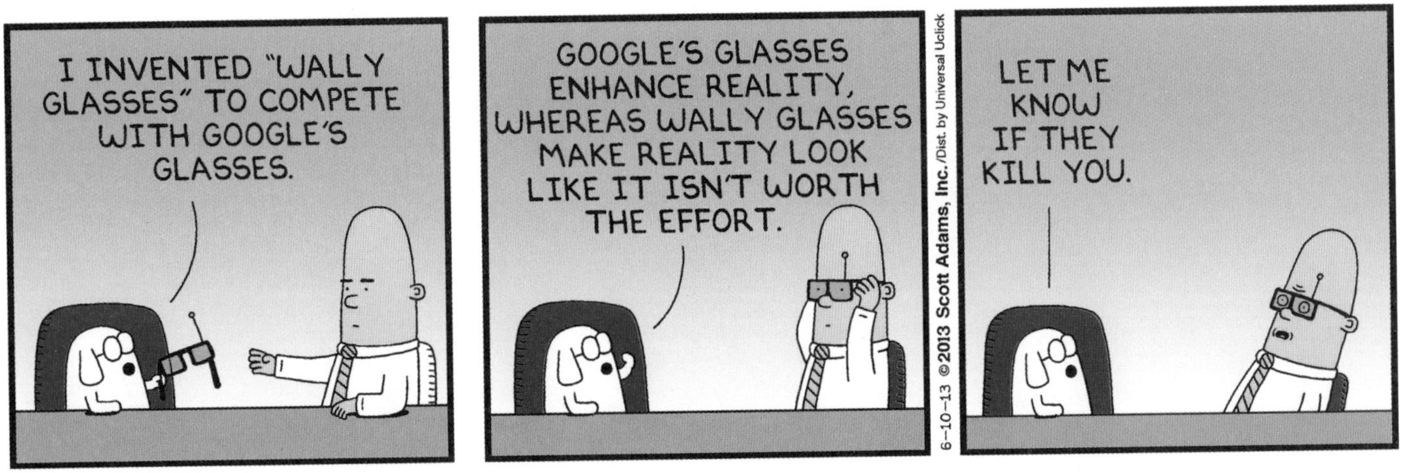
I INVENTED "WALLY GLASSES" TO COMPETE WITH GOOGLE'S GLASSES.
GOOGLE'S GLASSES ENHANCE REALITY, WHEREAS WALLY GLASSES MAKE REALITY LOOK LIKE IT ISN'T WORTH THE EFFORT.
6-10-13 ©2013 Scott Adams, Inc./Dist. by Universal Uclick
LET ME KNOW IF THEY KILL YOU.

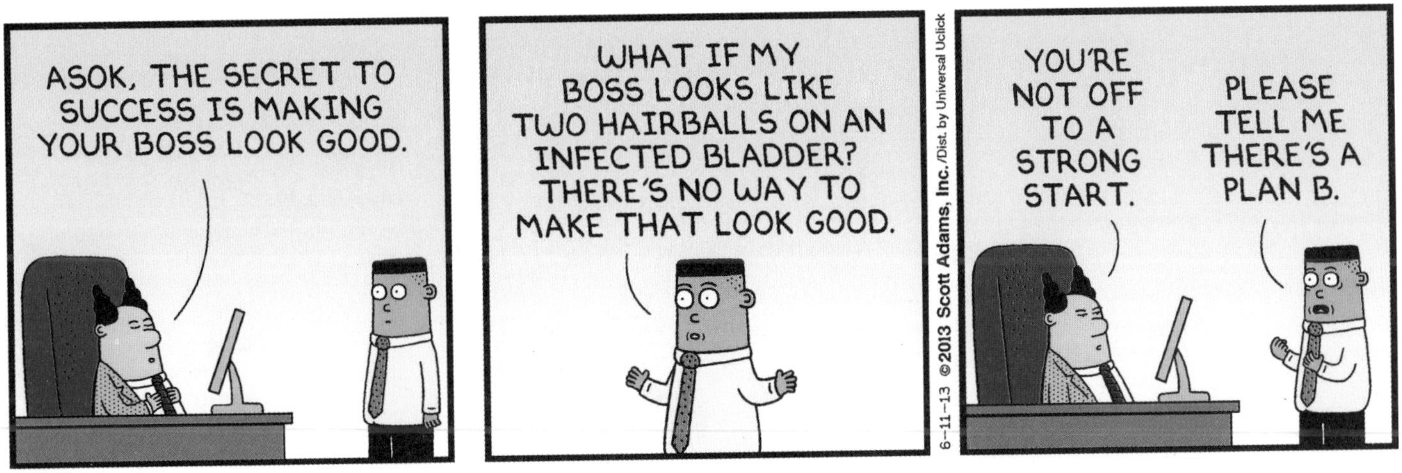
ASOK, THE SECRET TO SUCCESS IS MAKING YOUR BOSS LOOK GOOD.
WHAT IF MY BOSS LOOKS LIKE TWO HAIRBALLS ON AN INFECTED BLADDER? THERE'S NO WAY TO MAKE THAT LOOK GOOD.
6-11-13 ©2013 Scott Adams, Inc./Dist. by Universal Uclick
YOU'RE NOT OFF TO A STRONG START.
PLEASE TELL ME THERE'S A PLAN B.

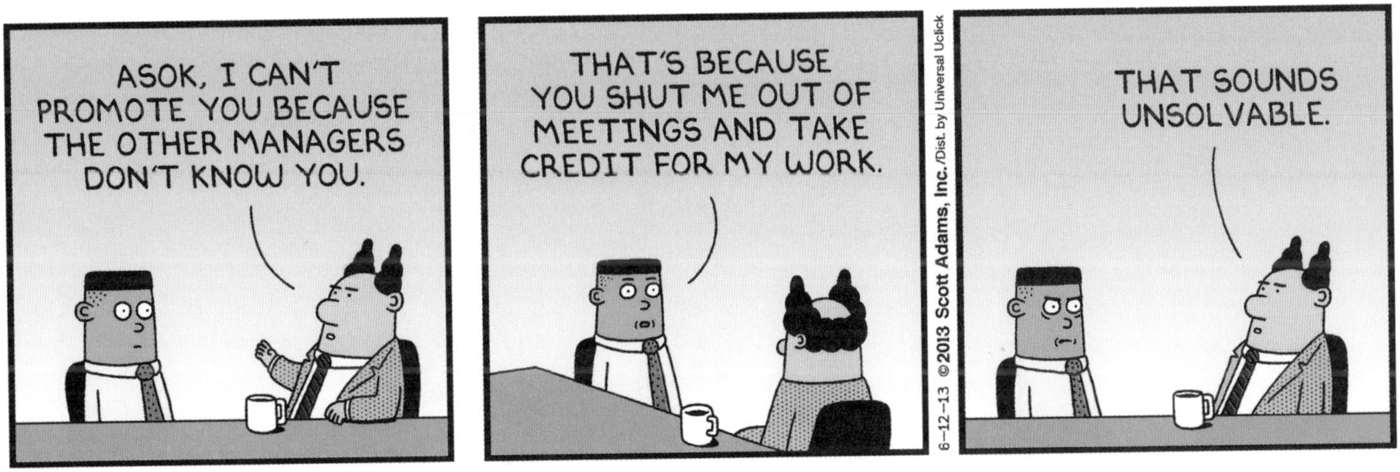
ASOK, I CAN'T PROMOTE YOU BECAUSE THE OTHER MANAGERS DON'T KNOW YOU.
THAT'S BECAUSE YOU SHUT ME OUT OF MEETINGS AND TAKE CREDIT FOR MY WORK.
6-12-13 ©2013 Scott Adams, Inc./Dist. by Universal Uclick
THAT SOUNDS UNSOLVABLE.

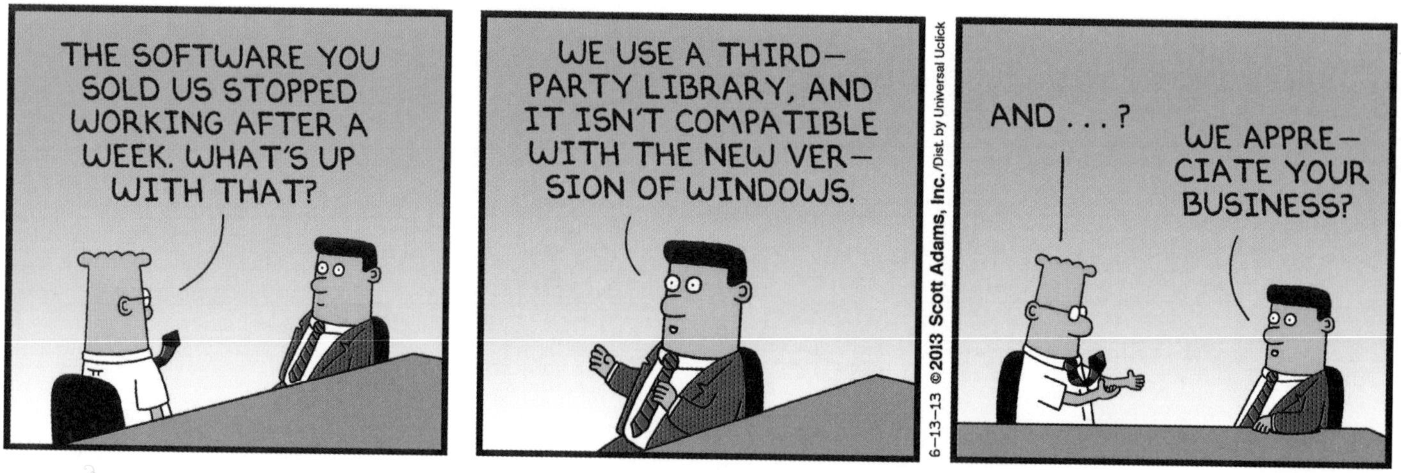
THE SOFTWARE YOU SOLD US STOPPED WORKING AFTER A WEEK. WHAT'S UP WITH THAT?
WE USE A THIRD-PARTY LIBRARY, AND IT ISN'T COMPATIBLE WITH THE NEW VERSION OF WINDOWS.
6-13-13 ©2013 Scott Adams, Inc./Dist. by Universal Uclick
AND . . . ?
WE APPRECIATE YOUR BUSINESS?

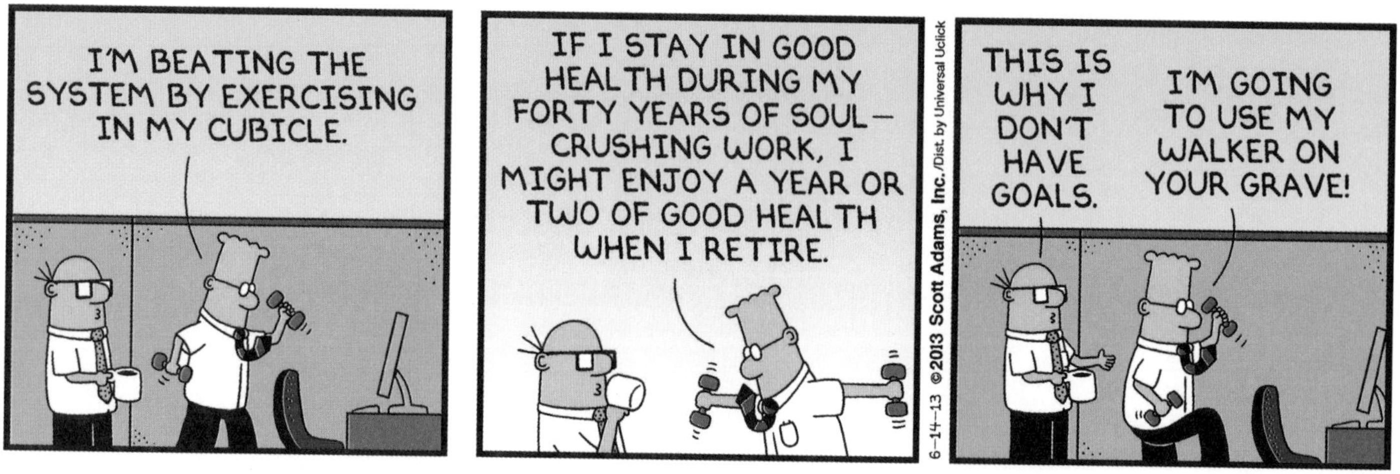
I'M BEATING THE SYSTEM BY EXERCISING IN MY CUBICLE.
IF I STAY IN GOOD HEALTH DURING MY FORTY YEARS OF SOUL-CRUSHING WORK, I MIGHT ENJOY A YEAR OR TWO OF GOOD HEALTH WHEN I RETIRE.
6-14-13 ©2013 Scott Adams, Inc./Dist. by Universal Uclick
THIS IS WHY I DON'T HAVE GOALS.
I'M GOING TO USE MY WALKER ON YOUR GRAVE!

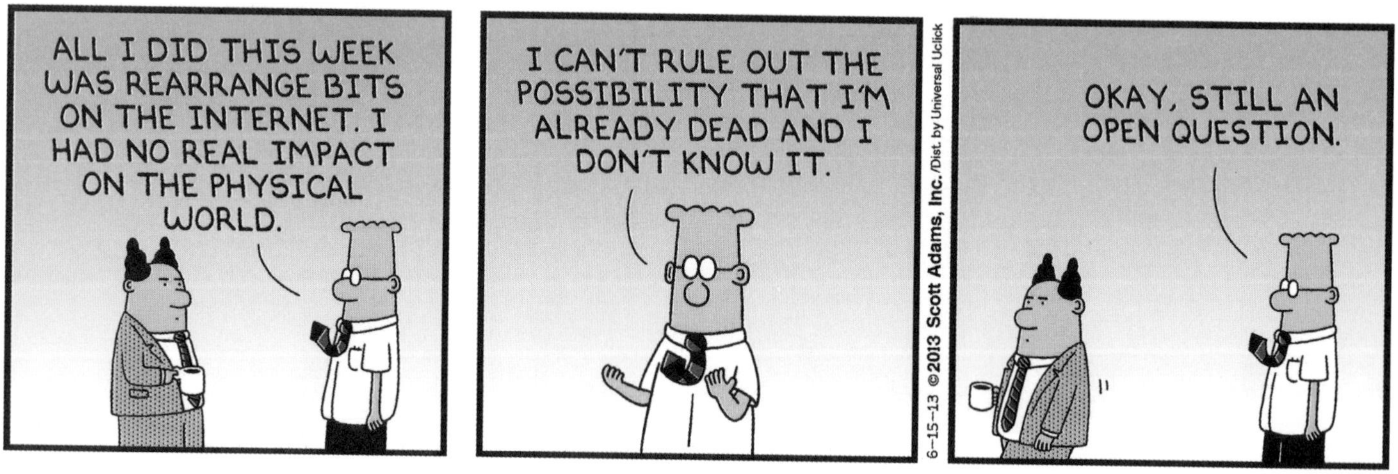
ALL I DID THIS WEEK WAS REARRANGE BITS ON THE INTERNET. I HAD NO REAL IMPACT ON THE PHYSICAL WORLD.
I CAN'T RULE OUT THE POSSIBILITY THAT I'M ALREADY DEAD AND I DON'T KNOW IT.
6-15-13 ©2013 Scott Adams, Inc./Dist. by Universal Uclick
OKAY, STILL AN OPEN QUESTION.

YOU LOOK GOOD ON PAPER, BUT HOW DO I KNOW YOU AREN'T LYING ABOUT YOUR SKILLS?
YOU SHOULD HOPE I AM LYING.
STUDIES SHOW THAT PEOPLE WHO EXAGGERATE THEIR CREDENTIALS TEND TO BE MORE EFFECTIVE ONCE HIRED.
THAT'S BECAUSE MIS-LEADING PEOPLE IS A VALUABLE BUSINESS SKILL.
FOR EXAMPLE, I MIGHT NEED TO CONVINCE OUR CUSTOMERS THAT OUR PRODUCTS ARE BETTER THAN THE COMPETITION.
OR I MIGHT NEED TO DUPE SOME IDIOT INTO LEAVING MY CUBICLE SO I CAN CONCENTRATE.
ANYONE CAN LEARN TECHNICAL SKILLS, BUT LYING IS AN ART FORM.
HE DOESN'T HAVE AN HONEST BONE IN HIS BODY.
PERFECT. I'LL TELL HUMAN RESOURCES TO SEND HIM AN OFFER.
© 2013 Scott Adams, Inc./Dist. by Universal Uclick
6-16-13

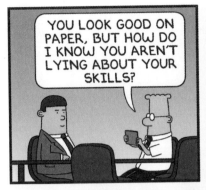

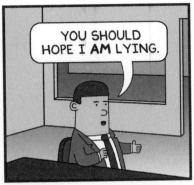

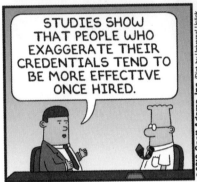

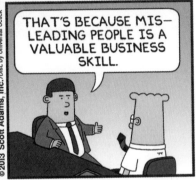

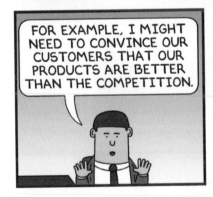

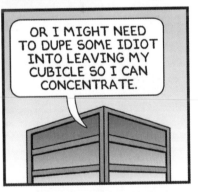

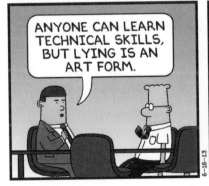

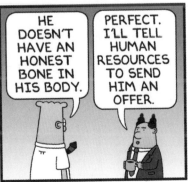

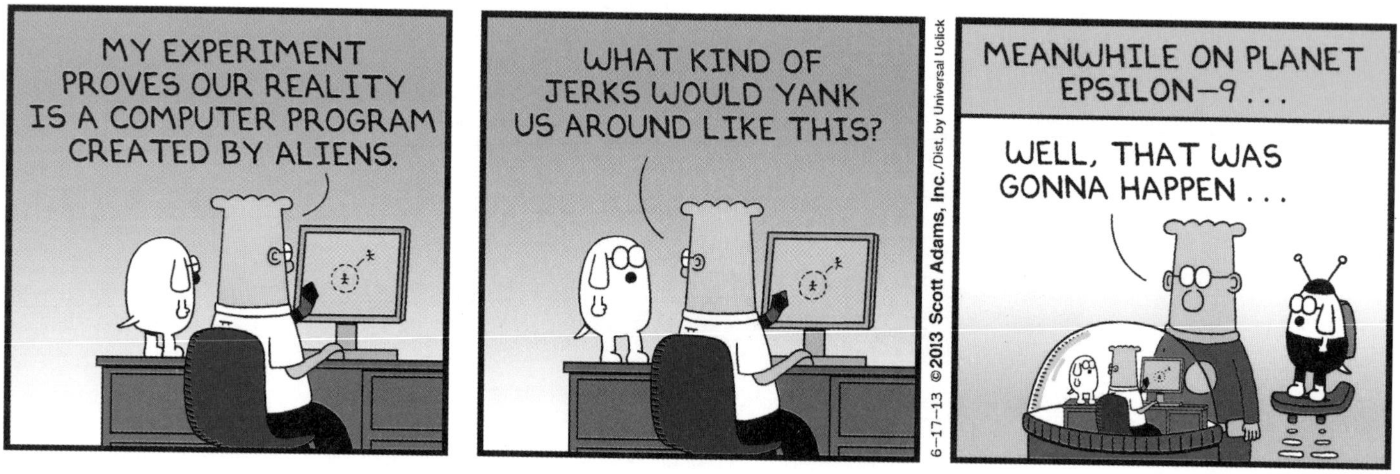
MY EXPERIMENT PROVES OUR REALITY IS A COMPUTER PROGRAM CREATED BY ALIENS.
WHAT KIND OF JERKS WOULD YANK US AROUND LIKE THIS?
6–17–13 ©2013 Scott Adams, Inc./Dist. by Universal Uclick
MEANWHILE ON PLANET EPSILON–9 . . .
WELL, THAT WAS GONNA HAPPEN . . .

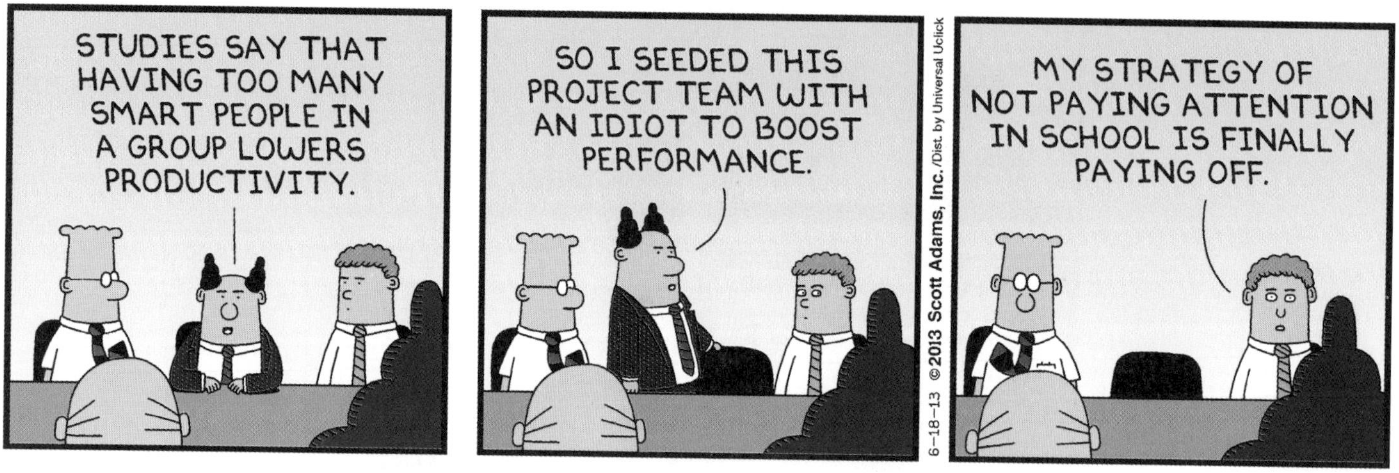
STUDIES SAY THAT HAVING TOO MANY SMART PEOPLE IN A GROUP LOWERS PRODUCTIVITY.
SO I SEEDED THIS PROJECT TEAM WITH AN IDIOT TO BOOST PERFORMANCE.
6–18–13 ©2013 Scott Adams, Inc./Dist. by Universal Uclick
MY STRATEGY OF NOT PAYING ATTENTION IN SCHOOL IS FINALLY PAYING OFF.

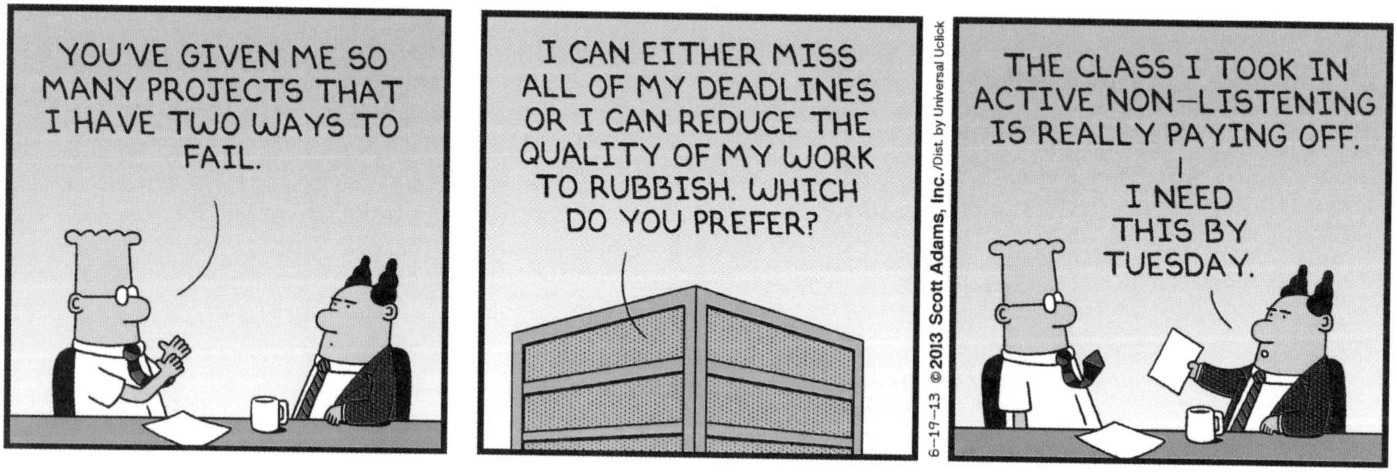
YOU'VE GIVEN ME SO MANY PROJECTS THAT I HAVE TWO WAYS TO FAIL.
I CAN EITHER MISS ALL OF MY DEADLINES OR I CAN REDUCE THE QUALITY OF MY WORK TO RUBBISH. WHICH DO YOU PREFER?
6–19–13 ©2013 Scott Adams, Inc./Dist. by Universal Uclick
THE CLASS I TOOK IN ACTIVE NON–LISTENING IS REALLY PAYING OFF.
I NEED THIS BY TUESDAY.

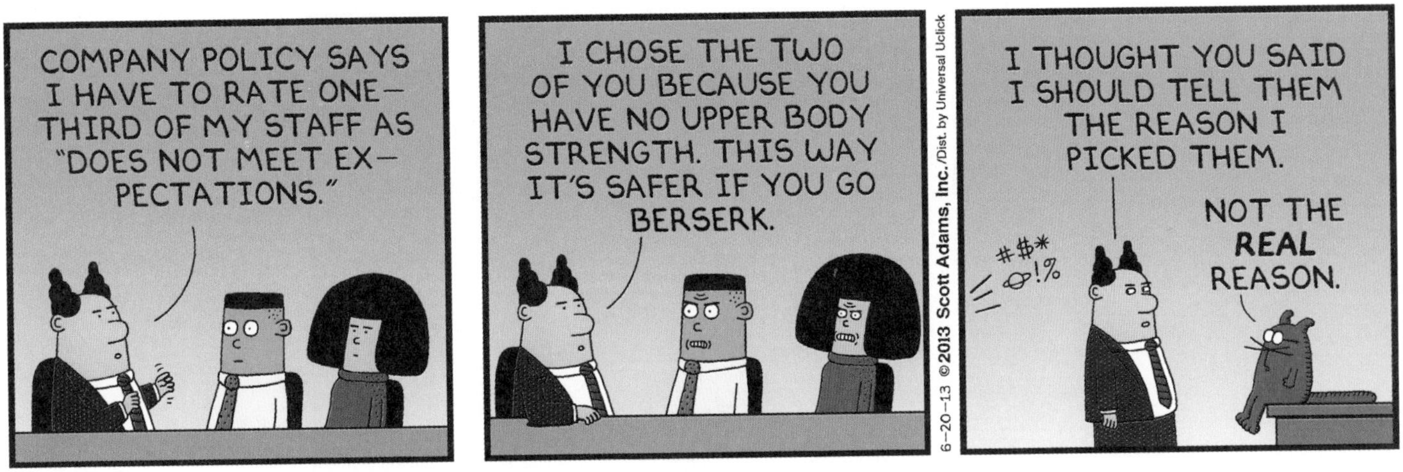
COMPANY POLICY SAYS I HAVE TO RATE ONE-THIRD OF MY STAFF AS "DOES NOT MEET EX-PECTATIONS."
I CHOSE THE TWO OF YOU BECAUSE YOU HAVE NO UPPER BODY STRENGTH. THIS WAY IT'S SAFER IF YOU GO BERSERK.
#$* !%
I THOUGHT YOU SAID I SHOULD TELL THEM THE REASON I PICKED THEM.
NOT THE **REAL** REASON.

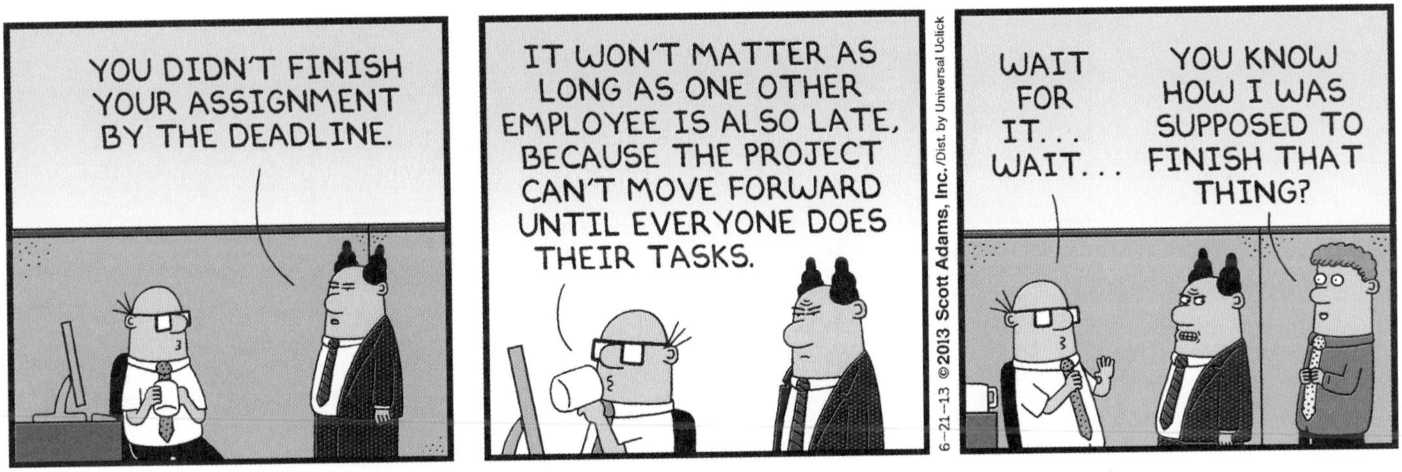
YOU DIDN'T FINISH YOUR ASSIGNMENT BY THE DEADLINE.
IT WON'T MATTER AS LONG AS ONE OTHER EMPLOYEE IS ALSO LATE, BECAUSE THE PROJECT CAN'T MOVE FORWARD UNTIL EVERYONE DOES THEIR TASKS.
WAIT FOR IT... WAIT...
YOU KNOW HOW I WAS SUPPOSED TO FINISH THAT THING?

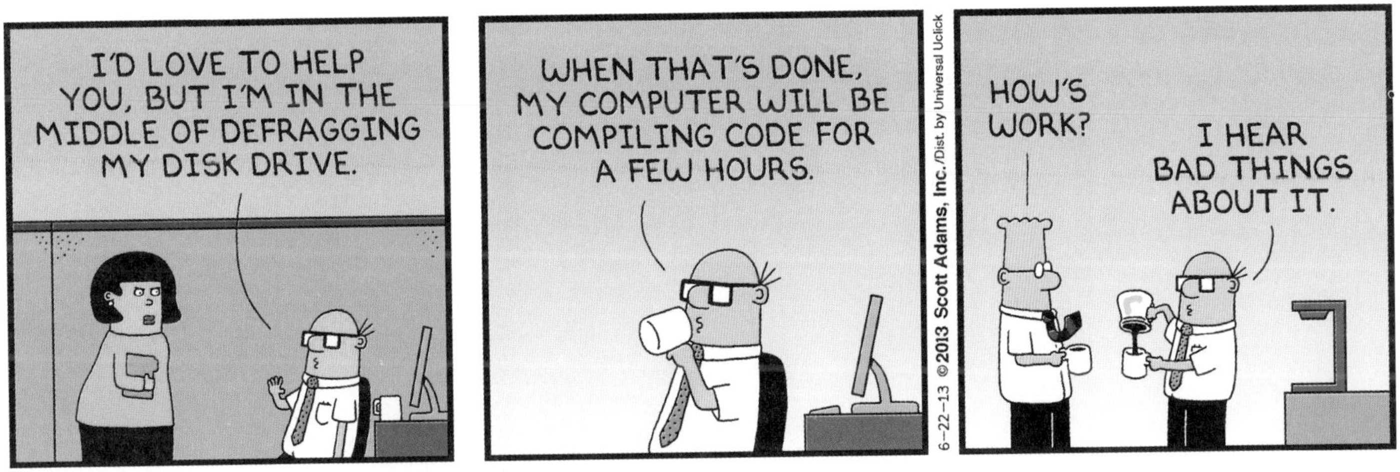
I'D LOVE TO HELP YOU, BUT I'M IN THE MIDDLE OF DEFRAGGING MY DISK DRIVE.
WHEN THAT'S DONE, MY COMPUTER WILL BE COMPILING CODE FOR A FEW HOURS.
HOW'S WORK?
I HEAR BAD THINGS ABOUT IT.

I'M ON A DEADLINE, SO DON'T LET ANYONE DISTURB ME FOR AT LEAST AN HOUR.
IF ANYONE GETS PAST YOU, YOU'RE FIRED.
TELL YOUR BOSS TO COME TO MY OFFICE NOW.
HE'LL FIRE ME IF I DISTURB HIM.
©2013 Scott Adams, Inc./Dist. by Universal Uclick
I'M YOUR CEO! DISTURB YOUR BOSS NOW OR ***I'LL*** FIRE YOU!
I HEARD THAT. AND IF YOU DISTURB ME, YOU'RE FIRED!
YOU'RE FIRED IF YOU DON'T!
YOU'RE FIRED IF YOU DO!
WHOA! HOLD ON! I'M GETTING A SUDDEN WAVE OF EUPHORIA.
ME TOO!
6-23-13
IS IT BECAUSE WE'RE OVER-PAID?
IT . . . IT FEELS . . . WONDER-FUL!

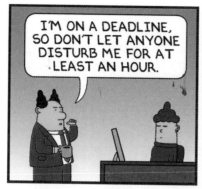

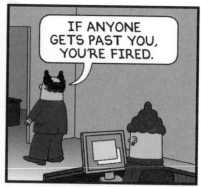

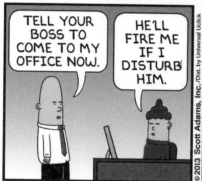

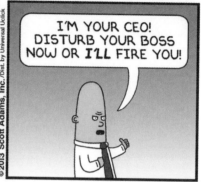

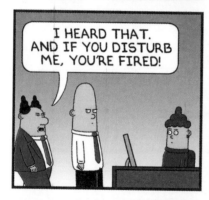

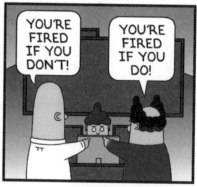

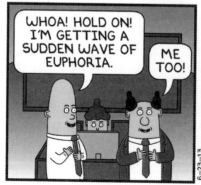

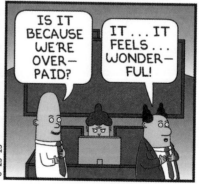

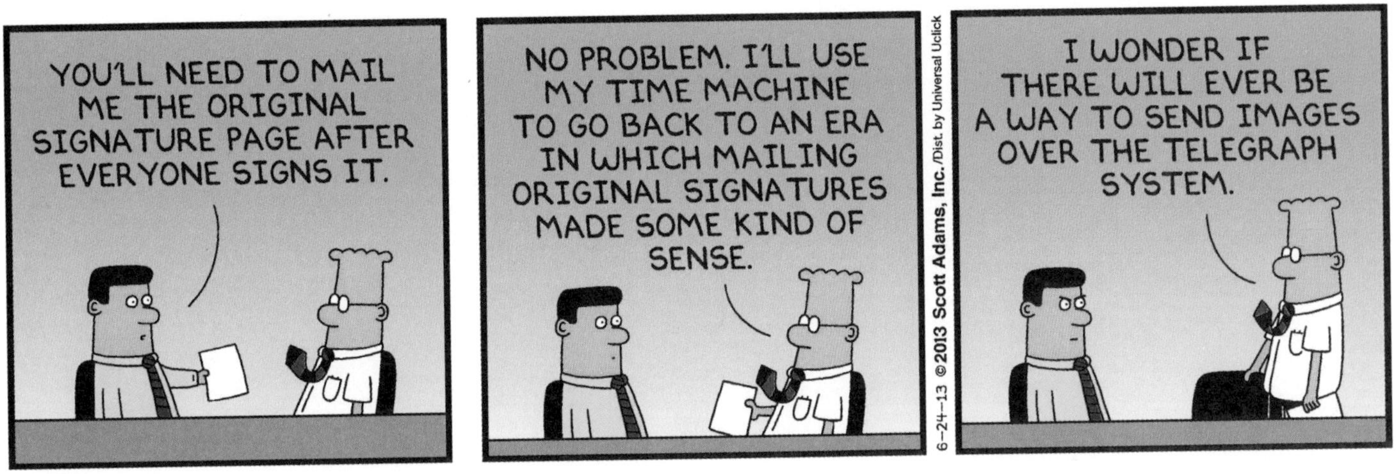
YOU'LL NEED TO MAIL ME THE ORIGINAL SIGNATURE PAGE AFTER EVERYONE SIGNS IT.
NO PROBLEM. I'LL USE MY TIME MACHINE TO GO BACK TO AN ERA IN WHICH MAILING ORIGINAL SIGNATURES MADE SOME KIND OF SENSE.
I WONDER IF THERE WILL EVER BE A WAY TO SEND IMAGES OVER THE TELEGRAPH SYSTEM.

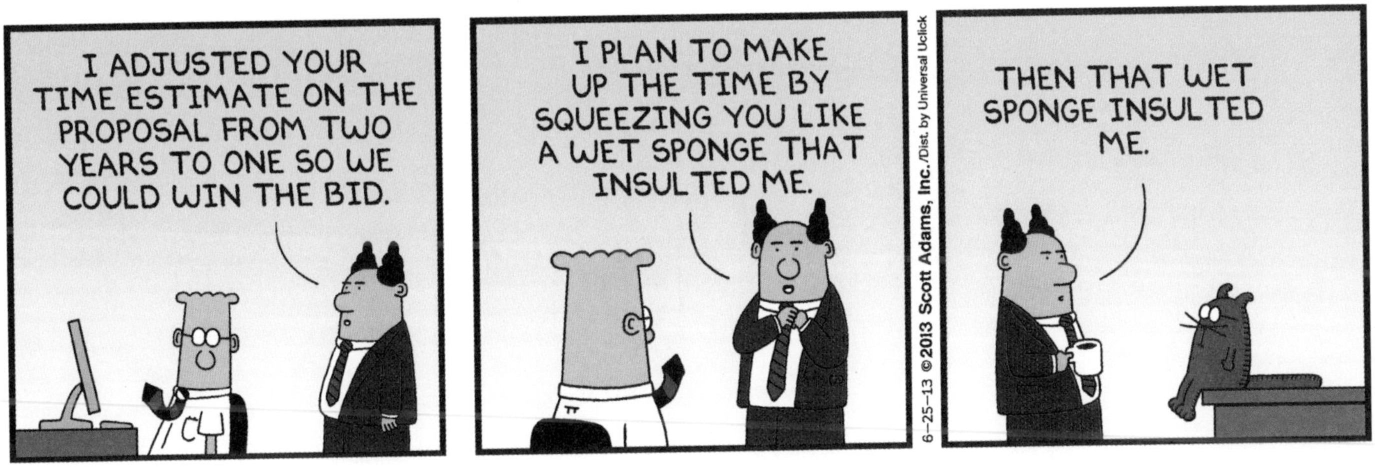
I ADJUSTED YOUR TIME ESTIMATE ON THE PROPOSAL FROM TWO YEARS TO ONE SO WE COULD WIN THE BID.
I PLAN TO MAKE UP THE TIME BY SQUEEZING YOU LIKE A WET SPONGE THAT INSULTED ME.
THEN THAT WET SPONGE INSULTED ME.

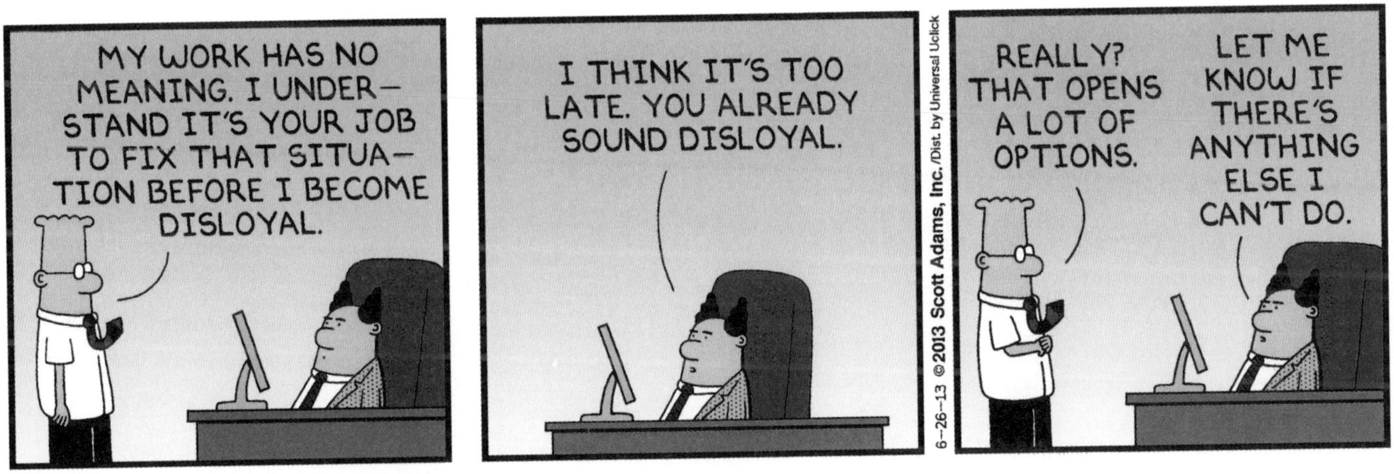
MY WORK HAS NO MEANING. I UNDER-STAND IT'S YOUR JOB TO FIX THAT SITUA-TION BEFORE I BECOME DISLOYAL.
I THINK IT'S TOO LATE. YOU ALREADY SOUND DISLOYAL.
REALLY? THAT OPENS A LOT OF OPTIONS.
LET ME KNOW IF THERE'S ANYTHING ELSE I CAN'T DO.

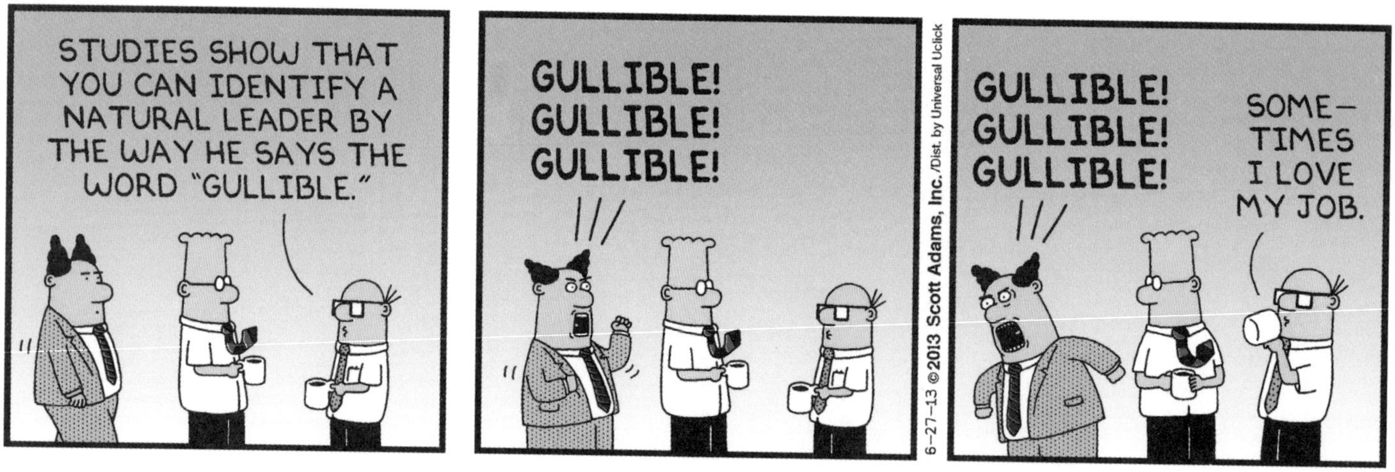
STUDIES SHOW THAT YOU CAN IDENTIFY A NATURAL LEADER BY THE WAY HE SAYS THE WORD "GULLIBLE."
GULLIBLE! GULLIBLE! GULLIBLE!
GULLIBLE! GULLIBLE! GULLIBLE!
SOME-TIMES I LOVE MY JOB.
6-27-13 ©2013 Scott Adams, Inc./Dist. by Universal Uclick

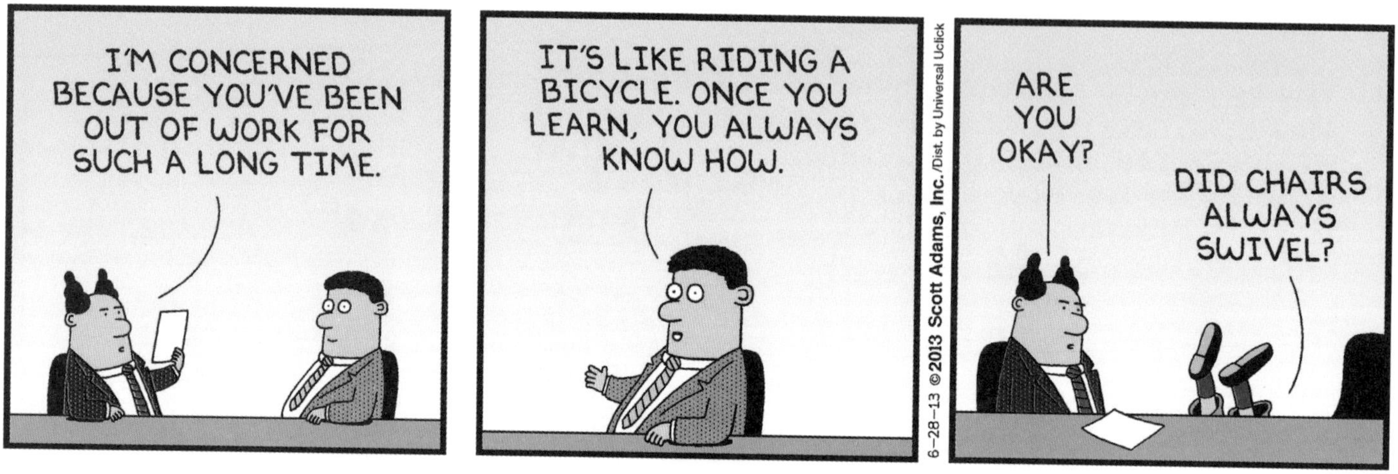
I'M CONCERNED BECAUSE YOU'VE BEEN OUT OF WORK FOR SUCH A LONG TIME.
IT'S LIKE RIDING A BICYCLE. ONCE YOU LEARN, YOU ALWAYS KNOW HOW.
ARE YOU OKAY?
DID CHAIRS ALWAYS SWIVEL?
6-28-13 ©2013 Scott Adams, Inc./Dist. by Universal Uclick

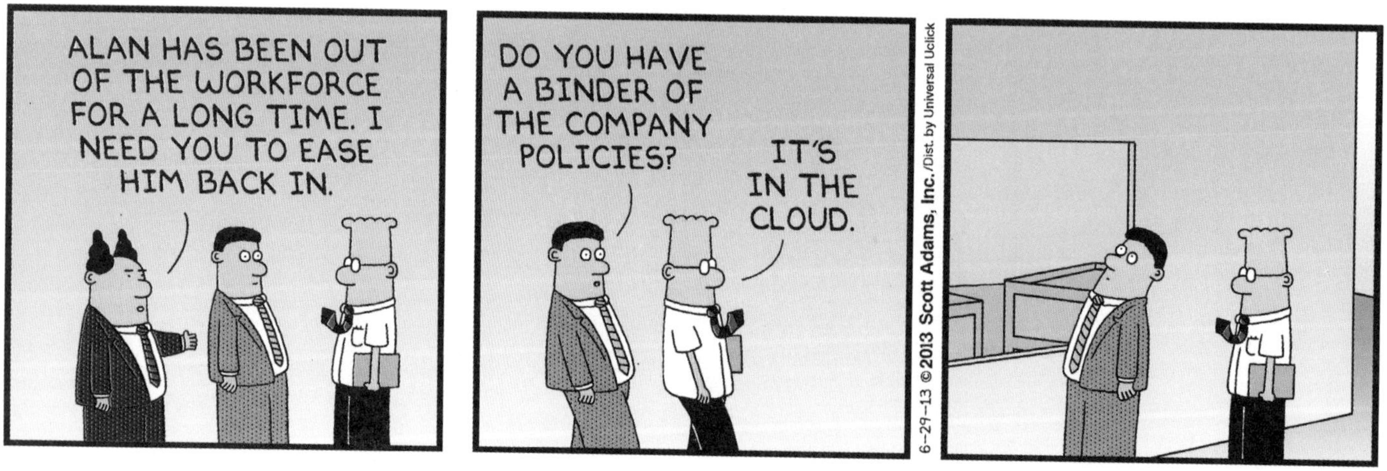
ALAN HAS BEEN OUT OF THE WORKFORCE FOR A LONG TIME. I NEED YOU TO EASE HIM BACK IN.
DO YOU HAVE A BINDER OF THE COMPANY POLICIES?
IT'S IN THE CLOUD.
6-29-13 ©2013 Scott Adams, Inc./Dist. by Universal Uclick

I'M READING A GREAT MANAGEMENT BOOK ABOUT THE RULES OF LEADERSHIP.
ALLOW ME TO PUT THAT IN CONTEXT.
THERE ARE PROBABLY 10,000 BOOKS ABOUT LEADERSHIP, AND EACH ONE HAS A DIFFERENT APPROACH.
AND THERE ARE MILLIONS OF REAL LEADERS, OF WHICH NO TWO ARE ALIKE.
MOREOVER, EVERY SITUATION IS UNIQUE AND REQUIRES A DIFFERENT TYPE OF LEADER.
AND YET, THIS ONE AUTHOR HAS FOUND A MAGIC FORMULA TO TRANSFORM YOU FROM A GULLIBLE BABOON INTO A GREAT LEADER.
AND THAT MAKES SENSE BECAUSE ALL GREAT LEADERS THROUGHOUT HISTORY ACHIEVED SUCCESS BY READING A RANDOM BOOK.
I DON'T LIKE CONTEXT.
IT ISN'T POPULAR.
©2013 Scott Adams, Inc./Dist. by Universal Uclick
6-30-13

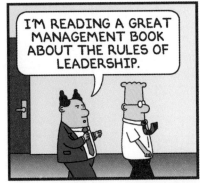

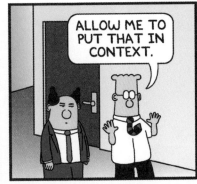

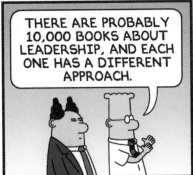

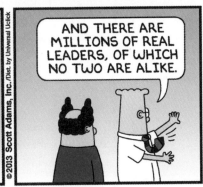

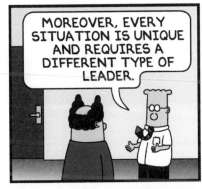

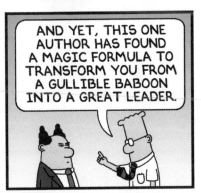

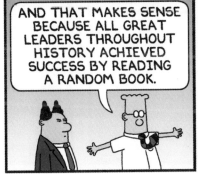

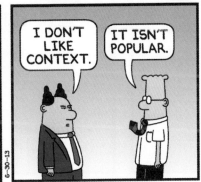

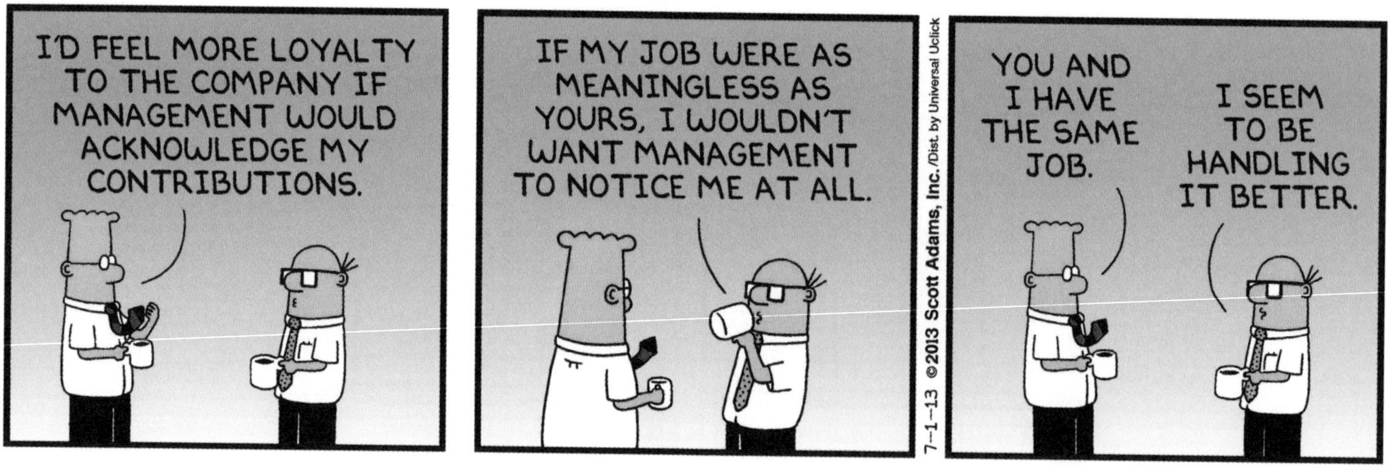
I'D FEEL MORE LOYALTY TO THE COMPANY IF MANAGEMENT WOULD ACKNOWLEDGE MY CONTRIBUTIONS.
IF MY JOB WERE AS MEANINGLESS AS YOURS, I WOULDN'T WANT MANAGEMENT TO NOTICE ME AT ALL.
7-1-13 ©2013 Scott Adams, Inc./Dist. by Universal Uclick
YOU AND I HAVE THE SAME JOB.
I SEEM TO BE HANDLING IT BETTER.

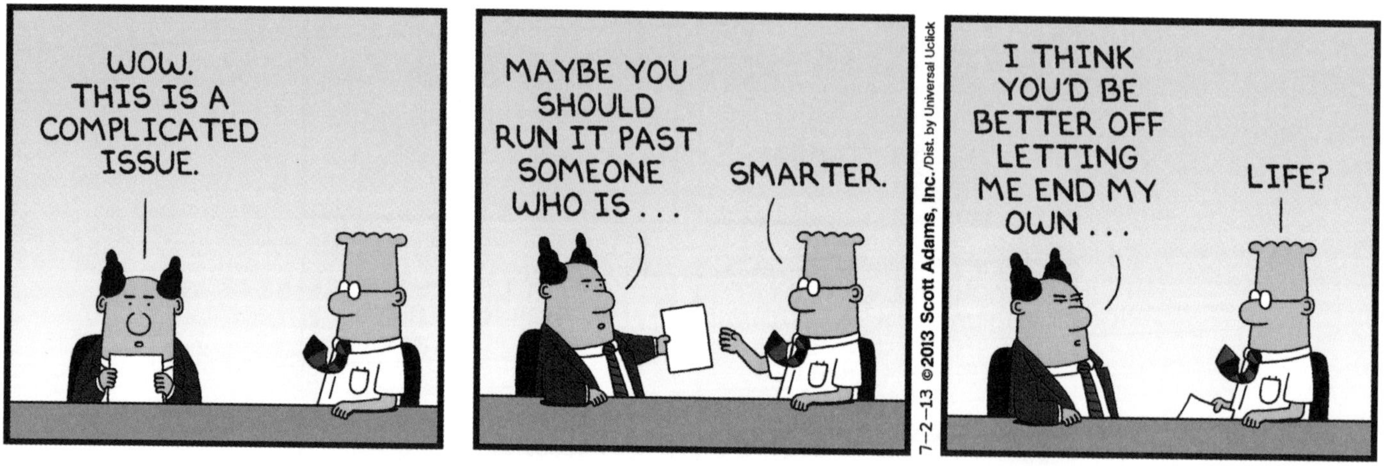
WOW. THIS IS A COMPLICATED ISSUE.
MAYBE YOU SHOULD RUN IT PAST SOMEONE WHO IS . . .
SMARTER.
7-2-13 ©2013 Scott Adams, Inc./Dist. by Universal Uclick
I THINK YOU'D BE BETTER OFF LETTING ME END MY OWN . . .
LIFE?

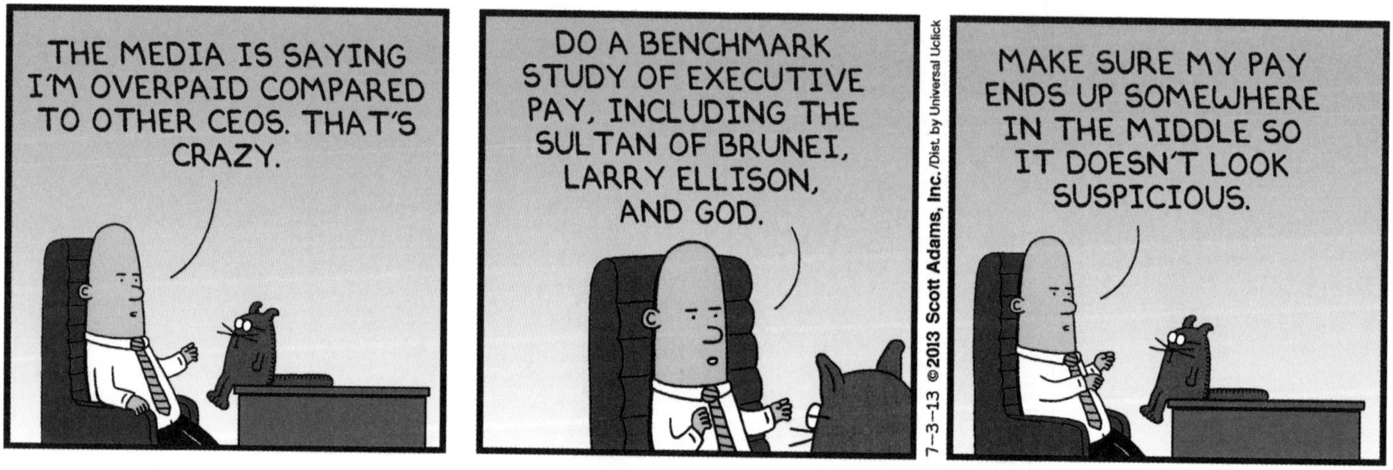
THE MEDIA IS SAYING I'M OVERPAID COMPARED TO OTHER CEOS. THAT'S CRAZY.
DO A BENCHMARK STUDY OF EXECUTIVE PAY, INCLUDING THE SULTAN OF BRUNEI, LARRY ELLISON, AND GOD.
7-3-13 ©2013 Scott Adams, Inc./Dist. by Universal Uclick
MAKE SURE MY PAY ENDS UP SOMEWHERE IN THE MIDDLE SO IT DOESN'T LOOK SUSPICIOUS.

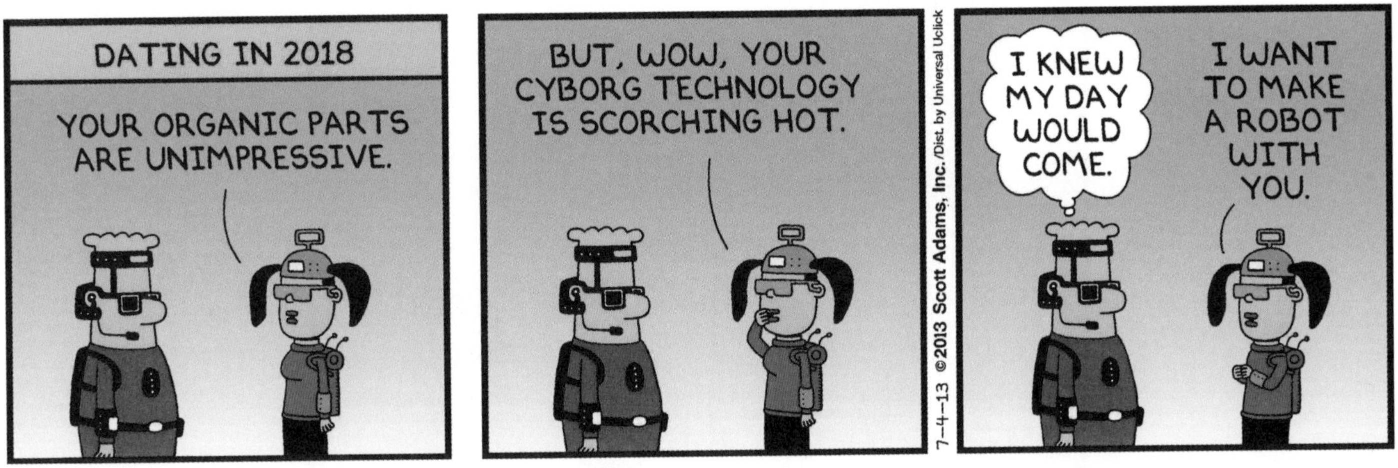
DATING IN 2018
YOUR ORGANIC PARTS ARE UNIMPRESSIVE.
BUT, WOW, YOUR CYBORG TECHNOLOGY IS SCORCHING HOT.
7-4-13 ©2013 Scott Adams, Inc./Dist. by Universal Uclick
I KNEW MY DAY WOULD COME.
I WANT TO MAKE A ROBOT WITH YOU.

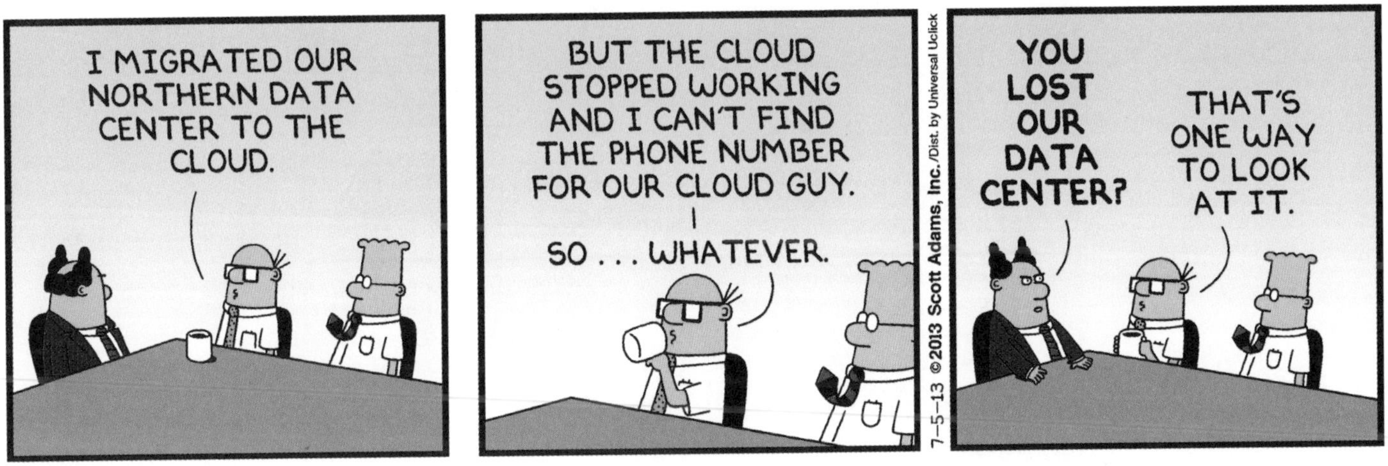
I MIGRATED OUR NORTHERN DATA CENTER TO THE CLOUD.
BUT THE CLOUD STOPPED WORKING AND I CAN'T FIND THE PHONE NUMBER FOR OUR CLOUD GUY.
SO . . . WHATEVER.
7-5-13 ©2013 Scott Adams, Inc./Dist. by Universal Uclick
YOU LOST OUR DATA CENTER?
THAT'S ONE WAY TO LOOK AT IT.

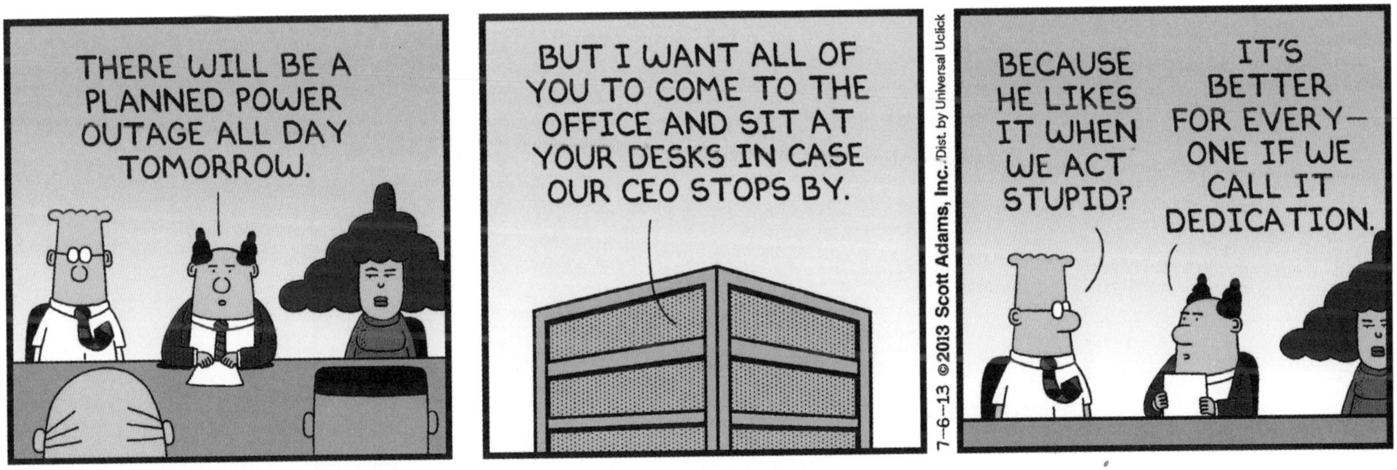
THERE WILL BE A PLANNED POWER OUTAGE ALL DAY TOMORROW.
BUT I WANT ALL OF YOU TO COME TO THE OFFICE AND SIT AT YOUR DESKS IN CASE OUR CEO STOPS BY.
7-6-13 ©2013 Scott Adams, Inc./Dist. by Universal Uclick
BECAUSE HE LIKES IT WHEN WE ACT STUPID?
IT'S BETTER FOR EVERY— ONE IF WE CALL IT DEDICATION.

OUR LAWYER SENT OVER A SIXTY-PAGE CONTRACT RENEWAL THAT I NEED YOU TO REVIEW.
MAKE SURE YOU COMPARE IT TO THE ORIGINAL CONTRACT AND ALL SIX OR SEVEN AMENDMENTS.
ARE THERE SIX OR . . . SEVEN?
NO ONE REALLY KNOWS.
CHECK OUT OUR OTHER NINE HUNDRED CONTRACTS TO MAKE SURE THIS ONE DOESN'T VIOLATE ANY OF THOSE.
KEEP IN MIND OUR FIVE-YEAR STRATEGIC PLAN AND ALL LIKELY CHANGES TO TAX LAW.
THEN GET BUY-IN FROM THE SEVENTEEN MANAGERS WHO HATE MY GUTS AND WILL TAKE IT OUT ON YOU.
BY TOMORROW.
GOOD LEADERS SET HIGH STANDARDS.
7-7-13

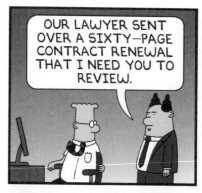

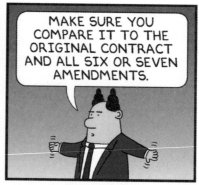

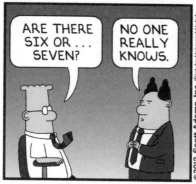

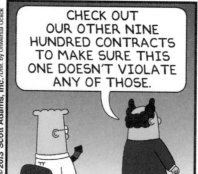

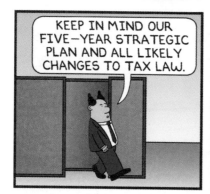

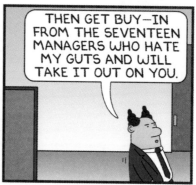

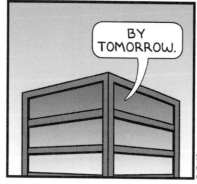

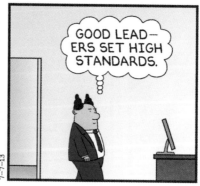

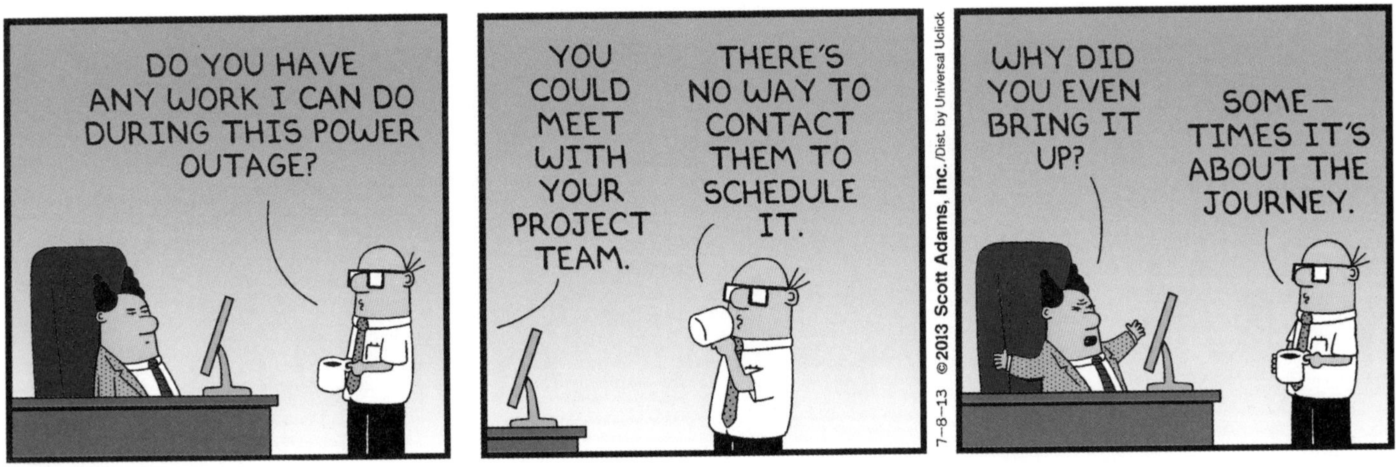
DO YOU HAVE ANY WORK I CAN DO DURING THIS POWER OUTAGE?
YOU COULD MEET WITH YOUR PROJECT TEAM.
THERE'S NO WAY TO CONTACT THEM TO SCHEDULE IT.
7–8–13 ©2013 Scott Adams, Inc./Dist. by Universal Uclick
WHY DID YOU EVEN BRING IT UP?
SOME-TIMES IT'S ABOUT THE JOURNEY.

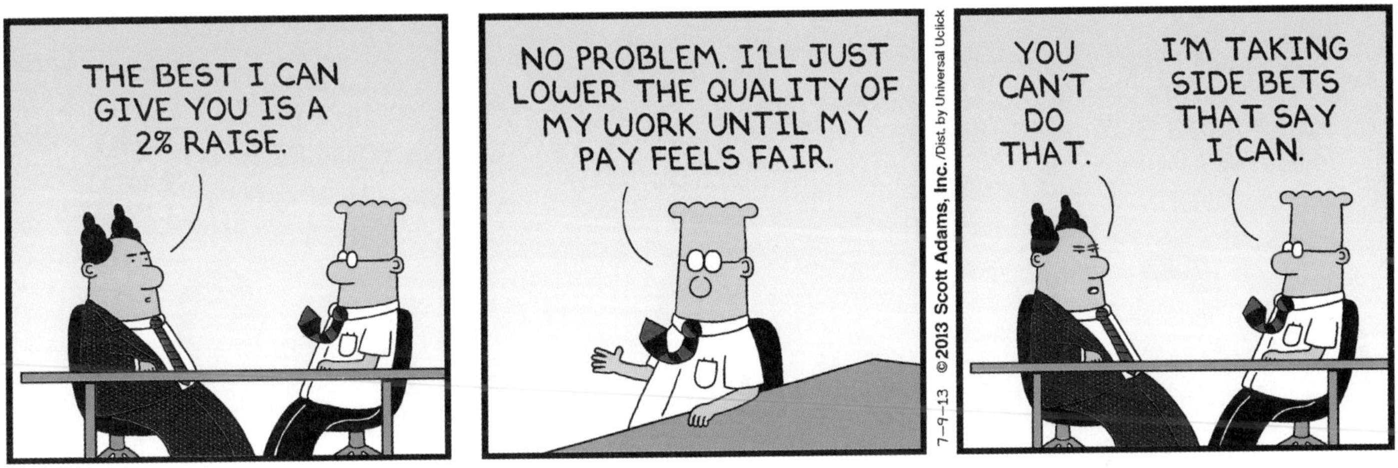
THE BEST I CAN GIVE YOU IS A 2% RAISE.
NO PROBLEM. I'LL JUST LOWER THE QUALITY OF MY WORK UNTIL MY PAY FEELS FAIR.
7–9–13 ©2013 Scott Adams, Inc./Dist. by Universal Uclick
YOU CAN'T DO THAT.
I'M TAKING SIDE BETS THAT SAY I CAN.

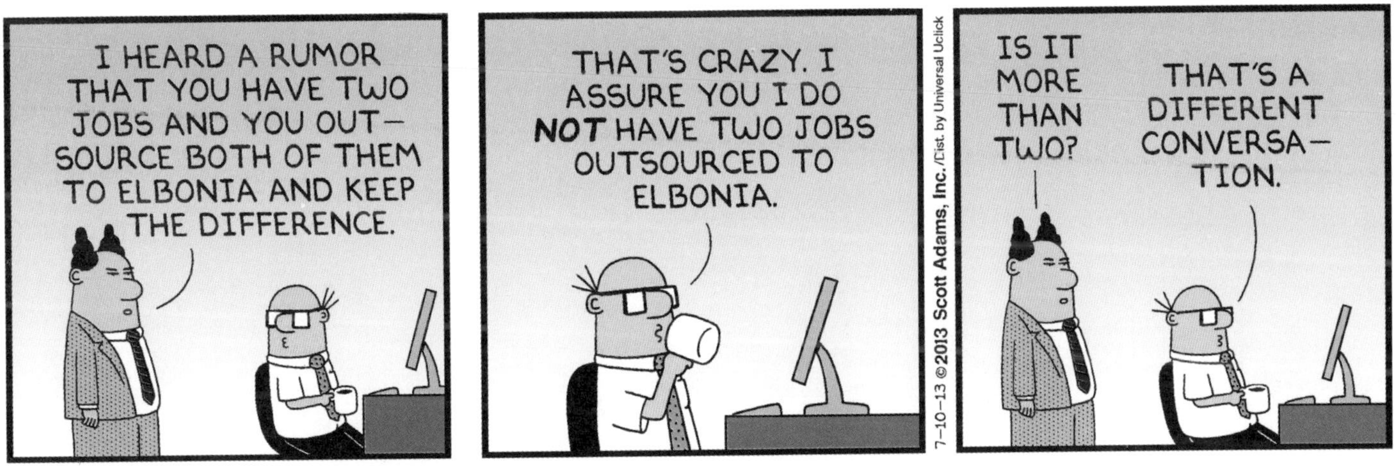
I HEARD A RUMOR THAT YOU HAVE TWO JOBS AND YOU OUT-SOURCE BOTH OF THEM TO ELBONIA AND KEEP THE DIFFERENCE.
THAT'S CRAZY. I ASSURE YOU I DO NOT HAVE TWO JOBS OUTSOURCED TO ELBONIA.
7–10–13 ©2013 Scott Adams, Inc./Dist. by Universal Uclick
IS IT MORE THAN TWO?
THAT'S A DIFFERENT CONVERSA-TION.

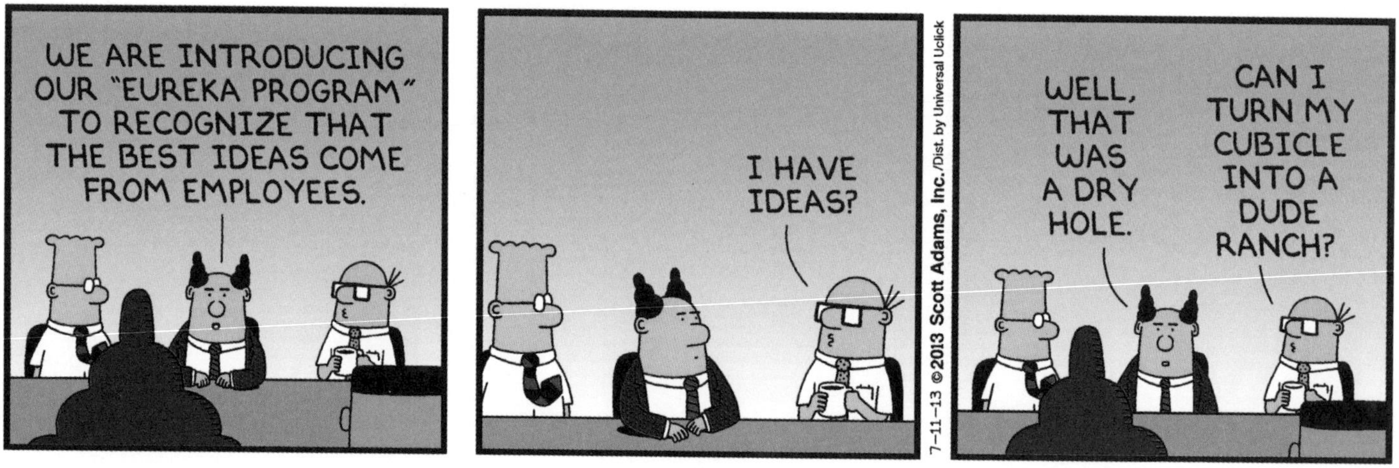
WE ARE INTRODUCING OUR "EUREKA PROGRAM" TO RECOGNIZE THAT THE BEST IDEAS COME FROM EMPLOYEES.
I HAVE IDEAS?
WELL, THAT WAS A DRY HOLE.
CAN I TURN MY CUBICLE INTO A DUDE RANCH?
7-11-13 ©2013 Scott Adams, Inc./Dist. by Universal Uclick

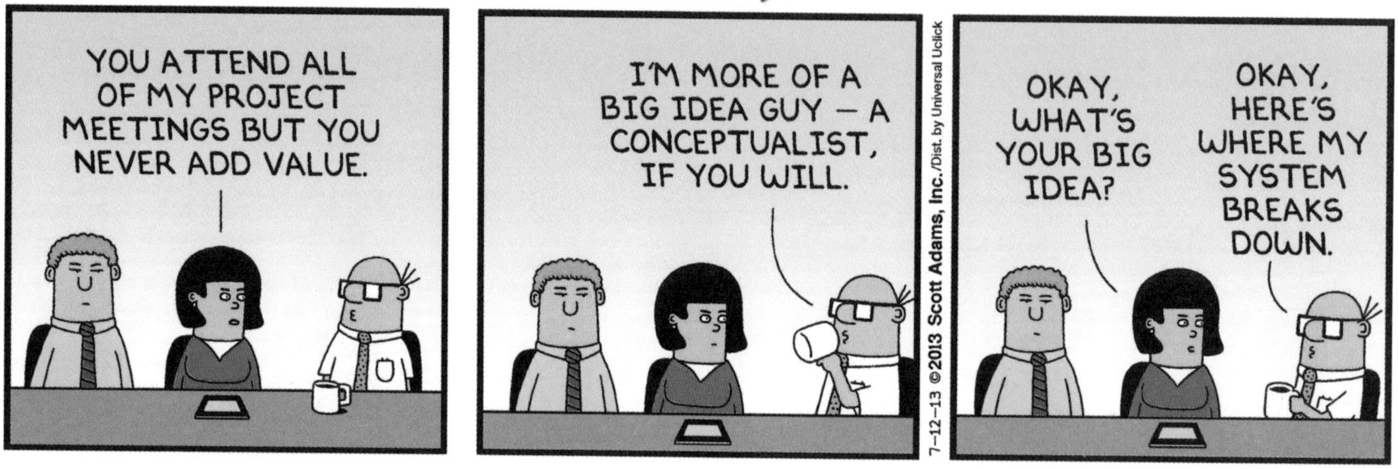
YOU ATTEND ALL OF MY PROJECT MEETINGS BUT YOU NEVER ADD VALUE.
I'M MORE OF A BIG IDEA GUY — A CONCEPTUALIST, IF YOU WILL.
OKAY, WHAT'S YOUR BIG IDEA?
OKAY, HERE'S WHERE MY SYSTEM BREAKS DOWN.
7-12-13 ©2013 Scott Adams, Inc./Dist. by Universal Uclick

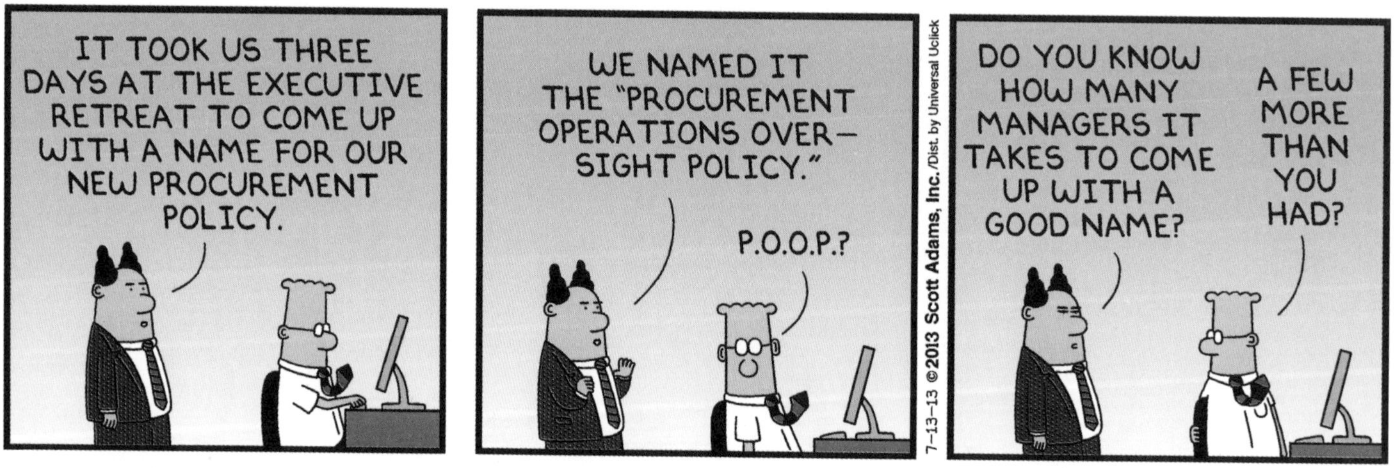
IT TOOK US THREE DAYS AT THE EXECUTIVE RETREAT TO COME UP WITH A NAME FOR OUR NEW PROCUREMENT POLICY.
WE NAMED IT THE "PROCUREMENT OPERATIONS OVER-SIGHT POLICY."
P.O.O.P.?
DO YOU KNOW HOW MANY MANAGERS IT TAKES TO COME UP WITH A GOOD NAME?
A FEW MORE THAN YOU HAD?
7-13-13 ©2013 Scott Adams, Inc./Dist. by Universal Uclick

THIS WEBSITE HAS BEEN BLOCKED BY YOUR COMPANY.
MORDAC, I NEED ACCESS TO A BLOCKED SITE FOR BUSINESS REASONS.
I CAN ONLY UNBLOCK THE SITE IF THE DIRECTOR OF HUMAN RESOURCES SENDS ME A WRITTEN APPROVAL.
©2013 Scott Adams, Inc./Dist. by Universal Uclick
I CAN ONLY MAKE RECOMMENDATIONS. OUR CIO STILL HAS TO APPROVE IT.
CHIEF INFORMATION OFFICER
HOW DARE YOU BOTHER ME WITH YOUR TRIVIAL WEBSITE PROBLEM!
CRAWL BACK INTO YOUR HOLE AND THINK ABOUT THE CAREER MISTAKE YOU JUST MADE!
7-14-13
CAN WE SKIP THE PART WHERE YOU ASK ME WHAT I ACCOMPLISHED THIS WEEK?

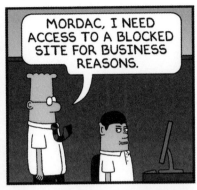